CONTRACT LAW WITHOUT FOUNDATIONS

Contract Law Without Foundations

Toward a Republican Theory of Contract Law

PRINCE SAPRAI

OXFORD
UNIVERSITY PRESS

OXFORD
UNIVERSITY PRESS

Great Clarendon Street, Oxford, OX2 6DP,
United Kingdom

Oxford University Press is a department of the University of Oxford.
It furthers the University's objective of excellence in research, scholarship,
and education by publishing worldwide. Oxford is a registered trade mark of
Oxford University Press in the UK and in certain other countries

First Edition published in 2019

Impression: 2

Published in the United States of America by Oxford University Press
198 Madison Avenue, New York, NY 10016, United States of America

British Library Cataloguing in Publication Data
Data available

Library of Congress Cataloging in Publication Data
Data available

ISBN 978–0–19–877901–8

Printed and bound by
CPI Group (UK) Ltd, Croydon, CR0 4YY

For Claudine, Constance, and Olivia

Preface

Looking back, the origins of this book lie, most likely anyway, in some remarks the late Peter Birks made in a BCL restitution seminar in 2002 that I attended during the course of my graduate studies at Oxford. They have stayed with me ever since. I can't remember the exact words or the precise context, and I really hope I'm not about to garble too much what he said. From what I remember, he said something like the following: law is unnecessarily complicated. This benefits no one but lawyers. It does not have to be this way, and indeed it should not be. Most people should be able to understand the law. The Roman jurists got this. Or something along those lines anyway (if there are any BCL students out there who were in that class and think I got this wrong, please get in touch!).

Peter was expressing here, I think, a very Benthamite sentiment, but Peter himself, of course, was no Benthamite. He did though, like Bentham, think that law should be guided by morals. But, for Peter, morality was not rooted in some utilitarian calculus, but—or so it seemed to me anyway—in common sense. With that in mind and with the conviction that the Roman jurists were right to make law as accessible to people at large as possible, he set about constructing and linking the basic categories of private law (contract, tort, and so forth) to everyday moral concerns including, for example, consenting or promising, making up for things when we wrong others, or giving things back that don't belong to us.

Many scholars will say (and indeed have said to me) that I get Peter and his work wrong here. He was a practically minded lawyer and certainly no philosopher. He thought law should be guided not by morals but just by, well, law. In a sense, these scholars are right. Sometimes Peter wrote like this, and indeed this may well have been his own self-conception. Nevertheless, I respectfully disagree with these interpretations.

This is a book about contract law, and more specifically the philosophy of contract law. The view that areas of private law should track common-sense moral concerns or intuitions found its most sophisticated articulation in contract law in the publication in 1981 of Charles Fried's seminal book, *Contract as Promise*.[1] Fried famously claimed that contract law should track the morality of promising. Since then, debate has raged among many brilliant philosophically minded contracts scholars about the extent to which contract law 'converges' or 'diverges' from the morality of promise. As will become apparent (and should already be apparent from the title of this book), I'm a sceptic about the idea that contract law has a 'foundation' in promissory morality or indeed any particular moral field. Nevertheless, I share with Peter the protestant or republican sense that the law should be accessible to people at large, and that the linkage between law and morality plays a key role in achieving this end.

[1] Charles Fried, *Contract as Promise: A Theory of Contractual Obligation* (Harvard University Press 1981).

This book is an attempt to reconcile my anti-foundationalism about contract law, with my republicanism about law in general.

As a student of the law, I've been incredibly lucky. Peter taught me restitution at Oxford, which for anyone who has taken that great course knows means that he taught me *all* of private law. John Gardner taught me jurisprudence both as an undergraduate at King's College in London and as a graduate student at Oxford. I still remember his undergraduate lectures about the problem of authority and anarchism vividly—at last, law became interesting. John is not, I think, an anarchist himself, but he is contrary. A bit of that has rubbed off on me and there is a streak of this in my book. As a graduate student, Mindy Chen-Wishart introduced me to the complexities of contract law—especially in relation to the undue influence doctrine—and the shortcomings of traditional and largely taken-for-granted conceptions of the field based on the idea that contract law serves some single principle, like autonomy, or consent, or promise, and so forth. This opened up a new world for me, and this book is just the latest attempt to make sense of it.

The influence that Peter, John, and Mindy have had on me—more than anything else—inspired this book, albeit there is much here that they would surely disagree with. I am indebted to them all.

A number of the chapters in the book are based on previously published material going back a number of years. In many cases, I have made fairly significant (and in some cases pretty radical) revisions and alterations to the published works (see *Acknowledgements* for full details). These changes largely reflect changes in my own view, unhappiness with the way I expressed things in the past, and adaptations made for the purposes of the book to bring my thoughts about the subject together. Chapters 2, 3, and 9 of the book are based on and largely reproduce the text of (with some revisions and adaptations), the text of two papers that I've co-written with my friend and colleague, George Letsas: 'Foundationalism About Contract Law: A Sceptical View', and 'Mitigation, Fairness, and Contract Law' (see *Acknowledgements* for full details). Thank you to George for kindly permitting me to use the text from these two papers. I've spent nearly a decade now talking to George about general jurisprudence. At the start, I did not really hold any strong views about the subject and indeed I wasn't really sure that I should care too much about it. George in contrast was a dyed-in-the-wool 'anti-positivist'. Over time, he did persuade me that general jurisprudence mattered and indeed affected how we should approach problems in particular jurisprudence. This changed profoundly how I think about law in general and contract law in particular, and I am hugely grateful to him for that.

I have made no attempt to make any arguments I advance in this book consistent with any of my writings in the past. Rather, my only aim has been to collect together the thoughts I *now* have about contract law and render them—as far as I can—coherent. The book has, as I have said, an underlying anti-foundationalist and broadly republican thesis about the morality of contract law. However, the chapters are largely designed so that they can be read on their own. So, the reader should feel free to dip into those parts of the book that seem to be of most interest or relevance.

Different bits of the book have been knocking around in various iterations or guises for about a decade or so now. Thank you to Alex Flach from Oxford

University Press for encouraging me—many years ago now—to put this material together, and to Eve Ryle-Hodges also from the Press for helping me through the production process. I have presented this material as discreet papers at conferences, workshops, and symposia here in England and abroad over the years. I have received incredibly helpful feedback from a great number of colleagues. I am indebted to them all. I will attempt here an alphabetical list of people to whom I know that I owe a debt: Thomas Adam, Aditi Bagchi, Roderick Bagshaw, Randy Barnett, Caspar Bartscherer, Hugh Beale, Richard Bronaugh, Kimberley Brownlee, Andrew Burrows, Robert Chambers, Mindy Chen-Wishart, Matthew Clayton, Lord Lawrence Collins, Hanoch Dagan, Stephen Darwall, Alison Diduck, Anthony Duff, Piet Eeckhout, Octavio Ferraz, Charles Fried, Andrew Gold, Amy Goymour, Les Green, Julius Grower, Birke Häcker, Christopher Hinchcliffe, Peter Jaffey, Larrisa Katz, Dori Kimel, Greg Klass, Dora Kostakopoulou, Dimitrios Kyritsis, Maria Lee, George Letsas, William Lucy, Paul MacMahon, Daniel Markovits, Nick McBride, Ben McFarlane, Claudio Michelon, Joanna Miles, Lucinda Miller, Chris Mills, Charles Mitchell, Paul Mitchell, Riz Mokal, Jonathan Morgan, Liam Murphy, Jason Neyers, Bill O'Brien, Maggie O'Brien, David Owens, James Penner, Dan Priel, Peggy Radin, Paul Raffield, Joseph Raz, the late Helen Reece, Joaquín Reyes Barros, Soléne Rowan, Michael Rush, Irit Samet, Joanne Scott, Scott Shapiro, Hanoch Sheinman, Seana Shiffrin, James Shirley, Adam Slavny, Steve Smith, Sandy Steele, Rob Stevens, Rebecca Stone, Andy Summers, Victor Tadros, John Tasioulas, Kevin Toh, Radosveta Vassileva, Emmanuel Voyiakis, Florian Wagner-von Papp, Stephen Watterson, Charlie Webb, Simon Whittaker, Fred Wilmot-Smith, and Ben Zipursky.

This is of course a non-exhaustive list. Due to the length of time involved I am sure I've inadvertently missed important people. I sincerely apologize if I have.

I could not have finished this book without the aid of outstanding research assistance from Simon Palmer, who worked tirelessly on the manuscript helping me to prepare it for publication. I owe him huge thanks for his work and for saving me from a number of errors—both stylistic and intellectual—which I had originally overlooked. Finally, I would like to thank the institution at which I work, the Faculty of Laws, UCL. I was lucky to come to UCL in 2009 at a very early stage in my academic career. It has provided me over the years with the resources, support, and sense of intellectual freedom to pursue my research interests in whatever direction I have seen fit. In this day and age, I don't take any of this for granted. It is a huge privilege to work at UCL. Thank you to all my brilliant colleagues and students over the years for challenging me to defend my views about the subject as clearly and cogently as I can.

I owe a great deal to all of these wonderful people. Any errors that remain in this book are of course mine.

Acknowledgements

Chapters 2 and 3 are based on and largely reproduce the text of, with some revisions and adaptations, an unpublished paper co-authored with George Letsas entitled 'Foundationalism About Contract Law: A Sceptical View', available at SSRN: <https://papers.ssrn.com/sol3/papers.cfm?abstract_id=3211283> accessed 7 November 2018. The text is used with kind permission of my co-author.

Chapter 5 is based on and largely reproduces, but with significant revisions and adaptations, the text of a previously published article of mine entitled '*Balfour v Balfour* and the Separation of Contract and Promise', which appeared in Legal Studies 37 (2017) 468, copyright © 2017 Society of Legal Scholars. The text is used with kind permission of John Wiley & Sons Ltd, subject to the following copyright notice: 'All rights reserved. No part of this publication may be reproduced, stored or transmitted in any form or by any means without the prior permission in writing from the copyright holder. Authorization to photocopy items for internal and personal use is granted by the copyright holder for libraries and other users registered with their local Reproduction Rights Organization (RRO), e.g. Copyright Clearance Center (CCC), 222 Rosewood Drive, Danvers, MA 01923, USA (www.copyright.com), provided the appropriate fee is paid directly to the RRO. This consent does not extend to other kinds of copying such as copying for general distribution, for advertising or promotional purposes, for republication, for creating new collective works or for resale. Permissions for such reuse can be obtained using the RightsLink "Request Permissions" link on Wiley Online Library. Special requests should be addressed to: permissions@wiley.com'.

Chapter 6 is based on and largely reproduces, but with some significant additions, revisions, and adaptations, the text of a previously published chapter of mine entitled 'Unconscionable Enrichment?', which appeared in Robert Chambers, Charles Mitchell, and James Penner (eds), *Philosophical Foundations of the Law of Unjust Enrichment* (Oxford University Press 2009) 417, copyright © The Several Contributors, 2009. The text is used with kind permission of Oxford University Press, and the editors of that volume.

Chapter 7 is based on and largely reproduces, but with significant additions, revisions, and adaptations, the text of a previously published article of mine entitled 'The Principle Against Self-Enslavement in Contract Law', which appeared in the Journal of Contract Law 26 (2009) 25, copyright © 2009 Reed International Books Australia Pty Limited. The text is used with kind permission of LEXISNEXIS (Australia).

Chapter 8 is based on and largely reproduces, but with some significant revisions and adaptations, the text of a previously published article of mine entitled 'The Penalties Rule and the Promise Theory of Contract', which appeared in The Canadian Journal of Law and Jurisprudence 26 (2013) 443, copyright © 2013

Canadian Journal of Law and Jurisprudence. The text is used with kind permission of Cambridge University Press.

Chapter 9 is based on and largely reproduces, but with some important revisions and adaptations, the text of a previously published chapter co-authored with George Letsas entitled 'Mitigation, Fairness, and Contract Law', which appeared in Gregory Klass, George Letsas, and Prince Saprai (eds), *Philosophical Foundations of Contract Law* (Oxford University Press 2014) 319, copyright © The several contributors 2014. The text is used with kind permission of my co-author, Oxford University Press, and the editors of that volume.

Chapter 10 is based on and largely reproduces, but with significant additions, revisions, and adaptations, the text of a previously published article: Prince Saprai, 'The Convergence of Contract Law in Europe and the Problem of Legitimacy: A Common Lawyer's Perspective'; in *European Review of Contract Law*, 12(2), Berlin/Boston: De Gruyter 2016, 96–135, copyright © 2016 Walter de Gruyter GmbH, Berlin/Boston. The text is used with kind permission of de Gruyter.

Contents

Contents

1

Introduction

1. The Promise Theory

The 'promise theory' has become in recent decades the dominant non-consequentialist account of contract law. The purpose of this book is to show that it is false, whilst acknowledging that its proponents have uncovered important truths about contract law and its central doctrines; and showing that rejecting the promise theory does not entail embracing the dominant consequentialist account of contract law—law and economics—which claims that the sole purpose of contract is to promote economic efficiency.

The promise theory is what I term throughout the book a 'foundationalist' account of an area of law. By this I mean that it relies on a deontic moral principle or concern to carve up an area of law. Foundationalism makes a metaphysical claim about the nature of law. According to it, certain moral principles are necessarily constitutive or built into the very fabric of the law of any legal system. They structure and shape certain core legal categories, like contract, tort, criminal law, property, and so forth. The rules and doctrines typically contained in these legal categories are magnetically drawn to these foundational principles. Such principles play a special role in justifying these particular doctrines, and in doing so render these legal categories coherent.

Foundationalism is now prevalent in private law scholarship. Peter Birks said 'It ought to be possible to take any legal subject and to cut away its detail so as to reveal the skeleton of principle which holds it together.'[1] That skeleton should serve both to justify an area of law and provides normative guidance on the shape that its doctrines and rules should take.[2] So, Birks argued that an array of rules and doctrines conventionally classified under the legal categories of contract, property, and trusts are in fact underlain by a principle of preventing unjust enrichment. In doing so, Birks attempted nothing less than the creation of a new legal category. More recently, Robert Stevens has claimed that the correction of rights infringements by wrongdoers holds tort law together.[3] Even more ambitiously, Ernest Weinrib has tried to explain the whole of private law using the principle of corrective justice.[4]

[1] Peter Birks, *An Introduction to the Law of Restitution* (Clarendon Press 1989).
[2] Seana Valentine Shiffrin, 'Is a Contract a Promise?' in Andrei Marmor (ed), *The Routledge Companion to Philosophy of Law* (Routledge 2012).
[3] Robert Stevens, *Torts and Rights* (Oxford University Press 2007) 2, 151.
[4] Ernest J Weinrib, *The Idea of Private Law* (Harvard University Press 1995).

In the context of contract law, it was Charles Fried who famously claimed that promise 'is the moral basis of contract law'.[5] That view quickly took root, especially among legal theorists seeking refuge from the imperialistic ambitions of law and economics which claimed that efficiency or wealth maximization lay behind not only contract law, but *all* law, and indeed the whole of morality.[6] Adherents to this promise-based theory of contract now include Jody Kraus,[7] Daniel Markovits,[8] Liam Murphy,[9] and Seana Shiffrin.[10]

These promise theorists disagree about the extent to which Anglo-American contract law in particular actually instantiates the promise principle. In a seminal article, Shiffrin claimed that the Anglo-American remedial regime for breach of contract diverged significantly from the requirements of promissory morality, in particular because the standard remedy of expectation damages, sends out the message that breach of contract is not a serious moral wrong, but is 'merely subject to a price'.[11] In response, Kraus argued that there is in fact no incompatibility with promise, because typically contracting parties do not promise to perform their contracts, but rather make alternative promises to 'perform or pay' the financial equivalent of performance.[12]

These sorts of disagreements have contributed to what has become known in the literature as the 'contract and promise debate', which concerns the extent to which contract law converges or diverges from promise. Despite these disagreements, these theorists at a fundamental level actually *agree* that promise *is* the foundation of contract law. In other words, they accept that the promise principle necessarily plays a special justificatory role when it comes to the evaluation of contract law rules and doctrines. Therefore, their disagreements are not deep or basic. Rather they are about what promissory morality entails, and the extent to which contract law reflects that morality.

I argue in this book that the promise theory of contract law is false. Metaphysically it is not true that there is necessarily a constitutive relationship between contract and promise. Contrary to what promise theorists say, promise does not necessarily

[5] Charles Fried, *Contract as Promise: A Theory of Contractual Obligation* (Harvard University Press 1981).

[6] Interestingly, in a recent paper Fried himself makes clear that when he wrote *Contract as Promise* he was not motivated to do so by law and economics, but rather was responding to the Critical Legal Studies ('CLS') movement that was dominant at the time when his book was written. Charles Fried, 'The Ambitions of *Contract as Promise*' in Gregory Klass, George Letsas, and Prince Saprai (eds), *Philosophical Foundations of Contract Law* (Oxford University Press 2014) 18–21. He acknowledges though that law and economics has since taken over as the dominant theory of contract law.

[7] Jody S Kraus, 'The Correspondence of Contract and Promise' (2009) 109 Columbia Law Review 1603.

[8] Daniel Markovits, 'Contract and Collaboration' (2004) 113 Yale Law Journal 1417.

[9] Liam Murphy, 'The Practice of Promise and Contract' in Gregory Klass, George Letsas, and Prince Saprai (eds), *Philosophical Foundations of Contract Law* (Oxford University Press 2014).

[10] Seana Valentine Shiffrin, 'The Divergence of Contract and Promise' (2007) 120 Harvard Law Review 708.

[11] ibid 724.

[12] Kraus, 'The Correspondence of Contract and Promise' (n 7) 1637. See similarly Daniel Markovits and Alan Schwartz, 'The Myth of Efficient Breach: New Defenses of the Expectation Interest' (2011) 97 Virginia Law Review 1939.

play any special justificatory role in contract law. This is not though to give up the game to law and economics. Rather, my contention will be that deontic moral principles such as promise do justify contract law rules and doctrines, but that no single principle or set of such principles *necessarily* plays a special role. The shape and structure that the contract law of any particular jurisdiction should take is a *contingent* matter, with contract law rules and doctrines being justified by the interaction between a multiplicity of moral principles and values, which cancel, qualify, defeat, and reinforce one another.

Much of the contract and promise debate has taken place on the terrain of Anglo-American contract law. My book roams over similar ground, but with a focus mainly on English contract law. My purpose though is to debunk promise theory, and to show that the contract and promise debate is in fact a pseudo debate. Promise theorists whether they repudiate (like Shiffrin) or attempt to justify (like Kraus) existing contract doctrine, fundamentally *agree* with one another that the immanent structure of contract law necessarily presupposes a preeminent justificatory role for the promise principle. I argue that promise plays no such role in contract, and that promise theorists often mishandle and misapply legal doctrine because they think it does. My book is a plea for a less 'top-heavy' theory of contract law; which builds from the 'ground-up' and shows greater sensitivity to the contours of actual contract law rules and doctrines.

Alongside these conceptual or interpretive worries, there is a further problem with the promise theory that I aim to explore. The promise theory purports to be a distinctly liberal theory of contract law, which emphasizes how contract law enhances the freedom or autonomy of contracting parties. The trouble though for such a view is justifying why the state in particular should involve itself in promoting promissory morality, and separately why it should do so using the coercive apparatus of the law. One might accept that contracting parties should keep their promises, whilst rejecting the idea that the state should be in any way involved in making sure this happens, or even if one accepts that the state has a legitimate role to play, one might deny that it should play a *coercive* role.[13]

The promise theory runs up here against the liberal aversion to the use of the law to enforce morals.[14] Promise theorists have not paid enough attention to this issue. It is a nettle though that needs to be grasped. Although I agree with the promise theorist that contracts are indeed promises, or to be more precise, involve the enforcement of promises, I will argue that the only way to draw the sting of the liberal objection to the enforcement of morality is by reaching beyond promissory morality to justify contract law.

[13] Antony R Duff, 'Penal Communications: Recent Work in the Philosophy of Punishment' (1996) 20 Crime and Justice 1, 9. Duff raises this objection in the context of the justification of state punishment. Making a similar point in the contractual context see Dori Kimel, 'The Morality of Contract and Moral Culpability in Breach' (2010) 21 King's Law Journal 213, 222; Randy E Barnett, 'Contract Is Not Promise; Contract Is Consent' in Gregory Klass, George Letsas, and Prince Saprai (eds), *Philosophical Foundations of Contract Law* (Oxford University Press 2014) 47: 'by justifying contract as a species of enforcing purely moral commitments, it seems tantamount to enforcing virtue'.

[14] John Stuart Mill, *On Liberty and Other Essays* (Oxford University Press 1998).

2. Normative Pluralism

As the title of this book suggests, my aims are avowedly anti-foundationalist in orientation. I deny not only that promise is the foundation of contract law, but more radically that *any* moral value or set of values necessarily provides a foundation for contract law (I would take issue then with Randy Barnett,[15] Dori Kimel,[16] and James Penner,[17] who all locate the value of contract in non-promissory deontic concerns).

My claim is motivated by the implications for contract law of what I call in this book 'interpretive pluralism' and 'value pluralism'. According to interpretive pluralism, there exist a multiplicity of eligible ways in which to interpret the requirements of moral values that play a role in contract law such as promise, fairness, corrective justice, altruism, and so forth. Value pluralism in this context is the thesis that there is a multiplicity of incommensurate values that bear on contract law rules and doctrines, and no single correct way to rank these values when they conflict.[18] I will use the phrase 'normative pluralism' in the book to capture both concepts, although at various points in the argument it will be necessary to distinguish between them.

It is not of course true to say that promise theorists have been completely blind to the existence of normative pluralism in contract law. So, for example, when Shiffrin attacked the mitigation doctrine, on the grounds of its incompatibility with promissory morality, Fried accused her of moral myopia. According to that doctrine, the innocent victim of a breach of contract may have a duty to find substitute performance. Fried accepted that from the perspective of the promise principle taken alone, this result might appear as Shiffrin claimed 'morally distasteful'.[19] Why should the innocent party have to clear up the mess that is the product of the other party's own moral wrongdoing? Perhaps the only explanation is efficiency?[20] However, Fried argued that Shiffrin failed to perceive the role that other moral principles play in shaping contract doctrine. In particular, he claimed that in the circumstances of breach, the innocent party might have an altruistic duty to assist the wrongdoer where it would be easy for the innocent party to do so.[21]

[15] Randy E Barnett, 'A Consent Theory of Contract' (1986) 86 Columbia Law Review 269; Barnett, 'Contract Is Not Promise; Contract Is Consent' (n 13).

[16] Dori Kimel, *From Promise to Contract: Towards a Liberal Theory of Contract* (Hart Publishing 2003).

[17] James E Penner, 'Voluntary Obligations and the Scope of the Law of Contract' (1996) 2 Legal Theory 325; James Penner, 'Promises, Agreements, and Contracts' in Gregory Klass, George Letsas, and Prince Saprai (eds), *Philosophical Foundations of Contract Law* (Oxford University Press 2014).

[18] On value pluralism see John Tasioulas, 'Human Rights, Legitimacy, and International Law' (2013) 58 The American Journal of Jurisprudence 1, 19.

[19] Shiffrin, 'The Divergence of Contract and Promise' (n 10) 725.

[20] An economic explanation for the doctrine has been defended by Charles J Goetz and Robert E Scott, 'The Mitigation Principle: Toward a General Theory of Contractual Obligation' (1983) 69 Virginia Law Review 967, 973.

[21] Charles Fried, 'The Convergence of Contract and Promise' (2007) 120 Harvard Law Review Forum 1, 7–8. Similarly in Fried, *Contract as Promise: A Theory of Contractual Obligation* (n 5) 61, Fried claimed that considerations of fairness justify the objective principle of contract interpretation. Promise alone would require only subjective meanings or intentions to be taken into account.

Few would argue that the promise principle alone could account for the array of rules and doctrines that we find in contract law. Doctrines like consideration, undue influence, frustration, remoteness, mitigation, and so forth, are no doubt shaped by promise, but they also bear the mark of other normative concerns, such as the prevention of exploitation, altruism, fairness, corrective justice, the protection of reliance, and so on. It is difficult for anyone who pays close attention to the actual practice of contract law to deny the relevance of these values. They should be obvious to anyone who flicks through a contract textbook.

My point is not that promise theorists deny the existence of normative pluralism in contract law (how could they?), but rather that despite their awareness promise theorists have failed to fully absorb, or completely confront the profound implications of normative pluralism for their conceptual claims and interpretive claims. My primary purpose in this book is to bring these implications to the fore, and show how and why they pose such a threat to the promise theory.

3. Contexts

As I have said, the central purpose of this book is to explore the implications of normative pluralism for the promise theory. However, I pursue that argument in three different but interrelated contexts, which I shall describe somewhat crudely as the domains of contract theory, contract doctrine, and comparative or transnational contract law. My aim is to bring out the implications of normative pluralism in each of these three contexts in which matters of contract law are often debated—whilst insisting on and acknowledging that the membrane between the three contexts is largely permeable.

3.1 Contract theory

The next three chapters of the book range largely over the terrain known as contract theory. The focus is on what I have called foundationalist accounts of contract law like the promise theory. I argue in these chapters that in the face of normative pluralism, the foundationalist struggles to explain the sense in which promise necessarily plays a special role in shaping contract law. It is not enough to say that promise justifies contract doctrine. That is true of *all* of the other principles that shape contract law. Attempts to carve out a special role for promise lead I argue ineluctably to a mishandling of contract law rules and doctrines.

Doctrine is mishandled, because by a variety of mechanisms the promise theorist artificially attempts to play up the justificatory role promise plays in contract, and in tandem with this play down the irreducible plurality of moral principles and values that actually bear on contract law. I discuss in this book three methods that the promise theorist might use to do this.

So, first, the promise theorist might argue that promise *necessarily* plays a part in the justification of *all* contract law rules and doctrines, although it may be defeated or qualified by other normative principles. I call this strategy 'justificatory necessity'. Second, the promise theorist may argue that promise plays the *primary* role in justifying doctrine, that is, those rules and doctrines incompatible with promise are objectionable.[22] I call this view 'justificatory primacy'. And, finally, there is the view that promise is special in contract, because there is an *epistemic* presumption that doctrines that are compatible with promise are justified, and those that conflict are unjustified.[23] I call this view 'justificatory presumptiveness'.

The trouble with these three responses to normative pluralism is that they lead the promise theorist to mishandle or misapply contract law doctrine. Adopting foundationalism either leads to the rejection of doctrine that is in fact justified (see, for example, Shiffrin's critique of the mitigation doctrine),[24] the acceptance of doctrine which should be rejected, or to misunderstandings about the rational basis of doctrine (consider Kraus' attempt discussed above to explain expectation damages by re-characterizing contractual performance as an alternative promise to perform or pay).[25]

This scepticism about foundationalism though does not mean that the widespread practice of carving out discreet areas of law undertaken by judges, lawyers, academics, and so forth, is a matter of mere convention or utility. Relying on some largely overlooked work by Ronald Dworkin, I go on to argue that at least some legal categories may be linked with aspects of conventional or popular morality to serve the republican ideal of encouraging citizen participation in social and political life. Legal categories Dworkin argued should 'allow ordinary people as well as hard-pressed judges to interpret law within practical boundaries that seem natural and intuitive'.[26] These connections though between legal categories and particular areas of moral concern are not *necessary* or *essential*, as the foundationalist would claim, but rather *contingent* and the product of local history, circumstances, and politics. Nevertheless, once these links take hold, I shall argue that the virtue of integrity, or principled consistency, in law, requires even these purely contingent connections to evolve in a coherent way.

To the extent that English contract law in particular does embody a distinct area of moral concern, I argue that it occupies the domain or serves the moral purpose of facilitating cooperation between citizens on the grounds of mutual trust and respect. In doing so, contract serves valuable instrumental and intrinsic ends. In contributing to a culture that promotes this specific type of cooperation between citizens, contract plays an important and indeed constitutive role in creating the necessary conditions

[22] For a statement of this view see Kraus, 'The Correspondence of Contract and Promise' (n 7) 1603: 'Correspondence accounts of the relationship between contract and promise hold either that contract law is justified to the extent it enforces a corresponding moral responsibility for a promise or unjustified to the extent it undermines promissory morality by refusing to enforce a corresponding moral responsibility for a promise.'

[23] So, for example, Fried says: 'It is because the legal institution of contract is grounded in the moral institution of promise ... that we both expect congruence between the two, but also demand an explanation when the two diverge.' Fried, 'The Convergence of Contract and Promise' (n 21) 4–5.

[24] Text to nn 18–21. [25] Text to nn 10–12.

[26] Ronald Dworkin, *Law's Empire* (Hart Publishing 1998) 252.

for a successful market economy, advancing social stability, and promoting a sense of solidarity. This provides an answer to the liberal objection about the enforcement of morals. The purpose of contract law is not to enforce private morality or promises per se, but to help forge a sense of community and collective endeavour, which is essential for the justification of any state or legal system.

Although this purpose of ensuring cooperation based on trust is in my view a constitutive part or goal of English contract law, it is important to stress and this is part of the anti-foundationalist message of the book that it may be the case that the contract law of other jurisdictions has evolved entirely differently to pursue other distinct ends and aims. English contract law could have gone in a different direction too. Therefore, unlike the foundationalist, my claim is that the nature of particular fields of law, and the values that they embrace, depend on the choices that particular legal systems have made at particular times.

To borrow some distinctions from Dworkin, I do not attempt to show in this book that securing cooperation based on trust is the 'authentic' purpose of English contract law, that is, the purpose that as a matter of historical or sociological fact, participants in the English legal system actually hold or have in the past pursued. Rather, my claim is that this purpose is 'complete', in that it provides a convincing account of English contract law rules and doctrines, and that this purpose is 'distinct' in providing a unique conception of that body of doctrine, which could not be offered by other theories such as, for example, law and economics.[27]

3.2 Contract doctrine

Chapters 5 to 9 of this book focus on the implications of normative pluralism for a range of contract law rules and doctrines relating to contract formation, vitiation, illegality, and remedies. I make three claims in particular. First, that promise theory by assigning a special role to promise in evaluating contract law has struggled to explain or has indeed mishandled these doctrines. Second, that efficiency is not the only other way to explain these doctrines. And, finally, that we get to the truth about the nature of contract law not by relying on a 'top-down' deontic or consequentialist theory according to which there is a uniquely correct answer to ethical or political questions, but rather by paying close attention to the actual practice of contract law, and the plurality of conflicting values and ethical concerns that shape it.[28] In this way, the theory of contract I present has a distinctly protestant or republican bent.

Promise theory has had an uneasy relationship with doctrine. Shiffrin's attacks on the Anglo-American remedial regime for breach of contract are a prominent example. By giving promise a central justificatory role the worry has been that rules and doctrines such as expectation damages and mitigation promote economic interests at the expense of moral concerns.

[27] Ronald Dworkin, 'Liberalism' in Stuart Hampshire (ed), *Public and Private Morality* (Cambridge University Press 1978) 121.

[28] John Tasioulas, 'Punishment and Repentance' (2006) 81 Philosophy 279, 280, 282–83, (making the point in relation to theories of punishment).

I will show why such views are mistaken. By embracing normative pluralism, we see that the promise principle is but one of a multiplicity of moral principles that bear on contract law. In these chapters on English contract law, I identify a doctrine that promise theory has struggled with in the past, and a salient non-promissory value that plays a key role in shaping and making sense of that doctrine.

As I have said above, by embracing normative pluralism, I do not mean to imply or suggest that contract law as a legal category is held together for purely instrumental or conventional purposes. In my view, English contract law has a constitutive purpose which is the facilitation of cooperation based on mutual trust and respect.

I should clarify what I mean here by a 'constitutive purpose'. Unlike consequentialist theories of contract law, like law and economics, in my view the relationship between contract law and the ends or goods it serves is not merely instrumental or causal. In other words, it is not the case that the value of contract law resides entirely in its instrumental contribution to an end that exists outside the practice itself, such as promoting economic efficiency. On such views, if there were better or less costly ways to serve that good, then that would be a sufficient reason to dispense with contract law as a means to it.[29]

Rather, on my view even though contract law may not necessarily succeed in serving its purpose of promoting trust-based cooperation, nevertheless it is not so easy to dispense with it as a means. This is because to borrow a phrase from Anthony Duff contract law is an 'intrinsically appropriate' mechanism for the pursuit of that distinct end. This provides a 'teleological' view of contract law. The goal of achieving trust-based cooperation requires that it be achieved in a particular way or through a particular means.[30] One such way in my view is contract. Contract law structures the relationship between parties who have typically exchanged promises with one another in a way that contributes intrinsically or constitutively to the distinct or independently specifiable good of trust-based cooperation.

I do not claim that contract law is the only way to secure trust-based cooperation. Most obviously, this type of cooperation might be achieved from the making and keeping of non-legally enforceable promises. Rather, my claim is that contract is one (very important) way of achieving this end, and that it is a distinct method which pursues the end by constituting a particular type of intrinsically valuable relation between contractual partners.

This teleological and distinctly republican approach to contract law diverges structurally from the consequentialism of law and economics, and it differs in at least four significant ways from the promise theory. First, on my view contract law serves a purpose that is distinct from the practice itself; it is *functional.* Foundationalists tend to make the structural assumption that the legal enforcement of promises is an intrinsically valuable end per se, or in and of its own right. In other words, the justification for the practice does not depend on the contribution it makes, whether

[29] I rely here on Duff's interpretation of consequentialist arguments. Duff, 'Penal Communications: Recent Work in the Philosophy of Punishment' (n 13) 4–6.

[30] ibid 8–9, (defining teleological views in these ways in the context of defending a theory of punishment).

instrumentally (the consequentialist view) or intrinsically (the teleological view), to the pursuit or promotion of a distinct or independently specifiable goal that is severable from the practice itself.[31] As I have said, I think this gets the foundationalist into the hot water of justifying the state enforcement of morality. I go on to show how the teleological view avoids these pitfalls, by focusing on the social benefits of contract.

Second, on my view the values that shape contract law are *contingent.* Most promise theorists claim that the enforcement of promissory morality is a necessary feature of contract law wherever and whenever it might be found. I make no such strong metaphysical claim. On my view, the existence of what I call contract law's constitutive purpose of promoting trust-based cooperation is an entirely contingent matter. The pursuit of that purpose is one way—I think the best way—of interpreting English contract law. But it may not provide the best account of the contract law of other jurisdictions, and therefore should not necessarily provide normative guidance for contract law rules and doctrines in these legal systems. The purpose or purposes of contract law may differ between jurisdictions and depend on local circumstances and the past political decisions made by the legal system in question.

Third, on my view the values that underpin contract law are *underdetermined.* Promise theorists tend to make ambitious claims about the normative guidance that their theories provide for how contract law rules are shaped and structured. They tend to assume that promissory morality is fairly determinate, and can be relied upon to make fairly specific recommendations about what contract law should or should not look like. I am highly sceptical of these claims, and I make no such claim for the constitutive good—the promotion of trust-based cooperation—that in my view animates English contract law.

This constitutive purpose despite being an organizing ideal that infuses decision-making in this area may be interpreted or specified in a variety of morally acceptable ways.[32] This gives those with primary responsibility for developing contract law rules and doctrines, for example, in England, the courts, a great deal of leeway in deciding exactly how they interpret, balance, and rank the often completing principles and values that bear on this area of moral concern. Therefore, even between legal systems that share trust-based cooperation as the organizing ideal of contract law, we should expect to see perfectly legitimate divergences between the rules and doctrines adopted in these jurisdictions.

These constitutive purposes due to their inherent under-determinacy function more like negative 'side-constraints' to condemn the creation or perpetuation of rules and doctrines that directly or egregiously contradict the values that these purposes instantiate, rather than positive sources of normative guidance about

[31] In this way, foundationalists share similarities with those who offer retributive theories of punishment. ibid 6–7.

[32] cf Nussbaum on the role and underdeterminacy of organizing values in the context of debates about what makes a distinctively human life. Martha C Nussbaum, 'Aristotle on Human Nature and the Foundations of Ethics' in JEJ Altham and Ross Harrison (eds), *World, Mind, and Ethics: Essays on the Ethical Philosophy of Bernard Williams* (Cambridge University Press 1995) 113–17, 123.

what contract law should look like, which is how promise theorists tend to treat promissory morality.[33]

Finally, there is no one single purpose of contract law; it has a *plurality* of purposes. Promise theorists tend to think that promissory morality exhausts the legitimate purposes and functions of contract law. I find such views both moralistic and underinclusive of the values that are actually at stake. Contract performs a variety of important ancillary or incidental functions, including promoting efficiency, ensuring fair terms of cooperation, preventing exploitation of bargaining power, protecting reliance, and so forth. Although I would claim that English contract law does have as a constitutive purpose the promotion of trust-based cooperation, which influences how these other incidental ends are pursued, we should be wary of downplaying these other functions, and recognize that they too play a significant role in the eventual shape that contract law rules and doctrines take. Like constitutive purposes, these incidental purposes or functions are underdetermined in nature too, and this adds to the legitimate variation in contract law rules and doctrines that we find between legal systems.

On this 'bottom-up' or republican view, and in contrast to the views of most promise theorists, the values that shape contract law are functional, contingent, underdetermined, and pluralistic. On this view, it is incumbent on those who seek to interpret contract law, to pay very close attention to its rules and doctrines and the particular ways in which courts have interpreted and balanced the multiplicity of values that bear on it.

In this book I apply this republican approach to a variety of doctrines, including undue influence, restraint of trade, the penalties rule, and mitigation, and show how the justification of each doctrine is linked in significant ways to at least one non-promissory value, such as fairness, corrective justice, freedom, the prevention of exploitation, and so forth. These doctrines are what I call 'composite' in character, that is, the product of the interaction between a multiplicity of deontic moral values and principles. Rejecting the promise theory, I argue, does not entail that only efficiency explains contract law doctrine.

3.3 Transnational contract law

In the final chapter of the book, my focus shifts to the topic of transnational contract law. In an era of globalization, free trade, and market liberalization, it is unsurprising given the important economic role that contracts play in any society, that there have been increasing global and regional efforts to bring about the harmonization of contract law regimes between jurisdictions to facilitate trade and reduce transaction costs.[34] These are important transnational initiatives that have the potential to

[33] I borrow the phrase 'side-constraint' here of course from Robert Nozick. Robert Nozick, *Anarchy, State, and Utopia* (Basil Blackwell 1974) 28–29.

[34] For example, UN Convention on Contracts for the International Sale of Goods (11 April 1980) 1489 UNTS 3, *entered into force* 1 January 1988 [CISG]; International Institute for the Unification of Private Law, *Principles of International Commercial Contracts* (3rd edn, Transnational 2010) [PICC]. Regional efforts include South America, Asia, and South Africa. For South America,

have far-reaching consequences for national contract laws. These developments have been largely driven by economic considerations, and philosophers of contract have tended to have little to say about them. My aim in this part of the book is to bridge this gap between contract theory and these political developments. This is important because controversies about the foundations of contract law are central to debates about the legitimacy of these transnational efforts. I argue at the end that the underlying theme of this book—the importance of normative pluralism—poses potentially a huge and insurmountable challenge to the legitimacy of these projects, because they overlook or are insufficiently attentive to the fact that the legitimacy of any contract law regime is rooted ultimately in local customs, circumstances, beliefs, and values.

I use European Union ('EU') efforts to bring about the harmonization of contract law in Europe as a case study to make these broader points. In 2001, the European Commission mooted the idea that contract law should converge in Europe.[35] Economic arguments were put centre stage. It was claimed that convergence would facilitate the creation of an internal market. However, the academic literature reveals the presence of certain foundationalist assumptions too, in particular the old idea that there exists an *ius commune* or one true contract law, discoverable by natural reason alone.[36]

I challenge these claims and argue that the existence of normative pluralism entails that there is no single correct way to interpret, order, or rank the values that play a role in contract law. The existence of this type of pluralism, explains in this context the value of state sovereignty. Due to the multiplicity of ways in which the values that shape contract doctrine can be interpreted and ranked, states should have the freedom or sovereignty to determine the shape their law will take. The value of that freedom, and in particular the role it plays in constituting and expressing a sense of national identity, gives rise to the central problem of the legitimacy of EU efforts to bring about convergence, to which I argue the EU at least has failed to provide an adequate answer.

see Rodrigo Momberg and Stefan Vogenauer (eds), *The Future of Contract Law in Latin America: The Principles of Latin American Contract Law* (Bloomsbury Publishing 2017); *Rodrigo Momberg and Stefan Vogenauer*, 'The Principles of Latin American Contract Law: Text, Translation, and Introduction' (2018) 23 Uniform Law Review 144. For Asia, see Shiyuan Han, 'Principles of Asian Contract Law: An Endeavor of Regional Harmonization of Contract Law in East Asia' (2013) 58 Villanova Law Review 589. For South Africa, see 'OHADA, Acte Uniform portant sur le Droit Commercial Général', OHADA Official Gazette, No 21 (15 February 2011), available at <http://www.ohada.org/index.php/en/official-gazette/official-gazette-n-21> accessed 5 July 2018, English translation available at <http://www.ohadalegis.com/anglais/audrtcomgb1.htm> accessed 5 July 2018.

[35] Commission, 'Communication from the Commission to the Council and the European Parliament on European Contract Law' COM (2001) 398 final.

[36] On the influence exerted by these foundationalist assumptions on contemporary debates about convergence see Hugh Collins, 'Cosmopolitanism and Transnational Private Law' (2012) 8 European Review of Contract Law 311.

4. Aims

These are the three contexts in which this book's argument are advanced. It seeks to address or fully comprehend the implications of normative pluralism in contract law in different ways, that is, theoretically, doctrinally, and politically. In doing so, I hope what emerges is a powerful critique of the promise theory and the foundationalist assumptions that underpin it.

Although this is a book about contract law, the critique I offer of the promise theory is also intended as a much broader critique of foundationalism. As I have said, foundationalism has had a huge influence in private law, but its influence is now being felt in many other areas too, such as environmental law, family law, labour law, constitutional law, criminal law, international law, and so forth.[37] If there is no meaningful sense in which the promise principle is the foundation of contract law, then there is reason to doubt in general that areas of law are differentiated in terms of their normative foundations. This is because few other areas of law have as tight a connection to a single moral principle as contract law has to promise.[38] Scepticism about foundationalism in contract law forces us to rethink why law generally is divided into different areas.

I do not dwell in this book on this broader critique of foundationalism. However, I believe my critique of foundationalism in contract law could—with appropriate modifications—be applied to these other areas too. Showing this though would go beyond the main purpose of this book, and indeed the limits of my own expertise. I leave it to others to take up that task.

[37] Reflected most recently in the popularity of a new series of edited collections by Oxford University Press on the philosophical foundations of various areas of law, see <https://global.oup.com/academic/content/series/p/philosophical-foundations-of-law-pf/?cc=gb&lang=en&> accessed 13 November 2018.

[38] It might be said that the law of unjust enrichment is based entirely on a single moral principle, bearing the same name. However, it is unclear whether any such principle exists in morality or whether instead it is just a placeholder for a range of normative concerns, see Hanoch Dagan, *The Law and Ethics of Restitution* (Cambridge University Press 2004); Charlie Webb, *Reason and Restitution: A Theory of Unjust Enrichment* (Oxford University Press 2016).

2

Foundationalism and the Promise Theory*

1. Introduction

In this short chapter, I define the main target of this book: the 'promise theory' of contract. I will argue that it is a 'foundationalist' theory of contract law, according to which the promise principle plays a special justificatory role in carving out this area of law and shaping the rules and doctrines that it contains. However, exactly what promise theorists take this special role for promise to be in contract law is largely obscure and underdeveloped in the literature. They tend to speak in metaphors like 'foundational' rather than define the role promise plays precisely. There are hints though of what they might mean. In this chapter, I set out three interpretations of what promise theorists could mean when they say promise plays a special or foundational role in contract law.

2. Foundationalism in Private Law

In his seminal *An Introduction to the Law of Restitution*, Peter Birks remarked that 'It ought to be possible to take any legal subject and to cut away its detail so as to reveal the skeleton of principle which holds it together.'[1] The idea that areas of law have a 'skeleton of principle' is intuitively very appealing. It allows us to abstract away from detailed rules and doctrines, many of which are ephemeral, and to seek a deeper understanding of what gives an area of law its distinct identity. It is also an intellectually stimulating task. The theorist delves into existing rules and doctrines and evaluates them, aiming to unmask the moral principles that serve as their foundation, whether or not officials or judges have explicitly articulated or endorsed them.[2] For convenience, let's call this type of project 'foundationalist'. Perhaps its

* This chapter is based on and largely reproduces the text of, with some revisions and adaptations, sections A and B of an unpublished paper co-authored with George Letsas entitled 'Foundationalism About Contract Law: A Sceptical View', available at SSRN: <https://papers.ssrn.com/sol3/papers.cfm?abstract_id=3211283> accessed 7 November 2018. The text is used with kind permission of my co-author.

[1] Peter Birks, *An Introduction to the Law of Restitution* (Clarendon Press 1989) 1.

[2] ibid. This was clearly Birks's project in the case of restitution, because he insisted on there being a distinct category of restitution even though judges did not systematically acknowledge its existence.

most appealing aspect is its critical edge. Once we know which moral principles hold an area of law together, we are also able to single out recalcitrant rules and doctrines with a view to making it more coherent.

In recent years, foundationalism has taken centre-stage in private law theory. Perhaps its best expression is found in the work of Charles Fried. Fried famously claimed that 'the promise principle . . . is the moral basis of contract law' and that 'a contract is first of all a promise'.[3] Similar approaches to private law have been very influential. Ernest Weinrib for instance has argued that private law is based on corrective justice,[4] and, more recently, Robert Stevens has claimed that the law of tort is underlain by the principle that wrongdoers ought to correct rights infringements.[5] Foundationalism is a *metaphysical* theory of areas of law. It claims that moral principles like promise, corrective justice, and unjust enrichment are *necessarily* built into the very fabric of every legal system, and are constitutive of particular areas of law, like tort, contract, and so on; and these moral principles magnetically attract the rules and doctrines contained in these areas of law.

Many of these foundationalist theories have emerged as a reaction to law and economics, and the claim that the doctrines of private law cannot be explained by any deontic moral principle, such as promise or corrective justice, but are rather grounded in the economics of efficiency.[6] And it is true that foundationalism sits uncomfortably with utilitarianism and other forms of consequentialism. Utilitarianism holds that the whole of morality boils down to a single moral aim, namely to maximize happiness. Since utilitarianism recognizes only one moral standard it must deny that each area of law has a separate moral foundation. If morality is reducible to a single moral concern there would be no principled basis for subdividing the law, though of course there could be other bases for doing so.[7]

So, one of the main motivations for foundationalism has been to show that—contrary to law and economics—deontic moral principles not only bear on the justification of legal doctrine, but can also justify a large number of existing doctrines and serve as a standard of excellence for particular areas of law. Seana Shiffrin remarks, for example, that behind the idea that contracts are enforceable promises is the thought that:

> if contracts have, at their foundations, the same moral relations that we describe as promises in our everyday social relations, that fact might provide the seedlings both of a justification for contract law and of a guide to the principles it should follow.[8]

[3] Charles Fried, *Contract as Promise: A Theory of Contractual Obligation* (Harvard University Press 1981) 1.

[4] Ernest J Weinrib, *The Idea of Private Law* (Harvard University Press 1995).

[5] Robert Stevens, *Torts and Rights* (Oxford University Press 2007) 2, 151.

[6] See the discussion in Charles Fried, 'The Convergence of Contract and Promise' (2007) 120 Harvard Law Review Forum 1, 1 (discussing law and economics and in relation to contract); and Seana Valentine Shiffrin, 'The Divergence of Contract and Promise' (2007) 120 Harvard Law Review 708, 724–26.

[7] Rule consequentialists might subdivide the law on the basis that compliance with certain rules, such as, for example, the rules of contract law, is a unique tool to maximize efficiency. But this way would not depend on the inherent moral significance of a particular area of law.

[8] Seana Valentine Shiffrin, 'Is a Contract a Promise?' in Andrei Marmor (ed), *The Routledge Companion to Philosophy of Law* (Routledge 2012) 242.

Another motivation behind foundationalism is the common lawyer's ambition to impose doctrinal coherence on the cases. Birks, for example, used the principle of unjust enrichment to gather together rules and doctrines that were conventionally thought to belong to other legal categories such as contract, tort, and trusts and to be explained by the principles found therein. The reason why he insisted on there being a distinct legal category individuated by the principle of unjust enrichment was that the principles found in those other areas were unable to explain cases of unjust enrichment and had led to mistakes about what claimants were entitled to. So, for example, Birks rejected the approach in *Sinclair v Brougham*, which blocked restitution on the ground that the claim depended on the existence of a valid contract, when in the case there was none. The mistake Birks thought was to identify restitution with contract law rather than its true basis in unjust enrichment.[9] Fried famously repudiated the consideration doctrine, because if as on his view contracts are promises there is no need for reciprocation to justify why they should be enforced.[10] This was despite the fact that conventionally consideration was seen as a central doctrine in contract law. And in tort, Weinrib has argued that strict liability is incompatible with corrective justice.[11]

Of course, foundationalism is not the only possible explanation for why there are different areas of law. According to what I call 'conventionalism', law is broken up by officials or participants in the legal system (that is, judges, legislators, lawyers, legal scholars, and so forth) for purely *epistemic* ends, such as to make the law more digestible, predictable, easier to teach, handle, and so on. On this view, legal categories exist if legal officials or legal actors happen to have taken a set of rules and doctrines to constitute a distinct field. It is conventionally understood, for example, that contract law is a separate area of law that contains doctrines such as offer and acceptance, consideration, intention to create legal relations, mitigation, and so forth. Conventionalism does not assume that the legal categories that exist have, or are supposed to have, some true normative principle as their foundation. A conventional category may reflect certain principles none of which is in any way foundational; or it may be based on an entirely immoral idea such as the category of 'slave law' in historic legal systems.

Conventional classification can be tremendously useful. As Birks argued the pursuit of certain valuable activities may be made easier by bringing together 'bits and pieces' of law which 'are kept apart in other ways of dividing up the law'.[12] Hence one finds textbooks and treatises on issues such as banking law, carriage of goods by sea, war law, sports law, or media law. These categories facilitate epistemic

[9] *Sinclair v Brougham* [1914] AC 398, 415. Birks, *An Introduction to the Law of Restitution* (n 1) 38: 'The question was whether, given the nullity of the contracts, restitution should nevertheless be ordered. So nothing could be less helpful than to begin the analysis with questions about promises.'

[10] Fried, *Contract as Promise: A Theory of Contractual Obligation* (n 3) 38: 'the doctrine of consideration offers no coherent alternative basis for the force of contracts, while still treating promise as necessary to it'.

[11] Weinrib, *The Idea of Private Law* (n 4) ch 7.

[12] Birks, *An Introduction to the Law of Restitution* (n 1) 74.

handling of the law, and promote rule of law values by making it easier for citizens to have notice of legal requirements.

Interestingly, both the law and economics school and foundationalism have tended to oppose the formalism embodied in conventionalist methods of differentiation. The economist rejects the very point of differentiating areas of law on the basis of distinct normative principles and subsumes everything under the test of efficiency or wealth maximization. The foundationalist by contrast takes differentiation by moral principle to be the antidote to arbitrary collections of doctrines and rules based on no other ground than the conventions of judges, officials, and textbook writers. Law and economics dominate private law scholarship in the US and foundationalism is now embedded in the literature in England and the Commonwealth. Both, however, take issue with formalistic or conventionalist accounts of private law, according to which, in Tony Weir's words, 'Tort is what is in the tort books, and the only thing holding it together is the binding.'[13]

So, in its typical form, foundationalism presupposes a deontological moral outlook as a mode of justifying legal doctrine. But it goes further than that, holding that areas of law have a particular deontic principle as their normative foundation. In the case of contract law, the main form of foundationalism is the idea that contract is underlain by the principle that promises ought to be kept, or the promise principle for short. Of all areas of law, contract is perhaps the one most closely associated with a single moral principle. As Shiffrin remarks: 'The language of promises, promisees and promisors saturates contract law'.[14] She cites the US *Restatement* which says that 'A contract is a promise or a set of promises for the breach of which the law gives a remedy, or the performance of which the law in some way recognizes as a duty.'[15] The idea that contracts are promises gained momentum after the publication of Fried's *Contract as Promise.* The number of promise theorists has grown steadily and the list now includes a number of leading legal theorists including Daniel Markovits,[16] Seana Shiffrin,[17] Liam Murphy,[18] and Jody Kraus.[19]

Promise theorists claim that there is some special connection between the promise principle and the task of justifying contract law doctrines. They engage with contract law doctrines, such as consideration, intention to create legal relations, expectation damages, the rule against penalties, mitigation, and so on and debate whether they converge or diverge from promissory morality.

[13] Tony Weir, *Tort Law* (Oxford University Press 2002) ix.

[14] Shiffrin, 'The Divergence of Contract and Promise' (n 6) 721.

[15] American Law Institute, *Restatement (Second) of Contracts* (American Law Institute Publishers 1981) s 1, cited by Shiffrin, 'The Divergence of Contract and Promise' (n 6) 721.

[16] Daniel Markovits, 'Contract and Collaboration' (2004) 113 Yale Law Journal 1417; Daniel Markovits, 'Promise as an Arm's Length Relation' in Hanoch Sheinman (ed), *Promises and Agreements: Philosophical Essays* (Oxford University Press 2011).

[17] Shiffrin, 'The Divergence of Contract and Promise' (n 6) 721.

[18] Liam Murphy, 'Contract and Promise' (2007) 120 Harvard Law Review Forum 10, available at <https://harvardlawreview.org/2009/10/contract-and-promise/> accessed 5 July 2018.

[19] Jody S Kraus, 'The Correspondence of Contract and Promise' (2009) 109 Columbia Law Review 1603.

In this chapter, I explore in more detail what is meant by the idea that promise is the moral foundation of contract law or—to use Birks's metaphor—its skeleton of principle. Though I recognize the intuitive appeal of this claim, it is not at all clear how these sorts of metaphor—used so often in the literature—should be unpacked. In particular, what exactly is the special role that the promise principle is meant to play in evaluating contract doctrine? Perhaps it plays no such role, in which case we should divorce foundationalism from the task of normatively assessing the law. The dominant view though is that foundationalism speaks to the normative justification of the law of contract and it is in this light that I approach it. My particular concern is with how different conceptions of contract law foundationalism play out in normative assessments of specific doctrines.

Below I distinguish three ways in which the claim that promise is the moral foundation of contract law might be cashed out: the promise principle can be said to enjoy either what I call 'justificatory necessity', or 'justificatory primacy', or 'justificatory presumptiveness'.

3. How Is Promise Special? Three Views

The claim that promise is the foundation of contract law is fairly abstract. Much depends on what one means by promise and what one means by contract law. To avoid confusion, I shall begin by taking promise to mean the moral principle that promises ought to be kept, while being agnostic about what best grounds the standing of this principle in morality. And I take contract law to mean all the legal rules and doctrines that are conventionally understood to constitute the law of contract in common law jurisdictions like the US and England, such as, consideration, duress, unconscionability, expectation damages, and so on. I propose to understand promise-based foundationalism as the claim that contract law doctrines are the *explanandum* and that the promise principle is the *explanans*. Moreover, I propose to take the kind of explanation to be involved here to be one of normative justification, not a causal or historical claim. One could be interested in the attitudes and beliefs of the officials that promulgated or enforced these doctrines. It could be the case, for example, that in doing so these officials were motivated by the promise principle. But this is not the kind of explanation that the foundationalist seems interested in. Foundationalists typically seek to assess the justifiability of doctrines, not to explain how they came about.

A cursory look at contract law doctrines reveals the presence of a number of considerations that go beyond the principle that promises should be kept. Contract law contains rules about which promises should be legally enforced (for example, consideration and the intention to create legal relations doctrine), when promises may be set-aside (duress, undue influence, unconscionability, and so on), and rules about remedies for breach of contract (expectation damages, remoteness, mitigation, and so forth). Few, if any, would argue that the promise principle, narrowly construed, could alone provide a complete normative explanation of all these doctrines. For example, moral considerations to do with preventing exploitation, security of transactions, reliance, fairness, and many others, clearly play a normative role in explaining the shape these doctrines take. In other words, the normative justification of most contract law doctrines, if one exists, turns on more than one principle. So-called 'normative pluralism' is something that most scholars now take for granted.[20] Therefore, the claim that promise is the foundation of contract must go beyond the idea that the promise principle is the only *explanans* of contract law doctrines. It must show that the promise principle plays a special role *within* a pluralistic framework.

Consider, for example, the doctrine that requires contracts to be interpreted according to their objective meaning. It has long been acknowledged that this requirement is not based on the promise principle, which would require the subjective meaning of the promisor to determine the content of the contractual duty. We would have to appeal to some other principle, like justice or fairness, to justify departures from the subjective intentions of the parties.[21] It should be uncontroversial, and indeed it is generally accepted, that a certain degree of normative pluralism is required in order to give a complete normative justification of contract law doctrines. Any theory that assigns to the promise principle a special role in justifying contract law doctrines must do so *given* this normative pluralism. Foundationalism cannot just be the view that the promise principle is the *only* one that bears on the justifiability of contract law doctrines, conventionally identified. Moreover, foundationalism must explain *how* the promise principle differs from others in the role that it plays in justifying contract law doctrines. It cannot just be special merely in virtue of justifying contract law doctrines, because other moral principles play the same role, such as fairness and justice.

There are at least three ways in which one can understand foundationalism. All of them relate to a special justificatory role that the promise principle might play given the existence of normative pluralism.

3.1 Justificatory necessity

According to the first view, the promise principle plays a *necessary* role in justifying each and every contract law doctrine. However, given the presence of other principles this role is not *sufficient*. On this view, all these other principles either qualify or defeat the promise principle. Consider, for example, the doctrine of illegality. The promise principle alone would be insufficient to explain why promises to do something illegal, or contrary to public policy, are invalid. What illegality does is to qualify the promise principle, by restricting the scope of legally enforceable promises. Likewise, consider the doctrine of frustration. The promise principle

[20] See, for example, Gregory Klass, 'Promise Etc.' (2012) 45 Suffolk University Law Review 695; Roy Kreitner, 'On the New Pluralism in Contract Theory' (2012) 45 Suffolk University Law Review 915; Robert A Hillman, *The Richness of Contract Law: An Analysis and Critique of Contemporary Theories of Contract Law* (Springer Science & Business Media 2012).

[21] Henry Sidgwick, *The Methods of Ethics* (Hackett Publishing 1907) 303–04; Fried, *Contract as Promise: A Theory of Contractual Obligation* (n 3) 61.

alone would be insufficient to explain why a valid promise is set aside because of subsequent events that either make the contract impossible or unfair to perform in the circumstances. The absence of illegality is a (negative) condition for the validity of a promise, whereas frustration defeats an otherwise valid promise. In both cases, the promise principle is necessary in order to offer a normative explanation of the doctrine, but it is not sufficient. Still, the promise principle can be said to be special in that, unlike other principles, it is *always* present in each and every contract law doctrine. All contract law doctrines can be said to be about the promise principle in the sense that they either instantiate, qualify, or defeat it. I call this view justificatory necessity.

3.2 Justificatory primacy

The second view holds that the promise principle is the primary basis for justifying contract law doctrines. Promissory morality is here taken to be the first virtue of contract law, in the same sense that John Rawls famously said that justice is the first virtue of social institutions. For Rawls, the primacy of justice means it is uncompromising: 'laws and institutions no matter how efficient and well-arranged must be reformed or abolished if they are unjust'.[22] If our social institutions fail the demands of justice, then no other principle can justify sustaining them. Likewise, the primacy of the promise principle means that contract law doctrines, no matter how efficient or fair, must be reformed or abolished, if they violate it. Here is what Kraus says about these types of view:

> Correspondence accounts of the relationship between contract and promise hold either that contract law is justified to the extent it enforces a corresponding moral responsibility for a promise or unjustified to the extent it undermines promissory morality by refusing to enforce a corresponding moral responsibility for a promise.[23]

The idea here is that either contract law doctrines converge with promissory morality, in which case they are justified, or they diverge from it, in which case they are objectionable and in need of reform. I call this view justificatory primacy.[24]

3.3 Justificatory presumptiveness

The third approach to the connection between the promise principle and the justification of contract law assigns to the promise principle a type of justificatory presumption. Here, the idea is that we should expect that contract law converges with promissory morality and presume that any divergence between contract and

[22] John Rawls, *A Theory of Justice* (rev edn, Oxford University Press 1999) 3.

[23] Kraus, 'The Correspondence of Contract and Promise' (n 19) 1603.

[24] I borrow this label from Jeremy Waldron's discussion of Rawls' claim that justice is the first virtue of social institutions; see Jeremy Waldron, 'The Primacy of Justice' (2003) 9 Legal Theory 269.

promise is prima facie objectionable.[25] So, for example, echoing such a view Fried describes his and Shiffrin's position as follows:

It is because the legal institution of contract is grounded in the moral institution of promise... that we both expect congruence between the two, but also demand an explanation when the two diverge.[26]

The upshot of this justificatory presumption is that doctrines that converge with promissory morality are presumed justified and those that diverge are presumed to be unjustified. So, the convergence of a doctrine with promissory morality is deemed sufficient to ground its justification, without the need to assess it in the light of non-promissory principles. In *Contract as Promise*, Fried argues, for example, that the doctrines of offer and acceptance, expectation damages, remoteness, and good faith in performance are all justified because they correspond with promissory morality. When, however, a doctrine diverges from promissory morality, this triggers a normative inquiry into whether the divergence can be justified. The normative inquiry might show that the divergence is the product of a justified compromise between the promise principle and other moral concerns. Shiffrin, for example, argues that certain legal doctrines that, on her view, offend the promise principle (such as expectation damages) may be justified in certain contexts by non-promissory considerations.[27] Unlike the second view, according to which the promise principle has justificatory primacy, this third position allows for the possibility that other considerations may justifiably compromise the application of the promise principle in contract. According to the second view, a contract doctrine that diverges from promissory morality is necessarily unjustified, as opposed to presumptively. On this third view, it is only if the divergence cannot be justified as a compromise that the doctrine should be rejected. For example, both Shiffrin and Fried reject the legal requirement that seriously intended promises are not enforceable in the absence of consideration.[28] I call this third view justificatory presumptiveness.

I should be clear here that I am not claiming that any single author endorses wholesale one or the other type of foundationalism, as sketched above. This is understandable, as few scholars address separately the question of what it means for any principle to serve as the foundation of an area of law. Rather my claim is that there are at least echoes of some of these views in the literature and that each of these three

[25] The presumption that contract law is objectionable is an epistemic presumption. Divergence creates the appearance that contract doctrine is unjustified, it does not mean that it actually is. On the distinction between prima facie and pro tanto reasons see Shelly Kagan, *The Limits of Morality* (Clarendon Press 1989) 17: 'a prima facie reason *appears* to be a reason, but may actually not be a reason at all, ... In contrast, a pro tanto reason is a genuine reason—with actual weight—but it may not be a *decisive* one in various cases.'

[26] Fried, 'The Convergence of Contract and Promise' (n 6) 4–5.

[27] Shiffrin, 'The Divergence of Contract and Promise' (n 6) 733. She calls such considerations distinctively legal arguments. These are moral arguments 'whose range is specifically tailored to the special, normatively salient properties of law and its appropriate content and shape'.

[28] Fried, *Contract as Promise: A Theory of Contractual Obligation* (n 3) 38: 'the doctrine of consideration offers no coherent alternative basis for the force of contracts, while still treating promise as necessary to it'; Fried, 'The Convergence of Contract and Promise' (n 6) 4; Shiffrin, 'The Divergence of Contract and Promise' (n 6) 736–37.

forms of foundationalism (justificatory necessity, primacy, and presumptiveness) are internally coherent and are worth examining on their own merits, as intelligible conceptions of how the promise principle holds contract law together.

4. Conclusion

In this short chapter, I have argued that the promise theory provides a foundationalist account of contract law, according to which the promise principle plays a special justificatory role in shaping contract law rules and doctrines. Foundationalism in recent times has emerged as the most influential non-consequentialist theory of areas of private law, like contract, tort, unjust enrichment, and so forth. However, in contract law the sense in which promise is meant to play a foundational role is imprecisely defined and under-discussed in the literature.

I have set out three plausible interpretations of what this role might be. Either promise plays a necessary role in the justification of every single contract law doctrine, a view I call justificatory necessity; or it plays an overriding or uncompromising role when it conflicts with other moral principles, which I call justificatory primacy; or, finally, it justifies an epistemic presumption that contract law rules and doctrines that diverge from promissory morality are prima facie unjustified, a view which I call justificatory presumptiveness. I do not mean to deny that there might be other ways of interpreting the special role that promise is meant to play in contract. Rather, my claim is that these three interpretations are distinct and plausible. Furthermore, some of these roles seem to be assumed or supported by promise theorists in the literature.

In the next chapter, I subject these three forms of foundationalism to detailed critical scrutiny, seeking to highlight their strengths and weaknesses. Ultimately, though, I argue that they fail to yield adequate accounts of contract doctrine. This is due to the stubborn fact of normative pluralism, that is, that more than one principle is required to justify contract law doctrines and rules. Given I argue further in the book that the promise principle is often defeated or qualified by other deontic principles, there is little sense in which promise—or any other single moral principle for that matter—is the foundation of contract law.

3

The Limits of Promise*

1. Introduction

In Chapter 2, I argued that promise theorists offer 'foundationalist' accounts of contract law. They claim that despite the existence of 'normative pluralism' the promise principle plays a special role in justifying contract doctrine. I distinguished three ways in which promise might play that role. According to 'justificatory necessity', promise plays a necessary role in justifying each and every contract law rule and doctrine. 'Justificatory primacy' holds that promise plays an overriding role when it conflicts with other deontic principles that bear on contract. Finally, 'justificatory presumptiveness' has it that the promise principle justifies an epistemic presumption that doctrines that diverge from promissory morality are prima facie unjustified.

In this chapter, I subject these three views to detailed critical scrutiny. I argue that normative pluralism is a stubborn fact that promise theorists have failed to take sufficiently seriously. As a result, these three conceptions of the special role that promise might play in contract law offer inadequate accounts of contract doctrine. They end up either repudiating doctrines that are justifiable from a deontic perspective, condoning doctrines that are unjustifiable, or, finally, offering the wrong explanation of why contract law doctrines are justified. To truly understand contract law, I argue that we have to reach beyond the promise theory.

2. Foundationalism as Justificatory Necessity

The idea that the promise principle is necessary but not sufficient in order to give a normative explanation of each and every contract law doctrine is intuitively appealing. The promise principle is often defeated by weightier moral considerations or qualified by moral considerations external to the promise principle. But if it is always present in the justification of each and every contract law doctrine, then its role is special enough to warrant the title of a foundation.

* This chapter is based on and largely reproduces the text of, with some revisions and adaptations, sections C, D, and E of an unpublished paper co-authored with George Letsas entitled 'Foundationalism About Contract Law: A Sceptical View', available at SSRN: <https://papers.ssrn.com/sol3/papers.cfm?abstract_id=3211283> accessed 7 November 2018. The text is used with kind permission of my co-author.

Yet as far as I know, no one has actually defended this view. This may be because it can very easily be challenged by pointing to contract law doctrines where promise plays no role. For example, pre-contractual liability, as its name readily suggests, imposes liability for reliance losses in anticipation of a promise, regardless of whether one is actually made. Charles Fried says that what justifies imposing liability on the party that induces pre-contractual reliance is not the promise principle, but rather the principle 'that people who give vague assurances that cause foreseeable harm to others should make compensation'.[1] On Fried's view, the justification of a number of contract law doctrines, as conventionally identified, has nothing to do with the promise principle. These include, as well as pre-contractual liability, doctrines such as mistake and fraud. There are, moreover, familiar remedial doctrines, such as remoteness, mitigation, causation, and contributory negligence which are triggered by a breach of promise yet their justification is independent of the nature of the wrong committed (evidenced by the fact that we find similar doctrines in, for example, tort law). Justificatory necessity overreaches as a conception of foundationalism.

It could however be argued that even though the promise principle is not necessary to justify each and every contract doctrine it is nevertheless always 'in the picture' within contract law. The idea here would be that in each and every contract law doctrine the promise principle features as a theme, even in cases where it plays no justificatory role. For example, in the context of mistake or pre-contractual liability there was *potentially* a promise, or in the case of fraud or misrepresentation there was an attempt to *procure* a promise. Likewise, it can be said that promise is the theme of other contract law remedies such as remoteness, mitigation, causation, and contributory negligence, in that they are triggered because of a breach of promise rather than some other moral wrong. Let's call this view 'thematic necessity'.

The problem with this alternative form of foundationalism *qua* thematic (as opposed to justificatory) necessity is that it is normatively inert. Foundationalism is supposed to help us in the task of providing a normative explanation of contract law doctrines. Merely knowing that the theme of an area of law is promise does nothing to assist us in assessing the justifiability of its doctrines. This is not only because some doctrines are the product of the interaction between the promise principle and other principles, but also because—as we saw—some of them have nothing to do with the promise principle. It is also hard to see how turning the theme of an area of law into its foundation illuminates our understanding of that area. We might for instance say that constitutionalism is both the theme and the foundation of constitutional law. But, at best, this statement would only serve to reiterate an uncontroversial starting point, namely that the value of constitutionalism is relevant in assessing constitutional law doctrines. But how exactly it is relevant would remain obscure.

There is potentially a further worry with respect to the idea of thematic necessity, which is that it can potentially mislead. It might lead us to infer, wrongly, that the

[1] Charles Fried, *Contract as Promise: A Theory of Contractual Obligation* (Harvard University Press 1981) 24, discussing *Hoffman v Red Owl Stores Inc* 26 Wis 2d 683, 133 NW 2d 267 (1965).

existence of a promise is necessary for contractual liability. Fried says that the classical exponents of contract as promise were 'supremely guilty' of making this error, as seen in 'their reluctance to grant relief for fraud or for mistakes that prevented a real agreement from coming into being'.[2] Such mistakes are, of course, not inevitable, but the fact that they are made suggests that foundationalism is inherently a thesis about the special justificatory force of a principle, not about its role as a central theme. The classical theorists were led astray because they took the claim that contracts are promises as a justificatory claim, and not simply as a claim about the theme of contract law. So, thematic necessity, as a conception of foundationalism, is at best incomplete and at worst misleading.

Before I move on, I should mention one final way in which the promise principle can be said to be necessary in justifying contract law doctrines. One could argue that, though not present in justifying each and every contract law doctrine, when it *is* present, the immorality of breaking a promise is always a pro tanto reason for legal enforcement.[3] On this 'moralistic' view, the various contract law doctrines (for example, undue influence, unconscionability, frustration, estoppel, and so forth) may be seen as being grounded on moral considerations (such as preventing exploitation, unfairness, and so on) that defeat a pro tanto reason for state enforcement.

A reason is pro tanto if, as Shelly Kagan writes, it 'has genuine weight, but nonetheless may be outweighed by other considerations'. Pro tanto reasons may be contrasted with prima facie reasons, which are *appearances* of reasons, and so may not have genuine normative weight.[4] A pro tanto reason or duty may be defeated by more weighty considerations but nevertheless it is, as Joseph Raz says, 'somehow still there, it somehow survives'.[5] This means that the fact that a reason has been defeated has normative consequences, ranging, for example, from secondary duties to make good the loss that one has caused, to duties to apologize or feel regret. So, this last view claims that most contract law doctrines are about considerations that defeat the pro tanto reason of the state to enforce promises.

I find this moralistic view problematic, because not all promises—whatever one's theory of promissory obligation is—give the state a pro tanto reason for enforcement. Consider, for example, certain kinds of promises between friends or intimates, such as the promise to be faithful to one's partner. Few would argue that such a promise ought to be legally enforceable, even if there was intention to create legal relations, and the partner has given consideration. And it is doubtful that the state has a pro tanto obligation to enforce the promise, which is defeated by considerations such as intimacy or autonomy. It seems clear that the law has no business intervening here in the first place, because the promise relates to an intimate aspect of one's personal relationships.[6] If it did then that would entail

[2] Fried, *Contract as Promise: A Theory of Contractual Obligation* (n 1) 24.
[3] Thank you to Hanoch Sheinman for alerting me to this possibility.
[4] Shelly Kagan, *The Limits of Morality* (Clarendon Press 1989) 17.
[5] Joseph Raz, *Practical Reason and Norms* (Oxford University Press 1999) 27 n 6.
[6] It is this kind of normative concern that I think motivates the thesis that the practice of promising performs a distinct function to contract. For a defence of this thesis, see Dori Kimel, *From Promise to Contract: Towards a Liberal Theory of Contract* (Hart Publishing 2003), claiming that contracts promote

that the law should regret not intervening, but that seems to misrepresent the normative situation.

People are responsible for the ethical success of their own lives, and the choices that they make in carrying out this responsibility include entering into personal relationships such as friendship, marriage, parenting, and so on. An important part of those relationships includes the making and keeping of promises.[7] These ideas are reflected in the long liberal tradition of opposing the state enforcement of morality, merely for the sake of making people comply with their moral obligations or improving their ethical character.[8] The state should respect the responsibility that people have for the ethical success of their own lives, and has a duty not to interfere with choices made within that domain of personal responsibility, including promises.[9] To use a legal metaphor, the state has no moral 'jurisdiction' over that domain. Hence, promises made within that domain do not even provide a pro tanto reason for enforcement, even though they are morally binding.

This is not to deny that how we define the boundaries of intimacy is a highly controversial matter with significant normative implications. My only point is that—wherever it is drawn—there is a boundary that separates the domain of intimacy from that of social and public life and within that private sphere the state has no right to interfere.

Besides, just like thematic necessity, this last view says nothing about how we are meant to account for the justifiability of the contract law doctrines that are meant to defeat this pro tanto reason of the state. In fact, it is not a view that even addresses the justifiability of those doctrines. This is because it makes a point about the promise principle which is hardly foundational: on a moralistic view of law, other moral principles—such as preventing exploitation or unfairness—would also be pro tanto grounds for the enforcement of contractual claims. Even if true, the claim that promises are a pro tanto ground for enforcement does not single out the promise principle as special in any way.

3. Foundationalism as Justificatory Primacy

Justificatory primacy is the view that the promise principle is the first virtue of contract law. If contract law doctrines are incompatible with the promise principle,

the intrinsic value of personal detachment. On why though this theory of contract is nevertheless misguided, see Chapter 5 of this book.

[7] Joseph Raz, 'Promises and Obligations' in PMS Hacker and J Raz (eds), *Law, Morality and Society: Essays in Honour of HLA Hart* (1977) 227–28; Stephen A Smith, 'Performance, Punishment and the Nature of Contractual Obligation' (1997) 60 Modern Law Review 360; Kimel, *From Promise to Contract: Towards a Liberal Theory of Contract* (n 6) 27–29; Seana Valentine Shiffrin, 'Promising, Intimate Relationships, and Conventionalism' (2008) 117 Philosophical Review 481.

[8] See the discussion in Liam Murphy, 'The Practice of Promise and Contract' in Gregory Klass, George Letsas, and Prince Saprai (eds), *Philosophical Foundations of Contract Law* (Oxford University Press 2014) 157.

[9] Ronald Dworkin, *Justice for Hedgehogs* (Harvard University Press 2011) ch 9.

no other virtue that they may have justifies sustaining them within the legal system. They need to be abolished or reformed. Justificatory primacy holds that in contract law the promise principle should not be subjected to any balancing against other considerations. This does not mean that other principles do not bear on the evaluation of contract law doctrines. On this conception of foundationalism, we have reason to strive to make contract law more efficient, well arranged, fair, stable, and so forth, and to applaud it when it is. None of these virtues however should ever outweigh the moral failure of contract law when it violates the promise principle.

What would it mean to say that contract law compromises the promise principle? One way to understand it is in terms of the law failing to enforce valid promises that fall within the moral jurisdiction of the law. But this is, I think, too strong a view to hold. Few would deny that there are cases where one is justified in breaking one's promise. I may be justified to break my promise to sell weapons to a foreign state, if my country declares war on that state. In legal terms, we would say that the outbreak of war frustrated the contract.[10] Likewise, I may be justified to break my promise to sell you my house if you extracted that promise from me by taking unfair advantage of the position of power that you had over me. In legal terms, we would say that the contract is voidable because of undue influence or unconscionability.[11] Just like the promise principle is a pro tanto reason to force promisors to perform, likewise principles of preventing exploitation or avoiding unfairness are pro tanto reasons not to force them to perform. The latter reasons may defeat the former, and indeed that is exactly what the doctrines of frustration and undue influence show.

Moreover, it is worth pointing out that there may be a justification for not enforcing a valid promise even when the promisor has no moral justification for breaching. For example, if I promise to sell you my car without consideration I am morally obligated to do so even though my promise would not be legally enforceable. It would be a mistake to infer from the fact that the promisor has no moral justification for breaching a valid promise, that the law has no justification for refusing to enforce the promise. Theorists attracted by justificatory primacy have often made precisely this inference. Fried for example in his early work criticized the doctrine of consideration for compromising the promise principle. However, in his most recent work he has acknowledged that the law may be justified in not enforcing valid promises. He says now that there are reasons to do with the administration of justice and the rule of law that justify not enforcing certain promises due to the absence of consideration.[12]

Justificatory primacy is an extremely strong view, because it would condemn most contract law doctrines. It would, for example, condemn doctrines like undue influence, frustration, and illegality, on the ground that the law fails to enforce a valid promise. But, few would mount a normative attack on these doctrines. Many have, however, been tempted to account for the moral considerations underlying

[10] *Fibrosa Spolka Akcyjna v Fairbairn Lawson Combe Barbour Ltd* [1943] AC 32.

[11] Of course, some might say that considerations such as frustration or exploitation *qualify* a promise rather than *defeat* it, such that there was no promissory obligation all along. See accompanying text to nn 13–21 for my response to this point.

[12] Charles Fried, 'The Ambitions of *Contract as Promise*' in Gregory Klass, George Letsas, and Prince Saprai (eds), *Philosophical Foundations of Contract Law* (Oxford University Press 2014) 33–36.

these doctrines by bringing them under the umbrella of the promise principle. For example, it has been argued that promises extracted under undue influence or emotional pressure impair the will of the promisor and thereby invalidate her promise.[13] Applying this logic to all contract doctrines would vindicate justificatory primacy by bringing all these considerations under the umbrella of the promise principle. By conceiving the promise principle broadly rather than narrowly, one may conclude that not enforcing these promises does not compromise the promise principle. Justificatory primacy then starts to look a lot more plausible and it is in this form that it has appealed to many theorists. However, bringing other principles under the umbrella of promise generates problems of its own. Conceiving the promise principle so broadly amounts to a form of 'inflation' that is worth examining in some detail. For it is questionable whether all doctrines that lead to a contract being set-aside, can be explained on the basis that there was never a valid promise.

3.1 Justificatory primacy by inflation

Let's consider the suggestion that the scope of the foundational principle of contract law is wide, encompassing other principles that underlie contract law doctrines. The idea here is that if the promise principle is understood in this wide sense, then it will have primacy because it will be the *only* principle in play. Exploitation, coercion, deceit, good faith, and so forth, can be understood as falling within the scope of the promise principle broadly understood. But can the promise principle be construed in this broad sense? Can the principle, thus understood, justify existing doctrines? My sense is that widening the scope of the promise principle in order to explain existing doctrine amounts to unwarranted inflation: not only does it distort the promise principle, but it also fails to justify doctrine because it loses sight of the obligation to perform one's promise. I will give two important examples of where this happens: the doctrines of voidability and expectation damages.

Voidability

Consider doctrines that make contracts voidable, such as undue influence or unconscionability. An employer has exploited a junior employee, extracting a promise from him to sell her a Picasso painting that he owns, way below its market value. One might argue that, due to exploitation, the employee has no contractual duty to perform because he has no pro tanto promissory obligation to do so. The argument may take one of two forms. First, that there was no genuine exercise of the employee's will, which is a condition for making a promise. Peter Birks and Chin Nyuk Yin, for

[13] Peter Birks and Nyuk Yin Chin, 'On the Nature of Undue Influence' in Jack Beatson and Daniel Friedman (eds), *Good Faith and Fault in Contract Law* (Clarendon Press 1995). Birks endorsed the will theory of contract, which is the intellectual ancestor of the promise theory. See also Daniel Markovits, 'Promise as an Arm's Length Relation' in Hanoch Sheinman (ed), *Promises and Agreements: Philosophical Essays* (Oxford University Press 2011) 316 n 36, claiming that unconscionability is 'designed to ensure that contracting parties' intentions are free rather than the product of manipulation'.

example, thought that undue influence vitiates the exercise of one's will: 'relief for undue influence is given ... on the ground of impaired judgmental capacity usually arising from morbid dependence on another'.[14] Alternatively, it might be argued that, even though there was a genuine exercise of the employee's will, nevertheless no promissory obligation came into being due to the existence of exploitation.[15] In either case, the 'promise' the employee made did not alter his moral profile or change the balance of reasons that applied to him: he has as much reason to sell the painting to his employer as he had before. This explanation is an example of inflation.

The problem with the above view is that, by inflating the promise principle, one loses sight completely of the duty to perform what was promised: the employee never acquired a duty to perform by his promise in the first place. In not performing he breached no duty, and therefore has nothing to justify.

But the existence of a duty to perform is essential in providing a correct normative account of the legal cases. If the view that exploitation negates the existence of a promissory obligation were correct, then one would not be able to justify the doctrine of voidability. According to this doctrine, the employer has a duty to perform (that is, pay the agreed sum) so long as the employee does not set the contract aside for undue influence. By contrast, the employer cannot invoke her own moral wrongdoing in order to set the contract aside. Their positions are asymmetrical. Moreover, unless the innocent party chooses to set the contract aside, voidable contracts, unlike void contracts, will have normative effects, for example, the passing of a good title to a third party, which courts will enforce.[16]

Now, if we say, with the inflationist, that due to exploitation the employee never really promised to sell, then we cannot explain why the employer has a duty to pay the agreed sum for the painting. This is because according to the most plausible view of agreements, they are conditional promises.[17] The condition consists in the existence of a valid promise on the part of the other party. In the example above, the employer promised to buy the painting for a specific sum on condition that the employee promises to sell it for that sum. They exchanged conditional promises and unless those conditions are met, that is, unless there is a valid promise made by each party, then there is no agreement. If the employee's promise to sell was invalid, because it was extracted through exploitation, and never came into existence, then the employer's promise to buy would not come into existence either and hence the employee would not be entitled to demand performance. Moreover, if the buyer's promise was invalid, it would be difficult to explain why the law allows, as in the case of English law, the possibility of passing good title before the seller rescinds.

[14] Birks and Chin, 'On the Nature of Undue Influence' (n 13) 85.

[15] Some philosophers take the view that defences like duress and misrepresentation invalidate one's promise, in the sense that breach of promise is not a wrong at all. See David Owens, 'Duress, Deception, and the Validity of a Promise' (2007) 116 Mind 293, 294, arguing that deception and coercion invalidate a promise in the sense that 'an invalid promise is one breach of which does not wrong the promisee'. The same argument can be made about exploitation.

[16] *Bainbrigge v Browne* (1881) 18 Ch D 188.

[17] On the claim that agreements can be created by conditional promises, see Joseph Raz, 'On the Nature of Rights' (1984) 93 Mind 194, 202–03.

By contrast, both the duty to perform and the possibility of passing good title can be explained directly, if we say that the employee's promise was valid *despite* the existence of exploitation. All that exploitation does is to equip the innocent party with a justification for breaching his promissory obligation.

An objection to the above analysis might be that, if agreements are conditional promises, then I cannot explain why the promisee is entitled to terminate a contract upon non-performance by the other party given that the relevant conditions are met (that is, the seller and buyer exchange valid promises). According to the view defended here, what conditions the existence of a valid contract is the exchange of valid *promises* to perform, rather than *performance* itself. I cannot therefore explain, the objection goes, why non-performance by one party entitles the other to do the same.[18] My view, however, is precisely that we should be able to appeal to non-promissory principles in order to explain why a promissory duty is not enforced. One could say, for instance, that it would be unfair to force promisees to perform their end of the bargain when the promisor has made it clear that she will not perform her end. Fairness or preventing unjust enrichment can explain why the law allows parties to terminate the contract when the other party refuses to perform.[19]

I don't mean to deny that there might be alternative accounts of voidability which are based on non-promissory principles.[20] Nor do I need to deny that the exercise of one's will is a condition for making a promise. Cases of insanity, brain injury, or intoxication, for example, may affect the exercise of one's will and prevent a promise from coming into existence. In some cases, moreover, like illegality, there is a genuine exercise of will but no valid promise is made. If I promise to torture someone, I exercise my will and make a genuine promise, and yet, nevertheless, my promise is invalid, creating no obligation.[21] My point is that at least some cases of voidable contracts, such as undue influence, are not cases of either defective exercise of the will or invalid promises. They are cases in which other principles defeat the promise principle and provide a justification for various legal rights, duties, and liabilities.

[18] James Penner makes the objection: James E Penner, 'Voluntary Obligations and the Scope of the Law of Contract' (1996) 2 Legal Theory 325, 333–34; James Penner, 'Promises, Agreements, and Contracts' in Gregory Klass, George Letsas, and Prince Saprai (eds), *Philosophical Foundations of Contract Law* (Oxford University Press 2014) 116, 119–20.

[19] Alternatively, one could argue that performance is what in law is called a 'condition subsequent', rather than a 'condition precedent'. In the latter case, no (promissory) duty comes into existence until such time as the other party has made a valid promise. By contrast, a condition subsequent brings a duty that has come into existence to an end because of a future event. Failure or refusal to perform can be seen as a condition subsequent, resulting in the termination of the promissory duty. Note, moreover, that it is difficult to cast exploitation as a condition subsequent. Unlike non-performance or frustration, exploitation is not an event that takes place *after* the promise is made. Rather, it usually takes place *before* a promise is made: the promise is the result of exploitation. So, if exploitation were to condition the validity of a promise, then it could not be a condition subsequent.

[20] So, one could argue, for example, that estoppel principles justify why the law should treat invalid promises as though they are valid.

[21] JEJ Altham, 'Wicked Promises' in *Exercises in Analysis: Essays by Students of Casimir Lewy* (Cambridge University Press 1985). For the contrary view see John R Searle, *Rationality in Action* (MIT Press 2001) 193–200; David Owens, *Shaping the Normative Landscape* (Oxford University Press 2012) 245–49.

The distinction between void and voidable contracts tracks, I think, the normatively important distinction between cases where there is no promise (or no valid promise) and cases where there is a justification to breach one's promise. Theorists may disagree about which promises fall on which side of the distinction. But we cannot wish away the distinction between factors that defeat a promise and factors that condition its existence or, if in existence, cancel it. To be sure, some cases of voidability can be explained in either way. Consider frustration for example. A radical and unexpected change in a promisor's circumstances can be seen as a factor that defeats his obligation to perform, or what lawyers call a 'condition subsequent' which cancels his obligations. As I have tried to show above in the case of undue influence, I do not think that one can explain all cases of voidability as cases of instances of one's promise being cancelled or qualified. But even if it is wrong to draw this conclusion regarding undue influence, the point remains that contract law cannot but be sensitive to the moral distinction between defeaters (which compromise the promise principle) and qualifiers (which do not). How this distinction maps onto the doctrinal distinction between void and voidable contracts is a different matter. My point is that the doctrinal distinction is meant to track the moral distinction.[22]

Expectation damages

Another example of the distorting effect that inflation has relates to expectation damages. Jody Kraus argues that most cases of efficient breach where promisors fail to perform in order to make a profit, are not really cases of breach because they did not promise to perform in the first place. Rather, according to Kraus, they should be taken to have made an 'alternative' promise to 'perform or pay' the monetary equivalent of performance unless they expressly intended a genuinely 'single' promise to perform.[23] He argues that 'most promisors who make legally enforceable single promises intend them to be morally alternative promises and that promisees understand them as such'.[24] He cites empirical evidence in support.[25] But even if that empirical fact is true, it is not clear what its relevance is with respect to legal doctrine. The law awards expectation damages even in cases where the parties intended no alternative promise to perform or pay, but simply a promise to perform. And it awards specific performance in cases where the goods are unique, regardless of whether the parties intended to agree on specific performance. Whether or not the law awards expectation damages over specific performance does not depend on the existence of an intention explicit or implicit to make an alternative promise.

[22] Even if one were to show, convincingly, that all the cases of voidable contracts in English law are cases of qualifiers or cancelling conditions, I would insist that there is another category of enforceable promises, call it voidable* contracts, in which the promisor's duty to perform is defeated. If the distinction between defeaters of a promise and qualifiers holds in morality, it will also hold in legally enforceable promises.

[23] Jody S Kraus, 'The Correspondence of Contract and Promise' (2009) 109 Columbia Law Review 1603, 1637.

[24] ibid.

[25] ibid 1638 n 67.

Sometimes the argument from 'perform or pay' takes a different shape. It says that parties *would* have agreed to perform or pay had they considered this at the time of contracting.[26] One could then argue that the fact that parties *would* have agreed to perform or pay means that they *should* be held to that hypothetical agreement. Arguments from presumed or hypothetical consent are familiar in the tradition of will theories in both legal and political philosophy.[27] But they face some very powerful objections. The fact that I would have promised to do something yesterday does not mean that I now have a promissory duty to do it. What these arguments do, as Ronald Dworkin pointed out, is introduce a separate normative consideration, disguised as what the parties would have agreed to:

> Suppose that you and I are playing poker and we find, in the middle of a hand, that the deck is one card short. You suggest that we throw the hand in, but I refuse because I know I am going to win and I want the money in the pot. You might say that I would certainly have agreed to that procedure had the possibility of the deck being short been raised in advance. But your point is not that I am somehow committed to throwing the hand in by an agreement I never made. Rather you use the device of a hypothetical agreement to make a point that might have been made without that device, which is that the solution is ... obviously fair and sensible ... the fact that I would have chosen it myself adds nothing of substance to that argument.[28]

Daniel Markovits and Alan Schwartz use the device of hypothetical agreements to try to reconcile the morality of promising with the idea of efficient breach. They argue that the regime of expectation damages maximizes the expected return of all promisees, compared to a regime of specific performance. At the stage of contract formation, this gives promisees a reason to make an alternative promise to perform or pay rather than simply perform. 'Promisees', they argue, 'should be taken to have made such contracts'.[29]

As Seana Shiffrin rightly objects, there is an illegitimate jump here between what parties *did* agree and what they *should* or *would* have agreed, were they rational maximizers of their interests.[30] One cannot infer one from the other because one cannot infer an *is* from a *should*. What this argument does is to introduce efficiency

[26] This seems to be the position taken by Daniel Markovits and Alan Schwartz, 'The Myth of Efficient Breach: New Defenses of the Expectation Interest' (2011) 97 Virginia Law Review 1939, 1987. In some places Kraus also seems to take a similar view: 'Expectation damages can be justified as the law's best guess about the remedial moral duty that most promisors *would* prefer.' Kraus, 'The Correspondence of Contract and Promise' (n 23) 1635 (emphasis added).

[27] They can be found for example in Hobbes, Locke, and Austin. Thomas Hobbes, *Leviathan: Revised Student Edition* (Richard Tuck ed, Cambridge University Press 1996); John Locke, *Two Treatises of Government* (Peter Laslett ed, Cambridge University Press 1988); John Austin, *The Province of Jurisprudence Determined and The Uses of the Study of Jurisprudence* (Hackett Publishing 1998).

[28] Ronald Dworkin, *Taking Rights Seriously* (Harvard University Press 1978) 151. See also Fried, *Contract as Promise: A Theory of Contractual Obligation* (n 1) 61: 'as we move further from actual intention the standard of presumed intention tends to merge into the other substantive standards used to solve the problems caused by a failure in the agreement'.

[29] Markovits and Schwartz, 'The Myth of Efficient Breach: New Defenses of the Expectation Interest' (n 26) 1987.

[30] Seana Valentine Shiffrin, 'Must I Mean What You Think I Should Have Said?' (2012) 98 Virginia Law Review 159, 169–74.

or preference satisfaction as a separate argument bearing on the justifiability of expectation damages while presenting it as an argument about what parties should be taken to have promised. But like the argument for throwing the hand in, in Dworkin's example, this argument cannot be premised on promise or agreement and is in need of a separate normative ground. Markovits and Schwartz must be taken to argue that the benefit all promisees receive from the legal regime of expectation damages justifies that regime, whether or not contractual parties in fact made an alternative promise. They must be taken to argue that this benefit justifies breach of contract. And the difference between this argument and the argument based on alternative promises is that in the latter case, unlike the former, no wrong has been committed. By presenting these cases as presumed alternative promises, the argument from alternative promises lets the promisor off the moral hook even though she has committed a moral wrong.

There is another reason why it is important not to conceive of all contracts as promises to perform or pay. Doing so would mean that non-performance does not necessarily entail breach of contract. One can always pay instead of performing, without breaching one's contractual duty. Yet, whether paying is part of performing one's contractual obligation or whether it is a remedy for breaching that obligation may make a huge practical difference in law. For example, if it is the former then rules relating to penalty clauses and mitigation would not apply.[31] Other doctrines too that typically limit the availability of damages for breach of contract would be inapplicable, such as remoteness, contributory negligence, causation, and so on. By construing all contracts as promises to perform or pay, one is bound to deny the applicability of doctrines that apply upon breach of contract, denying breaching parties the benefit of principles that bear on their normative situation.

Summary

In sum, inflation expands the scope of the promise principle so that cases of justified breach are presented as cases where there was no promissory obligation and no wrong committed. In undue influence, inflation has it that, because of exploitation, no promise (or no valid promise) was ever made. In expectation damages, inflation has it that, because of the gains promisees derive from the regime of expectation damages, there was no obligation to perform, only an obligation to perform or pay. In both cases, the promise principle is presented as having justificatory primacy within each and every contract law doctrine. In both cases, foundationalism by inflation makes the wrong of breaking one's promise disappear.

[31] See, for example, *Alder v Moore* [1961] 2 QB 57, (penalties rule not applicable where no breach of contract); *White & Carter (Councils) Ltd v McGregor* [1962] AC 413, (no requirement to mitigate loss where action is for the agreed sum).

3.2 The incompleteness of inflation

In section 3.1 I looked at contract law doctrines that relate to the interaction between the promise principle and other principles which are standard justifications or excuses (such as the exploitation principle). Inflation, which I took to be the most plausible way of assigning primacy to promise, seeks to bring all these principles under the umbrella of the promise principle. I tried to show that inflation distorts contract law because there are many cases, in both law and morality, in which a promisor has a justification to breach a valid promise. Though there may be disagreement as to which principles qualify the promise principle and which defeat it, one cannot deny that this distinction is salient in the morality of promising and that it maps onto the distinction between void and voidable contracts.

But suppose it was possible, contrary to my argument, to account for voidability or expectation damages using the promise principle broadly conceived, that is, including what we take to be principles that justify the breach of a valid promise. There would still be other contract law doctrines that cannot be explained in that way. Consideration and intention to create legal relations doctrines are about the law refusing to enforce a valid promise, even though the promisor has made a valid promise and has no justification to breach it. There are plenty of other examples. The mere passing of time may bar enforcement of an otherwise valid agreement. The law will not force promisors to perform, or hold them liable for not performing, if the promisee brings a claim outside the timeframe of the statute of limitations. The moral concern here is that without a time bar we risk holding innocent parties liable, based on stale evidence.[32]

The distinction between refusing to enforce a contract for reasons to do with the normative situation of the promisor, and reasons that are specific to the legal context within which promises are enforced seems to be of particular importance. In principle, the law may have moral reasons not to enforce promises, which have nothing to do with whether the promisor's promise is valid or with whether he has a moral justification to breach. This point is very often missed by theorists who criticize doctrines like consideration and intention to create legal relations. In fact, I suspect that conceiving of the promise principle in the broad sense and thereby achieving a type of justificatory primacy for the promise principle motivates the hostility toward these doctrines. Since they cannot be explained by the promise principle–no matter how broadly defined—they are seen as compromising the deontic idea of contracts as promises. But this is a mistake because there may be valid deontic reasons (for example, the administration of justice, the rule of law, procedural fairness, and so forth) why the institution of contract law should refrain from forcing a contractual party to perform an otherwise enforceable promise. Primacy by inflation is bound to repudiate such doctrines as incompatible with the foundation of contract law.

[32] Fried, 'The Ambitions of *Contract as Promise*' (n 12) 36.

4. Foundationalism as Justificatory Presumptiveness

Foundationalism as justificatory presumptiveness claims that promise is the foundation of contract law in the sense that any divergence between contract and promise should be presumed to be objectionable. Unlike justificatory primacy this position does not deny that the promise principle may be defeated by other deontic concerns. Justificatory presumptiveness is an epistemic rule. Given the link between contracts and promises we have reason to believe that contract should converge with promissory morality and that divergence is a cause for concern. Here is, for example, what Shiffrin says about the doctrine of expectation damages: 'Contract has a distinctive remedial regime that not only diverges from its moral counterpart, but also reflects an underlying view that promissory breach is not a wrong, or at least not a serious one.'[33] This has led to what is now known as 'the contract and promise debate', between those who argue that contract law diverges from promissory morality and those who claim that it converges.

The earlier discussion of contract doctrines challenges this presumption. Even though the promise principle is a necessary element in justifying several contract law doctrines, it is far from sufficient. Undue influence, rescission, voidability, mitigation, and expectation damages, are all examples of doctrines where the promise principle interacts with other principles. Given a set of facts, contract doctrines justify an outcome on the basis of more than one principle. If this is true, then there is no reason to presume that contract law should converge with what the promise principle, taken alone, requires. Nor is there a reason to presume that divergence between contract and promise is prima facie objectionable. As I have argued, deontic arguments may be available to justify doctrines, like undue influence or expectation damages, that seem to diverge from promise.

If promissory obligations may be defeated by other deontic concerns, such as the duty not to exploit in cases of undue influence, then why should we presume that in a contractual context a non-performed promise is a cause for moral concern? It may be objected that the presumption has no negative upshots. Even if it is true that many doctrines in contract law may be justified as a case of deontic defeaters, where is the harm in being concerned with divergence between contract and promise? After all, the inquiry into the divergence may show that there was valid justification for contract law to condone a breach of promise.

The problem with the presumption is that it is asymmetrical. There is cause for concern when there is divergence, triggering a moral inquiry, but no cause for concern when there is convergence. But this asymmetry is unjustified. A contract law doctrine that directly parallels promissory morality needn't be justified considered in the light of other competing principles. It would be wrong if contract law did not provide promisors with a defence in cases of unconscionability, misrepresentation,

[33] Seana Valentine Shiffrin, 'The Divergence of Contract and Promise' (2007) 120 Harvard Law Review 708, 724.

duress, or undue influence. The law would then impose the requirements of the promise principle other things being equal, but it would be unjustified to do so in the light of other competing principles. Likewise, if the law did not impose the requirement of consideration or intent to contract, it would converge with what the promise principle requires other things being equal. Whether or not one made a valid promise does not depend on the existence of consideration or an intention to create legal relations.[34] Arguably, however, the absence of the requirement of consideration or the intention to contract would be a cause for moral concern. Justificatory presumptiveness invites us to bring other principles to bear on the justifiability of contract doctrines in cases of divergence but not in cases of convergence. As a result, justificatory presumptiveness has the disadvantage of encouraging moral mistakes in evaluating contract law doctrines.

5. Shifting the Goalposts

So far, I have scrutinized the claim that the promise principle is the moral foundation of contract by observing two constraints. The first one is that the explanandum of the foundationalist claim is the body of contract law doctrines as they are conventionally defined in Anglo-American jurisprudence. The second one is that the explanans is the promise principle as understood in its deontic moral sense. I explored three ways in which the promise principle may play a special justificatory role in contract given these constraints, and I found that all three of them had some serious weaknesses. I now want to explore varieties of foundationalism that relax these constraints. The first, which I call 'stipulation', is the view that the explanandum should be understood narrowly so as to exclude contract law doctrines that cannot be justified by the promise principle taken alone. The second view, which I shall call 'holism', is that the explanans should be understood widely so as to include, alongside promise, all the non-promissory moral principles which bear on the practice of promising.

Both these views shift the goalposts, so to speak, in order to vindicate foundationalism. Stipulation seeks to account for doctrines in which non-promissory principles figure by relabelling them as non-contractual. And holism seeks to account for these doctrines by invoking non-promissory principles. My sense about these two moves is that they do not really achieve what foundationalism is meant to deliver, namely demonstrating that the promise principle plays a special justificatory role in explaining contract law.

5.1 Stipulation

Take stipulation first. Many promise theorists attempt to shrink the conventional category of contract law by excluding from it non-promissory principles. Fried takes

[34] Fried, *Contract as Promise: A Theory of Contractual Obligation* (n 1) ch 3; Shiffrin, 'The Divergence of Contract and Promise' (n 33) 728, 736–37.

the view that if the rule that shifts a loss is not justified by the promise principle, then it falls by definition outside the law of contract and belongs to some other area of law, such as tort law.[35] For example, Fried discusses the doctrine of mistake. In morality, he says, one should not be bound by a promise when, because of a mistake of fact, there was no exercise of one's will. The law however enforces contracts against those who made a unilateral mistake of fact.[36] Fried explains away this divergence in the following way: where there is a mistake about the terms of the contract the parties have failed to promise, due to the existence of divergent intentions. The conditions for the application of the promise principle are not met and hence there is no promissory obligation. On Fried's view, however, it is fair for a party who carelessly made a mistake to bear the loss that mistake causes. The principle of fairness justifies enforcing the contract against the party who made the mistake.[37] But the fact that the invoked justification here is non-promissory means, for Fried, that it is non-contractual. The doctrine of mistake is therefore not part of contract law. Fried takes a similar view about a number of other doctrines such as pre-contractual liability,[38] incapacity,[39] good faith ('honesty in fact'),[40] and the consequences of breach.[41] As a result, the field of contract law is shrunk to very few doctrines and rules, that is, the ones that on Fried's view can be explained by the promise principle alone, such as offer and acceptance, expectation damages,[42] remoteness, and good faith ('in performance').

It is not clear, however, what purpose is served by redrawing the conventional boundaries of contract law in this way. True, it is conceivable that legal categories can be carved up in different ways, as the taxonomical differences between civil law and common law readily suggest. But what stipulation effectively does is to restrict the domain of contract law to what the promise principle would require of contractual parties, other things being equal. All it says is that the promise principle is, other things being equal, a relevant moral principle bearing on legal rights and duties. It stipulates that there is a one-to-one correlation between a moral principle and an area of law and it takes the direction of this correlation to be from the moral principle to the area of law: the principle individuates the area. But then it would follow that there should be as many areas of law as there are moral principles bearing on legal rights and duties. The promise principle should individuate contract law,

[35] ibid 61. See also Fried's discussion of reliance at ibid 24. This is also how Jody Kraus reads Fried, see his 'The Correspondence of Contract and Promise' (n 23) 1607 nn 9–10, 1614 n 23: 'Fried argues that contract law, by definition enforces promises. He therefore concludes that any doctrine that fails to enforce a promise, or imposes nonpromissory liability, is either erroneous law or noncontract law.' See also Penner, 'Voluntary Obligations and the Scope of the Law of Contract' (n 18) 330–31 (identifying what I call stipulation as a problem for promise-based accounts of contract law in general).

[36] *Smith v Hughes* (1870–1871) LR 6 QB 597, 606–07.

[37] Fried, *Contract as Promise: A Theory of Contractual Obligation* (n 1) 61–63.

[38] ibid 24, 27, 55. [39] ibid 63. [40] ibid 81–82.

[41] ibid 114, 117–18, 125–26.

[42] It is puzzling why Fried thought that expectation damages, which is typically thought to be the doctrine that diverges the most from promissory morality, is what the promise principle requires upon breach of promise. Kimel, *From Promise to Contract: Towards a Liberal Theory of Contract* (n 6) 95; Shiffrin, 'The Divergence of Contract and Promise' (n 33) 710 n 2.

the fairness principle should individuate, say, tort law, the discrimination principle should individuate discrimination law, and so forth.

But this all sounds deeply counterintuitive. Law is not subdivided in that way and for good reason: the core areas of law (contract, tort, property, criminal, and so forth) are normatively pluralistic in the sense that they tell us how, in the eyes of the law, a moral principle should interact with other moral principles. This is important since the weight of principles depends—in morality and not just in law—on which other principle they interact with. Take for example the principle that no-one should profit from their own wrong. In property law, this principle is compromised, allowing the adverse possessor to benefit from trespassing, and to override the property right of the original owner. In the law of wills by contrast, this principle carries more weight than the principle of respecting the autonomy of the testator, as it prevents the beneficiary of a will from inheriting when he has murdered the testator.[43] If we classified areas of law on the basis of isolated principles then we would know very little about how existing doctrines weigh them up within the various conventional categories.

More importantly, stipulation does not show that the promise principle plays a special role in justifying the legal enforceability of promises, *given* normative pluralism. As it does not attend to how the promise principle may be defeated, qualified, supplemented, reinforced, and so on, it cannot even begin to assign such a role to the promise principle. Stipulation comes out not to be foundationalist at all—except in the tautological sense that the promise principle is the foundation of whatever in the law is explained by that principle alone.

5.2 Holism

How about the view that contract law is founded upon the promise principle plus all the other principles that interact with it? This view is an improvement on inflation, since it does not seek to subsume other principles that figure in contract law within promissory morality.[44] It is also an improvement on stipulation since it welcomes normative pluralism and seeks to attend to how the promise principle interacts with other principles. But this view, which I labelled holism, is hardly foundationalist either. This is because the whole of morality may bear on whether one should keep a contract. For example, duties of friendship or family may justify breaking a promise, including a legally valid contract. If the mere possibility of a principle interacting with the promise principle were the basis for individuating contract law, then the foundations of contract law would explode, encompassing the whole of morality.[45]

[43] See *Riggs v Palmer* 115 NY 506 (1889). Dworkin of course famously relied on the case to point out the differential weight of the principle in different areas of law. Dworkin, *Taking Rights Seriously* (n 28) ch 2.

[44] It is still vulnerable, however, to the same objection as inflation, namely that some principles that figure in contract law (such as rules of evidence or statutes of limitations) do not bear any special connection to promissory morality.

[45] I am very grateful to Les Green who drew my attention to the problem. He called it the 'exploding' problem and I have borrowed his metaphor.

There would then be no sense in which contract law forms a distinct area of law in virtue of its foundation. Nor would the promise principle play a special justificatory role within that holistic framework: the other principles with which it interacts would have the same deontic character, sometimes defeating or qualifying the promise principle and sometimes being outweighed by it. Holism may be the correct view to hold but, if anything, it is anti-foundationalist: it must reject the view that different areas of law are individuated in virtue of their foundation.

6. Conclusion

In this chapter, I have critically examined three ways in which one can unpack the claim that promise is the foundation of contract law. Foundationalism can be seen either as the view that the promise principle is necessary for justifying contract law (justificatory necessity), or as the view that the promise principle is uncompromising (justificatory primacy), or finally as the view that the promise principle is presumptively what justifies contract law doctrines (justificatory presumptiveness). I have argued that none of these conceptions provide plausible accounts of contract law. The promise principle is neither necessary, nor uncompromising, nor a proper presumption for justifying contract law doctrines. Attempts to vindicate foundationalism either by shrinking the conventional category of contract law doctrines or by welcoming other, non-promissory, moral principles end up, as I have shown, abandoning the very idea of foundationalism, rather than vindicating it.

Foundationalism, as an abstract idea, has the attraction of offering a simple and uniform theory of areas of law. Unlike conventional or utilitarian methods of differentiating areas of law, it seeks to impose principled order on what would otherwise be as Birks said a 'mass of cases' or 'bits and pieces' of rules that are held together for no obvious moral reason.[46] Though foundationalism has the attraction of the simplicity and uniformity it confers on our understanding of the relevant area of law, ultimately this is also the source of its main weakness.[47]

Must we then abandon inquiries into the moral foundations of contract law or other areas of law? Hardly. Contract law, like other areas of law, has a central theme and its doctrines are pluralistic, attending to the interaction between the promise principle and other principles. But which principles figure in that interaction and how they weigh up against the promise principle is not something that foundationalism can help us with. The idea we should guard against is that each area of law necessarily contains a principle (or more than one) which plays a special justificatory role within it. It is this sense of foundationalism that this chapter seeks primarily to challenge.

[46] Peter Birks, *An Introduction to the Law of Restitution* (Clarendon Press 1989) 2, 74.

[47] I echo here Herbert Hart's critique of Hans Kelsen's theory of law, teaching that purchasing 'uniformity of pattern' although 'pleasing' may come at 'too high a price'. HLA Hart, *The Concept of Law* (2nd edn, Clarendon Press 1994) 38.

We should not conclude that the shortcomings of foundationalism entail that the legal practice of dividing the law into different areas is merely conventional. Perhaps there are second-order moral reasons why the law should be divided into different areas. In some—largely overlooked—remarks in his book *Law's Empire*, Dworkin made just this sort of suggestion. Divisions between areas of law he argued are non-arbitrary when they facilitate people and judges in identifying correct moral principles at a local level and promote the integrity or coherence of law in the long-run.[48] Unlike the foundationalist, Dworkin did not think that connections between moral principles and legal categories were *necessary*, in the sense that particular moral principles necessarily played a special role in certain areas of law, whenever and wherever a legal system might be found. Rather, he thought the connections were *contingent* in nature. This gives rise to the possibility of an entirely distinct 'republican' theory of the individuation of areas of law. In the next chapter, I unearth Dworkin's views, and reveal some of the important insights about individuation that they contain.

[48] Ronald Dworkin, *Law's Empire* (Hart Publishing 1998) 252.

4
Republican Contract Law

> Liberty lies in the hearts of men and women; when it dies there, no constitution, no law, no court can even do much to help.
>
> Judge Learned Hand[1]

1. Law's Divisions

Looking at law in its entirety it seems we are presented with a sheet of glass broken into many shards, of different shapes and sizes. I use this metaphor to speak here of the way law is broken up into what lawyers usually call fields, departments, categories, areas, and so on. So, we have, for example, private law, public law, criminal law, international law, and so forth. These larger areas are subdivided. So, in private law, we distinguish obligations from property law. And we make many more cuts; for example, the law of obligations separates out contract from tort, and within contract we distinguish between insurance law, sale of goods, employment law, landlord and tenant, and so on. These distinctions are found not only in textbooks, but in the courses taught in law schools, the titles of law professors, the marketing of law firms, the branches of courts, and so on. The carving up of law in these ways is a pervasive feature of our legal system and more widely the legal culture that we occupy.

So far in this book, I have discussed the two most common reasons given for why laws are parcelled up or individuated in these ways. First, there is the view I have called 'conventionalism', according to which, these divisions reflect the practice of legal officials or participants in the legal system (judges, lawyers, legal academics, and so forth) over time. These legal actors break up the law into digestible chunks, making it more manageable, accessible, predictable, and easier to handle and follow. On this view, individuation achieves *epistemic* ends.

So, for example, Peter Birks argued that 'bits and pieces' of law might be brought together to facilitate the pursuit of certain valuable activities.[2] For instance, if you are an aeroplane pilot, it might be enormously helpful to have a textbook on 'aviation

[1] Irving Dillard (ed), *The Spirit of Liberty: Papers and Addresses of Learned Hand* (Alfred A Knopf, Inc 1959) 190.

[2] Peter Birks, *An Introduction to the Law of Restitution* (Clarendon Press 1989) 74.

law', which draws together the various rules, principles, and doctrines that govern the flying of aeroplanes; norms that would be 'kept apart in other ways of dividing up the law'.[3] We are familiar with such categories. They include, for example, sale of goods, sports law, carriage of goods by sea, and banking law.

On this view, these legal categories exist because of the common practice of legal officials, and they serve rule of law values, by making it easier for those to whom the law applies to have the notice they need of legal requirements. In this way, they facilitate epistemic access to the law. I call this view conventionalist, because the reason for the legal categories depends on the existence of conventions among lawyers.

The second theory is what I have called 'foundationalism'. According to this view, not all legal categories are convention-dependent. Some legal rules and doctrines are necessarily and magnetically drawn to certain moral principles whatever way they might have been classified in the past by lawyers, judges, or academics. These moral principles play a special justificatory role in the areas of law to which they are necessarily connected, and structure and shape the legal norms that these areas contain. Foundationalism is a *metaphysical* theory of individuation. According to it, these moral principles and the divisions that they create are constitutive or built into the very fabric of law.

It is logically possible that there may be other types of epistemic and metaphysical accounts of individuation. So, for example, one might argue that there are non-practice dependent epistemic justifications for dividing up the law. And one could argue for a metaphysical view of individuation that carves up the law not on the grounds of *moral* principles, but other sorts of principles or considerations. I don't deny these possibilities, but present foundationalism and conventionalism here because these are the views of individuation that have gained the most traction and influence in the literature.

In the previous chapter, I argued that despite the enormous influence it has had foundationalism as a theory of contract law is actually false. The most prominent foundationalist account of contract law—the 'promise theory'—fails in its attempts to show that the promise principle plays a special justificatory in contract law, because such theories pay insufficient regard to the interaction between the multiplicity of values that bear on and shape contract doctrine. As a result, promise theorists invariably mishandle contract doctrine.

Does this mean that contract law must be a conventional legal category? In my view, such a conclusion is too quick. My purpose in this chapter is to explore the possibility that contract law is neither a foundational nor a conventional category, but is rather a *tertium quid*. In *Law's Empire*, Ronald Dworkin suggested that there may be second-order moral values that shape legal categories.[4] Dworkin's account of individuation has been largely neglected in the academic commentary. This comes as little surprise, given that his remarks on individuation were sketchy and rather under-developed.

[3] ibid.
[4] Ronald Dworkin, *Law's Empire* (Hart Publishing 1998) 250–54, 402–03, 405, 406.

Nevertheless, I will argue in this chapter that they flow in important respects from his wider theory of law, and illustrate some of its implications. His interpretation of individuation in law was characteristically unique. Dworkin argued that legal categories are *contingently* connected with 'positive morality' or popular views about the moral principles, categories, and distinctions that legal categories implicate. This serves the purpose of involving ordinary citizens in legal and political decision-making about matters of principle, which are usually the preserve of the courts. It is a distinctly 'republican' account of differentiation in law. I will attempt to unpack and flesh out this embryonic theory, and draw out its implications for debates about the nature of contract law.

2. The Noble Dream

I will begin by setting out Dworkin's broader theory of law and political legitimacy relying both on his own work and on the work of others who have provided important and influential interpretations of Dworkin's legal and political theories. At the heart of *Law's Empire* is the age-old problem of the legitimacy of the state in circumstances of deep disagreement between members of a political community about the good and the requirements of justice. The orthodox picture, going back to Thomas Hobbes,[5] John Locke,[6] and Jean-Jacques Rousseau,[7] and taken up in recent times by John Rawls,[8] is that legitimacy rests on the consent of the people, constituting a social contract, and on state compliance with the explicit terms of that agreement. Members of the nascent political community possessed of overlapping interests would negotiate fair terms of social cooperation. An agreement would emerge laying down ground rules and expectations that would regulate the relations between citizens and between them and the state. Dworkin argued this account of political legitimacy gives rise to what he called the 'rule book' view of the rule of law: 'It insists that, so far as is possible, the power of the state should never be exercised against individual citizens except in accordance with rules explicitly set out in a public rule book available to all.'[9] Invariably the agreement would contain 'gaps', or areas where no agreement was reached, but these could be dealt with pragmatically *ex post*.

Dworkin was a sceptic about the argument from consent. What if some members of the community rejected the original agreement? In those circumstances, how could it reasonably be supposed that everyone consented? The claim that they consent tacitly, by not escaping the communities that they are in, seems wildly implausible; one can hardly assume, Dworkin argued, that such choices are fully voluntary,

[5] Thomas Hobbes, *Leviathan: Revised Student Edition* (Richard Tuck ed, Cambridge University Press 1996).

[6] John Locke, *Two Treatises of Government* (Peter Laslett ed, Cambridge University Press 1988).

[7] Jean-Jacques Rousseau, *'The Social Contract' and other Later Political Writings* (Victor Gourevitch ed, Cambridge University Press 1997).

[8] John Rawls, *A Theory of Justice* (rev edn, Oxford University Press 1999).

[9] Ronald Dworkin, 'Political Judges and the Rule of Law' (1980) 64 Proceedings of the British Academy 259, 261.

especially where people have built lives where they were born. Furthermore, they would merely be replacing the rule of one sovereign with that of another: 'he has no choice to be free from sovereigns altogether'.[10]

Instead, Dworkin sought to construct an argument for political community not on the basis of consent or contract, but instead on the ground of fraternity. The claim was that social obligations arise not only from shared interests and exercises of will, but also from our status as members of certain kinds of human association, such as family, friendship, and indeed political communities. He called these 'associative' obligations.[11] They arise when members of these groups regard the duties they owe to other members as *special* (owed specifically to other members), *personal* (owed individually to other members), as expressive of a more general *concern* for the wellbeing of other members, and, finally, they must show *equal* concern for the wellbeing of other members.[12] When those conditions, suitably tailored, are met in the context of a political community, 'a community of principle' emerges conferring legitimacy on that community's system of government and imposing a general duty on its citizens to obey the law.

But in what circumstances will these conditions be met in a political context, which as I have said is marked by widespread disagreement about the nature of the good and the requirements of justice? Dworkin's answer is that they are satisfied when the government personified as a moral agent behaves with integrity toward its citizens. By this he means that the government should aim 'to speak with one voice, to act in a principled and coherent manner toward all its citizens, to extend to everyone the substantive standards of justice or fairness it uses for some'.[13]

In concrete terms, this means that when the organs of the state make political decisions, they should do so with an eye on past political practice, to make sure that their actions exhibit principled consistency toward all citizens both past and present. In the context of adjudication, this commitment is manifested in the well-known doctrine of *stare decisis*, that is, that judges are duty bound to 'treat like cases alike'.[14]

Separately, Dworkin argues that law is an interpretive practice, and that integrity as well as supplying a theory of political obligation also supplies the best interpretation of legal practice.[15] In this way, integrity influences or shapes legal content.[16] On this picture, the law just is that set of moral and political principles that provide the most coherent account of past political practice, for example, constitutions, statutes, and court decisions.[17] So, Dworkin says:

[10] Dworkin, *Law's Empire* (n 4) 192–93. [11] ibid 195–96. [12] ibid 199–200.

[13] ibid 165. See also Stephen Perry, 'Associative Obligations and the Obligation to Obey the Law' in Scott Hershovitz (ed), *Exploring Law's Empire: The Jurisprudence of Ronald Dworkin* (Oxford University Press 2006) 188–89.

[14] Dworkin, *Law's Empire* (n 4) 165. See also Jeremy Waldron, 'Did Dworkin Ever Answer the Crits?' in Scott Hershovitz (ed), *Exploring Law's Empire: The Jurisprudence of Ronald Dworkin* (Oxford University Press 2006) 176–77.

[15] Dworkin, *Law's Empire* (n 4) chs 1–3, 7.

[16] Perry, 'Associative Obligations and the Obligation to Obey the Law' (n 13) 188–89.

[17] Joseph Raz, *Ethics in the Public Domain: Essays in the Morality of Law and Politics* (Clarendon Press 1995) 290–91; Silas Wasserstrom, 'The Empire's New Clothes' (1986–1987) 75 The Georgetown Law Review 199, 272.

If government relies on principles of majoritarian democracy to justify its decisions about who may vote, it must respect the same principles in designing voting districts. If it appeals to the principle that people have a right to compensation from those who injure them carelessly, as its reason why manufacturers are liable for defective automobiles, it must give full effect to that principle in deciding whether accountants are liable for their mistakes as well. If government says that a unanimous verdict is necessary for criminal conviction because special moral harm is suffered when someone is unjustly convicted of a crime, then it must take that special moral harm into account in considering, for example, the admissibility of confessions under various circumstances.[18]

The central idea here is that however much in the context of political community people disagree with others about ethics and the requirements of justice, they have a right when the state performs its political functions to be treated with equal concern and respect; a right on which state legitimacy depends.[19] In distributive terms, this means that when the state settles on a particular scheme of principle or theory of justice, it must ensure that the benefits and burdens of that regime are borne equally by its citizens. It should not be the case that rights conferred to some groups according to the scheme should be denied to others on arbitrary or capricious grounds.[20]

This is why *stare decisis* plays such a salient role in adjudication. In determining the rights and obligations of litigants in disputes, judges have to honour the scheme of principle already manifest in the past political practices of the community. This is what it means to show equal concern and respect to members of the same political community. As Scott Hershovitz says: 'A court displays integrity when its decisions reflect a commitment to a coherent and defensible view of the rights and duties people have under the law. Such a commitment can only be displayed by a pattern of decisions across time.'[21] If courts reached decisions on arbitrary, irrelevant, or capricious grounds, the state could no longer demonstrate how it shows equal concern and respect for its members; and would hence lose the argument for its own legitimacy.

Now, by integrity Dworkin does not mean mere consistency. His theory is not that judges should blindly or unquestioningly follow past precedents that seem to bear on the case at hand as closely as they can muster. Rather, the duty is to search out principles, or more accurately schemes of principle, that best explain the past cases and rely on those schemes to resolve the dispute in front of the judge. If a particular

[18] Dworkin, *Law's Empire* (n 4) 165.

[19] Ronald Dworkin, *Justice for Hedgehogs* (Harvard University Press 2011) 321–22, 330, (equal concern demands that each citizen's fate is regarded by the state as equally important, whilst equal respect means according equal value to the autonomy of each citizen). See also Wasserstrom, 'The Empire's New Clothes' (n 17) 226, 248, 257.

[20] Waldron, 'Did Dworkin Ever Answer the Crits?' (n 14) 177.

[21] Scott Hershovitz, 'Integrity and Stare Decisis' in Scott Hershovitz (ed), *Exploring Law's Empire: The Jurisprudence of Ronald Dworkin* (Oxford University Press 2006) 115. In the adversarial context, this means the parties are fighting it out to persuade the judge which side has the most coherent conception of the community's scheme of principle on their side. As Jeremy Waldron says, the basic idea is 'that in any given case, a judgment for the plaintiff, say, is to be defended by showing that it coheres better with existing legal materials than a judgment for the defendant would'. Waldron, 'Did Dworkin Ever Answer the Crits?' (n 14) 160. See also Jeremy Waldron, 'The Rule of Law as a Theater of Debate' in Justine Burley (ed), *Dworkin and his Critics: With Replies by Dworkin* (Blackwell Publishing 2004) 328–29.

line of precedent cannot be justified by that scheme, because, for example, these decisions have been taken on arbitrary or unfair grounds, then the judge may well have an obligation to overturn or depart from those cases.

So, for example, Dworkin thought it was not possible to justify past cases in English law which gave barristers immunity from liability for professional negligence:

> Consistency, narrowly understood, would have required continuing that exception, but integrity condemns the special treatment of barristers unless it can be justified in principle, which seems unlikely.[22]

Differential treatment of this sort is exactly what integrity or the commitment to equal concern and respect condemns.[23] It is not differential treatment per se which is the problem, for example, it may be perfectly legitimate to make the rich pay a higher rate of tax than the poor; rather, it is differential treatment that cannot be justified coherently with the scheme of principle embodied in the law as a whole. In the case of shielding barristers from negligence liability, it is hard to see what could justify treating barristers differently from other professions, such as doctors and teachers, who are liable to pay compensation for damage caused by their carelessness.

The picture that this account of political and legal obligation leaves us with is of a community of people who although divided on issues of justice and ethics nevertheless express, or at least strive to express, a more abstract commitment to treating one another with equal concern and respect. In the political context, this means that organs of the state, such as courts, have to make sure, when making decisions that bear on citizens' rights and obligations, that they respect the scheme of principle embodied or already endorsed in the past political practices of the community taken as a whole. Past decisions taken by political institutions should not be looked at in isolation, but rather interpreted in the context of how they fit this wider scheme of principle.[24] As Jeremy Waldron puts it, for Dworkin these communities are bound:

> when any particular issue comes up for present decision ... to delve relentlessly into the established terms of their association to ascertain how the present issue would best be decided in view of the deep commitments they think of themselves as having already taken on.[25]

What distinguishes a community of principle is the fact that its members and political institutions are committed to achieving coherence between present and past political decisions and the equal concern and respect that this practice manifests. It may be that they will fall short of this lofty ideal, but what matters is that they try; it is the striving and its expressive value that constitutes the special bond between members,

[22] Dworkin, *Law's Empire* (n 4) 220.

[23] This is why Dworkin objects to what he calls 'checkerboard' statutes, such as one that permits some women to have an abortion but not others on an arbitrary basis, by, for example, making abortion permissible but only if you were born in an even-numbered year. Although justice or fairness might require this sort of political compromise, it violates integrity because it asserts a right to abortion for some women, but denies it to others on an arbitrary basis. ibid 176–84.

[24] ibid 200. See also Wasserstrom, 'The Empire's New Clothes' (n 17) 201; Andrew Altman, 'Legal Realism, Critical Legal Studies, and Dworkin' (1986) 15 Philosophy and Public Affairs 205, 221.

[25] Waldron, 'The Rule of Law as a Theater of Debate' (n 21) 329.

and justifies the community's claim to legitimacy. Law as integrity, Dworkin said, 'consists in an approach, in questions rather than answers'.[26]

3. Climbing the Mountain

As I have explained, for Dworkin law as integrity is an ideal to which members of a political community aspire. By adopting it as an 'approach' toward other members of the community, a 'community of principle' is forged. This sounds though like a very demanding ideal, and this raises the question whether it is actually achievable. Standing at the bottom, the incline looks not just dizzying but impossible.

In essence what law as integrity requires is for the judge in settling a dispute to reach a decision that is coherent with the scheme of principle embodied in all of the community's past political practices. That means considering not only lines of authority that seem to bear on the *particular* dispute in front of the judge, but to ensure consistency in *all* lines of authority; to make sure that the correct moral and political principles are applied, and that they are interpreted, balanced, and ranked coherently in the law as a whole.

For any judge, this approach would require not only an extraordinary breadth of legal knowledge, grasp of legal and factual detail, and interpretive skill, but enormous amounts of energy, time, and resource. It is no surprise that to illustrate law as integrity in action, Dworkin conjures up the fictional judge, 'Hercules', who has 'superhuman intellectual power and patience'.[27] But is this not just law for the Gods? Given its exacting demands, would it make sense for real judges to actually adopt integrity as a standard?

It is important to be clear about what the exact nature of the challenge presented here is. The point is *not* that made by the Critical Legal Studies ('CLS') movement that past political practice is so riddled with political compromises between conflicting interest groups and intellectual tendencies, that no one, not even Hercules, could hope to make the record coherent. As Waldron says, on this view the community's political record 'is one of incoherence, in which the principles necessary to sustain some decisions are contradicted by the principles necessary to sustain others'.[28] This makes law inherently indeterminate; there is no right answer to any legal question.[29] Dworkin calls this critique 'internal scepticism' (which he distinguishes

[26] Dworkin, *Law's Empire* (n 4) 239, see also 190, 264, 413. See also Waldron, 'The Rule of Law as a Theater of Debate' (n 21) 329–30; Waldron, 'Did Dworkin Ever Answer the Crits?' (n 14) 179; Allan C Hutchinson, 'Indiana Dworkin and Law's Empire' (1987) 96 Yale Law Journal 637, 647.

[27] Dworkin, *Law's Empire* (n 4) 239.

[28] Waldron, 'Did Dworkin Ever Answer the Crits?' (n 14) 178.

[29] Roberto Mangabeira Unger, *What Should Legal Analysis Become?* (Verso 1996) 65–66; Duncan Kennedy, 'Form and Substance in Private Law Adjudication' (1975–1976) 89 Harvard Law Review 1685; Waldron, 'Did Dworkin Ever Answer the Crits?' (n 14) 162–65; Altman, 'Legal Realism, Critical Legal Studies, and Dworkin' (n 24) 217, 221–23. cf Joseph Raz who made the criticism that in the case of many regimes the political record is often the product 'of the rough-and-tumble of politics', which 'reflects the vagaries of pragmatic compromises, or changing fortunes of political forces, and the like. Their law, therefore, does not form a coherent body of principle and doctrine.' Raz, *Ethics in the Public Domain: Essays in the Morality of Law and Politics* (n 17) 298–99, and see 316: 'the existence of a plurality

from 'external scepticism', which is the metaphysical view that there are no objective moral values on which to ground interpretive claims), and important doubts have been expressed about his response to it.[30]

The objection I have in mind is of a different kind. Internal scepticism focuses on the impossibility of the task that judges are expected to perform. The political record is so internally compromised, that no judge, however good, could possibly make it coherent. This is a metaphysical point about the very nature of law. My point is not that the law is indeterminate or irreconcilable, but rather the moral claim that even if a judge with the Godlike powers of Hercules could set the political record straight, that is an impossible task for earthly judges who lack Hercules' superhuman capacities.[31]

In other words, this is the familiar 'ought implies can' objection. The claim is that human beings have limited capacities, relating, for example, to what they can will and know, and that moral standards or 'oughts' should, if they are to have any real-world traction, be tailored to them. Of course, there will be exceptional individuals, like Michael Jordan, Mother Teresa, Albert Einstein, or Nelson Mandela, who achieve acclaim precisely because they exceed, sometimes vastly, our expectations of what ordinary human beings can put up with and do. But our moral standards are calibrated not in the light of what exceptional individuals have achieved in the past or might achieve in the future, but instead against our understanding of the limitations and demands faced by ordinary people.[32] As James Griffin says, these limitations set the boundaries of what morality can demand: 'A moral standard that ignores human capacities is not an "ideal" standard, but no standard at all.'[33]

So, even if it is true, that a Learned Hand or a Lord Denning had what it takes to follow the trail of Hercules, it certainly would not be true for the overwhelming majority of ordinary judges. Against that background, the idea that law as integrity is something that the workaday judge should aspire to seems fanciful.

What if my view of the ought implies can standard is too democratic? Perhaps we should be aspiring, whatever our limitations, to the heights reached by the likes of Nelson Mandela, Learned Hand, or Michael Jordan? The vast majority of us are bound to fail of course, but perhaps that has no bearing on the moral standard? Provided in the course of human history it can be shown that someone achieved

of inconsistent views on moral, religious, social, and political issues in democratic (and in many other) societies, is likely to be reflected in a society's law.... it is likely to lead to legal rules and principles being in force reflecting the different outlooks of the people who fashioned them'.

[30] See in particular Altman, 'Legal Realism, Critical Legal Studies, and Dworkin' (n 24); Waldron, 'Did Dworkin Ever Answer the Crits?' (n 14); Hutchinson, 'Indiana Dworkin and Law's Empire' (n 26) 657–58; Wasserstrom, 'The Empire's New Clothes' (n 17) 275–78.

[31] cf Raz, *Ethics in the Public Domain: Essays in the Morality of Law and Politics* (n 17) 313 n 64: 'coherence is in fact very difficult to establish. It requires intellectual capacities, formal training, and a command of information about the law generally that is in excess of what is needed to reach decent decisions on most moral issues facing the courts.' Raz's point seems to be not only that judges lack these capacities, but also that they do not miss them.

[32] James Griffin, 'Moral Law, Positive Law' in John Tasioulas (ed), *Law, Values and Social Practices* (Dartmouth 1997) 41–42.

[33] ibid 45.

the standard, or realistically could do so in the future, that makes it an appropriate standard for everyone—however objectionably demanding, or in some cases elitist, that might seem. No one ever said morality or ethics was easy.

Even if the ought implies can objection could be overcome in this way, there would still be a problem for law as integrity. Determinations about what the law is would vary hugely depending on the particular skill or competence of the judge attempting to resolve a dispute. So, even if judges agreed broadly with what Dworkin calls the 'pre-interpretive stage', that is, on what constituted the basic political record (statutes, case law, and so forth), and on what would count as a good level of fit between principles and practice,[34] nevertheless they would be likely to give widely varying interpretations of the raw political material depending on their own abilities, knowledge, and grasp of legal and political principles. This would pose a serious threat to the rule of law and the ability of citizens to form settled expectations and order their lives according to them.[35]

Dworkin was aware of the challenge, but felt it could be overcome. He claimed the differences between Hercules and real judges were ones of degree and not of kind. Hercules is indeed more efficient, and because he is not burdened with a heavy caseload he has much more time. But real judges can become more efficient, and through good case management free up the time they need.[36]

If this was all that Dworkin's response to the ought implies can objection amounted to, we would rightly feel disappointed. No doubt real judges can be more efficient, but law as integrity seems to demand fields of vision and interpretive skill that seem to go far beyond what we might realistically expect from them. Moreover, this does not deal with the rule of law point, that interpretation of past political practice is likely to vary massively depending on the knowledge and skills of the particular judge deciding the dispute. However, Dworkin had more to say, and it related to the role that fields of law play in legal practice. The trouble was he did not say that much more, and what he did say seems sketchy and incomplete. We will have to do our best here.

4. Local Priority

In a 453-page book (including notes), which purports to offer an interpretive theory of legal practice, it is surprising, to say the least, that Dworkin only discusses the pervasive fact of the individuation of fields of law on eight of these pages. Nonetheless, what he does say is characteristically novel and interesting. It has been

[34] Dworkin cites these forms of consensus as important anchors for law as integrity. Dworkin, *Law's Empire* (n 4) 66–67.

[35] cf NE Simmonds, 'Protestant Jurisprudence and Modern Doctrinal Scholarship' (2001) 60 The Cambridge Law Journal 271, 293–94, making a similar point but about the uncertainty likely to arise from judges holding a diversity of moral views. See also Hutchinson, 'Indiana Dworkin and Law's Empire' (n 26) 658–60; Altman, 'Legal Realism, Critical Legal Studies, and Dworkin' (n 24) 230–31. Dworkin acknowledged the critique in Dworkin, 'Political Judges and the Rule of Law' (n 9) 263–64.

[36] Dworkin, *Law's Empire* (n 4) 264–65.

largely neglected in the academic commentary on *Law's Empire*, and in discussions about why law is broken up in these ways.

Individuation is introduced in *Law's Empire* toward the end of the chapter defending integrity as a theory of law. Given what we have been told about integrity, that it is the job of a judge deciding a case to apply that scheme of principles and policies that best justifies past political and legal decisions, the phenomenon of local priority is presented as a challenge to Dworkin's legal theory.

The practice of carving up law into various departments, such as public law, private law, sports law, war law, and so on, seems to make little sense on a model of law that requires judges to ensure that their particular decisions cohere not just with other cases in the same department or field, but with the entirety of law, where that is understood broadly to include not only case law, but legislation and other political acts.[37] For Dworkin, the judge is duty-bound to ensure that past political decisions, whatever department of law they might be found in, hang together or cohere with one another; to the extent that legal and political materials exhibit tensions, it is the judge's job to try to resolve them—she cannot shut her eyes and pretend that they do not exist.[38]

These tensions are bound to exist, because, as Dworkin argued in *Taking Rights Seriously*, principles and policies which lie behind past political rules and decisions, are not fixed apertures, but float free, and crop up in different areas of law, carrying weight which varies depending on the context.[39]

So, for example, the principle that you cannot profit from your own wrong played an important role in *Riggs v Palmer*,[40] but it also explains why restitution is given for certain breaches of contract,[41] or for interference with a restrictive covenant.[42] Even doctrines that seem to be inconsistent with that principle, by allowing in some cases profit from wrongdoing, are only fully explicable if we recognize that the principle nevertheless plays a role in the shape these doctrines take. So, for example, Dworkin said the fact that the no profit from wrongdoing principle carries some weight explains why, in the context of adverse possession, a trespasser has to wait a long time before acquiring a property right in another person's land.[43] The adverse possession doctrine has what I will call a 'composite' nature, that is, it is the product of the interaction of a multiplicity of moral values and concerns. As we shall see later in the book many contract law doctrines are composite in character.

In any case where the no profit from one's wrong principle is at stake, the judge, to ensure the coherence of the law, has to review these authorities, and no doubt there are many more, not only to check how that principle was interpreted in these cases, but also how it ranked (weighted) when up against other important moral and political principles, such as testamentary freedom (*Riggs*), property rights (adverse

[37] Ronald Dworkin, *Taking Rights Seriously* (Duckworth 1977) 119–20.
[38] Altman, 'Legal Realism, Critical Legal Studies, and Dworkin'(n 24) 220.
[39] Dworkin, *Taking Rights Seriously* (n 37) 22–28.
[40] *Riggs v Palmer* 115 NY 506 (1889).
[41] *Attorney General v Blake* [2001] 1 AC 268.
[42] *Wrotham Park Estate Co Ltd v Parkside Homes Ltd* [1974] 1 WLR 798.
[43] Dworkin, *Taking Rights Seriously* (n 37) 77.

possession), and corrective justice or compensation for harm (damages for breach of contract or covenant). When coherence is the aim, these decisions cannot be sidestepped but must be confronted and explained, or overruled where possible.

The reason law's compartments are such a puzzle for this view of law is not just that it is difficult to make sense of the practice of carving up the law if judges are expected to make it cohere as a whole, but because with compartmentalization comes what Dworkin calls 'local priority'. Judges assign particular weight or priority to ensuring that like cases are treated alike *within* the particular compartments of law that they are placed:

> Judicial opinions normally begin by assigning the case in hand to some department of law, and the precedents and statutes considered are usually drawn exclusively from that department. Often the initial classification is both controversial and crucial.[44]

What this means in practice is that judges should test their interpretations of the law that applies in a particular case 'in a series of concentric circles'.[45] So, for example, in the context of a case like *McLoughlin v O'Brian*,[46] about the circumstances in which damages are recoverable in negligence for psychological harm, the judge—first and foremost—has to interpret previous cases involving psychological harm, before she considers other areas, such as the principles that apply in cases of physical damage, economic harm, damage to reputation, and so on, and once she has exhausted the tort cases, the field will expand to contract, property, and so forth. The reason this practice presents a challenge is that the priority that challenges law as integrity is not of a *temporal* kind, that is, that we first have to consider emotional injury cases, second physical injury, third economic, and so on, but rather has a *substantive* dimension. If a candidate principle or theory does not fit the emotional injury cases, or, more widely, negligence law in general, then that fact, Dworkin says, 'counts dramatically against it as an eligible interpretation of that body of law, even if it fits other areas of the law superbly'.[47] If it does fit, the judge will usually not need to expand her inquiry into wider areas.

The difficulty is explaining why this kind of local priority attaches, given that law as integrity demands that any theory of law fit the entire body of the law. So, in *McLoughlin*, if the best interpretation of the cases on damages for negligently caused psychological harm sat very uneasily with the rest of private law, why not bring those psychiatric harm cases into line with the rest of private law? *Global* coherence is sacrificed at the altar of *local* coherence; and it's very unclear given what we know about law as integrity why this should be.[48]

Given that law is an interpretive practice, and law as integrity is a theory of law, the doctrine of local priority is a challenge that Dworkin cannot duck.[49] In the spirit of his interpretive enterprise, Dworkin offers a theory of compartmentalization and

[44] Dworkin, *Law's Empire* (n 4) 251. [45] ibid 250.

[46] *McLoughlin v O'Brian* [1983] 1 AC 410. [47] Dworkin, *Law's Empire* (n 4) 251.

[48] For a real-life example of the difficulties to which local priority might give rise see *Fisher v Bell* [1961] 1 QB 394, (priority attached to contract law definition of 'offer for sale' over layman's understanding controversially affecting criminal prosecution).

[49] Dworkin, *Law's Empire* (n 4) 251–52, 403.

the local priority that it entails. The account though is sketchy and itself open to interpretation. Here is the crucial passage:

> The boundaries between departments usually match popular opinion; many people think that intentional harm is more blameworthy than careless harm, that the state needs a very different kind of justification to declare someone guilty of a crime than it needs to require him to pay compensation for damage he has caused, that promises and other forms of explicit agreement or consent are a special kind of reason for state coercion, and so forth. Dividing departments of law to match that sort of opinion promotes predictability and guards against sudden official reinterpretations that uproot large areas of law, and it does this in a way that promotes a deeper aim of law as integrity. If legal compartments make sense to people at large, they encourage the protestant attitude integrity favors, because they allow ordinary people as well as hard-pressed judges to interpret law within practical boundaries that seem natural and intuitive.[50]

The emphasis in this passage is on the importance of the link between legal compartments and what Herbert Hart called 'positive' morality: 'the morality actually accepted and shared by a given social group'.[51] On this view, the distinctions between the departments of law should track popular sentiment about the importance of certain moral distinctions, such as that between intentional and negligently cased harm, or concepts, such as punishment, promise, consent, property, and so forth.[52]

However, Dworkin goes on to discuss the distinction between nuisance and negligence law. If the two areas were separated on the basis that for nuisance a 'natural user' test should be applied to determine liability, whereas for negligence economic tests were used, then Hercules might be required to unify these areas by applying the economic test to nuisance if he came to the view 'that the "natural use" test was silly, and the economic test much more just'.[53] This example is important, because the focus seems to shift now from the emphasis on popular or positive morality, to what Hart called 'critical' morality: 'the general moral principles used in the criticism of actual social institutions including positive morality'.[54] What matters is whether the distinction, however popular, is just 'silly' and whether there are 'much more just' ways of carving up the law.

There are some significant ambiguities here, which need to be teased out. In particular, it is crucial to see how the account, though sketchy and underdeveloped, differs from the traditional conventionalist and foundationalist interpretations of local priority, which I introduced earlier. Dworkin was doing the groundwork here for an entirely distinct 'republican' theory of individuation in law; which linked legal categorization to the broader project of civic participation in social and political life.

[50] ibid 252.
[51] HLA Hart, *Law, Liberty and Morality* (Stanford University Press 1963) 20.
[52] See also Dworkin, *Justice for Hedgehogs* (n 19) 322.
[53] Dworkin, *Law's Empire* (n 4) 254.
[54] Hart, *Law, Liberty and Morality* (n 51) 20.

4.1 Conventionalism

Recall, that according to the conventionalist picture of local priority, the law is broken up into smaller chunks by legal officials to promote epistemic access to the law and rule of law values, such as predictability, notice, transparency, enabling social coordination, and so on. Dworkin's account of local priority certainly has conventionalist overtones. In particular, there is the emphasis he places on legal boundaries tracking public opinion, which he justifies in the quote above on the basis that it 'promotes predictability and guards against sudden official reinterpretations that uproot large areas of law'.

Later on in the book he associates the doctrine of local priority with the virtue of 'procedural due process' because it encourages 'citizens to rely on doctrinal pronouncements and assumptions that it would be wrong to betray in judging them after the fact'.[55] These rule of law concerns, that is, the protection of settled expectations, notice, predictability, and so forth, are for Dworkin important centripetal forces; restraining the pursuit of global coherence or what he calls '*pure* integrity', that is, the pursuit of coherence without these sorts of constraints.[56]

He acknowledges the contingent nature of these forces, and that although 'we hope that departments of law will be rearranged, in professional and public understanding, to map true distinctions of principle, so that local priority presents no impediment to a judge seeking a natural flow of principle throughout the law', we know that it is by no means certain that it will track moral principles in these ways.[57]

There is then a clear conventionalist flavour to Dworkin's account. However, other elements sit far less easily with that interpretation. Most importantly, Dworkin says legal categories should track popular opinion about specifically *moral* principles and distinctions, or positive *morality*. Moreover, he says that when legal categories depart too significantly from moral requirements, and become arbitrary or 'silly', reasons of justice may require the judge to redraw them.[58]

Neither of these points makes sense to the conventionalist. One of the virtues of the conventionalist picture is that it explains the existence of legal divisions that do not track moral concepts and principles. So, for example, the conventionalist would have no problem with the existence of legal categories such as space law, banking law, aeroplane law, and so on, which have no moral cognates, or indeed even positively immoral categories, such as slave law, provided that they were the product of the practices of legal officials, carving up law in these ways, and they promoted *epistemic* access to the law and served rule of law values, such as notice, making the law more transparent, predictable, accessible, and so on.

[55] Dworkin, *Law's Empire* (n 4) 405.

[56] ibid 405–06. cf Raz, *Ethics in the Public Domain: Essays in the Morality of Law and Politics* (n 17) 318, relying partly on 'ordinary rule-of-law considerations' to justify 'pockets of coherence' in law: 'Only by adhering to one coherent policy can the law be made widely known and its application predictable.'

[57] Dworkin, *Law's Empire* (n 4) 406.

[58] ibid 253–54.

Although there are conventionalist elements here, the link Dworkin explicitly draws between legal categories and moral principles and distinctions elevates his account of local priority away from the conventionalist view.

4.2 Foundationalism

Is Dworkin's account foundationalist? Recall, that according to foundationalism legal categories should track true moral principles and distinctions, with which they are necessarily linked. Foundationalists collect together legal rules and doctrines using moral principles, such as promise and corrective justice, and use these moral principles to determine the content and shape of the legal categories that emerge.

Dworkin's account certainly has foundationalist elements. As I have said, he says it is important that legal categories reflect not just popular expectations, but more specifically popular *moral* expectations. He says that the doctrine of local priority has 'most force when the boundaries between traditional departments of law track widely held moral principles distinguishing types of fault or responsibility, and the substance of each department reflects these moral principles'.[59] And he says judges may have to redraw traditional legal boundaries where they become arbitrary or 'silly'. Although the emphasis is on legal categories reflecting popular or positive morality, Dworkin says when discussing the requirements of pure integrity or global coherence later in the book that, ultimately, we hope legal categories reflect 'true distinctions of principle' or critical morality.[60]

Nevertheless, the conventionalist aspects of Dworkin's account jar with the foundationalist picture. Foundationalists, like Charles Fried or Ernest Weinrib, link legal categories, like contract and tort, with *true* moral principles, like promise and corrective justice. They do not say that tort or contract are connected *contingently* with these moral concepts; that the link depends on what moral principles popular opinion at a particular time or place connects these legal categories with. Rather, the claims are universalist in nature. So, for example, according to the promise theory of contract, contract law whenever and in whatever jurisdiction we might find it, will have at its foundations the promise principle. The link is *necessary* or *essential*, not contingent.

Dworkin's account of local priority is not like Fried's or Weinrib's. For Dworkin, although we might hope that legal categories are connected with true moral categories and distinctions, they might not be, because they track lay and professional opinion about these aspects of morality, and those opinions in most cases have to be respected despite what global coherence or pure integrity might require.

4.3 Republicanism

Dworkin says in the quote above that according to law as integrity, one of the purposes of local priority is to promote settled expectations and to make the law

[59] ibid 252. [60] ibid 406.

more predictable. But that is not the whole story. He says the doctrine promotes epistemic access and these rule of law values in a particular way which advances a 'deeper aim':

> If legal compartments make sense to people at large, they encourage the protestant attitude integrity favors, because they allow ordinary people as well as hard-pressed judges to interpret law within practical boundaries that seem natural and intuitive.[61]

Dworkin here offers what I shall call a republican view of local priority, which requires judges to interpret existing or conventional legal categories in light of contingent public or popular views about the moral principles and categories that they implicate.

Although vague, the idea seems to be that there are areas of law or types of legal dispute that are generally seen to implicate certain moral principles, distinctions, practices, and so forth. The courts should take these popular views seriously, because by doing so they invite ordinary citizens to engage in legal reasoning, thus inculcating the 'protestant' attitude. Dworkin's account raises many questions. Surely, for example, there is a significant gap between knowing that a particular area of law is governed by a particular moral principle or concern, and understanding actual legal doctrine which seems to take account of an array of other moral, economic, political, and strategic considerations.[62] Furthermore, what if there are conflicting views in society about the morality of particular areas of law? So, for example, is the purpose of family law to promote the best interests of children, to protect marriage, or to prevent exploitation in trusting relationships? These are all plausible views, each of which is supported, I suspect, by different people. How are judges to tell which one is right? On Dworkin's view, should judges organize an opinion poll?

Dworkin makes no attempt to answer these questions. He sketches a theory of local priority, but leaves the detail incredibly vague. It goes beyond the scope of this chapter to speculate on how Dworkin might respond. Dworkin provides us with no more than a broad direction of travel. There are three important points though to take from what he does say. First, Dworkin shares with the conventionalist the epistemic concern that law should be transparent, predictable, accessible, and so on. The doctrine of local priority promotes these values, by breaking the law into smaller more digestible chunks.

As I have said, achieving the rule of law is particularly problematic for Dworkin, because law as integrity seems to require the impossible or nearly impossible from most earthly judges: they have to strive to make the law *as a whole* coherent, which requires huge intellectual resources, time, patience, and so on. It is likely that if every judge strove to achieve these standards, their interpretations of the law would vary significantly; this unevenness would result in law being less predictable, less accessible, and so on.

By defending local priority Dworkin is attempting to answer the ought implies can objection and the rule of law worries that follow in its wake. If judges only or

[61] ibid 252.

[62] cf Richard H Fallon Jr, *Implementing the Constitution* (Harvard University Press 2001) 28–29, 33, directing this criticism at Dworkin's more general theory of adjudication.

primarily have to achieve *local* coherence, or make particular compartments of law coherent, when deciding a dispute, then that takes a lot of the pressure of law as integrity off real judges, who Dworkin acknowledges are 'hard-pressed' anyway.

The second point is the reminder that it is not just judges, but 'ordinary people' too, who need to be able to know what the law is. The law after all aims to guide our conduct, and so it must be possible to work out what it roughly requires from us. That point may seem almost too obvious to mention. However, it is particularly important in the context of Dworkin's theory of law as integrity, which focuses so much attention on the role that judges play in adjudicating disputes in determining what the law requires. That makes sense; it is after all a key duty of judges to make authoritative interpretations of the law. But, we should not forget that we all have a duty to stay within the law. To comply with that obligation, we have to be able to work out what the law is. This raises once again the spectre of the ought implies can objection. In this context, the problem is much more acute for Dworkin given that laypersons are not professionally trained in the law in the way that judges and lawyers are. How can they possibly be expected to work out what the law requires when that exercise involves making the law as a whole coherent?

Dworkin responds to this worry by appealing to local priority, and in particular by saying that the doctrine requires judges to defer to popular views about the connection between moral principles and legal categories. Because they are operating with categories that seem 'natural and intuitive', it makes it easier for ordinary citizens to work out what the law requires; legal requirements should converge with popular views about what morality requires in particular cases.

The third point is the most fundamental. For Dworkin, his theory of law, law as integrity, is an attitude or approach to law that has to be cultivated not only among judges, lawyers, and public officials, but ordinary citizens too. That attitude has most chance of taking root when judges interpret legal categories in the light of ordinary or popular understandings of moral principles, categories, and distinctions. This is because, this interpretation makes law accessible to the public at large; and gives ordinary people an opportunity to engage with and respond to the law's requirements in their daily lives. This sort of continual engagement with the law's requirements will cultivate an attitude of respect for the law, and hence for people's rights, which is a constitutive duty that members of a community of principle owe to each other.

Recall, for Dworkin legal obligations are a species of 'associative' duties. They emerge when members of political communities regard themselves as owing duties of equal concern and respect to other members. In other words, they have to act with integrity. Crucial to the view is that these duties are owed not to the state, but individually to each and every other member. The state personifies the citizenry, and enforces the *moral* rights that they owe to one another, and indeed on behalf of citizens it may through legislation create new rights. In performing these functions, the state must, like citizens, ensure that it acts with integrity.[63] Thus the state itself

[63] Ronald Dworkin, 'Response' in Scott Hershovitz (ed), *Exploring Law's Empire: The Jurisprudence of Ronald Dworkin* (Oxford University Press 2006) 305.

as a collective entity owes duties toward citizens, and they are the source of *political* rights that citizens have against it.

Some of these political rights are *legislative* in nature, that is, they require the state to use its legislative power in certain ways, for example, to collect taxes, set up a police force, a health service, and so on. Alongside these legislative rights, there are *legal* rights, which citizens can enforce on demand through courts. It is the special responsibility of the courts to correctly identify these rights and to use the coercive apparatus of the state to ensure that they are upheld.[64] Unlike the rulebook view encountered earlier, this theory of legitimacy leads to what Dworkin calls the 'rights'-based view of the rule of law, which is 'the ideal of rule by an accurate public conception of individual rights'.[65] There are no gaps in law; judges have an integrity-based duty to go beyond the rulebook in novel cases to determine what rights people have, in accordance with the scheme of principle that makes best sense of past political decisions.[66]

This leads to a public culture where discussion of matters of principle and the rights that individual citizens have will take centre-stage. Dworkin acknowledges that this certainly comes with costs, in particular the pursuit of collective goals like efficiency is more likely to be challenged and setback, and potentially it may endanger the pursuit of a collective (rather than individual) ethos in society, where what matters most is the pursuit of the common good (this is because rights for Dworkin are to use his famous phrase 'trumps').[67] Nevertheless, he argues these costs should be borne, not only because as a matter of substantive outcomes it is more likely that individual rights will be protected, but perhaps more significantly because:

> It encourages each individual to suppose that his relations with other citizens and with his government are matters of justice and it encourages him and his fellow citizens to discuss as a community what justice requires these relationships to be.[68]

This procedural or participative aspect of Dworkin's account of law is often lost sight of in the literature.[69] A common critique has been that the rights-based view is elitist and profoundly anti-democratic in assigning so much power to the judiciary over the protection of rights and the pursuit of collective goals.[70] But this ignores

[64] Dworkin, *Justice for Hedgehogs* (n 19) 405.

[65] Dworkin, 'Political Judges and the Rule of Law' (n 9) 262, 281; Ronald Dworkin, 'The Forum of Principle' (1981) 56 New York University Law Review 469, 516.

[66] Dworkin, 'Political Judges and the Rule of Law' (n 9) 268.

[67] Dworkin, *Law's Empire* (n 4) 160.

[68] Dworkin, 'Political Judges and the Rule of Law' (n 9) 32; Dworkin, *Law's Empire* (n 4) 160–62, 413. See also Gerald J Postema, '"Protestant" Interpretation and Social Practices' (1987) 6 Law and Philosophy 283, 285.

[69] Waldron's work is a notable exception. See Waldron, 'Did Dworkin Ever Answer the Crits?' (n 14) 175, 176–77; Waldron, 'The Rule of Law as a Theater of Debate' (n 21) 326, 330–31.

[70] See, for example, Hutchinson, 'Indiana Dworkin and Law's Empire' (n 26) 655: '*Law's Empire* is about accepting and assuming political obligations and not about participating in the making of them. . . . For citizens, politics has become a spectator sport.'; Wasserstrom, 'The Empire's New Clothes' (n 17) 265. One way Dworkin answered the critique was to claim that judges will have this kind of power even if the more familiar rulebook model is adopted. See Dworkin, 'The Forum of Principle' (n 65).

the important role Dworkin saw courts playing as 'forums of principle', in which and around which citizens debated questions about what they owed to one another. For Dworkin, courts were laboratories for arguments of principle, which he hoped would help to cultivate a 'sense of justice' not only among judges and lawyers but ordinary citizens. Law as integrity was as important, possibly more important, as an approach that the state and individual citizens adopted toward fellow members of the political community, as it was about ensuring that moral and political rights were correctly captured and protected by the courts.[71]

It is against that political context that we have to interpret Dworkin's embryonic remarks about local priority. Law as integrity is a collective effort, which involves individual citizens striving toward relationships of respect with other members of their community. Given this, Dworkin attempts through the doctrine of local priority and in particular the emphasis he places on judges connecting legal categories with popular or positive morality an umbilical link between the arguments of principle about rights that we find in our highest courts and those that emerge around dinner tables, in pubs, coffeehouses, classrooms, and so forth when these cases are reported, discussed, and debated. Local priority for Dworkin not only makes law more digestible and predictable, but by connecting to popular moral sentiment it gives ordinary citizens the opportunity to share in the collective effort of determining what exactly the law in their particular society requires.

This raises a vital point. Dworkin is not merely saying that local priority is an epistemic device for promoting citizens' access to legal demands or requirements.[72] Rather, and more radically, he is making the metaphysical claim that local priority is built into the very fabric of law. This is because, for law as integrity, citizen participation in identifying legal rights and duties is an essential aspect of the legitimacy of any legal system.[73] For Dworkin, local priority secures this kind of citizen involvement by taking seriously people's ordinary moral beliefs and convictions about how legal disputes should be classified. In that way, those beliefs and the categories to which they give rise become part of, or constitute, the structure and shape that the law eventually takes, and this in turn influences the content of legal norms.[74]

[71] Dworkin, 'The Forum of Principle' (n 65) 517; Dworkin, *Taking Rights Seriously* (n 37) 186; Dworkin, *Law's Empire* (n 4) 190, 213. See also Waldron, 'The Rule of Law as a Theater of Debate' (n 21) 329–31.

[72] cf Fallon Jr, *Implementing the Constitution* (n 62) 40, (claiming that courts should take account in crafting legal doctrine of popular views about what the law requires for reasons of promoting efficiency, preventing resentment, and avoiding uncertainty).

[73] cf John Gardner's remarks about the importance of law achieving what he calls 'moral clarity': 'Moral clarity is secured ... by the adequate replication in the law of clear distinctions and significances which apply outside the law, together with reasonably clear indication (in the titles of Acts, the common names and classifications of offences, etc.) of which cluster of distinctions and significances people can expect to find replicated where.' John Gardner, *Offences and Defences: Selected Essays in the Philosophy of Criminal Law* (Oxford University Press 2007) 45. Moral clarity is for Gardner a standard that the law should seek to attain, but Gardner—unlike Dworkin—does not appear to justify it on republican grounds relating to the value of citizen participation in law. See ibid 44–45, 48.

[74] This is not to claim that this will happen easily. It is likely there will be conflict between the epistemic or rule of law goals of local priority and the metaphysical or republican aspects, when for example traditional legal categories conflict with popular moral views. Thank you to Benjamin Zipursky for making this point to me.

For Dworkin, law is not a 'top-down' phenomenon, presented on tablets of stone from on high. Rather, it is the other way around: law grows out of and is constituted by popular views about the moral principles and categories that should govern people's interactions and the resolution of disputes. To correctly identify and protect rights, judges must engage with the political and ethical beliefs of citizens. Law as integrity is an attitude that citizens take toward one another, and an ongoing collective effort which aims at realizing the ideal of fraternity in the context of the rough and tumble of everyday politics, where despite the entanglement of a people, past political practice has, as the CLS movement saw, been shaped by disagreement, conflicting interests, rival ideologies, and so on. The reality of politics is the breeding ground from which emerges the effort to achieve fraternity among those who though bound together, disagree about matters of fundamental ethical and political significance.[75]

These public or national debates about what integrity requires do not necessarily start and end with the adjudication of particular disputes in our highest courts. The civil rights movement predated *Brown v Board of Education*,[76] and the decision provoked violent backlashes. In a culture that embraces the rights-based conception of the rule of law and the system of judicial review it entails, these cases might just bring to the boil controversies that have been heating up in wider society.

In such a society, citizens are acutely aware of the central place of principle in resolving questions of what citizens owe to each other.[77] They play an active role in how controversies are settled. So, for example, Dworkin defended the rights of those who conscientiously objected to the Vietnam War on the ground that they were basing their resistance on plausible interpretations of the law, even though officials or courts took a different view about what it required. Courts, Dworkin argued, had to take seriously, not just for political but for *legal* reasons, ordinary people's views about the wrongness of the draft. This was for several reasons. First, allowing this kind of resistance to official views offers an opportunity to test the policy implications of particular decisions:

> If the question is whether a particular rule would have certain undesirable consequences, or whether these consequences would have limited or broad ramifications, then, before the issue is decided, it is useful to know what does in fact take place when some people proceed on that rule.[78]

Second, it made it more likely that the courts would get the law right. Dissenters gave reasons why they resisted the draft, and the public nature of their acts stimulated debate in society more widely, in newspapers, law schools, the legal profession, and so on.[79]

Third, these forms of resistance were important in and of themselves as 'a dramatic statement of the degree to which a court decision against the dissenter is felt to be

[75] See Jeremy Waldron, 'The Circumstances of Integrity' (1997) 3 Legal Theory 1.
[76] *Brown v Board of Education* 347 US 483 (1954).
[77] Dworkin, 'The Forum of Principle' (n 65) 517–18.
[78] Dworkin, *Taking Rights Seriously* (n 37) 212.
[79] ibid 213.

wrong, a demonstration that is surely pertinent to the question of whether it was right'.[80] Illustrating again the closeness of the link Dworkin drew between law and conventional or positive morality.

These reasons may persist even after a court, maybe even the highest court, has rejected the conscientious objector's interpretation of the law. It is true that integrity itself will require the citizen to attach weight, perhaps great weight, to the court's decision. The objector cannot ignore the decision, and it may significantly alter the plausibility of the objector's stance. However, even when the decision is taken by the highest of courts, that does not mean that it is necessarily the end of the matter: 'if the issue is one touching fundamental personal or political rights, and it is arguable that the Supreme Court has made a mistake, a man is within his social rights in refusing to accept that decision as conclusive'.[81] This is because for Dworkin: 'A citizen's allegiance is to the law, not to any particular person's view of what the law is, and he does not behave unfairly so long as he proceeds on his own considered and reasonable view of what the law requires.'[82]

Dworkin's views about conscientious objection are well known, but I rehearse them here because they illustrate vividly just how seriously, throughout his career, he took the idea that achieving the rule of law was a collective and interdependent effort, involving ordinary people and their own personal convictions about right and wrong (his essay on civil disobedience first appeared in *The New York Review of Books* in 1968,[83] nearly two decades before *Law's Empire* was published). As Gerald Postema says, this view unsettles the traditional 'unidirectional' view of law, where 'The influence moves entirely in one direction: top down. Law-making and law-interpreting, we think, is an exercise of power, and legislators and judges have all the power.'[84] In contrast, Postema argues, Dworkin emphasized the 'essentially interactive' nature of law: 'Judicial interpretive activity, while prominent and powerful, is nevertheless dependent in many ways on the interpretive activity of other, professional and lay, participants in legal practice.'[85]

This was not just about ensuring or making it more likely that courts got the law right, but, more fundamentally, it was about creating a particular kind of society, where all members tried in the course of their daily lives to treat other members with due regard and respect. As Dworkin said, this is a 'protestant' view of law, according to which political obligation is 'not just a matter of obeying the discreet political

[80] ibid 214. [81] ibid 214–15.

[82] ibid 214, 185; Ronald Dworkin, *A Matter of Principle* (Harvard University Press 1985) 115–16. And see Waldron, 'The Rule of Law as a Theater of Debate' (n 21), saying that on Dworkin's view: 'There is a truth about rights and justice that our public conceptions ought to embody, but that they might or might not embody accurately' (ibid 320), and further that 'Any principle of settlement is subordinated to the importance of the procedures that allow citizens as much as judges to pursue the possibility that the law is not what it says on the rule-books and that society has not kept faith—as its authoritative determinations claim to have kept faith—with principles of right and justice' (ibid 326).

[83] Ronald Dworkin, 'On Not Prosecuting Civil Disobedience' (1968) 10 The New York Review of Books 14.

[84] Gerald J Postema, '"Protestant" Interpretation and Social Practices' (n 68) 310, (pointing out the commonality in this regard between Dworkin and Lon Fuller).

[85] ibid.

decisions of the community one by one', but rather requires 'fidelity to a scheme of principle each citizen has a responsibility to identify, ultimately for himself, as his community's scheme'.[86]

This explains why local priority mattered so much for Dworkin. With its emphasis on respect for conventional or popular views about the moral distinctions legal categories should reflect, Dworkin was attempting to bring law down to earth—to facilitate everyday reasoning about rights and responsibilities among individual citizens, from whatever walk of life they might belong.

In a review of Gerald Gunther's biography of Judge Learned Hand, for whom Dworkin famously clerked, Dworkin describes Hand's political outlook as one of 'civic republicanism': 'he thought that a political community could not flourish, or its citizens develop and improve their own sense of moral responsibility, unless they participated in the community's deepest and most important decisions about justice'.[87] Dworkin took on the same view, but and this was Dworkin's distinctive contribution, he saw that it did not just entail citizens participating in decision-making about matters of *policy*, that is, decisions about public welfare or the common good usually reserved for legislatures, in which citizens could be involved through democratic decision-making processes designed primarily to elicit people's preferences.[88] That sort of involvement is of course important but (as Hand himself acknowledged) all too often illusory; how much difference, after all, can one vote make?[89] Rather, Dworkin emphasized the importance of citizens grappling with questions of *principle*, that is, those matters faced routinely by courts.[90] The civil rights movement, the protests over Vietnam, debates about abortion in the wake of *Roe v Wade*,[91] and so forth, illustrated for Dworkin exactly this point.

[86] Dworkin, *Law's Empire* (n 4) 190. See also Postema, '"Protestant" Interpretation and Social Practices' (n 68) 288–89. This approach explains, as Dworkin argued in *Law's Empire*, the argumentative nature of adjudication, but Nigel Simmonds makes the interesting point that it may also explain the authority that treatise writers and doctrinal scholars seem to have. On the positivist picture rules of adjudication explain why judges have authority to exercise discretion in hard cases, but that does not explain the authority treatise writers seem to have when they make pronouncements about how these cases should be decided. Simmonds, 'Protestant Jurisprudence and Modern Doctrinal Scholarship'(n 35) 273–74, 299. Treatise writers make arguments about what the law is, not predictions about what judges might do in the future: 'the scholar is thought of as drawing out the law's implicit content' (ibid 274). This practice makes more sense from the point of view of a theory of law that sees law not as a series of discreet rules or decisions made by judges and legislators, but rather as the scheme of principle that underpins these decisions. Simmonds concludes that the modern-day treatise must then be 'an heir to the tradition of modern natural law that began with Grotius' (ibid 273).

[87] Ronald Dworkin, *Freedom's Law: The Moral Reading of the American Constitution* (Oxford University Press 1999) 342.

[88] See Ronald Dworkin, 'What is Equality? Part 4: Political Equality' (1987) 22 University of San Francisco Law Review 1, 25.

[89] Learned Hand, *The Bill of Rights* (Atheneum 1965) 73–74, cited by Dworkin, *Freedom's Law: The Moral Reading of the American Constitution* (n 87) 342–43. This is not to diminish the undeniable symbolic importance of the vote, as an expression of equal standing. See Dworkin, 'What is Equality? Part 4: Political Equality' (n 88) 19.

[90] cf Griffin, 'Moral Law, Positive Law' (n 32) 54; Nigel E Simmonds, 'The Possibility of Private Law' in John Tasioulas (ed), *Law, Values and Social Practices* (Dartmouth 1997) 144.

[91] *Roe v Wade* 410 US 113 (1973).

Unlike in the legislative context, where matters of public welfare are at stake, what counted was not numbers, but rather the fact that citizens approached these issues of principle with the right attitude and gave them the seriousness and attention that they deserved. Dworkin argued that although citizens might not have *power* over judicial decisions in the way they might over legislative ones, nevertheless as moral agents they had a constitutional *role* in them: 'self-respect requires that people participate, as partners in a joint venture, in the moral argument over the rules under which they live'.[92] It was that citizens joined that moral argument, quite apart from any influence they might have on the final outcome or decision, which was of fundamental importance.[93]

In a recent article, Seana Shiffrin in discussing the advantages of using flexible and open-ended standards in law (which normally incorporate moral concepts and principles, such as, for example, the unconscionability doctrine in contract or the reasonable person test in tort) over clearer, more certain, rules, helpfully sheds light, I think, on the values that this sort of civic republicanism might implicate.[94] Although the price of flexibility is a degree of uncertainty, which may threaten a rulebook conception of the rule of law, it may be worth paying from the perspective of rights-based models. Not only are people more likely to behave morally (compared to episodic rule-following, people will be more alive to moral requirements in different contexts),[95] but, more fundamentally, it opens up deeper and more meaningful forms of human association in social and political life.[96]

This is because applying standards induces individual moral deliberation, which, firstly, promotes sympathetic understanding of other people's perspectives; secondly, exercises our moral capacities in a wide variety of contexts; and, finally, plays an important democratic role by educating citizens about the purpose of law. This last point chimes with Dworkin's claim that law as integrity provides a theory or interpretation of legal practice, which is essential for understanding what the law is. As Shiffrin says:

> As for most subjects for which understanding the foundations is necessary to grasp the surface, this engagement promotes an even fuller internalization and deeper mastery of the law. It also stimulates dialogue between citizens about the purpose of law and particular

[92] Dworkin, *Freedom's Law: The Moral Reading of the American Constitution* (n 87) 344. See also Dworkin, 'What is Equality? Part 4: Political Equality' (n 88) 5, 17.

[93] Dworkin, *Law's Empire* (n 4) 413. Although it may be that for minorities in particular joining such debates through conscientious objection or litigation could prove more influential than democratic decision procedures like voting which exclude them by weight of numbers alone. See Dworkin, 'What is Equality? Part 4: Political Equality' (n 88) 28; Aileen Kavanagh, 'Participation and Judicial Review: A Reply to Jeremy Waldron' (2003) 22 Law and Philosophy 451, 474, 482–84; Joseph Raz, 'Rights and Politics' (1995) 71 Indiana Law Journal 27, 43–44.

[94] Seana Valentine Shiffrin, 'Inducing Moral Deliberation: On the Occasional Virtues of Fog' (2010) 123 Harvard Law Review 1214.

[95] Shiffrin cites evidence showing that in certain situations accidents decrease when there are fewer traffic rules. ibid 1219–20. This is because when there are too many rules, 'We stop paying close attention to what we are doing, falsely secure in the sense that we are nested in a set of complex rules whose execution "guarantees" our safety' (ibid 1220).

[96] ibid 1222–23.

legal directives. These processes enable a richer form of democratic engagement and mutual understanding.[97]

This point about dialogue reminds us that on the rights-based view, the rule of law is as much about creating a particular kind of rights respecting culture or atmosphere in society, as it is about protecting people's entitlements. These three interlocking virtues of standards identified by Shiffrin are, I believe, entailments too of Dworkin's wider theory of law, which did so much to show the relevance of background standards for interpreting and justifying surface level legal rules. Shiffrin captures here (admittedly in a narrower context) the sorts of values that Dworkin's 'community of principle' sought to inculcate.

This culture of rights improves the quality of debate about matters of principle, and produces an atmosphere of respect for others crucial to the realization of 'a national sense of justice, and to keeping our spirit of liberty alive'.[98] But—and Dworkin took pains to emphasize the point—these public goods 'can be realised only when judges and the public cooperate in securing them'.[99] This explains the importance Dworkin attached to judicial decisions being expressed in less technical language, their wide-scale reporting in the news media, the significance of public participation in judicial selection processes,[100] and indeed the importance of popular opinion about moral questions when judges, lawyers, and legal scholars fashion our fields of law.[101]

5. Beyond the Determinatio

Local priority for Dworkin was about much more than just making the law more digestible. Unlike more common views, Dworkin offered a distinctively republican theory of local priority. He denied that legal categories were merely conventional in character and he rejected the view that they were shaped by critical morality alone. Rather, he argued, unlike the foundationalist, that they tracked conventions, but departing from the conventionalist he argued that those conventions were of a particular kind, that is, mapping popular views about specifically *moral* categories and principles.

Dworkin's account of local priority was motivated not just by the traditional natural law insight embraced in the concept of the determinatio that social conventions and law are necessary for rendering morality and moral requirements determinate.[102] So, for example, societies may be forced to choose between moral values, such as

[97] ibid 1224–25.

[98] Dworkin, *Freedom's Law: The Moral Reading of the American Constitution Law* (n 87) 346.

[99] ibid. [100] ibid.

[101] Shiffrin seems to take a similar view: 'how law is understood on the street by everyday citizens may actually, and rightly, have an important influence on its ultimate judicial interpretation'. Shiffrin, 'Inducing Moral Deliberation: On the Occasional Virtues of Fog' (n 94) 1225 and n 38.

[102] On the determinatio, see for example: Griffin, 'Moral Law, Positive Law' (n 32) 51–52; Simmonds, 'Protestant Jurisprudence and Modern Doctrinal Scholarship' (n 35) 292; Dworkin, *Justice for Hedgehogs* (n 19) 314.

promise, fairness, preventing exploitation, social solidarity, and so on, because they are incommensurable or irreducibly distinct and due to this will conflict with one another. When they do, we face choices between undefeated reasons, which reason alone cannot resolve. Instead, social or collective choices between these values have to be made to enable social coordination and cooperation.[103] Social conventions may express the choices that particular societies at particular times have made, and the law might track these. This is important, and no doubt one of the reasons Dworkin anchored his theory of local priority in positive morality. However, it is not the whole story. Dworkin was clear:

> When men disagree about moral rights, there will be no way for either side to prove its case, and some decision must stand if there is not to be anarchy. But that piece of orthodox wisdom must be the beginning and not the end of a philosophy of legislation and enforcement.[104]

The determinatio is 'the beginning and not the end' of a philosophy of local priority in two interlocking senses. First, once decisions between values are taken and made, the virtue of integrity requires the state to apply those decisions with principled consistency to *all* members and groups within society. This is not just for reasons of social coordination or cooperation, but rather it is about the expression of equal concern and respect.

Second, for that virtue to be embraced not just by officials but by each and every citizen, which is what Dworkin's theory of legitimacy required, the law had to be transparent, accessible, and available to the ordinary citizen. Citizens had to be in a position where they could engage with the law and legal requirements as they went about their daily lives. Dworkin's theory of local priority makes sense only against this background. He wanted to connect legal categories with popular morality, because it would enable ordinary citizens to join debates about matters of principle which are typically the preserve of the courts. This is not merely a point about epistemic access to the law, but rather for Dworkin it was a metaphysical point: legal categories and the ordinary moral beliefs that shape them, become part of the very fabric of law, because the legitimacy of the law depends on the kind of citizen involvement with law and legal requirements that local priority plays a crucial role in securing.

That form of political participation would not only enhance the quality of public debate about these issues, making justice more likely, but would be the tie that bound society together; it was the mark of Dworkin's distinctive brand of civic republicanism.

6. Toward Republican Contract Law

What are the implications of this republican theory of local priority for contract law? In my view, it offers a new way of thinking about the relationship that contract

[103] Raz, *Ethics in the Public Domain: Essays in the Morality of Law and Politics* (n 17) 317.
[104] Dworkin, *Taking Rights Seriously* (n 37) 186.

law has with morality. According to the foundationalist, contract is *necessarily* or *essentially* tied to a particular moral principle—the dominant view being that that principle is promise—which plays a special role in justifying contract law rules and doctrines. We saw in the previous chapter how this view falls short when it comes to explaining and handling actual contract law doctrine.

The difference on the republican view is that the link between contract law and the moral value or values that it serves is *contingent*. It depends on ordinary beliefs and customs about how contractual disputes should be handled or resolved.[105] Those conventional beliefs take root in the law to induce citizen participation in legal decision-making, which contributes to the creation and promotion of a rights-based culture, which, as Dworkin argued, is essential for political legitimacy.

If this background republican view of local priority and the conditions of state legitimacy is true—it goes beyond the scope of this book to argue for it in detail—then what follows for contract law is that we must as theorists and doctrinal lawyers approach contract law not as though it is a 'Platonic form', but rather as the particular law of a particular time and place; integrity requires that we investigate from the ground up local doctrines and rules to uncover the scheme of principle endorsed in that particular jurisdiction. On this view, it is possible and in fact highly likely that the contract law of different legal systems will—perfectly legitimately—diverge in embracing different values, purposes, and moral concerns. There is no one size fits all.

Dworkin only provided a sketch of a theory of local priority, and he did not in any way work systematically on contract law. My purpose in this book—especially in the chapters on doctrine that follow—is to develop a republican theory of English contract law which flows and is animated by Dworkin's admittedly brief remarks about local priority and his broader theory of law. The account I offer differs from this book's main target—the promise theory—in four main ways.

First, and as I have already said, the purpose of contract law on this republican view is *contingent*. It will depend on aspects of conventional morality and past political and legal practice. The job of the contract theorist or doctrinal lawyer is to uncover the particular scheme of principle embodied in the contract law of the particular jurisdiction that is the subject of study or interpretation.[106]

In the chapters on contract doctrine that follow, I argue that the best conception of the rules and doctrines of English contract law is that they embrace or embody the promotion of trust-based cooperation between contracting parties as the constitutive or characteristic purpose of this area of law. In making this claim, I do not argue—although I think it likely—that this is contract's *authentic* purpose, that is, one that actually motivated legal actors in the past when they fashioned contract law rules and doctrines. This would require historical or sociological research which

105 cf Stuart Hampshire, 'Morality and Pessimism' in Stuart Hampshire (ed), *Public and Private Morality* (Cambridge University Press 1978) 20–21; Stuart Hampshire, 'Public and Private Morality' in Stuart Hampshire (ed), *Public and Private Morality* (Cambridge University Press 1978) 44–47; and Ronald Dworkin, 'Liberalism' in Stuart Hampshire (ed), *Public and Private Morality* (Cambridge University Press 1978) 119–20.

106 cf Dworkin, 'Liberalism' (n 105) 119–20.

is beyond the scope of this book. Rather, the claim is that the purpose is *complete*, in that it provides a compelling or salient account of English contract law and doctrine and that it is *distinct*, because no rival theory provides the same account.[107]

Secondly, on the republican view contract law is *functional*. It serves a distinct or independently specifiable end or purpose, which for Anglo-American contract law is the promotion of trust-based cooperation between contractual partners. This view differs from consequentialism, in that contract law serves this function not instrumentally or causally but constitutively, by which I mean, following Anthony Duff's work on punishment, that contract law is an 'intrinsically appropriate' method for achieving this end.[108] This means that the goal of achieving trust-based cooperation sets limits or constraints on the means which can be used to achieve it. Contract law contributes constitutively to this goal by structuring through its rules and doctrines an intrinsically valuable relationship between contractual partners who have typically exchanged promises with one another.[109]

The difference with promise theory is structural. Promise theorists tend to assume that contract law serves no distinct end beyond itself, and that there is value per se in the legal enforcement of promises. But such views are in tension with the liberal aversion to the state enforcement of morality. Recall Dworkin's point earlier that included in the circumstances that bring the state into being are ones where there is deep disagreement between individuals and groups about the good and morality. It has been a central tenet of liberal thought that the state should stay neutral on such matters. When people make promises to one another, it is of course open to them to decide whether to keep them, but the state should not take a stance, and it certainly should not do so by using the coercive apparatus of the law to enforce the promises made.[110]

The key to unlocking the liberal dilemma about justifying the state in circumstances of disagreement about the good and the requirements of justice is finding principles or ends which diverse individuals and groups share or can reasonably agree to. Hobbes appealed to rational self-interest,[111] Rawls relied on 'the original position' as a device to unearth those principles that free and equal people would agree to,[112] and for Dworkin, as we have seen, the virtue of integrity expressed the liberal

[107] I borrow these distinctions from Dworkin. ibid 121.

[108] Antony R Duff, 'Penal Communications: Recent Work in the Philosophy of Punishment' (1996) 20 Crime and Justice 1, 8–9.

[109] See similarly Daniel Markovits, 'Contract and Collaboration' (2004) 113 Yale Law Journal 1417, 1419. Markovits here stresses the neglected importance of the relationship that contract law creates. He offers though a Kantian account of the value of this relation, which is at odds with the teleological theory of contract that I defend.

[110] Duff, 'Penal Communications: Recent Work in the Philosophy of Punishment' (n 108) 9. Duff makes the point in the context of justifying state punishment. Dori Kimel makes a similar point about contract law. Dori Kimel, 'The Morality of Contract and Moral Culpability in Breach' (2010) 21 King's Law Journal 213, 222. See similarly Randy E Barnett, 'Contract Is Not Promise; Contract Is Consent' in Gregory Klass, George Letsas, and Prince Saprai (eds), *Philosophical Foundations of Contract Law* (Oxford University Press 2014) 47: 'by justifying contract as a species of enforcing purely moral commitments, it seems tantamount to enforcing virtue'.

[111] Hobbes, *Leviathan: Revised Student Edition* (n 5).

[112] Rawls, *A Theory of Justice* (n 8) 15–19, ch 3.

commitment to equal concern and respect. On the republican view, to justify the state enforcement of promissory morality we have to look to a good that goes beyond promise itself. That good is the promotion of trust-based cooperation, and its status as a legitimate end for the state to pursue is secure because it is one of the essential or basic conditions for social cohesion, stability, and successful social cooperation.

I develop the point in much more depth in the next chapter, but it was Fried who made the point that promise is a way of invoking trust, and that cooperation and reliance based on trust is a much more secure method of achieving one's goals and predicting the behaviour of others than relying on their self-interest, the calculation of which may—depending on happenstance—change. Alongside these instrumental advantages, Fried rightly emphasized the intrinsic or inherent value of this type of cooperation.[113] It provides a way for people to enlist the support of others in pursuit of their own goals that brings people closer together; helping to foster a sense of neighbourliness or community which is an essential precondition for the existence of any state.

This could explain why the state might have a role in promoting the practice of promising, but it does not yet explain why the state should enforce promises using its legal apparatus. This is the point that Fried, and many other promise theorists, have missed or paid insufficient attention to. Contract law does not just enforce promissory morality *simpliciter*. It enforces it in a *distinctive* or *unique* way. Trust-based cooperation is a good that is pursued and secured through contract, but in a way that is different to how it is achieved in other contexts—most notably in promise.[114] Furthermore, the pursuit of that goal through contract is indispensable for creating a sense of social solidarity, achieving successful social cooperation, and so forth. It is the burden of the next chapter to put further flesh on the bones of this claim.

The third way the republican view differs from the promise theory is that promise theorists tend to assume that the values that contract law instantiates are fairly determinate in nature. They regard the norms of promissory morality to be largely clear, and they expect contract law to reflect or live up to them. This attitude is linked to the previous point just made that promise theorists tend to assume that the job of contract law is simply to enforce promissory morality. Fried and others have largely failed to notice the inherent or immanent value of the distinctive way in which contract law enforces promises. On the republican view, the *constitutive* or defining goal of English contract law—to promote trust-based cooperation—is

[113] Charles Fried, *Contract as Promise: A Theory of Contractual Obligation* (Harvard University Press 1981) 8, 13.

[114] The point has been missed or insufficiently attended to not only by promise theorists, but also by critics of the promise theory. See, for example, Kimel, 'The Morality of Contract and Moral Culpability in Breach' (n 110) 222: 'unless the function of contract law is viewed as that of enforcing the morality of promise-keeping *for its own sake*—something which would not only be illiberal and ill-advised on its own, but would also significantly undermine the propensity of contract law to fulfil the functions more commonly attributed to it—the threshold for legitimate remedial responses to a breach can only plausibly be harm'. Contra Kimel, I show in the next chapter that there is a plausible alternative to the harm principle, which is how liberals have traditionally responded to the anxiety about the state enforcement of morals.

largely *underdetermined*. There are innumerable and perfectly legitimate competing ways in which it might be specified or pursued by *derivative* or *strategic* legal rules and doctrines.[115] Unlike the promise theorist, the republican makes no strong claim that the values that underpin contract law provide positive guidance on the precise shape that contract law rules and doctrine should take. Rather, the courts are expected to interpret and fashion these more general and abstract principles and values in ways that take account of past political practice, local conditions, circumstances, and needs. Due to the relevance of these factors, there is likely to be perfectly legitimate divergences in the laws even of legal systems that share the promotion of trust-based cooperation as a constitutive end of contract law.

This shaping or moulding role that courts play is constitutive of the distinctive way in which Anglo-American contract law pursues the end of promoting trust-based cooperation. There is an asymmetry here with promissory morality, which I bring out further in the next chapter. This is not to say that on the republican view the constitutive end of contract law provides no guidance. Rather, the claim is that the guidance is broad and unspecific in nature, and typically operates *negatively* as a side-constraint on rules and doctrines that would directly or egregiously contradict that characteristic or defining purpose.[116]

Such a view—unlike promise theory—takes the 'normative pluralism' that I argued in the last chapter is such a feature of contract law seriously, by embracing the fact that there is no single eligible way—such as, for example, 'justificatory necessity', 'justificatory primacy', and so forth—in which the values or moral concerns that distinguish or organize contract law should feature in legal reasoning. Rather, and as I hope to show in the chapters on doctrine that follow, the context in which the constitutive purpose is pursued varies the weight of the principles—including the promise principle itself—that bear on how contractual disputes should be resolved.[117]

The final way that the republican view differs from the promise theory is that it is *pluralistic* about the purposes that contract law serves. Promise theorists tend to assume that the *only* purpose of contract is to enforce promissory morality. I have argued that such a view is under-inclusive of the values that actually shape contract

[115] On the distinction between constitutive and derivative principles and rules see Dworkin, 'Liberalism' (n 105) 116–17: 'In any coherent political program there are two elements: constitutive political positions that are valued for their own sake, and derivative positions that are valued as strategies, as means of achieving the constitutive positions' (116). And similarly on the under-determinacy of organizing ends, see Martha C Nussbaum, 'Aristotle on Human Nature and the Foundations of Ethics' in J E J Altham and Ross Harrison (eds), *World, Mind, and Ethics: Essays on the Ethical Philosophy of Bernard Williams* (Cambridge University Press 1995) 123; Hampshire, 'Morality and Pessimism' (n 105) 11–12.

[116] cf Hampshire, 'Morality and Pessimism' (n 105) 11–13, 16–19.

[117] This is not to deny that certain derivative legal principles or rules may be *insulated* from balancing exercises, because this makes it more likely down the line that the *constitutive* ends of contract law are achieved (it may be thought promise is such a principle, but I show in the chapters on doctrine that follow that it is often compromised by other moral concerns). This does not though necessarily mean that their status is *absolute* or that they could not be sacrificed where there is a clear and significant threat to a constitutive goal. I borrow this argument and these distinctions from Dworkin, 'Liberalism' (n 105) 116–17 n 1.

law and runs up against the liberal objection to the enforcement of morals. On the republican view, as I have argued, the purpose that contract law pursues is a contingent matter, dependent on past political practice, conventional morality, and so forth. Given this, there is no reason to assume in advance that contract law serves only one purpose or function. It will be a matter of local history and politics whether it serves only one or multiple purposes and functions.

I have argued that the promotion of trust-based cooperation is a *characteristic* or *constitutive* end of English contract law.[118] But Anglo-American contract law serves many other *incidental* functions too, such as preventing exploitation, promoting efficiency, ensuring fairness between contracting parties, and so forth. The constitutive end of contract does play an organizing or focal role in this area of law, and it affects or influences how these incidental functions are pursued.[119] That does not mean though that these ancillary functions do not play a significant role in the how contract law rules and doctrines are forged. Both the constitutive and these incidental purposes are underdetermined in nature and may be interpreted perfectly legitimately in innumerable ways by the courts. These ends may also conflict, and it is the job of national courts to authoritatively balance and rank these ends and the values they instantiate when they do. This leads to what I describe in the chapters on doctrine that follow to the formation of 'composite doctrines', that is, legal doctrines and rules that are the product of the interaction between a multiplicity of moral values and ends.[120] As I show, promise theorists consistently mishandle or misapply central contract law doctrines, because they are myopic about the values that actually bear on and shape contract law.

These four features of the republican theory—that it is contingent, functional, underdetermined, and pluralistic—distinguish it from the promise theory and reflect its nonfoundational nature as a 'bottom-up' theory of contract law; grounded in taking seriously the scheme of principle embodied in the rules and doctrines that constitute the contract law of particular legal systems. Such an account describes a contract law that the legal officials and citizens of these regimes would readily recognize; and invites them to participate in the process of interpreting and balancing the distinct set of values, organizing ideals, and incidental ends and purposes, that together shape this area of law. It is when citizens engage in this interpretive process

[118] In my view English contract law does not serve any other obvious specifically constitutive purpose. However, I do not mean to deny that in other legal systems contract law embraces multiple or even conflicting constitutive purposes. It is a matter of local history and politics whether this proves to be the case. See further ibid.

[119] I rely here on Martha Nussbaum's interpretation of Aristotle on the role of organizing principles in the leading of distinctively human lives. Nussbaum, 'Aristotle on Human Nature and the Foundations of Ethics' (n 115) 113–17. See also TH Irwin, 'The Metaphysical and Psychological Basis of Aristotle's Ethics' in Amélie Oksenberg Rorty (ed), *Essays on Aristotle's Ethics* (University of California Press 1980) 35–54; Kathleen V Wilkes, 'The Good Man and the Good for Man in Aristotle's Ethics' in Amélie Oksenberg Rorty (ed), *Essays on Aristotle's Ethics* (University of California Press 1980); John M Cooper, *Reason and Human Good in Aristotle* (Harvard University Press 1975); John M Cooper, 'Contemplation and Happiness: A Reconsideration' (1987) 72 Synthese 187. All sources cited by Nussbaum. See also, Hampshire, 'Morality and Pessimism' (n 105) 11–13.

[120] cf Hampshire, 'Morality and Pessimism' (n 105) 19.

that a culture that respects rights takes root in a particular society, and confers legitimacy on its system of law.

7. Conclusion

The key to understanding Dworkin's philosophy of law in general and his cryptic remarks on local priority is the problem of disagreement. Dworkin begins with the central problem of political philosophy: in any society people are likely to disagree profoundly about morality and the good life, and this will be a source of tension, conflict, and instability. How should we deal with this? Dworkin's answer is that the state which is charged with promoting the common good and creating, identifying, and enforcing the community's laws, should seek in performing its functions to ensure that it acts with integrity, and thereby avoids treating particular citizens or groups within society differently on arbitrary or capricious grounds. Whatever disagreements people have, they will recognize that they and others have a right to equal concern and respect.

In the context of adjudication, this view raises the ought implies can objection. Judges are not Gods, and they lack the time and intellectual resources required to make law as a whole coherent in the way that integrity requires. This is where local priority comes in for Dworkin. While *global* coherence looks like an impossible dream for earthly judges, *local* coherence—coherence *within* particular departments of law (contract, tort, trusts, and so forth)—is achievable.

In seeking local coherence though, the courts should, Dworkin argued, attempt to track popular views about the moral distinctions and concerns that demarcate conventional legal categories. The purpose of this for Dworkin was to invite citizens in general to participate in decision-making about matters of principle, which are the special responsibility of the courts. This was about creating a culture that respects rights in society which for Dworkin was an essential condition for the legitimacy of the state and its legal system. This went beyond promoting epistemic access to the law, but rather was a metaphysical claim about how conventional moral beliefs shape legal categories and become a part of the architecture of law.

Dworkin was here providing a sketch of a distinctively protestant or republican theory of the individuation of legal categories. In this chapter, I have begun to draw out some of the implications for debates about the morality of contract. In the context of the failure of foundationalism to handle or account adequately for legal doctrine, the republican view offers a way forward for a rival non-consequentialist account of contract law which—because it focuses on contract form the ground up—is more sensitive to the normative pluralism that forges contractual rules and doctrines. Such an account will, I have argued, reveal that contract law serves a constitutive or defining purpose or function, and that the values that underpin it are contingent to particular times and places, underdetermined, that is, subject to a multiplicity of reasonable interpretations and specifications, and irreducibly plural—meaning that it is the responsibility of the courts to balance and rank these competing values to suit local conditions and circumstances.

In the chapters on contract doctrine that follow, I defend a republican conception of English contract law—according to which it has as its constitutive purpose the promotion of the value of trust-based cooperation, which it serves in a distinctive way. I show how the promise theory of contract struggles to explain some important contract law doctrines. That does not though mean that we have to rely on the consequentialist view that the only purpose of contract law is to promote efficiency. Rather—by taking normative pluralism seriously—the republican view offers a compelling alternative to foundationalist and consequentialist theories of contract law.

5

Intent to Contract and Trust*

1. Introduction

In the preceding chapters on contract theory, I expressed some serious doubts about the plausibility of the 'promise theory' of contract law which is the dominant non-consequentialist account of contract law. According to the promise theory, promise necessarily plays a special justificatory role in contract law. I argued though that this is difficult to reconcile with the pervasive fact of 'normative pluralism' in contract law, that is, that there are an irreducible plurality of values that seem to bear on contract law and a multiplicity of ways in which they might legitimately be interpreted and ranked.

The promise theory offers a 'top-down' account of contract law. According to which, contract law is necessarily tied to promise, and promissory morality provides fairly specific guidance on how contract law doctrine is shaped. Indeed, promise theorists tend to argue that contract law should reflect or mirror promissory morality.[1] As well as raising liberal concerns about the state enforcement of morals,[2]

* This chapter is based on and largely reproduces, but with significant revisions and adaptations, the text of a previously published article of mine entitled '*Balfour v Balfour* and the Separation of Contract and Promise', which appeared in Legal Studies 37 (2017) 468, copyright © 2017 Society of Legal Scholars. The text is used with kind permission of John Wiley & Sons Ltd, subject to the following copyright notice: 'All rights reserved. No part of this publication may be reproduced, stored or transmitted in any form or by any means without the prior permission in writing from the copyright holder. Authorization to photocopy items for internal and personal use is granted by the copyright holder for libraries and other users registered with their local Reproduction Rights Organization (RRO), e.g. Copyright Clearance Center (CCC), 222 Rosewood Drive, Danvers, MA 01923, USA (www.copyright.com), provided the appropriate fee is paid directly to the RRO. This consent does not extend to other kinds of copying such as copying for general distribution, for advertising or promotional purposes, for republication, for creating new collective works or for resale. Permissions for such reuse can be obtained using the RightsLink "Request Permissions" link on Wiley Online Library. Special requests should be addressed to: permissions@wiley.com.'

[1] I borrow the reflection metaphor from Seana Shiffrin. See Seana Valentine Shiffrin, 'The Divergence of Contract and Promise' (2007) 120 Harvard Law Review 708, 713; Seana Valentine Shiffrin, 'Is a Contract a Promise?' in Andrei Marmor (ed), *The Routledge Companion to Philosophy of Law* (Routledge 2012) 250–56.

[2] Tangled up in the contract and promise debate are questions about the proper limits of the state and the enforcement of morality. See Shiffrin, 'The Divergence of Contract and Promise' (n 1) 713; Dori Kimel, 'The Morality of Contract and Moral Culpability in Breach' (2010) 21 King's Law Journal 213, 222; Randy E Barnett, 'Contract Is Not Promise; Contract Is Consent' in Gregory Klass, George Letsas, and Prince Saprai (eds), *Philosophical Foundations of Contract Law* (Oxford University Press 2014)

I argued that these structural assumptions lead promise theorists to mishandle actual contract doctrine; they exaggerate the role of promise and pay insufficient attention to the other values and moral principles that forge contract doctrine on the ground.

Instead, I set out in broad outline a republican theory of contract law, which approaches contract law rules and doctrines from the 'bottom-up'; looking for the particular scheme of principle by which they are underpinned. The republican view has four key characteristics. First, the connections between contract law and morality are *contingent*, or dependent on aspects of conventional morality or past political practice. Second, contract law is *functional* or serves a distinct or independently specifiable end, which in English contract law, I argue and hope to show, is the goal of promoting trust-based cooperation. It serves that goal constitutively (rather than instrumentally) by structuring intrinsically valuable relations between citizens who have made promises to one another. Third, that constitutive end is *underdetermined* and does not provide positive guidance on the shape that contract law rules and doctrines should take, but rather functions negatively as a side-constraint on doctrines that directly or egregiously contradict the value. And, finally, the republican view is *pluralistic*; it does not deny that contract may serve other incidental functions which play a significant role in forging contract doctrine.

These four characteristics of the republican view lead to a theory of contract that is better able to deal with the unarguable fact of normative pluralism in contract law, and provides an avenue by which citizens in particular jurisdictions can engage with contract doctrine on the ground and the scheme of principle by which it is underlain in their everyday lives. On the republican view, that kind of citizen engagement with the law is a condition for its legitimacy.

My purpose in the chapters on contract doctrine that follow is to put flesh on the bones of this republican account. Up to now I have focused on how normative pluralism impacted contract theory, but now I want to focus more narrowly on the detail of English contract doctrine. I will attempt to apply the republican theory I have outlined to interpret a variety of contract law doctrines and rules involving contract formation, vitiation, illegality, and remedies. The doctrines I will consider are: intent to contract, undue influence, restraint of trade, the penalties rule, and mitigation. I have specifically chosen these doctrines over others because the promise theory has struggled to explain them in the past, and they help to bring out important aspects of the republican interpretation of English contract law, in particular that contract law has in England the promotion of trust-based cooperation as its constitutive purpose.

In the chapters on doctrine that follow, I make three main claims. First, by exaggerating the role of the promise principle, the promise theory has mishandled contract doctrine. Second, the fact that the promise theory cannot account for these doctrines does not mean that we are left having to rely on economic or consequentialist theories to justify them. Third, that the best way to account for

47: 'by justifying contract as a species of enforcing purely moral commitments, it seems tantamount to enforcing virtue'.

these doctrines is from the bottom-up, that is, by taking seriously how they manifest themselves in law and their specific shape and contours.

The trouble with foundationalist and consequentialist theories of contract law is that they are *both* top-down in nature; and attempt to impose fairly specific normative requirements, relating to particular moral domains, such as efficiency or promissory morality, on the law. In doing so, they often lose sight of the nature of contract law rules and doctrines, their rootedness in particular jurisdictions, traditions, and cultures, and the normative pluralism that they reflect. Such rules and doctrines are often what I have called 'composite' in nature, that is, the product of the interaction between a multiplicity of normative values, concerns, and principles. The republican theory by seeking the scheme of principle that underpins the contract law of a particular jurisdiction is better able to capture this justificatory diversity.

To highlight the importance of normative pluralism in shaping contract law doctrine, I identify each of the rules and doctrines I discuss with a salient non-promissory moral concern, which plays a significant role in justifying the doctrine. So, for example, this chapter is titled 'Intent to Contract and Trust', Chapter 6 'Undue Influence and Exploitation', and Chapter 7 'Restraint of Trade and Freedom', and so forth.

My purpose in doing this is not to deny the important role that promise plays in shaping these doctrines—I think promise theorists have done valuable work in demonstrating this—and nor is it my purpose to deny that other non-promissory principles play a role in justifying these rules. Rather, my aim is largely strategic. The powerful influence of the promise theory, and its ancestor the nineteenth-century will theory, on the treatise writers has led generations of law students, lawyers, and judges, to strongly associate these doctrines with the promise principle, and to look to promissory morality alone to justify the shape they take. So, for example, vitiating factors, such as duress and undue influence, are widely thought to owe their explanation to the fact that they impair the exercise of the promisor's will. These are forms of what I called in Chapter 3 'justificatory primacy by inflation'.[3] These associations with promise have led to much confusion and mishandling of contract law doctrine.

I want to make an attempt at redressing the balance between promise and the other principles that play a normative role in shaping contract doctrine. Often these doctrines are the product of the interaction between more than one powerful normative concern or moral principle, that is, they are composite in nature. By associating these doctrines strongly with these other non-promissory principles, my aim is to shift attention onto them to highlight that they play a significant role in the shape that these doctrines take. My hope is that this might go a small way toward lessening some of the grip or hold that the promise theory has over contract lawyers. I am well aware though that this carries with it the risk of misinterpretation, that readers may think that I underplay the role of promise or other non-promissory concerns in contract. That is most certainly not my intention, but I accept that it may be an unfortunate side effect.

[3] See ch 3, s 3.1.

So much for the background to these chapters. Let's move onto the actual doctrine. The primary focus of this chapter is the intent to contract doctrine, according to which for a promise or agreement to be legally enforceable the parties must manifest an intention to be legally bound. The existence of the doctrine has played a central role in the arguments of those who want to drive a wedge between the realm of contract and that of promise.[4] On this 'divisionist' or 'separatist' picture, contract and promise pursue entirely distinct or even contrasting goals. The intent to contract doctrine is important for divisionists, because, they argue, it provides a portal between promise and contract. If Charles Fried was right that contracts *are* promises,[5] why have the portal? The doctrine suggests the existence of separate domains.

On the republican view, both the 'reflective' picture painted by the promise theory according to which contract law mirrors promissory morality, and the divisionist view according to which promise and contract pursue entirely distinct ends, are inaccurate.[6] Contra the divisionist, Fried was right to claim that contract law enforces promises, and he correctly perceived how the making of a promise invokes the trust of the promisee, and how important this was to facilitating cooperation. However, what he failed to see was how contract law pursues the value of promoting trust-based cooperation in a distinct way to how it is pursued in promissory morality simpliciter. This is a crucial point. Contra the divisionist, contract and promise do not serve fundamentally separate or contrasting ends, but rather they share the *same* value as a constitutive or characteristic end, but they serve that value in *distinct* ways. The intent to contract doctrine is central to understanding the link between contract law and the promotion of trust-based cooperation, and the unique way in which the practice serves that value.

In what follows, I set out the intent to contract doctrine and show how *Balfour v Balfour*, the case that brought intent to contract into existence, encouraged divisionist thinking with—as feminists have shown—damaging consequences for women.[7] I critically assess the arguments of Dori Kimel, who has offered a particularly sophisticated defence of the role that intent to contract plays in separating contract from promise. I hope to show some of the weaknesses in his view. They rest, I believe, on a mistaken understanding of freedom, according to which the value of freedom resides in *detachment*. Following Lon Fuller, I show that the exact opposite is true: freedom depends on *attachment* to others. With this view of freedom in place, it is possible to see how intent to contract might fit within a republican view of the relationship between contract and promise. The doctrine does not *separate* contract from promise. Rather, it provides a unique way for us to involve ourselves with others *through* promise.

[4] See, for example, Randy E Barnett, 'A Consent Theory of Contract' (1986) 86 Columbia Law Review 269, 304; Barnett, 'Contract Is Not Promise; Contract Is Consent' (n 2) 48–50; and Dori Kimel, *From Promise to Contract: Towards a Liberal Theory of Contract* (Hart Publishing 2003) 136–42.

[5] Charles Fried, *Contract as Promise: A Theory of Contractual Obligation* (Harvard University Press 1981).

[6] I borrow these metaphors from Shiffrin, 'The Divergence of Contract and Promise' (n 1) 713; Shiffrin, 'Is a Contract a Promise?' (n 1) 250–56.

[7] *Balfour v Balfour* [1919] 2 KB 571.

In the course of my critique of the divisionist view, I make two central claims. First, the republican theory can accommodate the intent to contract doctrine, without having to accept the divisionist claim that contract and promise are entirely distinct domains with their own unique ends or functions. Second, that it does so in a way that avoids some of the operational pitfalls of the divisionist picture, in particular that the divisionist view supports an evidential presumption against the enforcement of promises made in the social or domestic context, particularly between spouses, which is unfair on women. In light of this, I argue that judges should embrace the republican interpretation of the doctrine, and repudiate their use of the evidential presumption.

How the intent to contract doctrine is interpreted has other potentially far reaching doctrinal implications. So, for example, many argue that consideration is merely evidence of the existence of an intent to contract.[8] The view we take about intent to contract might affect what we think about consideration. It goes beyond the scope of this chapter to explore all of these ramifications; my aims are primarily theoretical. However, we should keep in mind that debates about intent to contract go to the heart of debates about the nature and purpose of contract law and doctrine in general.

2. *Balfour v Balfour*

According to intent to contract, an agreement is not legally enforceable unless the parties intended for it to be legally binding. The test for intention is an objective one, that is, whether a reasonable person would conclude that there was such an intention:

> The court has to consider what the parties said and wrote in the light of all the surrounding circumstances, and then decide whether the true inference is that the ordinary man and woman, speaking or writing thus in such circumstances, would have intended to create a legally binding agreement.[9]

There is a rebuttable presumption in English law that there is no such intention in the case of social or domestic agreements between, for example, friends, parents and children, husbands and wives, or co-habiting partners.[10] The opposite is presumed in commercial cases.[11]

[8] This view achieved considerable traction after the publication of Lon Fuller's paper 'Consideration and Form' (1941) 41 Columbia Law Review 799. There are good reasons though to doubt the link between consideration and intent to contract, in particular, as Mindy Chen-Wishart has argued, consideration is neither a necessary nor a sufficient condition for the existence of intent to contract. Mindy Chen-Wishart, 'Consideration and Serious Intention' (2009) Singapore Journal of Legal Studies 434, 441. Furthermore, I tend to agree with Chen-Wishart's argument in the same paper that consideration has its own rationale in notions of reciprocity. ibid 450–55.

[9] *Jones v Padavatton* [1969] 2 All ER 616, 621; Gregory Klass, 'Intent to Contract' (2009) 95 Virginia Law Review 1437, 1447–48; J Beatson, A Burrows, and J Cartwright, *Anson's Law of Contract* (29th edn, Oxford University Press 2010) 71.

[10] *Balfour v Balfour* (n 7) 578–80; *Jones v Padavatton* (n 9) 620; *Gould v Gould* [1970] 1 QB 275, 281; Edwin Peel, *The Law of Contract* (13th edn, Sweet & Maxwell 2011) 176–77.

[11] *Rose and Frank Co v J R Crompton & Bros Ltd* [1923] 2 KB 261, 288.

The doctrine entered English law in the Court of Appeal decision in *Balfour v Balfour*, decided in 1919. The case concerned a married couple. They both lived in Ceylon where the husband worked as Director of Irrigation. In November 1915, the husband was granted a period of leave from his work, and the couple moved back home to England. The leave ended in August 1916, but due to a health condition the wife was unable to return to Ceylon with her husband. Before leaving for Ceylon, the husband promised his wife that he would pay her £30 per month maintenance until he returned. While away, he wrote to say that it would be better for them not to get back together. They divorced, and the wife obtained an alimony award. She also sought to enforce the husband's promise to provide maintenance.

Sargant J upheld the wife's claim, finding consideration for the husband's promise in the commitment implicitly given by the wife not to rely on his credit for necessaries. However, a unanimous Court of Appeal reversed that judgment. Warrington LJ and Duke LJ did so mainly because they doubted that the wife gave consideration. Atkin LJ, on the other hand, invoked the intention to create legal relations doctrine to decide the case, a doctrine that up to that point could only be found in the textbooks.[12] He reasoned that it was routine for spouses to make arrangements such as the one in issue in the case, and that even with consideration such agreements should not be legally enforced 'because the parties did not intend that they should be attended by legal consequences'.[13] Atkin LJ did not, however, conduct a detailed investigation of the facts to ascertain whether such an intention was present.[14] Rather, he presumed that there was no intention, because of the nature of the relationship between the parties:

> Agreements such as these are outside the realm of contracts altogether. The common law does not regulate the form of agreements between spouses. Their promises are not sealed with seals and sealing wax. The consideration that really obtains for them is that natural love and affection which counts for so little in these cold Courts. The terms may be repudiated, varied or renewed as performance proceeds or as disagreements develop, and the principles of the common law as to exoneration and discharge and accord and satisfaction are such as find no place in the domestic code. The parties themselves are advocates, judges, Courts, sheriff's officer and reporter. In respect of these promises each house is a domain into which the King's writ does not seek to run, and to which his officers do not seek to be admitted.[15]

Although *Balfour* and many of the subsequent cases involved disputes between husbands and wives, the presumption, as I have mentioned, covers not only marital relations, but the domestic or social context more generally, including arrangements made between cohabitees, family members, and friends.

As Salmon LJ made clear in the later case of *Jones v Padavatton*, this is a factual, not a legal, presumption: 'It derives from experience of life and human nature which

[12] Stephen Martin Leake, *The Elements of the Law of Contracts* (Stevens and Sons 1867) 9; Frederick Pollock, *Principles of Contract at Law and in Equity* (Stevens and Sons 1876) 2; William R Anson, *Principles of the English Law of Contract* (Clarendon Press 1879) 14.

[13] *Balfour v Balfour* (n 7) 579.

[14] Klass, 'Intent to Contract' (n 9) 1491.

[15] *Balfour v Balfour* (n 7) 580.

shows that in such circumstances men and women usually do not intend to create legal rights and obligations, but intend to rely solely on family ties of mutual trust and affection.'[16]

Whatever the exact status of Atkin LJ's presumption, and indeed this is an issue on which there has been some controversy,[17] its effect has been to reinforce the sense that contractual and personal relations, like Venice and Belmont, are entirely separate realms. I allude of course to Shakespeare's *The Merchant of Venice*, which brings out beautifully the contrast between the worlds of commerce and intimacy. Making the same analogy, Roberto Unger describes the difference:

> In Venice people make contracts; in Belmont they exchange wedding rings. In Venice they are held together by combinations of interest, in Belmont by mutual affection. The wealth and power of Venice depend upon the willingness of its courts to hold men to their contracts. The charm of Belmont is to provide its inhabitants with a community in which contracts remain for the most part superfluous. Venice is tolerable because its citizens can flee occasionally to Belmont and appeal from Venetian justice to Belmontine mercy. But the very existence of Belmont presupposes the prosperity of Venice, from which the denizens of Belmont gain their livelihood.[18]

Though opposed, Venice and Belmont—commerce and intimacy—depend on each other. Commerce makes family life possible, and the family provides a refuge from the 'heartless world' of the market, where the pursuit of self-interest runs wild.[19] As Frances Olsen says: 'The market is the arena for work and the production of goods; the family is the arena for most forms of play and consumption.'[20] In *Balfour*, Atkin LJ endorsed this division of labour. The result was a vision of contract law that regulated trade, but largely stayed out of private and family life.[21]

[16] *Jones v Padavatton* (n 9) 621.

[17] Feminists, for example, have argued that the purpose of the presumption is not evidential, but reflects a policy choice by the courts to keep family life private. See Michael Freeman, 'Contracting in the Haven: *Balfour v Balfour* Revisited' in Roger Halson (ed), *Exploring the Boundaries of Contract* (Dartmouth 1996) 70; Mary Keyes and Kylie Burns, 'Contract and the Family: Whither Intention?' (2002) 26 Melbourne University Law Review 577, 595: 'Reference to the intentions of the parties in order to determine the enforceability of an agreement, ... makes no sense as the parties are unlikely to have considered the question. Quite clearly, the requirement of intention is based on a judicial policy that contract is "unfamiliar and undesirable" in the family context' (citing Steve Hedley, *Restitution: Its Division and Ordering* (Sweet & Maxwell 2001) 76). See similarly S Wheeler and J Shaw, *Contract Law: Cases, Materials and Commentary* (Clarendon Press 1994) 150.

[18] Roberto Mangabeira Unger, 'The Critical Legal Studies Movement' (1983) 96 Harvard Law Review 561, 622–23. For further reflections on the contrast drawn by the play and the implications for contract theory, see Alan Brudner, 'Reconstructing Contracts' (1993) 43 The University of Toronto Law Journal 1.

[19] I rely here of course on Christopher Lasch's famous metaphor: Christopher Lasch, *Haven in a Heartless World: The Family Besieged* (Basic Books 1977).

[20] Frances E Olsen, 'The Family and the Market: A Study of Ideology and Legal Reform' (1983) 96 Harvard Law Review 1497, 1564.

[21] Unger, 'The Critical Legal Studies Movement' (n 18) 623.

3. The Feminist Critique

The feminist critique of the *Balfour* doctrine has been trenchant. The problem is with the implications of the doctrine for women, who are still associated with roles at home and in family life; in contrast to men, who are identified with the market and the world of work.[22] In the past, privacy has been used to justify non-interference by the state to remedy injustice in the domestic context. As Michael Freeman says: 'The rhetoric of privacy has insulated the female world from the legal order and, in doing so, has sent an important ideological message to society. It devalues women by saying that they are not important enough to merit legal regulation.'[23]

This leaves women vulnerable to the exploitation and distributive unfairness that result when men break important promises (particularly when women rely on or confer benefits on the basis of these assurances).[24] For reasons of economic dependency and social pressure women are often the weaker party in intimate relationships.[25] These vulnerabilities exist both in the context of marriage and co-habitation. Seana Shiffrin has argued that promises perform a role of preventing exploitation in situations of power imbalance. Clearly then if the courts refuse to enforce those promises that may deprive women of what would otherwise be an important source of assurance.[26]

One might argue that the intent to contract doctrine does not prevent women from entering into contracts, and of course that is true, but that does not take account of the extent to which the doctrine privileges men over women. As Stephen

[22] Olsen, 'The Family and the Market: A Study of Ideology and Legal Reform' (n 20) 1576; Margaret Thornton, 'Intention to Contract: Public Act or Private Sentiment?' in Ngaire Naffine, Rosemary Owens, and John Williams (eds), *Intention in Law and Philosophy* (Ashgate 2001) 217; Keyes and Burns, 'Contract and the Family: Whither Intention?' (n 17) 578.

[23] Freeman, 'Contracting in the Haven: *Balfour v Balfour* Revisited' (n 17) 74. For similar arguments see Nadine Taub and Elizabeth Schneider, 'Women's Subordination and the Role of Law' in David Kairys (ed), *The Politics of Law: A Progressive Critique* (3rd edn, Basic Books 1998) 333–34. See also Keyes and Burns, 'Contract and the Family: Whither Intention?' (n 17) 578, arguing that the presumption against contract in domestic settings 'performs a powerful symbolic function delineating the realm of law from the realm of the family and the feminine, privileging the former over the latter'.

[24] Arguably the injustice in cases of detrimental reliance or the conferral of benefits may be mitigated to some degree by the application of reliance or restitution principles. Even though the promisee in these cases may not be able to enforce the agreement, and therefore protect her expectation interest, she may in cases where she has suffered losses or conferred benefits in reliance on the agreement claim compensation for losses suffered or restitution for the gain made by the promise breaker. See Kimel, *From Promise to Contract: Towards a Liberal Theory of Contract* (n 4) 140–41. However, the availability of these remedies in English law is severely restricted. Promissory estoppel cannot be used as a cause of action (*Combe v Combe* [1951] 2 KB 215). See John Wightman, 'Intimate Relationships, Relational Contract Theory, and the Reach of Contract' (2000) 8 Feminist Legal Studies 93, 95. For an unjust enrichment claim to succeed in this context, there has to be a 'total failure of consideration', see *Fibrosa Spolka Akcyjna v Fairbairn Lawson Combe Barbour Ltd* [1943] AC 32, 64–65; Peter Birks, *An Introduction to the Law of Restitution* (Clarendon Press 1989) 242–48; Frederick Wilmot-Smith, 'Reconsidering "Total" Failure' (2013) 72 The Cambridge Law Journal 414.

[25] Olsen, 'The Family and the Market: A Study of Ideology and Legal Reform' (n 20) 1519–20.

[26] Seana Valentine Shiffrin, 'Promising, Intimate Relationships, and Conventionalism' (2008) 117 Philosophical Review 481, 502–10.

Hedley has pointed out, in most cases, whether in the domestic or commercial sphere, parties will not have actively contemplated whether their agreement should be legally binding.[27] And yet, commercial parties are given a presumption that such an intention was present, while the opposite presumption applies in the domestic context.

That presumption against the existence of a contract creates a problem in those cases where the parties *did* intend to create a legal relationship. It places a burden on the promisee to show 'clear and convincing' evidence that there was a manifest intention to be legally bound when the agreement was reached.[28] This rule puts pressure on the promisee to be as clear as possible at the time of agreement that she intends legal enforceability.[29]

The trouble is that it may be very difficult for the promisee to achieve this level of clarity, and hence satisfy the manifest intent requirement, because being clear may involve a relational cost, incurred by the indication to the other party that they are not trusted by the promisee to perform.[30] This may happen even though the parties are operating on the assumption that they are making a legally enforceable agreement. As Gregory Klass says, 'Even where expectations or preferences regarding legal liability are mutually understood, those attitudes are often better left unspoken.'[31] Explicit articulation of those attitudes may evidence distrust or an overly litigious tendency that may harm the relationship and scupper the agreement.[32] Therefore, the promisee is placed in a dilemma by the law. Does she make explicit her preference for legal enforceability and risk the relationship and the agreement altogether, or does she stay silent and run the risk that the agreement is not legally binding? The likelihood is that she will take her chances and stay silent, but the danger of that course is that the agreement will not be legally binding, and the intentions of the parties not respected by the law.

A good example of the unfairness that results is the Court of Appeal decision in *Gould v Gould*.[33] The case concerned a husband who had separated from his wife,

[27] Stephen Hedley, 'Keeping Contract in Its Place: *Balfour v Balfour* and the Enforceability of Informal Agreements' (1985) 5 Oxford Journal of Legal Studies 391, 393–95. See also Keyes and Burns, 'Contract and the Family: Whither Intention?' (n 17) 581, 586–87, 595.

[28] *Gould v Gould* (n 10) 281.

[29] Gregory Klass distinguishes between rebuttal of the presumption against contract on the basis of showing the manifest intention to be legally bound and a rule that requires, as a formality, an express statement of an intention to create legal relations. Klass, 'Intent to Contract' (n 9) 1468, 1473–75. He is right to say that from the point of view of legal design these are two different ways of opting out of the presumption, with different costs and benefits. However, in practice, I suspect that the burden of the manifest intent requirement is so strong that it leads de facto to significant pressure on the promisee to make an express statement.

[30] ibid 1473–74.

[31] ibid at 1474. See also Ronald J Gilson, Charles F Sabel, and Robert E Scott, 'Braiding: The Interaction of Formal and Informal Contracting in Theory, Practice, and Doctrine' (2010) 110 Columbia Law Review 1377, 1401.

[32] cf Wightman, 'Intimate Relationships, Relational Contract Theory, and the Reach of Contract' (n 24) 108–09, making the point that it may be a feature of intimate relations that agreements are not explicitly spelt out; this may also reflect the presence of economic dependency: 'the backdrop to the day to day informality may be the power that a breadwinner can exert' (ibid 109).

[33] *Gould v Gould* (n 10).

leaving her to look after their two children. On breaking up, he promised to pay his wife £15 per week maintenance, with the proviso 'as long as he had it'. He failed to keep up with the payments, and his wife sought to enforce the promise. The Court of Appeal (with Lord Denning MR dissenting) held that there was a presumption against the legal effect of social and domestic arrangements, and that the onus was on the claimant to present 'clear and convincing' evidence of an intention to create a legal relation to rebut it.[34] The Court held that the husband's proviso that he would only pay the maintenance on condition that he was able to pay, created a lack of clarity about the terms of the agreement, which itself gave the strong indication that the parties did not intend legal relations.[35]

It is difficult to see here how the court arrived at the conclusion that there was no intention to create a legal relationship.[36] The agreement related to a serious matter, the parties had separated (unlike in *Balfour* where the parties were still in amity at the time of agreement),[37] and there was nothing about the husband's proviso that was particularly unclear or could not have been made clearer by the implication of further terms. For example, in his dissent, Lord Denning MR implied the term that 'if the husband found that he could not manage to keep up the payments, he could, on reasonable notice, determine the agreement'.[38]

Of course one might reply that all this shows is that sometimes courts fail to apply the law correctly; in this case, the facts suggest that the presumption should have been rebutted. However, the worry is that the intent to contract doctrine, or more specifically, the justification given for it in *Balfour* reinforces the existence of a dichotomy between the role of women in family and commercial life, which prejudices the judiciary in favour of the kind of unfairness we see in *Gould*.

By not recognizing the legal validity of the promise, the court left the wife vulnerable. Furthermore, the judicial reluctance to enforce agreements made in domestic settings leads to damaging distributive consequences for women. So, for example, women suffer disproportionately when agreements to perform domestic labour are not legally binding, because it is still women predominantly who carry out this work.[39] Non-intervention perpetuates existing inequalities, and leaves men with the power to dominate women.[40]

[34] ibid 281. [35] ibid.

[36] Freeman, 'Contracting in the Haven: *Balfour v Balfour* Revisited' (n 17) 71–72.

[37] Usually where the parties have separated the courts are quick to find an intention to contract. *Peters' Executors v Inland Revenue Commissioners* [1941] 2 All ER 620; *Merritt v Merritt* [1969] 2 All ER 760, 762: 'It is altogether different when the parties are not living in amity but are separated, or about to separate. They then bargain keenly. They do not rely on honourable understandings. They want everything cut and dried. It may safely be presumed that they intend to create legal relations', and see ibid 762–63.

[38] *Gould v Gould* (n 10) 280.

[39] Jill Elaine Hasday, 'Intimacy and Economic Exchange' (2005) 119 Harvard Law Review 491, 518–19; Klass, 'Intent to Contract' (n 9) 1494; Reva B Siegel, 'The Modernization of Marital Status Law: Adjudicating Wives' Rights to Earnings, 1860–1930' (1993) 82 The Georgetown Law Review 2127, 2209; Thornton, 'Intention to Contract: Public Act or Private Sentiment?' (n 22).

[40] Olsen, 'The Family and the Market: A Study of Ideology and Legal Reform' (n 20) 1510; Shulamith Firestone, *The Dialectic of Sex: The Case for Feminist Revolution* (William Morrow and Company, Inc 1970) 142–64.

Feminist critiques have shone a light on how this dualism, and the domination that results from it, affects the possibilities for human association. Women are left dependent on men, and feminists have questioned whether this 'makes true love between the sexes difficult, perhaps impossible'.[41] Love after all depends on relationships of equality, sharing, and respect.[42]

These economic and social inequalities that afflict women in particular are the source of the vulnerabilities that make the evidential presumption against legal enforcement problematic. It goes beyond the scope of this chapter to investigate whether similar inequalities exist in the context of other relationships covered by the presumption, such as gay marriage or those between parents and children. However, if it does, then the presumption is likely to have similarly damaging effects in these contexts too. Therefore, the feminist critique of the doctrine may extend beyond the injustices experienced by women.

It might be objected that the feminist critique of the doctrine that I present here is aimed at case law that has been gathering dust. Few cases in recent times raise intent to contract issues, and it may be that through developments in family law and changes in social and judicial attitudes the kinds of injustices that have arisen as a result of the presumption in the past are now of only theoretical interest and need no longer detain us. There are reasons though still to worry. First, it is not clear that the lack of case law is due to the lack of injustice, or whether the existence of injustice is the cause of the lack of case law. Arguably women and other vulnerable groups are deterred from bringing cases because of the presumption against enforcement and how it has been applied in cases like *Gould*. Second, the existence of the doctrine in the textbooks may carry symbolic or expressive significance, reinforcing gender stereotypes and roles, and potentially making exploitation by dominant parties more likely. These are genuine costs which flow from the failure to repudiate the presumption, and the false dichotomy between the domestic and commercial spheres which it both reflects and reinforces.

4. The Divisionist Defence

The feminist critique of the *Balfour* doctrine has shown how it might unfairly impact women and risk the possibility of intimacy between the sexes. The doctrine has though received a sophisticated divisionist defence.

The existence of the doctrine supports the central tenet of the divisionist position, which is that contracts and promises are very different things. Fried famously claimed that contracts are promises.[43] According to the promise theory, contract should reflect promissory morality. But if that is the case, it is difficult to explain why making a promise is not a sufficient condition for making a contract. Why does contract law require, in addition to the making of a promise, a separate intention

[41] Olsen, 'The Family and the Market: A Study of Ideology and Legal Reform' (n 20) 1572.
[42] Charles Fried, *Right and Wrong* (Harvard University Press 1978) 29–30.
[43] Fried, *Contract as Promise: A Theory of Contractual Obligation* (n 5).

that the parties intended to create a legal relationship? Contract law does seem to diverge from promissory morality here.[44]

Fried's response seems to be that the requirement exists to ensure that promises are made sincerely or seriously: 'The promisor must have been serious enough that subsequent legal enforcement was an aspect of what he should have contemplated at the time he promised.'[45] The thought appears to be that if the promisor contemplated legal enforcement, he must have made his promise seriously. The trouble is that if we consider cases like *Balfour* and *Gould*, it stretches reality to say that when the courts ruled that the parties lacked an intention to contract, they doubted the seriousness of the promises that were made.[46]

It is of course open to the promise theorist to repudiate the *Balfour* doctrine altogether, which is the strategy that Fried adopts with the consideration doctrine.[47] The suggestion may not be as radical as it as first appears. Although the matter is controversial, there seems to be no intent to contract requirement in U.S. contract law. Section 21 of the Second Restatement of Contracts says: 'Neither real nor apparent intention that a promise be legally binding is essential to the formation of a contract'.[48] In England, the operation of the factual presumption that intent to contract exists in commercial transactions led Patrick Atiyah to the view that in the majority of cases 'no positive intention to enter into legal relations needs to be shown'.[49]

The difficulties for the reflective view are not then necessarily doctrinal. Rather, the greater difficulty is that divisionists provide credible explanations for the doctrine. Consider for example the arguments of Dori Kimel.

Kimel claims that the doctrine promotes two types of valuable freedom, by giving parties the right to decide whether to create a legally enforceable obligation, rather than a purely moral obligation.

First, there is freedom *from* contract, which is valuable because legal enforceability might change the relational significance of compliance with voluntary undertakings. The making and keeping of promises normally conveys the existence of trust and respect in relationships.[50] However, those messages get disrupted when promises

[44] Barnett, 'A Consent Theory of Contract' (n 4) 304–05; Barnett, 'Contract Is Not Promise; Contract Is Consent' (n 4) 47, arguing that Fried's theory 'commits courts to enforcing promissory commitments that the parties themselves may never have contemplated as "contractual" or legally enforceable'.

[45] Fried, *Contract as Promise: A Theory of Contractual Obligation* (n 5) 38. I follow Kimel's reading of Fried here. Kimel, *From Promise to Contract: Towards a Liberal Theory of Contract* (n 4) 137–38. Fuller gave a similar explanation for the doctrine of consideration, by claiming it performed a cautionary function. See his Fuller, 'Consideration and Form' (n 8) 816–17.

[46] cf Kimel, *From Promise to Contract: Towards a Liberal Theory of Contract* (n 4) 137–38.

[47] Fried, *Contract as Promise: A Theory of Contractual Obligation* (n 5) ch 2.

[48] Randy Barnett rejects the standard interpretation of this section, arguing that it only applies in cases where consideration is absent. For Barnett, consideration is evidence of the existence of an intent to contract. Randy E Barnett, *The Oxford Introductions to U.S. Law: Contracts* (Oxford University Press 2010) 165. See also Klass, 'Intent to Contract' (n 9) 1438, setting out the various exceptions to section 21.

[49] PS Atiyah, *An Introduction to the Law of Contract* (5th edn, Clarendon Press 1995) cited by Klass, 'Intent to Contract' (n 9) 1438.

[50] cf James Penner, 'Promises, Agreements, and Contracts' in Gregory Klass, George Letsas, and Prince Saprai (eds), *Philosophical Foundations of Contract Law* (Oxford University Press 2014) 116,

are made legally enforceable, because promisors are given independent reasons to perform, which may either corrupt their motives or create the impression of corruption in the mind of promisees: 'The availability of remedies seriously and manifestly reduces the likelihood that, and at any rate the extent to which, a party would benefit from a breach, significantly undermining the expressive potential of contractual fidelity in the process.'[51] As a result, promise won't convey the attitudes of trust and respect, on which personal relationships hinge.[52] Therefore, parties might choose to do without the added reassurance that legal enforceability brings, so as to create an opportunity to express these attitudes, and to foster and deepen their relationships.[53]

Second, freedom *to* contract is promoted, in particular where there is an absence of trust between the parties. In that context, contract through the mechanism of legal enforcement enables the parties to enter into a mutually beneficial exchange without being, or having to enter into, a personal relationship with one another, thus promoting their freedom to remain detached.[54]

Thus, on Kimel's view, the *Balfour* doctrine promotes *both* the values of personal *attachment* and *detachment*, by giving parties the right to decide whether to steer clear of law and depend instead on their personal relationships to secure the benefits of cooperative activity, or alternatively to invoke the law and thereby avoid having to rely for reassurance on the presence of existing or future personal ties. The resonance with Atkin LJ's justification in *Balfour* is clear.

There are though problems with both of Kimel's arguments for the doctrine, and with the underlying dichotomy between contract and promise that they reflect and defend.

4.1 Freedom from contract and the value of personal attachment

Kimel's first argument relies on the damage done to personal relationships and the value of personal attachment, by the effect that legal enforcement has on corrupting the motives of promisors, or by giving promisees the impression that the promisor is acting out of self-interest. The danger is that the expressive quality of making, relying on, and keeping promises will be lost, or 'crowded out'.[55] The argument has

123 (discussing the expressive role that agreements—which he distinguishes from promises—play in ongoing relationships).

[51] Kimel, *From Promise to Contract: Towards a Liberal Theory of Contract* (n 4) 75.

[52] ibid 29, 74–77.

[53] ibid 138. See similarly Chen-Wishart, 'Consideration and Serious Intention' (n 8) 452–53.

[54] Kimel, *From Promise to Contract: Towards a Liberal Theory of Contract* (n 4) 78–80, 141–42. cf James E Penner, 'Voluntary Obligations and the Scope of the Law of Contract' (1996) 2 Legal Theory 325, 335–39 (distinguishing the contractual realm from other relational contexts within which agreements are made on the ground that trust is not involved in the same way at least in the contractual context. Saying at ibid 339: 'What characterizes bargains is not that they occur between strangers, but that they *can* occur between strangers').

[55] Kimel, *From Promise to Contract: Towards a Liberal Theory of Contract* (n 4) 29. cf Michael Sandel, *What Money Can't Buy: The Moral Limits of Markets* (Allen Lane 2012), who relies on this notion of corruption and crowding out to justify ethical limitations on the market.

a distinctly 'empirical cast'.[56] It focuses on the *effect* that legal enforcement has on personal relationships.

I follow Shiffrin in finding this type of argument unconvincing. There are at least two problems. First, Kimel does not present any empirical evidence which supports his claim that moral motivations would be displaced by legal incentives, or the claim that promisees would have this impression. Certainly, our experience of other legal domains suggests the contrary. As Shiffrin says:

> In the case of tort, there is little serious concern that legal regulations on bodily contact have come to dominate the motives of citizens or that citizens believe their safe passage across the streets is generally a matter attributable to law and not to basic civic decency.[57]

It is quite possible that the law is only providing a 'backstop' to reassure promisees, in case the motivations that normally govern the practice of promising fail.[58]

It is beyond the scope of this chapter to review the empirical evidence that does exist. Although there is some empirical support for the existence of crowding out,[59] there are studies that go in the other direction, and which show that notions of fairness and reciprocity play a significant role in explaining contractual performance.[60]

Even if, arguendo, the empirical effects Kimel describes are shown to exist, there is a second problem. It might be possible, Shiffrin argues, to manage these effects. So, for example, to prevent the corruption of motives, or the perception of such corruption, the courts could make clear that the purpose of contractual remedies is merely to provide a backstop, and not to displace relational motives.[61]

As well as the assumptions that Kimel makes about the effects of contract on promise, he also makes assumptions about the effects of the moral practice

[56] Shiffrin distinguishes between empirical and expressive versions of this type of argument. Shiffrin, 'Is a Contract a Promise?' (n 1) 251–52. According to the expressive view, the damage is done by the message that the law sends out about the type of norms that should govern these relationships, rather than the effects of that message. Aditi Bagchi makes this type of argument in 'Separating Contract and Promise' (2010) 38 Florida State University Law Review 709.

[57] Shiffrin, 'Is a Contract a Promise?' (n 1) 253.

[58] ibid. cf Lon L Fuller, *The Law in Quest of Itself* (Beacon Press 1966) 137: 'the effective deterrents which shape the average man's conduct derive from morality, from a sense of right and wrong'; Stewart Macaulay, 'Non-Contractual Relations in Business: A Preliminary Study' (1963) 28 American Sociological Review 55, 65–66. See also Antony R Duff, 'Penal Communications: Recent Work in the Philosophy of Punishment' (1996) 20 Crime and Justice 1, 41–42, saying that prudential incentives '*supplement*, rather than *replace*, the moral reasons that would ideally be sufficient' (42).

[59] Gary Charness, 'Responsibility and Effort in an Experimental Labor Market' (2000) 42 Journal of Economic Behavior & Organization 375, 375; Iris Bohnet, Bruno S Frey, and Steffen Huck, 'More Order with Less Law: On Contract Enforcement, Trust, and Crowding' (2006) 95 American Political Science Review 131, 132; Uri Gneezy and Aldo Rustichini, 'A Fine is a Price' (2000) 29 The Journal of Legal Studies 1, 3; Carl Mellström and Magnus Johannesson, 'Crowding Out in Blood Donation: Was Titmuss Right?' (2008) 6 Journal of the European Economic Association 845.

[60] Ernst Fehr, Simon Gächter, and Georg Kirchsteiger, 'Reciprocity as a Contract Enforcement Device: Experimental Evidence' (1997) 65 Econometrica 833; Martin Dufwenberg and Georg Kirchsteiger, 'A Theory of Sequential Reciprocity' (2004) 47 Games and Economic Behavior 268, 290–91; David K Levine, 'Modeling Altruism and Spitefulness in Experiments' (1998) 1 Review of Economic Dynamics 593, 595; Macaulay, 'Non-Contractual Relations in Business: A Preliminary Study' (n 58) 64.

[61] Shiffrin, 'Is a Contract a Promise?' (n 1) 253–54.

of promising on individual acts of making, relying on, and keeping promises. He assumes that *social* pressure, unlike *legal* pressure, *won't* ordinarily affect the relational motivations and attitudes that should govern promising or will largely only do so as a contingent matter.[62] It is unclear that this is true, or at least that there should be an asymmetry in this context between legal and social pressure. Depending on the community, there may be significant social pressure to keep one's word.[63] Moreover, there is empirical evidence showing that the reputational damage done by breach, and the chance that future cooperation will be endangered, are significant reasons motivating performance.[64] In such a context, it may be that people keep their promises for fear of the negative reactions others have toward breach, or at least it may be that this is the perception of promisees. This might displace relational motives and attitudes, just as much as Kimel argues that legal pressure does. Furthermore, there is a significant sense in which the existence of legal pressure following a breach of contract is importantly contingent; dependent as it is of course on the willingness of the innocent party to bear the costs and risks of litigation, including, for example, the vagaries of the judicial assessment of damages.

In conclusion, Kimel does not show that legal enforcement necessarily undermines the expressive quality of promising, and nor is it clear that absent legal enforcement promise has this expressive quality anyway. Therefore, Kimel's claim that the *Balfour* doctrine promotes freedom *from* contract is unconvincing.

[62] Kimel, *From Promise to Contract: Towards a Liberal Theory of Contract* (n 4) 76–77.

[63] Alan Schwartz and Robert E Scott, 'Contract Theory and the Limits of Contract Law' (2003) 113 Yale Law Journal 541, 557: 'reputations work best in small trading communities, especially those with ethnically homogenous members, where everything that happens soon becomes common knowledge, and boycotts of bad actors are easy to enforce'. Citing Janet T Landa, 'A Theory of the Ethnically Homogeneous Middleman Group: An Institutional Alternative to Contract Law' (1981) 10 The Journal of Legal Studies 349. There are no doubt cultural differences at play too. The importance that the French attach to keeping one's promises may be one of the reasons for the significant divergences that exist between English and French contract law. French contract law attaches enormous importance to upholding the agreement, which is reflected in key doctrines, such as the greater availability of specific performance and damages for cost of cure and non-pecuniary loss, the enforceability of penalty clauses, restrictions on the right to terminate, and the absence of a duty to mitigate loss. See Solène Rowan, *Remedies for Breach of Contract: A Comparative Analysis of the Protection of Performance* (Oxford University Press 2012); Lucinda Miller, 'Specific Performance in the Common and Civil Law: Some Lessons for Harmonisation' in Paula Giliker (ed), *Re-examining Contract and Unjust Enrichment: Anglo-Canadian Perspectives* (Martinus Nijhoff Publishers 2007); Lucinda Miller, 'Penalty Clauses In England And France: A Comparative Study' (2004) 53 International and Comparative Law Quarterly 79. The doctrinal differences with English contract law reflect the contingent nature of the values and the weight attached to them that shape contract law. I return to this theme of divergence between the contract law of different jurisdictions and its normative implications in Chapter 10.

[64] Benjamin Klein and Keith B Leffler, 'The Role of Market Forces in Assuring Contractual Performance' (1981) 89 Journal of Political Economy 615, 616; Lisa Bernstein, 'Merchant Law in a Merchant Court: Rethinking the Code's Search for Immanent Business Norms' (1996) 144 University of Pennsylvania Law Review 1765, 1787–88; Macaulay, 'Non-Contractual Relations in Business: A Preliminary Study' (n 58) 55, 64.

4.2 Freedom to contract and the value of personal detachment

There are problems too with Kimel's argument that the *Balfour* doctrine promotes freedom to contract and the value of personal detachment. There are three interconnected difficulties. First, it is not obvious that it offers a plausible interpretation of contract law. Second, I doubt that personal detachment has value. And, third, it is unclear that personal detachment is even possible in the contractual context.

Is contract based on personal detachment?

First, it is unclear that contract law is a realm of detachment. My point is not the same as that which has been made by relational contract theory, according to which some, many, or even most, contracts involve relationships, with the result that relational norms might in certain cases displace, or at least shape (qualify, defeat, reinforce, supplement, and so forth) contractual norms.[65] Kimel deals with relational contract theory not by doubting how many contracts have relational elements, but rather by insisting that contract gives parties the freedom to allow relational norms to play these roles if they want them to. Parties can insist that contractual norms govern, and in some cases, the existence of that freedom may actually facilitate the emergence and success of close relationships:

> it is the very fact that the contract provides for some more or less certain, enforceable fundamentals, that liberates the parties from dependence on the creation or maintenance of personal relations for the realisation of such fundamentals; and this liberty, in turn, is often indispensable in enabling the parties to develop, possibly over time, a relationship that far transcends that set of legally binding rights and duties which the contract constituted or recorded in the first place.[66]

So, for example, in the context of academic employment:

> A dean, for instance, or head of department, would likely find herself rather inhibited in her efforts to develop an informal friendship with a new appointee, if she knows that their interactions invariably lead to understandings or expectations pertaining to those issues that formal contract settles.[67]

Kimel's response to relational contract theory is fine as far as it goes, but it fails to address a related but altogether more radical critique. It is problematic to claim that detachment is the prevalent mode of contract law, not because relational norms *displace* or *supervene* on contractual norms, but rather because it is unclear that *contractual* norms uphold the value of detachment.

[65] See Ian R Macneil, 'The Many Futures of Contracts' (1973) 47 University of South California Law Review 691; Charles J Goetz and Robert E Scott, 'Principles of Relational Contracts' (1981) 67 Virginia Law Review 1089; Melvin A Eisenberg, 'Relational Contracts' in Jack Beatson and Daniel Friedmann (eds), *Good Faith and Fault in Contract Law* (Clarendon Press 1995) 291.

[66] Kimel, *From Promise to Contract: Towards a Liberal Theory of Contract* (n 4) 83.

[67] ibid 85.

This is a deeper point that emerged from Lon Fuller's work in the 1950s and 1960s, and in particular in his broader response to Herbert Hart's *The Concept of Law*.[68] Its significance was blurred in the 1970s by Ian Macneil's work, and the ensuing runaway success of relational contract theory.[69] Fuller's central claim was that *contract* norms, that is, the rules, doctrines, principles, and so forth, that govern the practice of making and keeping promises and agreements are *driven* by relational considerations, and far from promoting detachment, actually promote attachment. This is the nerve of the republican view that contract law has as its constitutive end the promotion of trust-based cooperation.

This connects with the scepticism expressed earlier that contractual enforcement necessarily disrupts the expressive quality and relational significance of promising. It may merely provide a backstop of reassurance for the promisee, in case the ordinary motivations that should preside over the practice fail. These sorts of prudential incentives are concessions to human frailty or weakness of will.[70]

Other structural features of contracting support this relational interpretation of the practice. Fuller placed particular emphasis on the centrality of negotiation or bargaining in contract. Successful negotiation requires an accommodation of potentially conflicting interests. Parties have to be prepared to engage sympathetically with each other, and indeed to reveal to one another something about their interests and desires, and the weight that they attach to them. Agreement will not be reached without at least some degree of give and take:

> the creation of a complex contractual relationship through explicit negotiations requires a certain attitude of mind and spirit on the part of the participants; ... Each must seek to understand why the other makes the demands he does even as he strives to resist or qualify those demands.... Explicit bargaining involves, then, an uneasy blend of collaboration and resistance.[71]

By engaging in this process, the parties do not of course become friends, but nor are they strangers. They become Fuller said 'friendly strangers'.[72] There is a type

[68] HLA Hart, *The Concept of Law* (2nd edn, Clarendon Press 1994); Lon L Fuller, 'Freedom: A Suggested Analysis' (1955) 68 Harvard Law Review 1305; Lon L Fuller, *The Morality of Law* (rev edn, Yale University Press 1969); Lon L Fuller, 'Human Interaction and the Law' (1969) 14 The American Journal of Jurisprudence 1. For a recent articulation of the implications of these views for debates in general jurisprudence see Nigel Simmonds, *Law as a Moral Idea* (Oxford University Press 2007).

[69] See Macneil's seminal paper 'The Many Futures of Contracts' (n 65). Fuller's point was not completely submerged; it resurfaced and found its clearest expression in Charles Fried's *Contract as Promise: A Theory of Contractual Obligation* (n 5).

[70] See in the context of punishment: Duff, 'Penal Communications: Recent Work in the Philosophy of Punishment' (n 58) 41–42; Uma Narayan, 'Appropriate Responses and Preventive Benefits: Justifying Censure and Hard Treatment in Legal Punishment' (1993) 13 Oxford Journal of Legal Studies 166, 181.

[71] Lon L Fuller, 'The Role of Contract in the Ordering Processes of Society Generally' in *The Principles of Social Order: Selected Essays of Lon L Fuller* (Kenneth Winston ed, rev edn, Hart Publishing 2002), 203. See also Fuller, 'Human Interaction and the Law' (n 68) 28–29; Fuller, 'Irrigation and Tyranny' in *The Principles of Social Order: Selected Essays of Lon L. Fuller* (Kenneth Winston ed, rev edn, Hart Publishing 2002), 220–21.

[72] Fuller, 'Human Interaction and the Law' (n 68) 27. cf James E Penner, 'Voluntary Obligations and the Scope of the Law of Contract' (n 54) 335–38 (identifying a spectrum of relational contexts within which agreements are made), and James Penner, 'Promises, Agreements, and Contracts' in Gregory Klass, George Letsas, and Prince Saprai (eds), *Philosophical Foundations of Contract Law* (Oxford University Press 2014) 116, 131–34 (explaining the existence of trust between strangers on the grounds of the basic human capacity to respond to reasons).

of association here that is not captured by the dichotomy between close relations (friends, intimates, and so forth) and strangers.[73] This was an important insight, which promise theorists have largely neglected or only been dimly aware of—Fried for example recently said contracting parties are 'neighbors rather than strangers'.[74] Unlike the divisionist who assumes that the contractual relation is based on distrust, the promise theorist tends to assume the opposite: that contracts involve the same or a very similar kind of trust that obtains between friends, intimates, and so on. In truth, as Fuller noticed, the contractual relation lies somewhere in between.

This spirit of cooperation does not cease when bargaining comes to an end. When parties reach agreement, they repose trust in one another and embark on a joint project whereby to achieve their aims each has to assist the other.[75] This feature of the practice creates room for seriously doubting the relevance of personal detachment. How can parties be said to be detached from one another, when, *first and foremost*, they have to *trust* and *depend* on one another for the pursuit of their respective ends?[76] Trust is essential for assurance and reliance; otherwise the agreement is based merely on predictions about what the other will do. This was Fried's great insight.[77]

These relational norms and moral attitudes play a central role in explaining not only how contracts are formed, but also how they are interpreted, vitiated, and remedied when they are broken. So, for example, even business transactions, Fuller argued, might involve relations of 'heavy and complex interdependence'.[78] Parties may have to make reasonable adjustments in the light, for example, of technological advancements: 'Here fidelity to explicit contractual commitments must be tempered by a sense of reciprocal dependence and a willingness to meet unexpected developments in a spirit of cooperation.'[79]

The efficacy of contract as a mechanism of social order depends upon a recognition of these realities, and indeed they are reflected in the canons of contractual interpretation.[80] Plausibly, these relations of trust and mutual dependency have a role to play in explaining other central contract doctrines, such as undue influence,[81] unconscionability, economic duress,[82] the duty to mitigate (which Fried has argued

[73] ibid 27–28.

[74] Charles Fried, 'The Convergence of Contract and Promise' (2007) 120 Harvard Law Review Forum 1, 8.

[75] Fried, *Contract as Promise: A Theory of Contractual Obligation* (n 5) 8; Fried, 'The Convergence of Contract and Promise' (n 74) 8.

[76] Fuller, 'Freedom: A Suggested Analysis' (n 68) 1313; Fried, *Contract as Promise: A Theory of Contractual Obligation* (n 5) 13.

[77] Fried, *Contract as Promise: A Theory of Contractual Obligation* (n 5) 8, 13.

[78] Fuller, 'The Role of Contract in the Ordering Processes of Society Generally' (n 71) 200.

[79] ibid 201. See also Fried, *Contract as Promise: A Theory of Contractual Obligation* (n 5) 89.

[80] *Investors Compensation Scheme Ltd v West Bromwich Building Society (No 1)* [1998] 1 All ER 98, 114–15; *L Schuler AG v Wickman Machine Tool Sales Ltd* [1974] AC 235, 251; *Pink Floyd Music v EMI Records Ltd* [2010] EWHC 533 [55].

[81] Mindy Chen-Wishart, 'Undue Influence: Vindicating Relationships of Influence' (2006) 59 Current Legal Problems 231.

[82] Andrew Burrows, *Remedies for Torts and Breach of Contract* (3rd edn, Oxford University Press 2004) 664.

is an altruistic duty triggered by the relationship between the parties),[83] and restrictions on the right to affirm for repudiatory breach.[84] I return in more depth to some of these possible connections in the chapters that follow.

In conclusion, it is unclear that the institutional features of contract law, such as legal enforcement, and contractual rules and doctrines support Kimel's claim that the mark of contract is personal detachment.

Is personal detachment a value?

The purpose of the last section was interpretive: to cast doubt on Kimel's claim that the best way to understand contract law is through the prism of the value of personal detachment. In this section, I make a more radical claim. I doubt that an interpretation of contract law in terms of personal detachment even gets off the ground, because it is far from clear that personal detachment has any value at all.

Kimel says that, in the contractual context, the value of personal detachment consists in the ability to enter into exchanges with other people, without having to be in a pre-existing relationship with them, and without having to commit to entering such a relationship in the future.[85] He says that it is a value that is 'diametrically opposed' to the value of personal relationships, which is the value that animates promising. Like the value of personal relationships, personal detachment has intrinsic value, which he argues is 'easy to see'.[86]

Contra Kimel, that value is far from being easy to see. The difficulty is related to Fuller's concerns about John Stuart Mill's theory of freedom:

> Mill seems to assume that the ideal condition would be one in which, unhampered by social arrangements of any kind, the individual would, in effect, choose everything for himself—his satisfactions, his mode of life, his relations with others. Only the unfortunate circumstance that his actions may impinge harmfully on others makes it necessary to qualify this ideal.[87]

This is a negative, distinctly English, conception of freedom, according to which 'freedom means primarily privacy', or 'the right to be let alone'. Fuller contrasted it with the American, more positive, republican version, where freedom entails involvement in social and political life.[88]

[83] Fried, 'The Convergence of Contract and Promise' (n 74) 8. Explaining the altruistic nature of the duty, Fried says: 'a promise may call for sacrifices far in excess of what residual, background nonpromissory principles of fairness and decency require'. Fried, *Contract as Promise: A Theory of Contractual Obligation* (n 5) 131.

[84] *MSC Mediterranean Shipping Company SA v Cottonex Anstalt* [2015] EWHC 283, (imposing a good faith restriction on the right to affirm).

[85] Kimel, *From Promise to Contract: Towards a Liberal Theory of Contract* (n 4) 78.

[86] ibid 79.

[87] Fuller, 'Freedom: A Suggested Analysis' (n 68) 1310. Fuller's works on freedom are largely forgotten. Thank you to Dan Priel for bringing them to my attention. Dan Priel, 'Lon Fuller's Political Jurisprudence of Freedom' (2014) 10 Jerusalem Review of Legal Studies 18.

[88] Fuller, 'The Case Against Freedom' in *The Principles of Social Order: Selected Essays of Lon L. Fuller* (Kenneth Winston ed, rev edn, Hart Publishing 2002) 323, citing Hart who brought out the contrast after his visit to Harvard between 1956–1957; HLA Hart, 'A View of America' (16 January 1958) 59 The Listener 89; Lon L Fuller, 'Freedom as a Problem of Allocating Choice' (1968) 112 Proceedings of the American Philosophical Society 101, 103.

Fuller could not see the value in being left totally alone. He calls this 'freedom in a void', deriding its 'worthlessness'. He used Chester Barnard's example of a solitary rower adrift in the centre of a foggy lake to make his point:

> Such a man is utterly free to row in any direction he sees fit. He is even free from the burden of decision, since he is in a situation where it is impossible to reach any intelligent decision as to the direction he should take. Completely without shackles, duties or obligations, such a man ought to feel free—if to be free is to be unfettered by restraints.[89]

But, of course, he is not free in any meaningful way.[90] Freedom, Fuller argued, of the kind we value requires 'effective participation in the affairs of the family, the tribe, or the nation'.[91] It is a republican ideal that depends on background social institutions, which channel our creative energies. He used the right to vote as an example. A freedom which depends on 'a machinery of election':

> This machinery will in turn carry with it its own compulsions, for instance, against voting twice. Not only that, but the forms through which choice is channeled by an election law will of necessity exclude other forms of choice. Thus, if the election is to be by the system known as proportional representation (PR), the electorate must necessarily forego the form of choice involved in election by a simple majority.[92]

For Fuller, there are a battery of social forms behind the exercise of any valuable freedom. Kimel does not endorse a negative conception of freedom, preferring instead Joseph Raz's view of freedom as personal autonomy, or the 'ideal of self-creation, of people exerting control over their destinies', by freely choosing and pursuing valuable 'activities, goals and relationships'. As a matter of political philosophy, government should, on this view, create the conditions for autonomy, by making such options available, and respect the decisions that citizens make about how to live.[93]

Nevertheless, Kimel does support making personal detachment available as a valuable option in people's lives. In doing so, he links detachment to the value of freedom, and opens himself up to Fuller's critique of Mill. Absent restraint, freedom is not worth the candle.[94] Thus, far from being dependent on personal detachment, the value of freedom is inimical to it.

[89] Fuller, 'The Case Against Freedom' (n 88) 321.

[90] Fuller, 'Freedom: A Suggested Analysis' (n 68) 1312.

[91] Fuller, 'Freedom as a Problem of Allocating Choice' (n 88) 103; Fuller, 'The Case Against Freedom' (n 88) 320.

[92] Fuller, 'Freedom: A Suggested Analysis' (n 68) 1312.

[93] Kimel, *From Promise to Contract: Towards a Liberal Theory of Contract* (n 4) 126.

[94] Fuller, 'The Case Against Freedom' (n 88) 319–20; Fuller, 'Freedom: A Suggested Analysis' (n 68) 1311–12: 'The complex network of institutional ways by which the bulk of our energies is directed and channeled is not an unfortunate limitation on freedom. It is essential to freedom itself.'; Fuller, 'Freedom as a Problem of Allocating Choice' (n 88) 102–03; Lon L Fuller, 'Law as an Instrument of Social Control and Law as a Facilitation of Human Interaction' [1975] Brigham Young University Law Review 89, 89–90; Priel, 'Lon Fuller's Political Jurisprudence of Freedom' (n 87) 23.

Is personal detachment possible?

It follows from what I have said above that I doubt whether personal detachment in any meaningful sense is actually possible. One might reply that though this appears to be true in the case of the solitary rower, there are other cases that plausibly indicate that personal detachment has value. Timothy Macklem has argued that privacy or personal detachment has value in the context of artistic expression, such as the writing of poetry. It enables certain forms of creativity, which shape and express character:

> It is in isolation from other people, and the supports they offer and the freedoms they make possible, that a person is forced to confront the constraints of his or her circumstances, as best he or she can, with whatever resources, personal and practical, he or she cannot only call upon but develop, through the exercise of his or her imagination, strength and will, in short, through the exercise of creativity.[95]

It sounds plausible that detachment has value in this context. However, it is important to bear in mind a point that Fuller made, which is that due to over-familiarity, we have a real tendency to take for granted, or overlook, the presence of social forms.[96] Indeed, Macklem is quick to uncover some of these relations:

> Even poetry . . . one of the purest expressions of individual consciousness and endeavour, is a recognized social form in itself and relies upon structures that are intelligible and accessible to its audience, be they sonnet forms or free verse. Poetry also depends upon a literary culture, in the form of publishers, reviewers, booksellers and readers, for the achievement of its purpose, and full realization of its value.[97]

Poetry depends on social forms. However, it may be that the background existence of these forms means that there is space for a form of personal detachment in poetry, and perhaps other forms of artistic expression. Whatever the case might be in these contexts, it's clear there is no such possibility for detachment in contract. Contracts are inherently relational. As I have argued, contractual parties depend on the trust they repose in each other to achieve their ends. Unlike poetry, that dependence is upfront and of immediate concern to both of the parties. Contra Kimel, it is this relation and not the threat of legal enforcement, which merely provides a backstop or supplement, which is central.

[95] Timothy Macklem, *Independence of Mind* (Oxford University Press 2006) 67.

[96] Fuller, 'The Case Against Freedom' (n 88) 323, 325. There are ways though to bring the centrality of those forms to the fore. Samuel Scheffler asks us to imagine the implications of knowing that the entire human race would be wiped out soon after we die. Many activities such as music or academic research would lose their value, he argues, because they presuppose the persistence of human institutions and practices. Samuel Scheffler, *Death and the Afterlife* (Niko Kolodny ed, Oxford University Press 2013).

[97] Macklem, *Independence of Mind* (n 95) 37.

Summary

In summary, I have challenged Kimel's divisionist defence of the *Balfour* doctrine. I doubt that a contracting party's right to decide whether a promise should be legally binding promotes attachment or freedom from contract, because it is not clear legal enforcement would necessarily disrupt the expressive quality of promising. Nor is it evident that the intent to contract doctrine promotes personal detachment or freedom to contract. It is far from obvious, for the reasons Fuller gives, that this is a value worth serving, or that contract law does or even could serve it.

The underlying problem with Kimel's approach is that it reinforces the *Balfour* contrast between the personal and commercial sphere. The assumption is that personal relations involve attachment, and a lack of constraint, whilst in the commercial realm people are detached, and constrained by the mechanism of legal enforcement. The contrast is false, and, as feminists have shown, potentially highly damaging. It is based on a mistaken conception of freedom. As Fuller argued, the value of freedom involves attachment and that depends on a morality of constraint. Social forms facilitate valuable human interaction by subjecting the pursuit of our ends to the recognition of our common humanity.[98] On this republican view, there is no separation between contract and promise. They are both forms of attachment, and they both involve constraint. The divisionist obscures this reality, and crudely restricts the possibilities for human association.

Fuller saw that there exists a spectrum of human relations: 'running from intimacy, at the one end, to hostility, at the other, with a stopping place midway that can be described as the habitat of friendly strangers'.[99] That realm of friendly strangers includes contractual relations. It is a different kind of relation to friendship or love, but nevertheless it is premised on trust and attachment. We lose sight of this at our peril. Commenting on this divisionist picture, Unger says: 'The most remarkable feature of this vision is its exclusion of the more morally ambitious models of human connection from the prosaic activities and institutions that absorb most people most of the time.'[100] Contract is, primarily, an opportunity for human association, rather than an escape from it.

The dichotomy threatens both the possibility of intimacy, by, as feminists have argued, creating relations of dependency and need rather than equality and respect, and the neighbourly relations that underpin contract. For these reasons, it should be rejected. Does this mean abandoning the intent to contract doctrine too? It does not, but it may mean having to turn away from the reflective view or promise theory

98 As Fried says, this is a principle of natural law: 'by the norm of human nature a person in his dealings with others may not deny either his own or any other person's capacity for free and rational action. To do so is always to act irrationally—that is, a failure to make a true judgment of reality the ground for one's acts—and therefore to act contrary to one's nature.' Charles Fried, 'Natural Law and the Concept of Justice' (1964) 74 Ethics 237, 248. See also Fried, *Right and Wrong* (n 42) 29; Fuller, 'Law as an Instrument of Social Control and Law as a Facilitation of Human Interaction' (n 94) 89.

99 Fuller, 'Human Interaction and the Law' (n 68) 27. See also Fried, *Right and Wrong* (n 42) 30. cf Clare Dalton, 'An Essay in the Deconstruction of Contract Doctrine' (1985) 94 Yale Law Journal 997, 1098–1100.

100 Unger, 'The Critical Legal Studies Movement' (n 18) 623.

of contract. The trouble with the reflective view has been that whereas the divisionist has been too quick to drive a wedge between contract and promise, the promise theorist by assuming contract must mirror promise has failed to take seriously the structural differences between the two practices. This is why the promise theory has struggled with the intent to contract doctrine.

Fried was right to notice that contract like promise involves cooperation based on the values of attachment and trust. He failed though to see how contract as a social form served these ends in a fundamentally different way to promise. This is the advantage of a bottom-up republican approach to contract, which won't just assume that contract reflects promise. On this view, the constitutive purpose of contract is to promote trust-based cooperation, but the requirements of that ideal are not set in stone. Rather, they are underdetermined and allow considerable flexibility in how it is pursued in different institutional contexts. Promise theorists tend to assume that the moral values in play in contract provide fairly determinate or specific guidance on the shape contract law must take, but this is a mistake which leads to insensitivity to the differences between promissory morality and contract. In the next section, I show how the republican framework I defended in Chapter 4 is better able to account for the intent to contract doctrine.

5. The Republican Vision

5.1 Kimel's challenge

The promise theory or reflective view of contract seems, as I have said, to struggle with the intent to contract doctrine. If contracts are promises, it is unclear why seriously intended promises should not be contracts, whether or not there was a further intention to create legal relations. Kimel puts the challenge in the following way:

> For the 'separate requirement' of an intention to create legal relations to be significant or even explicable, it should be possible to think of a reason why not to have such an intention in the relevant circumstances, or at least why not to ascribe it systematically to rational agents (in these circumstances) ... And if it is thought that there is no pertinent difference between contractual and promissory relations, and even more so if the former are thought to be but an improved version of the latter—if contracts are understood to offer all the benefits of promises (or exchanges of promises) with the additional bonus of enforceability—then the chances of finding such reasons look rather slim.[101]

In other words, Kimel asks what does the reflective view have to lose? If contracts are promises, there seem to be only upsides to legal recognition, that is, the additional assurance provided by legal enforcement.

Kimel's puzzlement here about what the promise theorist would have against the repudiation of the intent to contract requirement rests in the key assumption he identifies that promise theorists tend to make that there is 'no pertinent difference

[101] Kimel, *From Promise to Contract: Towards a Liberal Theory of Contract* (n 4) 137.

between contractual and promissory relations'. This is the product of their general view that promissory morality is fairly determinate, and contract law should seek to reflect or mirror it. If that is true, Kimel is right that there is no convincing reason why the promise theorist should insist on intent to contract as a distinct requirement.

Kimel hopes of course by discrediting the promise theory to show that the only plausible explanation for intent to contract is that contract law pursues its own unique end or purpose, which Kimel argues is the promotion of personal detachment. I have already set out my doubts about his claims. There is an alternative. It involves moving away both from the view that contract mirrors promissory morality and the claim that it pursues its own separate purposes. This is the republican theory of contract according to which contract and promise *share* the promotion of trust-based cooperation as a constitutive end but pursue this purpose in *distinct* ways. This is made possible by the inherent under-determinacy and flexibility of that moral purpose. There is then a 'pertinent difference' between the two realms, but it does not rest in the pursuit of entirely distinct or contrasting ends. In this section, I want to respond to Kimel's challenge by embracing the republican vision. As well as the upsides, there are significant downsides to contracts, even if contracts do indeed enforce promises.

5.2 Pluralism and the determinatio

Historically, it has been a feature of positivist thinking about the nature of law to focus on its coercive nature. This, together with the idea of the sovereign, creates a top-down model of the law, which loses sight of the moral value of the relations that the law facilitates.[102] As Fuller said, the law is not just 'a system of minimum restraints designed to keep the bad man in check, but is in fact helping to create a body of common morality which will define the good man'.[103]

In the contractual context, Kimel too focuses on the reassurance that legal enforcement provides, and the detachment this creates between the parties. What's missed here is the moral quality of the relations that contract law structures. There are two in particular: the relations between the contracting parties and those between the parties and the state.

The relations between the contracting parties are based on promise and trust. As Fried said, when we make a promise we invite trust, and when that promise is accepted we are trusted to do what we say. Breaking a promise is an abuse of trust, which shows a lack of respect for the promisee.[104] The sense that relations based on trust are what are at stake here is brought out by a homely example used by Shiffrin:

[102] There are of course positivist thinkers, like Hart, who are exceptions, but the claim here has Thomas Hobbes, John Austin, and Hans Kelsen in mind. Charles Fried, *An Anatomy of Values: Problems of Personal and Social Choice* (Harvard University Press 1970) 249–50; Fuller, *The Law in Quest of Itself* (n 58) 137.

[103] Fuller, *The Law in Quest of Itself* (n 58) 137.

[104] Fried, *Contract as Promise: A Theory of Contractual Obligation* (n 5) 16–17.

It is not uncommon, as many of us know, for plumbers or contractors to commit to appear to do a job but then fail to appear. You wait for hours, they don't call, and then you must reschedule and wait again, apprehensive that the scene will recur. Most people who are subject to this sort of treatment are enraged. I find those who are not enraged a little alien: they seem either sedated or to have made a heavy investment in honing their meditative techniques.[105]

The source of that anger is not just the fact that you have not received the service you were promised and the inconvenience this causes. Imagine, for example, that the plumber called in advance to warn you that she was not going to make it, she got a better job elsewhere, but that, quite fortuitously, at that very same moment another plumber knocks on your door to say that she can do the job for the very same price. You might feel less angry, but I suspect that for most people there would still be some residual resentment toward the first plumber. Although you receive the service you were expecting, you do not receive it *from* the first plumber. She has let you down; abused your trust. You might be less likely to hire that plumber again, regardless of whatever assurance legal enforcement provides. This is because, as Fried saw, trust provides a firmer ground for acts of reliance, than the shifting sands of self-interest.[106]

This is why Fried said 'a contract is first of all a promise'.[107] Note though, he did not say that a contract is *only* a promise.[108] The claim is that contracts are promises, not that all promises are contracts.[109] The two practices, contract and promise, are both based on promise, but it is possible to differentiate them. This creates space for choice. There may be reasons for preferring one practice over the other and *vice versa*. Here are the seedlings of a response to Kimel's challenge.

The trouble was that Fried himself and many of the promise theorists who have followed him have said very little about how the practices might be distinguished or the grounds on which lines between them might be drawn. The reasons are not I believe difficult to find. The promise theory is a justificatory theory of contract, which seeks to provide normative guidance on the shape contract law and doctrine should take. Promise theorists have in the past strongly tended to assume that contract should just track promise, and that promissory morality is a source of fairly determinate norms. One explanation for these tendencies may have been the felt need to present a fairly united and concrete alternative to economic analysis which has dominated contract theory in the past few decades. Efficiency theorists have always lauded, as a distinct advantage of their approach, that they could provide clear economic solutions to difficult legal questions and issues.

[105] Shiffrin uses the example to illustrate that usually when we make promises they are not promises to perform or pay the monetary equivalent of performance, rather the expectation is that we will perform what we promised. So, the example continues: 'If the no-show plumber were to appear next time matter-of-factly presenting you with a check or a discount reflecting the value of your time that was wasted, I suspect that, after emerging from shock, the resentment would not fully dissipate.' Seana Shiffrin, '*Could* Breach of Contract Be Immoral?' (2009) 107 Michigan Law Review 1551, 1564.

[106] Fried, *Contract as Promise: A Theory of Contractual Obligation* (n 5) 8, 13.

[107] ibid 17. Similarly, Shiffrin says that promise is 'the fundamental component of a contract'. See Shiffrin, '*Could* Breach of Contract Be Immoral?' (n 105) at 1551–52.

[108] Fried, *Contract as Promise: A Theory of Contractual Obligation* (n 5) 17.

[109] ibid.

Whatever the motivations, because of these practical commitments to providing fairly specific normative guidance, promise theorists have in the past generally struggled to explicate Fried's intuition that contract though built on promise, is not the same as promise. In my view, without shedding some of these commitments and embracing something like the republican framework, which emphasizes the contingency of contractual ordering, the characteristic functions of contract law, the inherent underdeterminacy and pluralism of the values that shape contract and so forth, the reflective view cannot sensibly account for how contract law differs from promise.

How are they differentiated on the republican view? Promise, unlike contract, is what I shall call an 'open' or largely underdetermined system of norms. This is contrary to the usual picture of promise painted by the promise theory. The underdeterminacy is due to the existence of what I have called in earlier chapters 'normative pluralism'. There are in fact two types of pluralism captured by this concept: let's call them 'interpretive' and 'value pluralism'.

By interpretive pluralism, I mean that there is an irreducible plurality of ways in which to interpret values. Values that bear on promising include promise, altruism, fairness, corrective justice, and so forth. When we make a promise, it is fairly clear what we should do. Having made a promise, we now have an obligation to keep it, or to do what we said we would do. The existence of this fundamental norm of promising is pretty uncontroversial. However, due to interpretive pluralism, many of the other requirements of the practice are much less clear, and to a large degree dependent on context.[110]

So, for example, it is far less clear what the promise principle requires when a promise is broken. To a fairly large degree it will depend on the nature and history of the relationship we have with the promisee and the context. If I promise my daughter that I will go to the cinema with her on Tuesday, but end up breaking that promise, because, say, I get stuck in traffic, it is not obvious what promissory logic now requires. Some people say promise or the interests it protects require me to perform my promise at the next available opportunity.[111] I am far less sure. What if instead of offering to go to the next showing of the movie, I buy a DVD of another movie for us to watch together at home, or I suggest we go for dinner, or I say 'I am really sorry' and leave it at that? Although promise requires me to do something when I breach, it is not clear that any of these potential responses necessarily has priority over any of the others.[112] Instead, the parties have to decide between themselves which response is most appropriate.

[110] Tony Honoré argues that the duty to perform one's promise is an example of 'subsumption' where 'a particular instance can be subsumed under a wider principle', but as he rightly goes on to point out 'in many situations there is no simple connection with a moral principle, because the principle involved, for example that we should act with due concern for others, is not specific enough'. Tony Honoré, 'The Dependence of Morality on Law' (1993) 13 Oxford Journal of Legal Studies 1, 6.

[111] Shiffrin, 'The Divergence of Contract and Promise' (n 1) 724; Rowan, *Remedies for Breach of Contract: A Comparative Analysis of the Protection of Performance* (n 63) 118–20; Kimel, *From Promise to Contract: Towards a Liberal Theory of Contract* (n 4) 95; John Gardner, 'What is Tort Law For? Part 1. The Place of Corrective Justice' (2011) 30 Law and Philosophy 1, 28–29.

[112] cf John Tasioulas, 'Human Rights, Legitimacy, and International Law' (2013) 58 The American Journal of Jurisprudence 1, 20; Allen Buchanan, 'The Legitimacy of International Law' in Samantha

This is not to say promissory morality exerts no influence on which option to take. So, for example, it might rule out some obviously inappropriate responses to my breach, such as agreeing to take my daughter on an all-expenses-paid world trip. The point is only that there is no uniquely appropriate response, but rather a range of rationally defensible courses of action.[113]

Another source of under-determinacy in promise is value pluralism. According to value pluralism, there are an irreducible plurality of moral values and no single correct way of resolving conflict between them. Rather, there exist a multiplicity of legitimate rankings.[114] So, for example, imagine I promise to drive my friend to the airport tomorrow so she can make a flight. However, I forget to set my alarm clock and my friend misses the flight. When I failed to turn up, my friend could easily have taken a taxi to the airport, but instead she chose to stay at home and wait for me. How should I feel about my friend missing the flight? Should I feel guilty? Or perhaps resent that she did not call a taxi? What should I do? Say 'sorry'? Tell my friend off? Offer to pay the cost of the flight?

These and many other normative questions arise. There are a multiplicity of values that bear on the situation, including promise, corrective justice, fairness, altruism, friendship, and so on. Those values might conflict. So, for example, corrective justice might require me to compensate my friend for missing the flight. However, fairness might require my friend to take some share of the responsibility.[115] According to value pluralism, there is no single correct answer.

How the parties interpret these values, and how they navigate and resolve conflicts between them, will say something about the weight they attach to the values at stake and the character of their relationship; indeed, it will shape it. As Fried says:

> It is clear enough that after we have taken care to render to others their fair share and have taken care also to avoid doing wrong, there remains during the whole course of our lives a large measure of discretion. In filling this discretionary space we make a life which is characteristically our own.[116]

The source of that 'discretionary space' is the existence of interpretive and value pluralism. In contrast to promise, contract manages pluralism in a different way. It is a 'closed' or largely determined system of norms. By this I mean that the decisions about the interpretation and ranking of values that are left to the parties themselves in the context of promise, are authoritatively settled for the parties by legal institutions, such as courts and legislatures.

For natural lawyers, this is the key function of law.[117] On account of interpretive and value pluralism, many of the requirements of natural law are too vague to

Besson and John Tasioulas (eds), *The Philosophy of International Law* (Oxford University Press 2010) 95. Both discussing the multiple ways in which human rights might be interpreted.

113 Thank you to Fred Wilmot-Smith for helping me to clarify this point.

114 For a general discussion of the thesis see Tasioulas, 'Human Rights, Legitimacy, and International Law' (n 112) 19.

115 I argue in Chapter 9 that this is the best way to interpret the mitigation doctrine.

116 Fried, *Right and Wrong* (n 42) 167.

117 Fried, *An Anatomy of Values: Problems of Personal and Social Choice* (n 102) 122: 'the function of concretizing the constraints of justice is the most characteristic function of law'.

provide practical guidance. They have to be concretized by systems of positive law. They call this role the determinatio.[118]

In the context of promise, it is contract law that fleshes out the requirements of natural law. As I have said, there are a number of perfectly eligible ways that those requirements might be interpreted and balanced. So, for example, English law embraces the requirement that on breach of contract, the promisee has a duty to take reasonable steps to mitigate any loss caused by, for example, obtaining substitute performance. In doing so, English law seems to attach priority to non-promissory values, such as altruism, loss avoidance, or fairness.[119] In contrast, French law eschews the existence of such a requirement, thus attaching greater weight to the duty to perform one's promises.[120] Neither interpretation of the practice is necessarily wrong. They are both rationally defensible interpretations and rankings of the values at stake.

Whichever way the law chooses to interpret the practice, it facilitates or provides a framework for a new type of relation. Participants are given the choice, through the intent to contract doctrine, of having their relation governed or structured by the largely open or underdetermined practice of promising, or the relatively closed or determinate system of contract law. How they choose depends on the circumstances and what sort of relation they want. Do they want greater flexibility and room for manoeuvre or would they prefer the certainty and predictability of bright line rules?[121] Do they want greater control over the rules that govern their interaction, or would they prefer for this to be out of their hands?[122] And so on. There are advantages and disadvantages here that need to be weighed up. So, for example, flexibility is preferable where the future is difficult to predict. Flexibility avoids the costs of renegotiating contracts due to change of circumstances. However, flexibility has its drawbacks too, such as lack of predictability, and the risk of moral hazard arising from the tendency of parties to interpret their agreements in ways that suit their own interests.[123]

[118] Jeremy Waldron, 'Torture, Suicide and Determinatio' (2010) 55 The American Journal of Jurisprudence 1, 2, 9–10; JM Finnis, 'On "The Critical Legal Studies Movement"' (1985) 30 The American Journal of Jurisprudence 21, 43; Fried, *An Anatomy of Values: Problems of Personal and Social Choice* (n 102) 121–22.

[119] For a critique of this choice see Shiffrin, 'The Divergence of Contract and Promise' (n 1) 725. For a defence of the English position see Chapter 9 of this book (relying on the principle of fairness); Fried, 'The Convergence of Contract and Promise' (n 74) 7–8, (relying on altruism); Charles J Goetz and Robert E Scott, 'The Mitigation Principle: Toward a General Theory of Contractual Obligation' (1983) 69 Virginia Law Review 967, 973, (defending loss avoidance as the rationale).

[120] Rowan, *Remedies for Breach of Contract: A Comparative Analysis of the Protection of Performance* (n 63) 147–51.

[121] See Gilson, Sabel, and Scott, 'Braiding: The Interaction of Formal and Informal Contracting in Theory, Practice, and Doctrine' (n 31) 1391–92. See also Robert E Scott, 'The Death of Contract Law' (2004) 54 The University of Toronto Law Journal 369, 372, 374.

[122] Robert Scott reports that in the US context, parties increasingly opt for less costly and more flexible informal enforcement: 'The result is that *the law* of contract is suffering from stagnation and, even more embarrassingly, from irrelevance.' Scott, 'The Death of Contract Law' (n 121) 370.

[123] Gilson, Sabel, and Scott, 'Braiding: The Interaction of Formal and Informal Contracting in Theory, Practice, and Doctrine' (n 31) 1391–92; Scott, 'The Death of Contract Law' (n 121) 372, 374, 385–86; Macaulay, 'Non-Contractual Relations in Business: A Preliminary Study' (n 58) 64–65.

This was the step that Fried failed to take. His great insight was to see that contract was based on promise, trust, and attachment. But he did not see or fully appreciate how these values although shared with promise, could be pursued perfectly legitimately in ways distinct from promise. On the republican view, contract and promise both have the pursuit of trust-based cooperation as a constitutive end, but they structure the relations between those who have made promises to one another in competing ways. This is possible because the republican view recognizes that the constitutive end of contract law is underdetermined and capable of being interpreted in a multiplicity of ways.

The value of the choice between the competing forms of association structured by contract and promise explains how the republican view responds to Kimel's challenge. Despite the advantages of legal enforcement, the parties might quite reasonably prefer to have their relation structured by the practice of promising rather than contract, because of the flexibility, freedom, and opportunity for moral development that it provides. None of this means that contractual relationships are not based on promise or trust. In the same way that the framework provided by the legal institution of marriage hardly indicates that those who marry do not love or trust one another.[124]

5.3 The citizen and the state

There is potentially another advantage to avoiding contract, which the republican view helps to bring out. For contract law, as well as providing a different kind of framework for the relationship between the parties themselves, one that is governed by a more rigid and determinate set of norms, also involves the parties in a relationship with the state.[125] As I argued in Chapter 4, the republican picture of contract is rooted in a theory of the state according to which the legitimacy of the state depends on citizens being treated with equal concern and respect.

That relationship, like any other, has its own distinctive set of what Fuller called 'interactional expectancies'.[126] In other words, it creates rights and duties for both parties. The state has authority over the contracting parties. It decides how to interpret and balance the values that govern their interaction. However, that power has to be exercised legitimately.[127] In particular, the state must ensure that it treats its citizens with equal concern and respect in its decision-making, which includes a duty to publish its decisions and rules, and to act with principled consistency.[128] In other words, the state must comply with the rule of law. In return, citizens have an obligation to obey the law.[129] The relationship depends on reciprocity. As Fuller

124 Fried, *An Anatomy of Values: Problems of Personal and Social Choice* (n 102) 118–19.

125 Michel Rosenfeld, 'Contract and Justice: The Relation between Classical Contract Law and Social Contract Theory' (1984) 70 Iowa Law Review 769, 880–81.

126 Fuller, 'Human Interaction and the Law' (n 68) 24.

127 Priel, 'Lon Fuller's Political Jurisprudence of Freedom' (n 87) 26.

128 On the importance of the publication requirement for contracting parties see Scott, 'The Death of Contract Law' (n 121) 379–80.

129 Ronald Dworkin, *Law's Empire* (Hart Publishing 1998) ch 7; Fuller, 'Human Interaction and the Law' (n 68) 24–25.

says: 'If the lawgiver wants his subjects to accept and act by his rules, he must himself display some minimum respect for those rules in his actions toward his subjects'.[130] Despite its benefits, citizens might legitimately, at least in the context of promise, want to avoid this morally charged relationship; preferring instead to make decisions themselves.

6. Conclusion

In this chapter, I have explored how the *Balfour* doctrine and the sophisticated defence of it given by Kimel has reinforced a damaging separation between contract and promise, which threatens both relationships of intimacy between the sexes, and the neighbourly relations which should underpin contract.

The divisionist defence is based on a mistaken conception of freedom, according to which the value of freedom resides in the right to be let alone, and an undue focus on the coercive aspects of contract law, at the expense of the moral quality of the relationships that contract law structures.

Freedom does not depend on an absence of constraint, but rather on social forms, such as promise and contract, which provide a framework for human interaction. Promise theorists were right to point out the relationship between contract and promise, but their tendency to assume that promissory morality provided contract with fairly determinate normative guidance, clouded their ability to perceive the differences between the two practices. The differences come into view if we adopt the republican framework, which accepts Fried's insight that contract is based on the values of promise and trust, but at the same time does not assume that these values can be interpreted in only one or a narrow range of ways. Rather, on the republican picture both contract and promise have the promotion of trust-based cooperation as a constitutive or characteristic value, but due to the different ways that they manage the pervasive influence of interpretive and value pluralism on our lives, the two practices constitute and sustain different kinds of relation.

Promissory relations are open and flexible, providing greater room for moral development. Contractual relations, on the other hand, are closed and relatively rigid, due not least to the constraints that the principle of fairness imposes on the relations between the citizen and the state that they necessarily involve. The difference in the moral quality of the relations that these two practices facilitate creates room for the republican account to justify the existence of a separate intent to contract requirement, without having to let go of the view that contracts enforce promises.

My aim in this chapter has been to set out this republican defence of the intent to contract requirement, which as I have shown both the divisionist and reflective theory of contract mishandle. The values that underpin and sustain it, promise,

[130] Fuller, 'The Role of Contract in the Ordering Processes of Society Generally' (n 71) 190. See also James Boyle, 'Legal Realism and the Social Contract: Fuller's Public Jurisprudence of Form Private Jurisprudence of Substance' (1992) 78 Cornell Law Review 371, 377.

trust, respect, attachment, human association, are the polar opposite of those that motivate the divisionist view. They are pursued though in contract in a distinct way to how they are instantiated in promise, and this is the key to the advance in understanding made by the republican view over the reflective conception.

This does not yet though deal with the objections made by feminists about how the doctrine operates in practice. This is true, but it is important to see that the answer to the operational question depends on how the doctrine is justified in the first place. I cannot spell out all of the doctrinal or practical implications of the republican view here. Instead, I have chosen to focus on the broader philosophical issues. I will though mention one very important implication.

The dichotomy between contract and promise embraced by the divisionist supports the evidential presumption against intent to contract in the context of promises made in the domestic or social sphere. If these promises were legally enforced that would, Kimel argues, threaten the expressive quality of promissory relations. I have questioned the plausibility of these claims. Moreover, this presumption is one that, as the feminist critique has shown, creates the risk of unfairness, distributive injustice, and relationships of dependency. Given these effects, that presumption is clearly incompatible with the values of trust, equality, and respect that I have argued underpin *both* promise and contract. In light of this, whatever practical benefits the presumption may have (resolving evidential difficulties, saving judicial time, and so forth), they cannot justify interference with the principles of a morality of contract that enforces promises and pursues trust-based cooperation as a constitutive end. This is an example of what I described in Chapter 4 as the negative role that trust-based cooperation plays as a side-constraint on contractual rules and doctrines that directly or egregiously contradict the value. Given this conflict with contract's constitutive purpose, there can be no doubt that the presumption should go.

6

Undue Influence and Exploitation*

1. Thick Trust

In Chapter 5 I argued against the 'divisionist' view that contract and promise occupy different realms. As we saw, Dori Kimel argues that whilst promises usually take place in the context of trusting relationships, contracts typically occupy the sphere of transactions between strangers. Such dichotomies are not only misleading, but have, as feminists have shown, damaging consequences for women. Instead, I defended the republican view that contract and promise *both* involve invocations of trust, and aim constitutively at the promotion of the value of trust-based cooperation, but they pursue that value in different ways.

The relationships of trust that obtain between contracting parties are not though typically the same as those that we associate with intimates, that is, friends, siblings, married couples, parents and children, and so forth. As I argued, in these contractual cases the relations are as Lon Fuller said more like those between 'friendly strangers'.[1] Promise theorists have largely neglected this point, or only been dimly aware of it. So, for example, in recent work Charles Fried likened contractual relations to those that exist between neighbours.[2] However, in the bulk of his work Fried has made little of Fuller's insight—like most other promise theorists he assumes that the trust that obtains between contractual parties is the same or a very similar type of trust that obtains in the promissory realm between close relations like intimates

* This chapter is based on and largely reproduces, but with some significant additions, revisions, and adaptations, the text of a previously published chapter of mine entitled 'Unconscionable Enrichment?', which appeared in Robert Chambers, Charles Mitchell, and James Penner (eds), *Philosophical Foundations of The Law of Unjust Enrichment* (Oxford University Press 2009) 417, copyright © The Several Contributors, 2009. The text is used with kind permission of Oxford University Press, and the editors of that volume.

[1] Lon L Fuller, 'Human Interaction and the Law' (1969) 14 The American Journal of Jurisprudence 1, 27. cf James E Penner, 'Voluntary Obligations and the Scope of the Law of Contract' (1996) 2 Legal Theory 325, 335–39 (identifying a spectrum of contexts in which agreements are made and the different relations of trust that form the backdrop for them), and James Penner, 'Promises, Agreements, and Contracts' in Gregory Klass, George Letsas, and Prince Saprai (eds), *Philosophical Foundations of Contract Law* (Oxford University Press 2014) 116, 131–34 (explaining the existence of trust between strangers on the grounds of the basic human capacity to respond to reasons).

[2] Charles Fried, 'The Convergence of Contract and Promise' (2007) 120 Harvard Law Review Forum 1, 8.

and friends. This is a mistake, which has led these promise theorists to mishandle contract doctrine.

In truth, Fuller was right—there is a 'thinner' type of trust in contract than the 'thick' trust we find in the context of relations between intimates. We trust intimates more; this is just to say that some of our relationships are closer than others. This has significant normative implications, the most important of which is that we owe duties of altruism to the people we are closest to. However, contra Kimel, this does not mean that normally no trust obtains between contractual partners. There is trust, albeit in a thin rather than thick sense. In contract, promisors invoke the trust of the promisee; but it is a *restricted* kind of trust, which invites the promisee to trust that the promisor will perform his contractual obligations.[3] *To this extent*, he will serve the promisee's interests or ends. However, the promisor has no duty to go beyond this.

In this sense, because of this relation, and contra Kimel, the promisee is no stranger. However, she is no intimate either; the trust invoked relates specifically to the performance of the promisor's contractual obligations. This is what I mean when I say that contracts involve thin trust.[4] My purpose in this chapter is to explore what happens in those less typical cases when contracts take place in the context, or against the backdrop, of pre-existing relationships of thick trust between the parties. The law cares very much about these cases, because they give rise to the danger that the promisee will exploit the close relationship to secure an unfair advantage for herself. The close relationship between the parties triggers an altruistic duty on the promisee to look out for the promisor's interests, or alternatively—if the promisee wants to deal self-interestedly with the promisor—to delegate that responsibility to an independent third party (usually a lawyer).[5] If the promisee instead takes advantage of the influence she has then she will have exercised undue influence, which gives the promisor a defence to her contractual claim.

As I set out in Chapter 9 on the mitigation doctrine, Fried thought that these altruistic duties arose in every contract, but I argue this was a mistake. It was a product of his broader claim that contract law should reflect promissory morality.

[3] I do not mean to suggest here of course that this is trust in what Kimel calls the 'trivial' sense, which is based on the 'basic rationality' of the promisor, that is, that due to the remedial regime for breach of contract, the promisor is highly unlikely to benefit from breach. Dori Kimel, *From Promise to Contract: Towards a Liberal Theory of Contract* (Hart Publishing 2003) 57–60. I follow Fried in thinking that what Kimel has in mind is not even a kind of trust, because trust depends on the belief that the person trusted 'will do what is right (not just what is prudent)'. Charles Fried, *Contract as Promise: A Theory of Contractual Obligation* (Harvard University Press 1981) 8. In contract, when the promisor invites the promisee to trust that he will perform, he is asking her to believe that he will perform for *moral* rather than *prudential* reasons.

[4] cf Daniel Markovits, 'Good Faith as Contract's Core Value' in Gregory Klass, George Letsas, and Prince Saprai (eds), *Philosophical Foundations of Contract Law* (Oxford University Press 2014) 292. See similarly James E Penner, 'Voluntary Obligations and the Scope of the Law of Contract' (n 1) 2 Legal Theory 337–38, 354.

[5] Mindy Chen-Wishart, 'Undue Influence: *Beyond* Impaired Consent and Wrongdoing towards a Relational Analysis' in Andrew Burrows and Lord Rodger (eds), *Mapping the Law: Essays in Memory of Peter Birks* (Oxford University Press 2006) 220–21. cf James E Penner, 'Voluntary Obligations and the Scope of the Law of Contract' (n 1) 2 Legal Theory 343.

Fried and promise theorists who followed him failed to adequately perceive the differences that Fuller recognized between the thick trust typical of close and intimate relations and the thinner type of trust that obtains in contractual relations. It is only when contracts take place in the context of pre-existing relationships of thick trust, like friendships or relationships between family members, that these altruistic duties are triggered. Absent these background relationships, the only trust at stake in contract is thin: the commitment made by the promisor to perform his contractual obligations.

Due to its commitment to the idea that promise plays a special role in justifying contract doctrine, I argue here that the 'promise theory' has also seriously mishandled the undue influence defence. This 'top-down' approach overlooks, underplays, or misunderstands the role that other values play in shaping contract law. The republican approach which accepts the contingency, under-determinacy, and irreducible plurality of the values that shape contract law is more sensitive to the contours of these doctrines. By adopting this 'bottom-up' approach, I aim to show that the undue influence doctrine is a 'composite doctrine', that is, the product of the interaction between more than one normative concern. In this case, the relevant concerns are promise and the prevention of exploitation. Of course, there are many different ways in which we might exploit others. It should come as no surprise though that a contract law which has as its characteristic or focal concern the promotion of trust-based cooperation will attach particular salience to forms of exploitation which involve abuse of trust. When contract balances normative concerns and values in forging its rules and doctrines, it does so against the backdrop of this constitutive end.

2. Exploitation and the Law

Undue influence is a particular form of exploitation, and exploitation is a form of moral wrongdoing. In contract, when a promisee exercises undue influence the complaint is that she has unfairly benefited from a contract by taking advantage of a pre-existing relationship she had with the promisor (that is, she has exploited the thick trust that existed between the parties). Undue influence is a central doctrine in contract law, but there are other types of exploitation which are dealt with in contract under the broader unconscionability principle. Unconscionability is the legal cognate of the moral principle against exploitation. So, when lawyers say that certain types of conduct are unconscionable, what they mean is that they are unfairly exploitative.

Before we discuss in greater depth the species of exploitation known in law as undue influence, it is important to get clear the broader concept of exploitation. When is conduct exploitative? Exploitation involves seizing opportunities or taking advantage of things, people, situations, places, and so forth. So, for example, I might exploit my friend's intimate knowledge of the New York restaurant scene to work out where best to go for a meal, or I might take advantage of a day off work to spend more time with my daughter. These are examples of course of non-wrongful advantage-taking. There is nothing bad—let alone wrongful—in taking advantage of my friend's local knowledge or a day off work.

When moral philosophers and lawyers speak of exploitation, they are normally interested in the pejorative sense of that concept. There is nothing wrong per se with advantage-taking or the seizing of opportunities, rather the concern is about cases where advantages or opportunities are *unfairly* seized.[6] Typically, E exploits V unfairly when four conditions are satisfied: first, E takes advantage of V's attributes or situation, which vis-à-vis E are weaknesses; second, E benefits from this behaviour; third, E's gain is made at V's expense; and, finally, the transaction is substantively unfair to V or harmful to his interests.

There are many examples of unfair exploitation. They range from the multinational which makes use of sweatshops in underdeveloped parts of the world; the 'friend' who is happy to receive favours and gifts, but not to give them in return; the 'quack' doctor who sells so-called 'miracle' cures to the desperately ill; and the circus owner who exhibits the grossly deformed to sell more tickets for his shows.[7]

Arguably some of these cases involve elements of coercion or fraud. Many think coercion and fraud are central instances of exploitation.[8] However, it is important to distinguish exploitation from these cases. It is certainly true that coercive or fraudulent behaviour is often described as being exploitative. But, it is important to notice that these forms of conduct are independently wrongful, that is, they are wrongful quite aside from the fact that they might involve exploitation. Although it is not a misuse of words to say that profitable torture, rape, genocide, or blackmail are forms of exploitation, it may make us lose sight of the fact that these acts are independently wrongful too.[9] Even if they all involve exploitation, they involve other distinct wrongs too.

It is better to reserve the label of exploitation in the pejorative sense for those cases where we use the term for actions that are *not* wrongful on independent grounds, like coercion and fraud. Now, one might argue that there are no such cases; that exploitation necessarily involves profiting from forms of conduct that are independently wrongful on other grounds. That though seems unlikely. Although many cases of exploitation do involve conduct that is independently wrongful, such as fraud and coercion, there are examples where they don't. So, for example, the circus owner who makes money from exhibiting deformed people exploits those people even if they fully consent to being taken advantage of in this way. Focusing on such cases reveals an important difference between exploiters and other types of wrongdoer such as rapists, blackmailers, torturers, and so forth. The exploiter is an opportunist. As Joel Feinberg says, they typically 'extract advantage from situations

[6] Richard Arneson, 'Exploitation' in Lawrence C Becker and Charlotte B Becker (eds), *Encyclopedia of Ethics* (Routledge 1992) 350–51; Joel Feinberg, *The Moral Limits of the Criminal Law: Harmless Wrongdoing* (Oxford University Press 1988) 177; Alan Wertheimer, *Exploitation* (Princeton University Press 1999) 10; John Lawrence Hill, 'Exploitation' (1994) 79 Cornell Law Review 631, 684.

[7] I borrow the last example from Feinberg, *The Moral Limits of the Criminal Law: Harmless Wrongdoing* (n 6) 184.

[8] ibid 178.

[9] Arneson, 'Exploitation' (n 6) 351; Wertheimer, *Exploitation* (n 6) 16.

that are not of their own making'; unlike coercers or fraudsters who are usually 'makers rather than discoverers and users of opportunities'.[10]

This conception of exploitation picks out types of conduct that resemble the sorts of behaviour that common lawyers describe as instances of undue influence or unconscionability. There does appear to be a very good fit between the moral wrong of exploitation and the legal principle of unconscionability and its species the doctrine of undue influence. There are three reasons for making the link. First, the application criteria or factors that trigger the defences of undue influence or unconscionability seem to reflect or mirror those that make conduct outside of the law exploitative.

In law, it is normally the case that for a defence of unconscionability or undue influence to be successful four things have to be shown. First, the promisor must have been at a serious situational or personal disadvantage vis-à-vis the promisee. In unconscionability cases, this includes relative poverty, immaturity, or ignorance. In undue influence, the disadvantage arises out of the background relationship between the parties and consists in the promisor's relational dependency on the promisee. In other words, the thick trust that is constitutive of the relationship between the two parties is also the source of the promisor's vulnerability to the promisee. Second, the promisee must be shown to have 'fraudulently' (either actually or constructively) taken advantage of the promisor's weakness to secure the transaction. Third, the transaction must be substantively unfair for the promisor. And, finally, the promisor must have entered the transaction without the benefit of adequate and independent legal advice.[11]

These four elements usually make up the application criteria for the unconscionability and undue influence defences. The structure of these defences matches the moral structure of exploitation. This suggests that the justificatory rationale lying behind these defences is to prevent the promisee from exploiting certain types of ascendency she has over the promisor.

The second reason for the link to exploitation is the language the courts often employ to justify these defences.[12] The House of Lords has referred to the exercise of undue influence as a type of wrongful conduct,[13] 'a species of fraud',[14] and as a form of 'victimization'.[15]

[10] Feinberg, *The Moral Limits of the Criminal Law: Harmless Wrongdoing* (n 6) 184. See also Hill, 'Exploitation' (n 6) 684–85.

[11] *Boustany v Pigott* (1995) 69 P & CR 298; Nicholas Bamforth, 'Unconscionability as a Vitiating Factor' (1995) Lloyd's Maritime and Commercial Law Quarterly 538, 559.

[12] Peter Birks and Nyuk Yin Chin, 'On the Nature of Undue Influence' in Jack Beatson and Daniel Friedman (eds), *Good Faith and Fault in Contract Law* (Clarendon Press 1995) 58–59.

[13] *Barclays Bank plc v O'Brien* [1994] AC 180, 189: 'A person who has been induced to enter into a transaction by the undue influence of another ("the wrongdoer") is entitled to set the transaction aside as against the wrongdoer.'

[14] *CIBC Mortgages v Pitt* [1994] AC 200, 209.

[15] *National Westminster Bank plc v Morgan* [1985] AC 686, 705. Relying on Lindley LJ in *Allcard v Skinner* [1887] 36 Ch 145, 182–83: 'to protect people from being forced, tricked or misled in any way by others into parting with their property is one of the most legitimate objects of all laws; and the equitable doctrine of undue influence has grown out of and been developed by the necessity of grappling with insidious forms of spiritual tyranny and with the infinite varieties of fraud'. See also *Re the Estate*

Thirdly, such an analysis is supported at the level of the facts and outcomes of cases where these defences have been successfully invoked. If we look closely at these cases, it's clear to see that the behaviour of the promisee (or transferee where there was no contract) was exploitative. The courts in the past refused to enforce extortionate loans made by unscrupulous moneylenders who preyed on young and inexperienced expectant heirs. This was regardless of whether the creditor used fraud, but rather about was about preventing 'an unconscientious use of the power arising out of these circumstances and conditions'.[16] Similarly, the courts would not assist a vendee who took advantage of the poverty and ignorance of two brothers to buy their reversionary interests in land at a massively discounted price.[17] In both cases, the promisors did not receive adequate and impartial legal advice.

In these cases, the ascendant party has taken advantage of the personal traits or circumstances of the promisor, which relative to the promisee are weaknesses to be exploited. The Courts have also shown themselves to be keen to protect parties, where the vulnerability arises from the presence of a pre-existing relationship of thick trust between the promisor and promisee. So, for example, in *Backhouse v Backhouse*, the Court granted relief to a wife who during the course of going through a divorce, transferred to her husband her share in the matrimonial home for nothing in return. Even though she was a smart business woman, the court granted a remedy, because she was under a 'great emotional strain':

> When a marriage has broken down, both parties are liable to be in an emotional state. The party remaining in the matrimonial home, as the husband did in this case, has an advantage. The wife is no doubt in circumstances of great emotional strain. It seems to me that she should at least be encouraged to take independent advice so that she may know whether or not it is right for her—whatever the circumstances of the break-down of the marriage may be—to transfer away what is her only substantial capital asset.[18]

The Australian case of *Louth v Diprose* provides another example of the how the courts step in to prevent this kind of relational abuse or advantage-taking. In that case, the court granted equitable relief to a lovesick solicitor who had bought a house for a woman with whom he had become infatuated. The High Court of Australia held that the woman had:

> deliberately used [the claimant's] love or infatuation and her own deceit to create a situation in which she could unconscientiously manipulate [the claimant] to part with a large proportion of his property. The intervention of equity is not merely to relieve the plaintiff from the consequences of his own foolishness. It is to prevent his victimisation.[19]

These cases, the application criteria of the unconscionability and undue influence doctrines, and the language of the courts provide at the very least strong prima

of Brocklehurst [1978] Ch 14, 39–42, 48; *Royal Bank of Scotland Plc v Etridge (No 2)* [2002] 2 AC 773, [6]–[7].

16 *Earl of Aylesford v Morris* (1873) 8 Ch App 484, 491.

17 *Fry v Lane* (1888) 40 Ch D 312. See also *Cresswell v Potter* [1978] 1 WLR 255.

18 *Backhouse v Backhouse* [1978] 1 WLR 243, 251.

19 *Louth v Diprose* (1992) 175 CLR 621, 638.

facie evidence that the moral injunction against exploitation plays a significant role in justifying these defences in contract law. Nevertheless, there has been strong resistance to this interpretation. In my view, much of this is the product of the huge influence that the promise theory of contract, and its nineteenth-century ancestor the will theory of contract, has had on lawyers and legal scholarship. There are three main types of objection that might be made to the exploitation analysis of these cases that I defend. First, that the promise theory offers a more plausible interpretation of these cases. Second, that the requirement of wrongdoing is too restrictive a constraint on the type of cases covered by these doctrines, and, finally, that the substantive unfairness requirement for exploitation fails to explain the cases. In what follows, I will argue that all of these concerns are without merit.

2.1 Why not promise?

The promise theory has attempted to explain these undue influence cases by adopting the strategy I called in Chapter 3 'justificatory primacy by inflation'. They widen or 'inflate' the scope of the promise principle to justify the defence. I argued in that chapter that these strategies lose sight of the duty to perform in these cases and distort the promise principle.[20]

The main argument of this kind that the promise theorist makes in the context of undue influence is that the presence of undue influence vitiates the exercise of the promisor's will, and this prevents a valid promise being made. The absence of a genuine promise explains the existence of the undue influence or unconscionability defence. This argument was famously made by Peter Birks and Nyuk Yin Chin. They claimed that 'relief for undue influence is given ... on the ground of impaired judgmental capacity usually arising from morbid dependence on another'.[21] This interpretation of the doctrine was in keeping with a broader commitment to the will theory of contract, which is the nineteenth-century intellectual ancestor of the promise theory.

I have already defended what I consider to be a decisive objection to these kinds of explanation for defences like undue influence, duress, misrepresentation, and so forth. They cannot explain the legal concept of voidability.[22] Briefly, according to these views when a promise is made under undue influence no valid promise or contract comes into being. However, it is clear from the cases that the victim of the undue influence does incur a pro tanto promissory obligation. Indeed, that is the only way to explain why the other party to the contract has a contractual obligation in the circumstances. The existence of the promisee's duty is premised on the fact that the promisor is under a valid contractual duty. It is true that the innocent party

[20] See ch 3, s 3.

[21] Birks and Chin, 'On the Nature of Undue Influence' (n 12) 85. Daniel Markovits, 'Promise as an Arm's Length Relation' in Hanoch Sheinman (ed), *Promises and Agreements: Philosophical Essays* (Oxford University Press 2011) 316 fn 36, claiming that unconscionability is 'designed to ensure that contracting parties' intentions are free rather than the product of manipulation'.

[22] See ch 3, s 3.1, 'Voidability'. On the application of these arguments to the duress doctrine see my paper 'Promising Under Duress' (unpublished, on file with author).

is free—subject to certain conditions—to set the transaction aside by raising the defence of undue influence. However, if he chooses not to, then the transaction stands as a valid contract.

By inflating the promise principle, the promise theorist loses sight of the underlying validity of the contract, which is necessary to explain why absent rescission by the innocent party, the guilty party has a contractual obligation to perform and why good title to property transferred under the contract may pass to third parties.[23] In other words, if we follow the account of undue influence offered by the promise theory, we would expect to find the contract to be void rather than voidable. It is open of course to the promise theorist to say that the law has gone astray here. In contrast, the bottom up republican approach that I endorse is able to explain the legal position here because of its greater sensitivity to the plurality of moral concerns and values that forge contract doctrine. On the republican view, exploitation does not vitiate the promise, thus making the contract void. Rather, the contract is valid, but due to the exploitation, the innocent promisor has a justification for breaching that pro tanto duty, which he can exercise or rely upon by rescinding the contract.

The promise theorist, by inflating the promise principle, loses sight of the role of undue influence as a justification for breach, because on this view there was no valid promise in the first place and so no breach of contract to justify. By contrast, the republican view by taking seriously the specific way that the exploitation principle interacts with the promise principle as a matter of law is better able to account for or explain the precise shape that the legal doctrine actually takes. The doctrine of undue influence is a composite doctrine, that is, the product of the interaction between multiple normative concerns.

In the literature on undue influence, promise theorists have paid insufficient attention to the general structure of the defence, and the fact that a key component of it is that it makes contracts voidable. Rather, they have tended to focus their energies on the support for their view given by the case law. So, for example, Birks and Yin relied on the Australian case of *Stivactas v Michaletos (No 2)*.[24] Not long after having suffered a cerebral haemorrhage, an elderly lady transferred her real estate to her great-nephew for virtually nothing in return. After making a fuller recovery, she regretted the transfer and brought proceedings to get the property back. Despite the fact that she had initiated the transfer and that the defendant nephew had ensured that she received independent legal advice, the New South Wales Court of Appeal declared it null and void and granted recovery. Kirby P and Shaller JA for the majority, gave as their reason that in the circumstances there was a presumption that the aunt's consent was impaired. The defendant could not show that his aunt gave the property through her own 'free will and informed exercise of judgment'.[25] They found that at the time the property was transferred that her condition due to

[23] *Bainbrigge v Browne* (1881) 18 Ch D 188.

[24] *Stivactas v Michaletos (No 2)* (1993) Court of Appeal of NSW, 31 August 1993, BC930187. Birks and Chin, 'On the Nature of Undue Influence' (n 12) 72–73.

[25] *Stivactas v Michaeletos (No 2)* (n 24) 5.

the haemorrhage was still very severe, and that the independent lawyer had not given her all the information she needed.

The importance of the case for Birks and Yin rests on the fact that the defendant here appears not to have done anything wrongful, and that the crucial issue for the court was that the aunt's consent to the transfers was impaired or vitiated by her condition. They use the case to argue that wrongdoing or exploitation is not part of the justification for the undue influence defence. I though am far less persuaded that this is what the case shows. First, it's far from clear that the defendant was entirely innocent in the circumstances. For instance, Mahoney JA rested his judgment for the aunt on the unconscionable behaviour of the defendant, which he argued consisted in the fact that the nephew proceeded with the transaction despite being fully aware of the frailty of his aunt's condition. Surely in these circumstances the nephew should have refused to participate? As Mahoney JA said:

> In such a case, the inequity lies, in my opinion in his participation in what she proposed to do notwithstanding what he knew of her condition and circumstances, and in his retaining the benefit of what she had done.[26]

Even if we put aside the question of whether the defendant's conduct was entirely innocent in this case, there is a deeper issue which calls into question the Birks and Yin analysis. To argue as I do that the rationale for the undue influence defence resides in the moral concern to prevent the exploitation of relationships of pre-existing thick trust that obtain between contracting parties, is not to deny that there may be cases perhaps decided under the rubric of undue influence or unconscionability where the real issue is not wrongdoing but the impairment of the promisor's will to the transaction. Cases of insanity, severe intoxication, and, as in *Stivactas*, brain injury may well be like this. That *Stivactas* might be a case of this kind seems plausible, and indeed this interpretation coheres well with the judicial explanations for the decision given by the majority in the case and the fact that the transaction was found to be null and void, rather than voidable. My central claim is not to deny the possibility of such cases—it is of course true that in some cases there is no contract because the will of the promisor was defectively exercised; rather, my argument is that there will be *other* cases—the majority I think—where the explanation for the defence is not that no promise came into being, but that a perfectly valid promise came into being, which was defeated by the presence of exploitation on the promisee's part.

Indeed, this last point is precisely what is shown by the classic undue influence case of *Allcard v Skinner*.[27] Over the course of eighteenth months, a young woman became a full member of a sisterhood. She agreed to abide by the order's rules which included commitments to chastity, poverty, and obedience. After joining, the novice nun received a substantial bequest, which in compliance with the rules of the order she gave over to the Mother Superior. These rules required that members of the order give up their property, treat the voice of the Mother Superior as the voice of God, and never to seek external advice without the Mother Superior's permission.

[26] ibid 19. [27] *Allcard v Skinner* (n 15).

Eventually the novice left the sisterhood and went to court to recover some of the property she had transferred. She rested the claim on the undue influence of the Mother Superior. Although her claim was time-barred, the court agreed with the novice that as matter of principle there had been undue influence.

According to Birks and Yin, the explanation is the impairment of the novice's will, caused by her being 'excessively dependent' on the Mother Superior.[28] On this view, the novice, due to the vitiation of her will, simply did not consent to transfer the property to the order.[29] The trouble though with this analysis is that it seems implausible to say on a review of the facts of the case that the novice did not consent. There are three ways in which it might be argued that the novice's will was impaired. One might claim that she did not act *intentionally*, or that she did not act *knowingly*, or, finally, that her decision was not the exercise of a *free choice*.[30] These arguments may also of course be combined. However, it seems clear from the facts of the case that her consent was not impaired in any of these ways.

There is no doubt that she acted intentionally. She was certainly capable of rational action.[31] As the Court found: 'though infatuated, there is no evidence to shew that she was in such a state of mental imbecility as to justify the inference that she was unable to take care of herself or to manage her own affairs'.[32] Unlike the aunt in *Stivactas*, the novice suffered 'no want of mental power'.[33] Furthermore, she exercised her rational powers. She acted in light of the reasons she perceived herself to have.[34] As the Court said, her actions were 'referable to her own willing submission to the vows she took and to the rules which she approved, and to her own enthusiastic devotion to the life and work of the sisterhood'.[35] It was the value of joining this particular religious community which drove her to transfer the property. Against the light of these goals which she set for herself her conduct in transferring the assets to the Mother Superior seems perfectly rational.

Nor is there any doubt that she acted *knowingly*. She was an associate of the convent for eighteen months before joining as a full member. During this time, she became familiar with the rules of the sisterhood, and what was required of full members. Despite receiving advice from her family against joining, she decided to take the plunge. The Court found that she 'possessed intelligence, educated intelligence, above the average'.[36] She knew exactly what she was doing.

By acting intentionally and knowingly, the nun certainly exercised a choice, but was it a *free* choice? The court was clear that she was not the victim of coercion or

[28] Birks and Chin, 'On the Nature of Undue Influence' (n 12) 68.

[29] The relevant normative power in this case where a gift was made is consent rather than promise. However, the issue is the same: whether the will to exercise the power is impaired?

[30] cf WNR Lucy, 'Contract as a Mechanism of Distributive Justice' (1989) 9 Oxford Journal of Legal Studies 132, 137–39.

[31] Mindy Chen-Wishart, 'Undue Influence: Vindicating Relationships of Influence' (2006) 59 Current Legal Problems 231, 238; Chen-Wishart, 'Undue Influence: *Beyond* Impaired Consent and Wrongdoing towards a Relational Analysis' (n 5) 219.

[32] *Allcard v Skinner* (n 15) 178. [33] ibid 189. [34] ibid 137. [35] ibid 184.

[36] ibid 165.

manipulation. But was her choice free in the broader sense that she had reasonable alternative courses of action or options to choose between?[37] This is an important requirement. The victim of a highwayman is free when she hands over her purse in the sense that she acts intentionally and knowingly, but we would not say she is free in the richer sense of that word, by which we mean that she has viable alternative courses of action open to her. Did the novice have reasonable options to choose between?

It is clear that she did. She turned to the sisterhood because she was unhappy at home and wanted to dedicate her life to good works. It hardly needs saying that joining a nunnery is not the only way to free yourself from your family and make a difference. Therefore, she had a choice; she could have pursued her goals in a different way. In Lindley LJ's words, she 'chose it as the best for herself',[38] and not because she had to because of the circumstances she found herself in, or because she had no alternative.[39]

One might object that the relevant point for assessing whether the novice had a free choice is not *before* she enters the sisterhood as a full-member, but rather *after*, when she actually transferred the property.[40] At this point, she had turned away from her family, and had bound herself to the rules and expectations of the order. At that point, can we say she exercised a free choice? I believe that we can. Although she was bound by the rules of the order, she had a legal right to leave, and the rules of the order themselves were clear that she could leave if she wanted. Given this, and the fact that she had just received a substantial bequest, it seems implausible to say that at the time she transferred the property she had no viable alternative courses of action open to her.

One might argue that this takes no account of the fact that after joining she would have attached special weight to remaining in the sisterhood. Having become a full-member, living up to the expectations of the order became one of her central or overriding goals. By that point, complying with the order's rules was central to her wellbeing and sense of self. This would have exerted considerable ethical and psychological pressure, making it hard to exercise a free choice. From the point of view of a nun, which is what she had committed to be, she had to make the gift: any alternative course of action would have seriously compromised her personal integrity. Therefore, the argument goes, she had no real choice but to transfer the property.

[37] For defences of free choice in this sense as accounts of voluntary action or responsibility see Lucy, 'Contract as a Mechanism of Distributive Justice' (n 30) 133, 139; Stephen A Smith, 'Contracting under Pressure: A Theory of Duress' (1997) 56 The Cambridge Law Journal 343, 361; HLA Hart, *Punishment and Responsibility: Essays in the Philosophy of Law* (Clarendon Press 1968) 152; J Beatson, A Burrows, and J Cartwright, *Anson's Law of Contract* (28th edn, Oxford University Press 2002) 280–81; Ewan McKendrick, 'The Further Trevails of Duress' in Andrew Burrows and Lord Rodger (eds), *Mapping the Law: Essays in Memory of Peter Birks* (Oxford University Press 2006) 190–92.

[38] *Allcard v Skinner* (n 15) 178.

[39] Chen-Wishart, 'Undue Influence: Vindicating Relationships of Influence' (n 31) 238; Chen-Wishart, 'Undue Influence: *Beyond* Impaired Consent and Wrongdoing towards a Relational Analysis' (n 5) 201, 207, 219.

[40] This was the view of the Court of Appeal, *Allcard v Skinner* (n 15) 178, though not of Kakewich J, who was the judge at first instance.

The trouble with this argument is that it takes no account of the value of the freedom to change one's mind.[41] It is true that from the point of view of a nun, there is no real choice but to comply with the rules of the order. But we should evaluate the nun's actions from an *all things considered* perspective. From that point of view, even though her commitment to the order would have given her special reasons to transfer the property, that does not mean that there won't have existed viable alternative courses of action for her to choose, and indeed in certain circumstances she might have a duty to compromise her personal integrity to pursue these other ends.

What would be the result of the view that in circumstances like these that there was a lack of reasonable alternatives? It would commit one to saying that even though the novice thought she was acting charitably, her actions were not because they were involuntary. She had no choice but to act in the way she did. This seems not only untrue but insulting.[42]

Contra Birks and Yin, on no plausible account of how the novice's will might have been impaired is it possible to say on the facts that she did not consent to transfer the property. Her actions were intentional, she knew what she was doing, and she exercised her choice freely. As Lindley LJ said in the case: 'she chose the life and work; such fetters as bound her were voluntarily put upon by herself; she could shake them off at any time had she thought fit, and had she had the courage so to do'.[43]

In summary, attempts by promise theorists (or more broadly their intellectual ancestors the will theorists) of contract to justify the undue influence doctrine by inflating the promise principle fail. Not only does this strategy lose sight of the pro tanto obligation to perform one's promise in these cases, reflected in the fact that typically these transactions are voidable rather than void; but, furthermore, achieving the primacy of promise by inflation sits uncomfortably with the facts of the leading case in this area, *Allcard v Skinner*, where there is no doubt that the will of the victim of undue influence was not impaired.

2.2 Is wrongdoing necessary?

I have argued that the promise theory does not offer a plausible alternative justification for the undue influence defence. Rather, on the republican view the doctrine has a composite nature: it is the product of the interaction between the promise principle and the principle against exploitation. One of the problems with the promise-based account is that it is under-inclusive. It cannot explain cases like

[41] For a discussion of this value see Dori Kimel, 'Personal Autonomy and Change of Mind in Promise and in Contract' in Gregory Klass, George Letsas, and Prince Saprai (eds), *Philosophical Foundations of Contract Law* (Oxford University Press 2014); John Gardner, *From Personal Life to Private Law* (Oxford University Press 2018) ch 5.

[42] We can make an analogy with other walks of life: does a teacher teach because she has no alternative? Hill, 'Exploitation' (n 6) 668: 'if social conditioning vitiates free and consensual action, then everyone is unfree as all behavior is the product of each individual's own psychological history, itself a function of the totality of the individual's interaction with the external world'; Chen-Wishart, 'Undue Influence: Vindicating Relationships of Influence' (n 31) 238; Chen-Wishart, 'Undue Influence: *Beyond* Impaired Consent and Wrongdoing towards a Relational Analysis' (n 5) 201, 207, 208.

[43] *Allcard v Skinner* (n 15) 184.

Allcard, where it is clear that the novice's will to transfer the assets was not impaired. However, one might object that the republican account that I defend suffers from an under-inclusivity problem too.

This is because it is usually thought that exploitation requires *active* advantage-taking. As Joel Feinberg argues, normally we think of the exploiter as someone who 'plays on' the weaknesses of the victim, to achieve a benefit for himself.[44] So, for example, he might 'offer inducements, employ flattery, beg or beseech; he can try alluring portrayals or seductive suggestions; he can appeal to duty, sympathy, friendship, or greed, probing constantly for the character trait whose cultivation will yield the desired response'.[45] This though seems to present a problem for the republican account of undue influence, because there are cases where undue influence has been found even though there was no evidence of this kind of shabby behaviour on the part of the alleged exploiter.

Allcard is a case in point. The court went to great lengths to emphasize that the Mother Superior's behaviour was beyond reproach.[46] She did not seek to profit personally from the transaction, but received the gifts believing that she was serving the novice's own best interests.[47]

Another good example is the three-party case of *Credit Lyonnais Bank Nederland NV v Burch*.[48] The defendant, Helen Burch, worked in a junior capacity for Andrea Pelosi's tour operating company. Pelosi wanted to increase the company overdraft facility from £250,000 to £270,000. Pelosi knew Burch personally: she had visited his family in Italy and London and occasionally she babysat for him. Pelosi asked her whether she would stand as surety for the increased company overdraft he wanted to take out with the claimant bank. She agreed to Pelosi's proposal, and gave to the bank an unlimited second charge over her flat, and a without limit all moneys personal guarantee. This was despite the fact she did not receive independent legal advice and that she did not know the extent of the company's indebtedness, or the extent of the overdraft facility Pelosi was seeking. Subsequently, the company went into liquidation owing some £60,000 to the claimant bank. Not being able to recover the money from the company, the bank called in the security with Burch. Burch though refused to pay, and this led the bank to bring proceedings for possession of her flat. Burch raised a defence on the grounds that Pelosi had exercised undue influence to get her to agree to the terms of the suretyship, and that the defendant bank had constructive notice of his actions. The Court of Appeal agreed with Burch and relieved her of the duty to perform the contract.

It is difficult to account for Burch's right to rescind the transaction on the ground that the bank behaved in a reprehensible manner. The bank's solicitor wrote twice to Birch to advise her of the unlimited nature of the charge, questioning whether

[44] Feinberg, *The Moral Limits of the Criminal Law: Harmless Wrongdoing* (n 6) 178–79.

[45] ibid 181. [46] *Allcard v Skinner* (n 15) 214–15.

[47] Birks and Chin, 'On the Nature of Undue Influence' (n 12) 67–68; Chen-Wishart, 'Undue Influence: Vindicating Relationships of Influence' (n 31) at 237–38, 259–60; Chen-Wishart, 'Undue Influence: *Beyond* Impaired Consent and Wrongdoing towards a Relational Analysis' (n 5) 201, 206–07, 214–15.

[48] *Credit Lyonnais Bank Nederland NV v Burch* [1997] 1 All ER 144.

this was 'actually what had been agreed?', and encouraged her to seek independent legal advice. Burch wrote back saying independent advice wasn't necessary. Despite this, the court ruled that Burch had the right to set the agreement aside. Moreover, Millet LJ suggested that even if she had got independent advice and followed it, this would not have been enough to save the agreement. The advice would need to be competent, and 'no competent solicitor could advise her to enter into the guarantee in the terms she did'. In other words, the transaction would need to be substantively fair for the court to enforce it.[49]

Neither the Mother Superior in *Allcard*, nor the bank in *Burch*, appear to have played on or actively taken advantage of the weaknesses of the other party. Does this mean that we cannot say that they acted exploitatively, and that the justification for the right to rescind in these cases must lie elsewhere? In my view, it does not. In his account of exploitation, Feinberg makes an important distinction between the 'active' variety of exploitation, where the exploiter deliberately procures an unjust benefit by playing on the weaknesses of the other party, and 'passive' exploitation, where the exploiter's receipt of her unjust gain is unplanned or not the product of the exploiter's deliberate manipulation of the vulnerabilities of the other party, and instead 'comes through the inadvertent receiving of benefits and consequent refusal to make restitution'.[50]

With passive exploitation, the unfairness consists in the *retention* of benefits or gains in circumstances where the recipient is aware of some morally relevant weakness on the part of the transferor which caused the transfer. It does not require, unlike active exploitation, the recipient to have deliberately manipulated the transferor to procure the benefit: 'The enrichment is often more like a windfall than it is like reaping the fruits of one's larceny, burglary, or fraud.'[51] This *passive* variety of exploitation, which (Feinberg's important contribution aside) is largely neglected in the philosophical literature, plays an extremely important role in law.

It was recognized as a concern by the courts as long ago as the eighteenth century, in the case of *Bridgemann v Green*, where due to the undue influence of his butler, a man gifted money to the butler's wife and brother. Despite the fact that the wife and brother were not involved in the butler's exercise of undue influence, they were nevertheless required by the court to make restitution of the money they received. Speaking for the court, Lord Wilmot enunciated the following principle to justify the result: 'Let the hand receiving it be ever so chaste, yet if it comes through a corrupt polluted channel, the obligation of restitution will follow it.'[52]

Why is this a variety of exploitation? The reason is that by retaining a benefit in circumstances where the recipient is aware of some morally relevant weakness on the part of the transferor which caused the transfer, the recipient is exploiting,

[49] ibid 155. Chen-Wishart Mindy, 'The *O'Brien* Principle and Substantive Unfairness' (1997) 56 The Cambridge Law Journal 60; Birks and Chin, 'On the Nature of Undue Influence'(n 12) 83.

[50] Feinberg, *The Moral Limits of the Criminal Law: Harmless Wrongdoing* (n 6)196.

[51] ibid 198.

[52] *Bridgeman v Green* (1757) Wilm 56, 64–65; 97 ER 22, 25.

or deliberately taking advantage of, that weakness.[53] It does not matter that the recipient did not deliberately manipulate the transferor to procure the benefit, by, for example, exercising undue influence, as the butler did in *Bridgemann*. In this way, as Feinberg argues, 'From the moral point of view, the failure to return … hardly differs from deliberate fraud'.[54]

With this concept of passive exploitation in place, we can see how both the Mother Superior in *Allcard* and the bank in *Burch*, by refusing to give up gains which they received due to relational vulnerabilities on the part of the transferors were at the point of retention taking advantage of those weaknesses (even though they did not play on these vulnerabilities to procure the transfers in the first place). We all have a duty not to exploit people, the Mother Superior's and the bank's retention of gains in spite of the fact that they know they have been received from the transferors because of some morally relevant weakness is a breach of that duty, which grounds an obligation on their part to make restitution.

Although I call this type of exploitation passive, following Feinberg, it is important to clarify that even passive exploitation has an active element. This is because passive exploitation requires retention, that is, a decision on the part of the transferee to keep the gain, despite knowing that it has been made as a result of some morally relevant weakness on the transferor's part. The primary duty not to exploit the transferor is breached at the point of retention, and this is what triggers the transferee's secondary or remedial duty to make restitution of the gain or its value. Therefore, for liability to be triggered the transferee must know of the receipt of the benefit and the morally dubious circumstances in which the transfer took place. These facts trigger the primary duty not to exploit.[55] At this point, the transferee has a decision to make. Does she return the benefit received, or does she instead take advantage of the morally relevant weakness that caused the transfer by holding onto or retaining the benefit in spite of what she knows? If she chooses the latter course of action, she breaches her duty not to exploit the transferor, and this triggers the remedial duty to make restitution of the benefit received or its value.

I present the concept of passive exploitation here as a way of explaining using the exploitation rationale of the defence of undue influence in cases like *Allcard*, *Burch*, and *Bridgemann*, where the promisee or transferee (as the case may be) did not deliberately take advantage of the weaknesses of the other party to *procure* the transfer. In these passive cases, the breach of the duty not to exploit takes place not when the transfer is procured, but when the recipients hold onto or *retain* the benefits received despite knowing that the circumstances in which the transfer was

[53] The requirement that the weakness be morally relevant is an important one. So, for example, there is no passive exploitation when I gain because a seller is spontaneously mistaken about the value of his goods.

[54] Feinberg, *The Moral Limits of the Criminal Law: Harmless Wrongdoing* (n 6) 210. And see Lord Eldon's affirmation of the principle a century later in *Huguenin v Baseley* (1807) 14 Ves Jun 273, 289; 33 ER 526, 532.

[55] The duty cannot be triggered without these forms of knowledge, because otherwise it would be a duty with which we cannot comply—violating the 'ought implies can' injunction. See further Prince Saprai, 'Restitution Without Corrective Justice' (2006) 14 Restitution Law Review 41, 46–47.

made were morally dubious, for example, because a third party has exercised undue influence on the transferor (*Burch* or *Bridgemann*), or because the transferee has failed to comply with her altruistic duty to look out for the interests of the other party (*Allcard*). Although my purposes here are restricted to explaining undue influence and more broadly unconscionability defences in the law of contract, it is important to note that the use of the concept of passive exploitation to explain some of these cases may have broader implications. For Birks and Yin doctrines like undue influence and unconscionability are underpinned by a broader principle of preventing unjust enrichment.

In my view, an unjust enrichment analysis or interpretation of these cases does not rival my exploitation-based account. This is because unjust enrichment law itself is best understood as animated by a principle of preventing exploitation. It goes beyond the scope of this book to argue for this view fully. However, it is worth making some brief remarks. The core case of unjust enrichment is generally taken to be the case of the mistaken payment.[56] Jack pays money into Jill's bank without her knowledge. Jack thought he owed her the money. It turned out that he did not. Jack had made a mistake. As a matter of law, in these circumstances, Jill comes under a duty to make restitution of the money or its value. Birks argued this is because Jill has been unjustly enriched at Jack's expense. However, it is difficult to see what the moral basis for this legal claim is. After all, Jill was not at fault for receiving the money, and it was Jack who made the mistake. The balance of the equities appears if anything to be in Jill's favour, and yet the law imposes a duty on her to make restitution.

These justificatory difficulties disappear though once we recognize the relevance of passive exploitation in such cases. As in cases like *Allcard* and *Burch*, although Jill has done nothing wrong in how she came by the money, she will be at fault if she refuses to return the money or its value once she is aware of Jack's mistake. This is because by holding onto the money in these circumstances she is passively exploiting Jack's mistake.

Unjust enrichment lawyers have been largely dismissive of so called 'defendant-sided' accounts of the law of unjust enrichment, such as the exploitation analysis defended here, and have preferred instead 'claimant-sided' approaches which focus on the impaired will or defective consent of the transferor (as we have seen with Birks and Yin's account of undue influence). Three-party cases (loosely based on *Bridgemann v Green*) are routinely used in the classroom to show why the defendant-sided view is wrong: A points gun at B, and says to B 'pay money to C, or else I shoot'. B pays over the money. C has a duty to make restitution of the money received from B or its value, even though C was not implicated in A's duress. Therefore, it must surely follow that C's liability depends on B's lack of consent to the transfer, rather than any wrongdoing on C's part? No. Even if C was not implicated in A's duress, if she chose to hang onto the gain, even after becoming aware that it was received as a result of A's duress, then she would at that point be guilty of passively exploiting,

[56] Peter Birks, *Unjust Enrichment* (2nd edn, Oxford University Press 2005) 5–9.

or taking advantage of, the fact that B had a gun to his head when he transferred the money.

This exploitation-based account of unjust enrichment is not only appealing in the sense of providing a moral justification for these cases of restitution, but also has longstanding support in the case law. Take, for example, the classic case of *Kelly v Solari*.[57] This is usually the first case a student will learn on a restitution course. The Court of Exchequer held that where money is paid because of a liability mistake (such as in my hypothetical *Jack v Jill* above), and where absent the mistake the money would not have been transferred, the payer is entitled to restitution from the recipient. When we look closely though at the reasons the court gave for why restitution should be ordered, we do not find support for the dominant claimant-sided account of unjust enrichment. Rather, the court's reasoning supports the republican exploitation-based analysis that I defend here. Parke B said that where a mistaken payment is made, 'an action will lie to recover it back, and it is against conscience to retain it; though a demand may be necessary in those cases in which the party receiving may have been ignorant of the mistake'.[58]

It could not be clearer that the basis of the decision was the fact that the recipient was unconscientiously taking advantage of the payer's mistake by holding onto the payment despite knowing that the payer was mistaken. This explains why Parke B says a 'demand may be necessary' where the payee receives the money ignorant of the mistake. The demand makes the payee aware of the mistake, and if in spite of that knowledge the payee refuses to return the money, there will be a clear breach of the duty not to exploit.

Similarly, Lord Mansfield said, over a century before *Kelly v Solari*, that the action for recovery of a mistaken payment—the action for 'money had and received'—was 'a liberal action in the nature of a bill of equity; and if, under the circumstances of the case, it appears that the defendant cannot in conscience retain what is the subject matter of it, the plaintiff may well support this action'.[59] More recently, this interpretation of the action was affirmed by the High Court of Australia in *Roxborough v Rothmans of Pall Mall Australia Ltd*.[60] Gummow J insisted that the basis of the action was the prevention of unconscionable conduct. In a money had and received case, he argued the central question was whether it was unconscionable for the recipient to retain moneys she was never intended to receive.[61] This interference with the claimant's rights explains why the law attributes responsibility to the recipient in particular rather than someone else to make restitution to the claimant.[62] Exploitation and its legal cognate unconscionability explain the normative connection between the parties. It is the recipient's breach of her primary duty not to exploit the claimant, which explains her secondary or remedial duty to make restitution.

[57] *Kelly v Solari* (1841) 9 M & W 54; 152 ER24. [58] ibid 58; 26.

[59] *Clarke v Shee* (1774) 1 Cowp 197, 199–200; 98 ER 1041, 1042.

[60] *Roxborough v Rothmans of Pall Mall Australia Ltd* (2001) 76 ALJR 203. [61] ibid 225.

[62] ibid 217. Following Paul Finn, 'Equitable Doctrine and Discretion in Remedies' in WR Cornish, Richard Nolan, and Janet O'Sullivan (eds), *Restitution Past, Present and Future: Essays in Honour of Gareth Jones* (Hart Publishing 1998) 252. See also Ben Kremer, 'Restitution and Unconscientiousness: Another View' (2003) 119 Law Quarterly Review 188, 189.

Of course, Birks had no truck with the idea that unconscionability in the sense I have developed it in this chapter played any justificatory role in unjust enrichment cases.[63] He brushed under the carpet awkward references in cases like *Kelly v Solari*, by insisting that what the courts had in mind was merely what he called 'unconscionability *ex post*'. The basis of the money had and received claim was not—despite appearances to the contrary—unconscionable conduct by the recipient. Rather, liability was strict: arising either because the recipient was not entitled to the money due to a failure of the transfer's basis, or because of the impairment of the transferor's will. On Birks' view, fault by the defendant played no role in the claim. The reason the courts used the language of unconscionability could be explained, he argued, by the fact that in circumstances where there is already strict liability to make restitution, it becomes unconscionable for the recipient to retain the money in defiance of a pre-existing legal duty. This is unconscientiousness ex post: 'which is no more than a reflection of the prior determination that other facts require restitution to be made'.[64]

Birks' explanation of the language of unconscionability in the cases is both contrived and reductive. There is a simpler and more natural interpretation and it is that when the courts justified restitution on the grounds of the defendant's unconscionable conduct, they were invoking the moral principle of preventing exploitation to justify the law. As I have argued, exploitation has both active and passive varieties. Passive exploitation plays a central role in explaining liability for unjust enrichment. Contra Birks, the duty to make restitution in these cases does not pre-exist the recipient's awareness of the morally dubious circumstances in which benefits have been conferred, but rather arises when the recipient becomes aware of these facts and despite this knowledge chooses to hold onto or retain these benefits. In that context, the recipient breaches her duty not to exploit the weaknesses of the other party; and it is the unconscionable nature of this action which makes the enrichment unjust and justifies the legal obligation to make restitution.

In summary, I have argued in this section that the concept of passive exploitation helps to explain restitution or rescission in those cases of undue influence like *Allcard*, *Burch*, and *Bridgemann*, where the promisee or transferee does not actively manipulate the weaknesses of the other party to procure the promise or transfer. Given this, we can reject the objection that an exploitation-based analysis of undue influence is under-inclusive at the level of explaining the case law. Although I cannot develop the argument fully here, I have argued that unjust enrichment is not a rival

[63] Although he did at one time argue that there were a category of unjust enrichment cases involving 'free acceptance' that did have defendant-sided considerations as their rationale. Peter Birks, *An Introduction to the Law of Restitution* (Clarendon Press 1989) 265–93. However, he subsequently changed his view on this. Peter Birks, 'In Defence of Free Acceptance' in Andrew Burrows (ed), *Understanding the Law of Obligations: Essays on Contract, Tort and Restitution* (Clarendon Press 1991).

[64] Birks, *Unjust Enrichment* (n 56) 5–6. The view of unconscionability taken—either as on my view constitutive of the cause of action or on Birks' as merely reflecting the existence of a pre-existing strict duty to make restitution—may have important remedial consequences. See Mitchell McInnes, 'Unjust Enrichment: A Reply to Professor Weinrib' [2001] Restitution Law Review 29, 42–43.

theory of these cases, but rather as an area or category of law is itself best interpreted or justified by a moral concern to prevent exploitation.

2.3 Undue influence without substantive unfairness?

For a transaction to be exploitative, it has to be substantively unfair or contrary to the promisor's or transferor's interests.[65] So, for example, if I say to my children 'I will let you play video games, provided you promise to do your homework', I am clearly taking advantage of their desire to play video games to achieve my own ends which are to get them to do their homework. However, one would not say that the transaction is exploitative in the pejorative sense of that term. This is because the transaction is not substantively unfair or harmful to my children. They are not harmed by having to do their homework; far from it, they benefit.[66]

This raises a potential objection to my exploitation-based interpretation of the undue influence and more broadly unconscionability doctrines in contract law. There appear to be cases where transactions have been set-aside for undue influence and unconscionability where it seems there was *no* substantive unfairness. This brings into question whether substantive unfairness is really a requirement for undue influence or unconscionability.

The objection though is based on an important confusion of thought. One of the difficulties with substantive unfairness as a requirement of exploitation is that we cannot know whether a particular transaction is harmful without having in place a background moral theory. The result, as Richard Arneson has pointed out, is that there will 'be as many competing conceptions of exploitation as theories of what persons owe to each other'.[67]

The trouble is that many lawyers have lost sight of this important truth. Instead, they have come to strongly associate substantive unfairness with the ancient idea of the *laesio enormis* ('abnormal harm') which allowed a promisor to rescind an agreement where the exchange of values was significantly one-sided in the other party's favour. This helped to ensure that contracts took place at an *iustum pretium* ('just price'). These principles of achieving equality of exchange have been enormously influential and have significantly influenced how lawyers interpret the substantive unfairness requirement when applying doctrines like undue influence and unconscionability. It has become almost an unshakeable truth in Anglo-American contract law that a contract is substantively unfair when significantly unequal values have been exchanged, or when the weaker party buys a good or service at significantly more than its market price, or sells at significantly less.[68] In the absence of inequality of

[65] Wertheimer, *Exploitation* (n 6) at 6, 22, 51, 208; Hill, 'Exploitation' (n 6) 641, 680, 689; Feinberg, *The Moral Limits of the Criminal Law: Harmless Wrongdoing* (n 6) 193–94.

[66] Mindy Chen-Wishart, *Contract Law* (2nd edn, Oxford University Press 2008) 349; Feinberg, *The Moral Limits of the Criminal Law: Harmless Wrongdoing* (n 6) 180, 184.

[67] Arneson, 'Exploitation' (n 6) 350. See also Wertheimer, *Exploitation* (n 6) 10; Hill, 'Exploitation' (n 6) 641, 680.

[68] Stephen Smith, *Atiyah's Introduction to the Law of Contract* (6th edn, Oxford University Press 2006) 321; Hugh Collins, *The Law of Contract* (4th edn, LexisNexis Butterworths 2003) 270; Hugh Collins, *Regulating Contracts* (Oxford University Press 1999) 256, 259–60; Hugh Collins, 'Good Faith

exchange of this kind, it is generally thought that, even when the other elements of exploitation are present, contracts should be enforced. As an account of substantive unfairness, inequality of exchange has been defended on a variety of grounds, including Hegelian, teleological, and Marxist.[69]

It is inequality of exchange as an interpretation of the substantive unfairness requirement, which might lead some to doubt the relevance of the exploitation analysis of undue influence and unconscionability that I defend in this chapter. This is because there are cases where the courts have refused to enforce transactions on the grounds of undue influence or unconscionability despite the fact that they did not involve unequal exchanges. Take, for example, the Canadian case *Morrison v Coast Finance Ltd*, where as security for a small loan, an elderly lady mortgaged her home which was her only substantial asset. Even though the transaction took place on normal banking terms, it was set-aside on grounds of unconscionability.[70] Similarly, there are many three-party surety cases involving wives who put up their matrimonial homes to secure the business debts of their husbands, which the courts have rescinded on the grounds of undue influence even though the transactions took place at market rates.[71]

These cases are important, but they do not actually cast doubt on my claim that substantive unfairness is a requirement for undue influence or unconscionability. The claim that they do rests on the widely shared assumption among lawyers that substantive unfairness and inequality of exchange are synonymous. This though is a fallacy. Inequality of exchange is a theory of substantive unfairness, or an account of why a contract might cause the promisor harm. The cases above cast doubt on whether inequality of exchange is adequate as a theory. However, this does not mean that substantive unfairness is not a requirement in these cases. If the transactions above are not substantively unfair, because they do not involve unequal exchanges, nevertheless they may be substantively unfair or harmful to the promisors involved on other grounds, or from the point of view of alternative theories of substantive

in European Contract Law' (1994) 14 Oxford Journal of Legal Studies 229, 249; Ewan McKendrick, *Contract Law* (2nd edn, Oxford University Press 2005) 793; Beatson, Burrows, and Cartwright, *Anson's Law of Contract* (n 37) 297–98, 305. cf Chen-Wishart, *Contract Law* (n 66) 377–78, who adopts a notion of substantive unfairness that goes beyond mere inequality of exchange.

[69] For Hegelian accounts see Peter Benson, 'Abstract Right and the Possibility of a Nondistributive Conception of Contract: Hegel and Contemporary Contract Theory' (1989) 10 Cardozo Law Review 1077; Alan Brudner, 'Reconstructing Contracts' (1993) 43 The University of Toronto Law Journal 1. Teleological theories have been defended by James Gordley, 'Contract Law in the Aristotelian Tradition' in Peter Benson (ed), *The Theory of Contract Law: New Essays* (Cambridge University Press 2001); Stephen Smith, 'In Defence of Substantive Fairness' (1996) 112 Law Quarterly Review 128. For a critique of these Hegelian and Aristotelian accounts see Prince Saprai, 'Against Equality of Exchange' (2010) 21 King's Law Journal 71. On the Marxist interpretation see Richard J Arneson, 'What's Wrong with Exploitation?' (1981) 91 Ethics 202, 210. However, Robert Nozick argued that the labour theory of value is incompatible with equality of exchange. Robert Nozick, *Anarchy, State, and Utopia* (Basil Blackwell 1974) 256–60. See also Wertheimer, *Exploitation* (n 6) 229, 231.

[70] *Morrison v Coast Finance Ltd* (1965) 55 DLR (2d) 710.

[71] See, for example, *Barclays Bank plc v O'Brien* (n 13). See also Chen-Wishart, *Contract Law* (n 66) 377.

unfairness. In other words, accepting this objection to the exploitation-based theory of undue influence would be to throw out the baby with the bathwater.

I am not going to attempt here to provide an alternative theory of substantive fairness. As Arneson said, this would require an entire moral theory, and that task goes beyond the scope of this book. Rather, my central purpose here is to make the more modest claim that the inadequacies of inequality of exchange as a theory of substantive unfairness do not necessarily mean that the fundamental moral concern in these cases is not exploitation.

3. Conclusion

As I argued in the previous chapter, *both* divisionists and promise theorists are mistaken about the precise type of relation that contract law involves. Divisionists, like Kimel, associate contract law with the realm of strangers, whilst promise theorists like Fried tend to assume that the same or a very similar kind of trust that obtains in promise between intimates, friends, and so forth, is also invoked in contract. Both views are mistaken. As Fuller argued, contractual partners are neither strangers nor intimates. Rather, they are 'friendly strangers'.[72] Contractual relations typically involve a thinner kind of trust than the thick trust we normally find in close relations between, for example, friends and intimates. In contract, the trust invoked by the promisor is restricted to the contractual relation: the promisor invites the promisee to trust that he will perform his contractual obligations.

The distinction between thin and thick trust is important, because it affects in significant ways what the parties to these relations owe to each other. This is brought out in the context of undue influence cases. When a contract takes place in the context of a pre-existing relationship of thick trust, the existence of that level of trust between the parties triggers a duty in the promisee to look out for the interests of the other party, or alternatively if she wishes to deal self-interestedly—to delegate that responsibility to an independent third party like a lawyer.[73] The danger is that the promisee, in disregard of her altruistic duty, might exploit the thick trust between the parties to secure advantages for herself. A republican theory of contract law, according to which contract law has as a constitutive end the promotion of trust-based cooperation between the parties, will be acutely alive to this risk. On the republican view, the purpose of the defence of undue influence is to prevent the abuse of thick trust when contracts take place between close relations, intimates, friends, family, and so forth.

I have argued that the application criteria for the defence, the language the courts use when applying it, and the facts and outcomes of undue influence cases strongly support the republican interpretation. Due to its top-down nature, the promise theory is insufficiently sensitive to these facts about the law on the ground. Instead,

72 Fuller, 'Human Interaction and the Law' (n 1) 27.

73 Chen-Wishart, 'Undue Influence: *Beyond* Impaired Consent and Wrongdoing towards a Relational Analysis' (n 5) 201, 220–21.

the promise theorist artificially inflates the role of the promise principle to achieve its justificatory primacy by claiming that when contracts are rescinded for undue influence the relevant normative concern is the impairment of the promisor's will to make the promise. But this loses sight of the promisor's pro tanto duty to perform the contract which is subject to his right to rescind. In other words, it cannot explain the fact that typically in undue influence cases the contract is voidable rather than void, that is, it is perfectly valid unless the promisor chooses to set it aside. Furthermore, the promise theory cannot account for the classic undue influence case of *Allcard v Skinner*, where there it is clear that the novice's will was not impaired, and yet undue influence was nevertheless found.

As I have argued in previous chapters, on the republican view the ends of contract law are contingent, underdetermined, and pluralistic. Due to these features, it is better able to work with contract doctrine from the bottom up. Applying this approach, we see that undue influence is a composite doctrine, which is the product of the interaction between the promise principle and the principle against exploitation. The presence of undue influence does not usually impair the will of the promisor, but it does provide him with a right to set the contract aside should he wish to do so.

The worries that this exploitation-based account is under-inclusive of the law are misplaced. First, the concept of passive exploitation explains cases of undue influence like *Allcard*, *Burch*, and *Bridgemann*, where the promisee or transferee does not actively take advantage of her influence over the other party to procure the transaction. It is sufficient for this passive variety of exploitation that the promisee refuses to give up a gain which she now knows she received in circumstances involving undue influence. Secondly, the fact that undue influence has been found in cases like *Morrison*, where there is no inequality of exchange, does not mean that exploitation is not present. It is a requirement of exploitation that a transaction be substantively unfair or harmful to the promisor. Inequality of exchange is one particularly influential conception of substantive unfairness. Its apparent inadequacies though, even if true, do not call into doubt the possibility that there are other rival conceptions of substantive unfairness that can explain these difficult cases.

This exploitation-based rationale provides a compelling account of the undue influence defence. Preventing exploitation has always been a concern of republican theories of freedom, which have traditionally emphasized the ideal of non-domination by others. One should have control over one's life, and not be the plaything of others—even if this means that one lives a materially worse life as a result. Better to be free than a contented slave. This broader republican concern plays an important role in shaping another important contractual doctrine: restraint of trade. It is to consideration of this doctrine and its relationship to the value of freedom that I turn to in Chapter 7.

7

Restraint of Trade and Freedom*

Political liberty in a citizen is that tranquillity of spirit which comes from the opinion each one has of his security, and in order for him to have this liberty the government must be such that one citizen cannot fear another citizen.

Montesquieu[1]

1. Republican Freedom

In Chapter 5 I defended the republican notion of freedom as participation in social and political life, against the traditional liberal view that freedom consists in non-interference from others. Against liberals like John Stuart Mill, I followed Lon Fuller arguing that the liberal ideal leads ultimately to the pursuit of a solitary and atomized existence lacking in the restraints necessary to make human life worth living.

In political life, the source of these restraints are the legal and political rights of others; rights which these fellow members of the political community are entitled to demand on account of their status as free and equal citizens. As I argued in Chapter 4, the legitimacy of a state and its law depends ultimately on the extent to which individual citizens and the political institutions that represent them correctly identify, observe, and enforce these rights.

On this republican conception of freedom, it is not interference with others per se that is morally problematic. Rather, the trouble begins when we, or the political institutions that represent us, interfere with other members of the political community on an arbitrary or unprincipled basis, that is, in a way that is inconsistent or incompatible with their rights to equal concern and respect.

* This chapter is based on and largely reproduces, but with significant additions, revisions, and adaptations, the text of a previously published article of mine entitled 'The Principle Against Self-Enslavement in Contract Law', which appeared in the Journal of Contract Law 26 (2009) 25, copyright © 2009 Reed International Books Australia Pty Limited. The text is used with kind permission of LEXISNEXIS (Australia).

[1] Charles de Secondat baron de Montesquieu, *The Spirit of the Laws* (Anne M Cohler, Basia C Miller, and Harold S Stone trs, Cambridge University Press 1989) 157.

In recent times, the philosopher Philip Pettit has done more than anyone else to revive this distinctively republican account of the value of freedom.[2] At the heart of his conception is the ideal of what he calls 'non-domination', by which he means that to be truly free people should not have to live their lives subject to the arbitrary judgment of others, such that at any moment these others have the unrestrained power to set them back or make their lives go worse. Even if such powers are never exercised, and lives never set back, there is a sense in which the freedom of those subjected to the possible or potential exercise of these powers has been fundamentally compromised. It is this grievance that the republican view of freedom (in contrast to the liberal conception of freedom as non-interference or absence of coercion) highlights. As Pettit says:

> It is the grievance expressed by the wife who finds herself in a position where her husband can beat her at will, and without any possibility of redress; by the employee who dare not raise a complaint against an employer, and who is vulnerable to any range of abuses, some petty, some serious, that the employer may choose to perpetrate; by the debtor who has to depend on the grace of the moneylender, or the bank official, for avoiding utter destitution and ruin; and by the welfare dependent who finds that they are vulnerable to the caprice of a counter clerk for whether or not their children will receive meal vouchers.[3]

In each of these cases, whether or not the more powerful party exercises their power, the weaker party's freedom is fatally undermined. They are all in the position of what the Romans called the *servus* or slave, that is, subject to the arbitrary will or judgment of their master, in contrast to the *liber* or true Roman citizen who as the bearer of civil and political rights was protected from precisely this type of interference by another. Whilst the slave's status was one of being *dominated* by her master, the citizen was free in the republican sense, in that she was *non-dominated*, or, in other words, could not be subject to another's arbitrary will or judgment.[4]

Unlike the slave, the citizen does not 'live at the mercy' or 'in the shadow' of anyone else.[5] This status of non-domination breeds a sense of security or resilience in the citizen that the slave will forever lack.[6] The source of the citizen's confidence is that because of her status, others lack the capacity to interfere on arbitrary grounds with her life or prospects. By contrast, the slave has to live a life of perpetual uncertainty about what her master might do, which might require her to deploy strategic deference, that is, 'to fawn or toady or flatter' her master to improve her prospects. Unlike the citizen, the slave cannot 'look the other in the eye', and is demeaned or degraded by her dependency.[7]

Going back to Fuller's point discussed in Chapter 5, this republican account of freedom is a world away from the Millian ideal of freedom as isolation, which Fuller derided as 'freedom in a void'.[8] Whereas the liberal traditionally has sought the freedom of the heath, for the republican true freedom lies in the city, with the *presence*

[2] Philip Pettit, *Republicanism: A Theory of Freedom and Government* (Oxford University Press 1997).
[3] ibid 5. [4] ibid 31–32. [5] ibid 4–5. [6] ibid 24–26.
[7] ibid 5, 85–88.
[8] Lon L Fuller, 'The Case Against Freedom' in *The Principles of Social Order: Selected Essays of Lon L Fuller* (Kenneth Winston ed, rev edn, Hart Publishing 2002) 321.

rather than the *absence* of others. The conditions of social and political life require a form of *civil* rather than *natural* freedom, which is *constituted* by the protection given to each and every citizen by the due observance, recognition, and enforcement of their civil and political rights. As Pettit says: 'Non-domination ... is the position that someone enjoys when they live in the presence of other people and when, by virtue of social design, none of those others dominates them.'[9] Acknowledging its Roman origins, Pettit captures the view with the phrase: '*libertas* is *civitas*'.[10] Unlike the slave, the citizen is 'a somebody' with respect to others 'and not a nobody'.[11]

There are two kinds of threat to freedom as non-domination. First, there is the risk that the state might attempt to abuse its power by subjecting individual citizens or groups of citizens to arbitrary interference. This type of domination is known as *imperium* in the republican tradition.[12] It is prevented when the state upholds laws and pursues policies that reflect and express equal concern and respect toward its citizens; rather than laws and policies that prefer the interests of particular individuals or groups over others. To achieve this end, the state must take account of and be guided by the shared or common interests of the group and the group's self-understanding of what these interests are.[13] As I argued in Chapter 4, a system of law that shows equal concern and respect toward its citizens is legitimate; it can command the loyalty or allegiance of these citizens or justify an obligation to obey the law.

Such a system of law on the republican view although a form of interference with the *natural* liberty of citizens, does not compromise (even pro tanto) their freedom in the republican sense of that ideal; rather, it is constitutive of the *civil* liberty that those citizens enjoy.[14] However, and as again I argued in Chapter 4, central to the realization of a rule of law that shows equal concern and respect and upholds the principle of integrity is the creation of a rights-respecting culture, where individual citizens and groups are able to contest on the grounds of principle potentially arbitrary exercises of state power. It is here that doctrines like local priority, the separation of powers, and the availability of judicial review play such a critical role.[15]

The second threat to the ideal of non-domination is known as *dominium*. This is the danger that one might be subject to the arbitrary control not of the state but rather other individuals or groups.[16] Contract law is one way in which private individuals or groups might amass dominium or the capacity to control on arbitrary grounds the lives of others. There are two ways that contract could do this.

First, it might make a *causal* contribution. As Robert Nozick showed contract law can create great inequalities of wealth and resources in society. Imagine, Nozick

[9] Pettit, *Republicanism: A Theory of Freedom and Government* (n 2) 67. Pettit makes clear that the relationship between social institutions and the ideal of non-domination is constitutive and not causal: 'the institutions which promote people's freedom as non-domination go to constitute that freedom, not to cause it; the doctrine does not countenance any temporal or causal gulf between civic institutions and the freedom of citizens' (ibid 81). See also ibid 106–09.

[10] ibid 66. [11] ibid 71. [12] ibid 13.

[13] ibid 35–37. Although note that Pettit does not put his arguments in the terms of the state having to show equal concern and respect. However, I believe his arguments are compatible with this Dworkinian reading.

[14] ibid 35–36. [15] ibid 63. [16] ibid 12–13.

famously argued, that goods are initially distributed equally in society. Along comes Wilt Chamberlain—a great basketball player—who has it in his contract with his basketball club that he is to receive a commission from the admission price for every home game he plays. Such is Wilt's popularity that huge numbers of people buy tickets to see him play and he ends up incredibly rich. Nozick argued that the resulting distribution of wealth is—despite the gross inequality—just, because people freely chose to spend their money on going to see Wilt.[17]

Nozick was of course a libertarian, and although the resulting distribution might appear just from that perspective, for the republican such inequalities are a source of consternation. These uneven distributions create power imbalances that lead to the better off being able to exert dominium or arbitrary control over those who have much less. For the republican, the state has a duty to protect citizens from these forms of domination. Whether that should be done through the use of progressive taxation or price regulation is a different question not pursued here.

In the above example, contract law makes a *causal* contribution to the creation of conditions of vast inequalities of resources and wealth that lead to relationships of dominium. My main purpose in this chapter though is with another way contract law creates dominium. As well as its causal role, contract law may play a *constitutive* role in creating relationships of dominium. This occurs when the 'power-conferring' rules of contract law are used by the contractual parties to structure a relationship of dominium between them.[18] Such relations come about when one of the parties transfers too many rights or cedes too much control over central aspects of her life to the other.

Recall that I argued in Chapter 5 that the constitutive function of contract law is to bring about the intrinsically valuable good of trust-based cooperation between the parties. It does this in a unique and distinct way by using legal rules and doctrines to render determinate the terms or structure of the relationship or interaction between the parties. The trouble is that the parties might themselves, relying on freedom of contract or the promise principle and the powers conferred on them by contract law to set the terms of the transaction, structure a relationship that is deeply at odds or subverts the constitutive function of contract law.

Rather than structuring—as it is meant to—intrinsically valuable relationships, contract law and the powers it confers on the parties might be abused to create relationships not built on trust, equality, respect, and so forth, but rather control, inequality, and subjugation. On the republican view, the state through the courts has a duty to step in and prevent the purpose of contract law from being subverted in this way. This is an example—perhaps the prime example—of where the constitutive purpose of contract law although largely underdetermined and capable of being legitimately pursued in a multiplicity of ways by derivative legal rules and doctrines, does *at the limit* function as a negative side-constraint or brake on legal rules and doctrines and the use of contract law in ways that directly or egregiously contradicts

[17] Robert Nozick, *Anarchy, State, and Utopia* (Basil Blackwell 1974) 160–64.

[18] On the power-conferring nature of contract law, see famously HLA Hart, *The Concept of Law* (2nd edn, Clarendon Press 1994) 27–28, 41.

that purpose.[19] Contracts or contract clauses that attempt to structure relationships of domination and subjugation are on the republican view null and void because they are incompatible with contract law's focal or constitutive function. The courts have a legal duty *not* to uphold or enforce them.

Whether a contract creates a relationship of dominium is a matter of degree.[20] The risk of subjugation increases depending on factors such as: whether there are any limits or controls on the discretion of the dominant party;[21] how central the activities the dominant party has control over are to the wellbeing of the weaker party; the geographical domain over which that control ranges; and, the length of the period over which the dominant party has control. Broadly speaking, the less control there is over the discretion of the stronger party (the more 'intense' it is), and the greater its sphere of influence (the larger its 'extent'), the more likely it is that it creates a relationship of dominium or ownership between the two parties.[22] It does not matter whether the dominant party does actually exercise this power. The fact that the dominant party has the capacity to exercise arbitrary judgment over the weaker party compromises, on the republican view, the weaker party's freedom and sense of security and self-respect.

Whether a contract that creates a relationship of domination or servitude is entered into voluntarily by both of the parties does not change the fact that the contract compromises the weaker party's right to be free from domination. This is because, for the republican, the ideal of liberty is based on non-domination.[23] In contrast, for the liberal, what matters is absence of interference, and it has traditionally been a central tenet of liberalism that interference is not impermissible if it was invited consensually or willingly (indeed it may not in such circumstances even amount to interference). This all stems from the priority attached by liberals to the value of personal sovereignty or autonomy.

My purpose in this chapter is to show that this republican stance against contracts that constitutively bring about relationships of subjugation or servitude is reflected in English contract doctrine. I show most prominently in the context of the doctrine of restraint of trade that English courts refuse to enforce or uphold contracts or contract clauses which lead to the self-enslavement of one or both of the contracting parties. This is because the state cannot through its courts lend a hand to promisees who seek, by abusing the practice of contract, to achieve ends that are inimical to the constitutive purpose of contract law which is to promote trust-based cooperation. If such contracts or contract clauses were valid and enforced that would make the state complicit in these forms of domination.

These doctrines cannot be explained by the promise principle alone. If that were all that mattered, then such contracts should be enforced because typically they are

[19] See ch 4, text to nn 111–14.

[20] Pettit, *Republicanism: A Theory of Freedom and Government* (n 2) 77.

[21] See the distinction between strong and weak discretion made by Ronald Dworkin, *Taking Rights Seriously* (Duckworth 1977) 31–33.

[22] This distinction between 'intensity' and 'extent' of control is taken from Pettit, *Republicanism: A Theory of Freedom and Government* (n 2) 57–58.

[23] ibid 62.

entered into voluntarily. Rather, we have to reach beyond the promise principle to the characteristic function of contract law to justify the doctrine. Contracts or contract clauses which create servitude or self-enslavement are void and not enforced by courts because they contradict the focal purpose of contract law which is to structure relationships of cooperation based on trust, equality, and respect.

Nor, as this chapter shows, can such doctrines be explained away on economic grounds. Rather, to do justice to the doctrine in this context we have to appeal to the distinctly republican value of non-domination, which once in place in our interpretative scheme helps to bring out instructive similarities between cases and doctrines that are all too often kept apart. Recognizing the existence of the principle of non-domination and the important role it plays in shaping contract doctrines is essential for achieving integrity or coherence in this area of law.

2. The Principle of Non-Domination

There is a broad principle against domination in contract law that has been alluded to and relied on in the cases. The principle was cited obiter by Cotton LJ in the late-nineteenth-century case, *Re Clarke*,[24] and applied in *Horwood v Millar's Timber and Trading Co*.[25] In *Horwood*, the promisor entered into a moneylending contract, agreeing that he could not, without the lender's consent: quit his job, borrow money, sell or give away any of his property, obtain credit, incur any obligation (legal or moral), or change his address. Lord Cozens-Hardy MR said that the fact that the borrower was an adult man, to whom undue pressure had not been applied, did not mean that he could 'be allowed to enter into any contract he thinks fit affecting his own liberty of action'.[26] In particular, he could not self-enslave himself: the common law would not uphold a 'servile incident', or let the moneylender 'get his clutches round' the borrower:

> Possibly slavery is too strong a word, but it certainly seems to me to savour of serfdom to say 'You shall not leave the house in which you are living without my consent; you shall not dispose of a chair or a table in your house in which I have no charge without my consent, and if you do the whole amount of principal and interest will immediately become payable instead of being payable by instalments.'[27]

In line with the republican interpretation of contract law, the contract in this case was held void because the borrower had 'put himself . . . almost body and soul in the power of this money-lender'.[28] The Court refused to enforce the contract because of its antipathy toward self-enslavement. The contract gave too much control over

[24] *Re Clarke* (1887) 36 Ch D 348, 352. See also Fry LJ's *dictum* in the same case at 357–58.

[25] *Horwood v Millar's Timber and Trading Co* [1917] 1 KB 305.

[26] ibid 311.

[27] ibid 312. cf Scrutton LJ: 'it is not using overstrained or poetical language to say that it [the contract] made this unfortunate man the slave of the money-lender' (ibid 317).

[28] ibid 314.

central areas of the borrower's life to the lender; creating a situation of inequality whereby the borrower was subject to the arbitrary will of the lender.[29]

3. Restraint of Trade

In this section, I show how this broader principle of preventing dominium explains the common law doctrine of restraint of trade. The courts interfere with restraints of trade where they unduly cede too much control over the promisor's central activities to the promisee, with the result that the promisee has the power to subject the promisor to her arbitrary will and judgment. This explains, I will argue, the difference in the way that the courts treat employer-employee restraints and those in business sales. I then go on to refute alternative explanations for the restraint of trade doctrine.

According to restraint of trade, any agreement that restrains a person from the lawful exercise of her trade or employment is prima facie contrary to public policy.[30] Such restraints can only be enforced where they are reasonable in the interests of the contracting parties and of the public.

3.1 Employer-employee restraints

Agreements caught by restraint of trade include those that restrain an employee from setting up a business or working for a rival after she has left the service of an employer. Such agreements are prima facie void. An employer cannot prevent competition from a former employee, or the use by the employee of her own skill and experience, even when gained from the employer: in *Ward v Byrne*,[31] a restraint on a coal merchant's clerk required that once the clerk had left his master's employment he could not either set up business as a coal merchant or work, in any capacity, for another coal merchant in England for nine months. The agreement was in restraint of trade because it violated the 'the right of every man to be at liberty to struggle for his own existence'.[32]

[29] cf *Denny (Trustee) v Denny & Warr* [1919] 1 KB 583, where the Court also recognized the existence of a principle against non-domination but distinguished the case from *Horwood* on the basis that the contract at issue did not restrain personal freedom to the same extent that the contract in *Horwood* did. Interestingly, the Court in *Denny* said that the object, as well as the content, of the agreement was relevant to its enforceability. Whereas the lender in *Horwood* entered into the contract for purely selfish reasons, in *Denny* a father tried by way of the contract to restrict his son's freedom in order to save the son 'from ruin and to induce him to become, if possible, an honourable and useful citizen' (ibid 588). On republican views, such motivational considerations are irrelevant as what matters is whether the contract subjects the weaker party to the other's arbitrary will and judgment.

[30] *Nordenfelt v Maxim Nordenfelt Guns and Ammunition Co Ltd* [1894] AC 535, 565; *Mason v Provident Clothing & Supply Co Ltd* [1913] AC 724.

[31] *Ward v Byrne* (1839) 5 M & W 547; 151 ER 232.

[32] ibid 559; 237. See also: *Bromley v Smith* [1909] 2 KB 235, (agreement to restrain a baker's employee from setting up his own restaurant, held void); *Mineral Water Bottle Exchange and Trade Protection Society v Booth* (1887) 36 Ch 465, (a rule of a society set up to promote the interests of mineral water manufacturers said that 'No member of the society shall employ any traveller, carman or outdoor *employee*, who has left the service of another member, without the consent in writing of

In *Herbert Morris Ltd v Saxelby*,[33] the claimant, who manufactured and sold lifting machinery, in particular: pulley blocks, runways, and travelling cranes sought to enforce an agreement with the defendant who had worked as an engineer for the claimant since leaving school. The defendant had covenanted that he would not:

> at any time during a period of seven years from the date of his ceasing to be employed by the company ... either in the United Kingdom of Great Britain or Ireland carry on either as principal agent servant or otherwise alone or jointly or in connection with any other person firm or company or be concerned or assist directly or indirectly whether for reward or otherwise in the sale or manufacture of pulley blocks hand overhead runways electric overhead runways hand overhead travelling cranes.[34]

Despite the fact that there was no fraud, misrepresentation, deceit, or duress, the covenant was held to be void, as it was an unreasonable restraint of trade. The trouble was that the agreement aimed to take away from the defendant his skill and experience. By doing that it turned the defendant into the property or slave of the employer:

> a man's aptitudes, his skill, his dexterity, his manual or mental ability—all those things which in sound philosophical language are not objective, but subjective—they may and they ought not to be relinquished by a servant; they are not his master's property; they are his own property; they are himself.[35]

By relinquishing these subjective attributes, the defendant had put himself in a situation of 'bondage in regard to his own labour',[36] such that the defendant could not seek any other employment without fear of losing his trade and livelihood. This is why such agreements attract the language of slavery. They deter employees from ever leaving their employment; leaving them at the mercy or control of their employers.

The fact that these agreements have this 'chilling' effect has been explicitly referred to in the case law. In *Mason v Provident Clothing & Supply Co*,[37] a canvasser in the Islington branch of a company agreed that he would not for three years after his employment with the company enter the same or a similar business within twenty-five miles of London. The restraint applied even if he were only employed by the company for a fortnight. It was declared void. The trouble was that the restraint was designed to create disincentives for the man to leave. The drafters of the covenant

his late employer, until after the expiration of two years from his leaving such service.' The rule was a hidden employer-employee covenant which the court refused to enforce because it was an unreasonable restraint of trade); *Eastham v Newcastle United Football Club Ltd* [1964] Ch 413; *Greig v Insole* [1978] 1 WLR 302.

[33] *Herbert Morris Ltd v Saxelby* [1916] 1 AC 688.
[34] ibid 690.
[35] ibid 714. See also *Mason v Provident Clothing & Supply Co Ltd* (n 30) 740–41; *Faccenda Chicken Ltd v Fowler* [1987] Ch 117; *Office Angels Ltd v Rainer-Thomas and O'Connor* [1991] IRLR 214; *Universal Thermosensors Ltd v Hibben* [1992] 1 WLR 840. PS Atiyah, *An Introduction to the Law of Contract* (5th edn, Clarendon Press 1995) 328: 'The skills or experience obtained by an employee do not belong to the employer—they are assets of the employee alone.'
[36] *Herbert Morris Ltd v Saxelby* (n 33) 718.
[37] *Mason v Provident Clothing & Supply Co Ltd* (n 30).

'hoped by means of it to paralyse the earning capabilities of the man if and when he left their service'.[38] Therefore, the restraint was 'penal', 'coercive', and 'tyrannous'; the employee could not 'risk a movement towards his own advancement'.[39]

In *M & S Drapers Ltd v Reynolds*,[40] a drapery firm's collector salesman promised that he would not canvass his employer's customers for five years after the end of his employment. Although the employer had a proprietary right to protect his customers, it was held that the length of the restraint was unreasonable given the lowly position previously occupied by the employee. Denning LJ said that the courts have power to declare such covenants unenforceable because they have a chilling effect:

> if these covenants were given full force, they would tend to reduce his [an employee's] freedom to seek better conditions, even by asking for a rise in wages: because if he is not allowed to get work elsewhere, he is very much at the mercy of his employer.[41]

Lord Denning's words support my claim that what is objectionable about these kinds of restraints is that they give employers dominium over central aspects of the lives of their employees. If the employee cannot, as the court said in *Mason*, 'risk a movement towards his own advancement' he is then, to use Lord Denning's phrase, 'at the mercy of his employer'; the employer has no incentive to treat the employee fairly, or to improve his pay or conditions. Instead, the employer has the power to exercise his arbitrary will and judgment over the employee, with the risk that it will be exercised adversely against the employee. It is the desire of the courts to prevent contract being used to create unequal and controlling relationships of this kind.

Not all employer-employee restraints are invalid. As I said, they are only prima facie void. They can be enforced if they are reasonable in the interests of the parties and of the public. Factors relevant to reasonableness include:[42] whether the employer is trying to protect a legitimate interest (for example, a trade secret);[43] the scope of the restraint (what does the restraint prevent the employee from doing?);[44] the geographical area covered by the restraint (where does it prevent the employee from working?);[45] the length of the restraint;[46] the position occupied by the employee (how senior is the employee?);[47] and whether the restraint is in the public interest.[48]

On the balance of these factors, restraints of trade can be upheld.[49] This is in keeping with the republican view that the existence of dominium is a matter of degree. It will vary depending on the intensity and extent of the discretion that the dominant party has over the weaker.[50] Nor do I deny that that there may be cases where the presence of a degree of dominium has to be balanced in light of the other legitimate aims of contract law or the broader public interest.

[38] ibid 746.
[39] ibid 741.
[40] *M & S Drapers Ltd v Reynolds* [1957] 1 WLR 9.
[41] ibid 18.
[42] Jack Beatson, *Anson's Law of Contract* (28th edn, Oxford University Press 2002) 372–75 citing cases referred to in nn 43–48.
[43] *Faccenda Chicken Ltd v Fowler* (n 35) 137.
[44] *Baker v Hedgecock* (1888) 39 Ch D 520.
[45] *Mason v Provident Clothing & Supply Co Ltd* (n 30).
[46] *M & S Drapers Ltd v Reynolds* (n 40).
[47] ibid.
[48] *Wyatt v Kreglinger and Fernau* [1933] 1 KB 793.
[49] See, for example, *Home Counties Dairies Ltd v Skilton* [1970] 1 WLR 526.
[50] See text to nn 19–23.

Rather, my central claim about restraint of trade is that in those cases where restraints are held invalid, the reason for the invalidity is that the restraint, because of factors such as its scope, the area it covers, and its length, unjustifiably gives the employer too much control over the employee: it denies the employee access to her skill and experience for her own advancement, and therefore deters her from seeking employment elsewhere; the result is that she is locked into an unequal and inherently oppressive relationship with her employer. In general, if a restraint is very wide in scope, covers a large geographical area, and lasts a long time, the greater the extent of the control that the employer will have and the more likely it is that the restraint will be held invalid: when these factors are present the restraint is more likely to have a chilling effect and subject the employee to the arbitrary will and judgment of her employer over central aspects of her well-being.

3.2 Restraints in business sales

This prevention of domination rationale of restraint of trade is consistent with the law relating to restraints which arise out of the seller of a business ensuring its goodwill. In these cases, the seller of a business agrees not to carry on a business after the sale which will compete with the buyer's. The buyer is entitled to protect the goodwill of the business. The courts, in general, are far more likely to declare such agreements reasonable than they are employer-employee restraints of trade.[51] I am not suggesting that such restraints can never be unreasonable. As with employer-employee restraints, this depends on the balance of considerations, for example, the scope of the restraint, the area it covers, and so forth. Rather, the point is that the courts have a marked tendency to uphold such restraints. I shall argue that the reason for this relates to the fact that such covenants are less likely than employer-employee covenants to create situations of bondage or slavery.

So, for example, in *Nordenfelt v Maxim Nordenfelt Guns and Ammunition Co Ltd*, a maker and inventor of guns and ammunition sold his business. To ensure the goodwill of the business he agreed that he would not engage, except on behalf of the company, in the business of gun or ammunition manufacture for twenty-five years. He reserved the right, by express agreement, to deal in: explosives other than gunpowder, torpedoes, submarine boats, and forgings. The House of Lords held that the restraint was reasonable to the extent that it protected the business sold: 'without it the purchasers could not have been protected in the possession of what they wished to buy'.[52]

Their Lordships relied on an economic consideration to uphold the restraint: the restraint protected the value of property; and without such restraints people would not buy businesses. This raises the question why isn't similar economic reasoning

[51] *Mitchel v Reynolds* (1711) 1 P Wms 181; 24 ER 347; *Nordenfelt v Maxim Nordenfelt Guns and Ammunition Co Ltd* (n 30).

[52] *Nordenfelt v Maxim Nordenfelt Guns and Ammunition Co Ltd* (n 30) 574. See also *Herbert Morris Ltd v Saxelby* (n 33) 708–09; *Mason v Provident Clothing & Supply Co Ltd* (n 30) 738; Atiyah, *An Introduction to the Law of Contract* (n 35) 324–26.

used by the courts to justify employer-employee covenants?' Shouldn't the courts uphold employer-employee covenants on the basis that without them employers may be reluctant to take on apprentices?[53] In *Nordenfelt*, Lord Macnaghten tried to explain the distinction:

> To a certain extent, different considerations must apply in cases of apprenticeship and cases of that sort, on the one hand, and cases of the sale of a business or dissolution of partnership on the other. A man is bound an apprentice because he wishes to learn a trade and to practise it. A man may sell because he is getting too old for the strain and worry of business, or because he wishes for some other reason to retire from business altogether. Then there is obviously more freedom of contract between buyer and seller than between master and servant or between an employer and a person seeking employment.[54]

The difficulty with Lord Macnaghten's distinction is that it is under-inclusive: it may be the case that someone sells her business because she wishes to give up business. But it may not be: someone may sell a business, for example, to pay off debts or to pay school fees, and yet even in these cases the courts are more likely to find reasonableness than they are in employer-employee covenants. Therefore, Lord Macnaghten's distinction does not explain all the cases.

An approach based on the principle of preventing domination explains the distinction between restraints in the employer-employee context and in the sale of a business context. In the former, as has been shown, restraints may have the effect of chilling the employee into working for the employer; thereby creating a relationship of subjugation between employer and employee, as in *Ward v Byrne*, and *Herbert Morris Ltd v Saxelby*.

In such circumstances, it is inappropriate for the courts to use economic reasoning to determine reasonableness: so, for example, the courts should not ask themselves whether without the restraint the employer would have employed the employee. Such reasoning is inappropriate because of what it implies about the attitude of the courts to the person subject to the restraint. It suggests that the courts *would* uphold the restraint if that maximized wealth even if the contract constituted a relationship of domination.

In contrast, the promisor's interest at stake in the sale of a business context is not as great: the seller does give up her freedom to carry on her trade, but she is not left in a situation of subjugation to another; she is not effectively forced to be under the power or control of another.

This is not to say that the autonomy interest of the business seller is trivial. It is not, and the courts are protective of it: in *Nordenfelt*, it was crucial to the question of reasonableness that the seller had received a large sum of money, and that he had

[53] '[T]hough in one sense no doubt it is contrary to the interests of the covenantor to subject himself to any restraint, still it may be for his advantage to be able so to subject himself in cases where, if he could not do so, he would lose other advantages, such as the possibility of obtaining the best terms on the sale of an existing business or the possibility of obtaining employment or training under competent employers'. *Herbert Morris Ltd v Saxelby* (n 33) 707.

[54] *Nordenfelt v Maxim Nordenfelt Guns and Ammunition Co Ltd* (n 30) 566. Similar reasoning was used by Dodderidge J in *Jollie v Broad* (1676) 2 Rolle 201, 203; 81 ER 750, 751; and Lord Macclesfield in *Mitchel v Reynolds* (n 51) 191; 350.

reserved for himself the right to deal in explosives other than gunpowder, torpedoes, submarine boats, and forgings. This meant that he could still employ his inventive and manufacturing skills.

However, the autonomy interest at stake in the business sale context is not as weighty as the employee's interest in the employer-employee context. This is because of the element of subjugation and slavery in the employer-employee context.

This explains why the courts are more likely to intervene in employer-employee cases than in business sale cases, and it is why economic reasoning relating to the protection of property and encouragement of transactions is justified in the sale of business context, but not in employer-employee cases.

3.3 An economic doctrine?

Jack Beatson has said, extra judicially, that he is tempted to think that restraint of trade has an economic, rather than moral, justification: it aims at preventing agreements that damage the economy by restricting competition. However, he acknowledges that there are serious obstacles to such an interpretation of the doctrine.[55] In my view, economic analysis does not or cannot alone explain restraint of trade. Preventing anticompetitive agreements is not the only motivation for the doctrine. There are three reasons for this.

First, as Beatson says, 'there is no judicial authority for this formulation'.[56] In contrast, a prevention of domination approach has judicial backing. The cases are littered with references to preventing 'oppressive', 'coercive', 'tyrannous', or 'penal' agreements that create situations of 'slavery', 'servitude', and 'bondage'. Judicial language fits a non-domination or prevention of self-enslavement rationale.

Secondly, the law and economics approach has been explicitly rejected in the case law. In *Texaco Ltd v Mulberry Filling Station Ltd*,[57] Ungoed Thomas J said that general economic considerations were irrelevant to determining whether a restraint was reasonable in the interests of the public. Rather, the public interest limb of the reasonableness test was, he said:

> part of the doctrine of restraint of trade which is based on and directed to securing the liberty of the subject and not the utmost economic advantage. It is part of a doctrine of the common law and not of economics.[58]

Thirdly, the economic approach may not be able to explain the facts and outcomes in some of the cases. Take, for example, *A Schroeder Music Publishing Ltd v Macaulay*:[59] a young aspiring songwriter assigned to a music publisher the copyright in his present and future musical works for five years, a period that was automatically extendable by a further five years if royalties exceeded £5,000. The publisher could terminate the agreement with one month's notice and assign it. The songwriter had no such

[55] Beatson, *Anson's Law of Contract* (n 42) 367. [56] ibid.
[57] *Texaco Ltd v Mulberry Filling Station Ltd* [1972] 1 WLR 814.
[58] ibid 827. cf *A Schroeder Music Publishing Ltd v Macaulay* [1974] 1 WLR 1308, 1315.
[59] *A Schroeder Music Publishing Ltd v Macaulay* [1974] 1 WLR 1308, 1315.

rights. The publisher was also under no obligation to publish any of the songwriter's works. The House of Lords held that the agreement 'sterilised' the songwriter, and was an 'oppressive' and 'unreasonable' restraint on his trade.

The prevention of domination rationale can explain the result: the agreement effectively locked the songwriter in with the publisher for potentially ten years, and during that period the publisher was under no duty to publish any of the songwriter's work. The songwriter's freedom to practice his chosen trade was severely restricted, which gave the employer an undue degree of control or dominium over central aspects of the songwriter's wellbeing.

As Michael Trebilcock has argued, the economic approach cannot explain the result in this case.[60] This is because the music industry is inherently risky; the chances of an unknown songwriter achieving success are low. Therefore, the terms that publishers offer songwriters reflect that risk. They recoup their losses on all those songwriters who do not achieve success from the few who do. If publishers are prevented from offering terms such as those in *Schroeder*, they would not be able to recoup their losses; and, therefore, they would be less likely to take on unknown songwriters. This is inefficient because profits that could have been made would not be.[61]

Accordingly, from the point of view of economic analysis, *Schroeder* was wrongly decided. Preventing domination can, however, explain the case: economic considerations were not taken into consideration because they cannot be relied on or used to justify a contract that constitutes a relationship of servitude or subjugation.[62]

One reply to this is that economic analysis can explain the result because the restraint prevented *other* music publishers from exploiting the talent of the songwriter. Such restraints might 'sterilise' talent, and that may have bad economic implications: valuable resources will not be tapped, and it may have anticompetitive effects.

I find such an argument plausible and I would suggest that despite Trebilcock's claims about the case, an economic justification might exist to justify the decision. The fact that restraints of trade may have damaging economic implications, not least because of their anticompetitive effects, is arguably one reason why they should not be enforced. However, as I have shown, there are other reasons which seem to move the courts. These are that such restraints may constitute relationships of domination. A purely economic analysis of these cases misses these other reasons and gives an incomplete picture of what underlies the doctrine. This may be significant, because in some cases, perhaps as in *Schroeder* itself, the fact that a restraint may be efficient does not mean that it should be enforced. This is because such restraints compromise freedom in the republican sense.

In conclusion, judicial language, the explicit rejection of economic analysis by the courts, and the fact that economic analysis might struggle to explain all of the cases

[60] M J Trebilcock, 'The Doctrine of Inequality of Bargaining Power: Post-Benthamite Economics in the House of Lords' (1976) 26 University of Toronto Law Journal 359. See also, relying on Trebilcock's arguments, Beatson, *Anson's Law of Contract* (n 42) 383.

[61] Trebilcock, 'The Doctrine of Inequality of Bargaining Power: Post-Benthamite Economics in the House of Lords' (n 60) 381.

[62] cf Beatson, *Anson's Law of Contract* (n 42) 383.

shows that the restraint of trade doctrine is not only or even principally motivated by economic concerns. The deeper explanation is one of preventing the domination of one contractual party by the other.

4. Equitable Relief

This section shows that there are echoes of the non-domination principle and how it is applied in restraint of trade cases when the courts exercise their equitable discretion to award specific performance for breach of contracts of employment or injunctions to restrain the breach of negative obligations in employment contracts. It also rejects economic explanations of these cases.

4.1 Specific performance

Against an employee

The Trade Union and Labour Relations (Consolidation) Act 1992, s 236, states that no court shall by an order for specific performance 'compel an employee to do any work or attend at any place for the doing of any work'. Accordingly, the courts have no power to make an employee specifically perform an employment contract. This is true whether or not specific performance was stipulated as a remedy for breach by the contracting parties.[63]

Specific performance is an equitable remedy which enforces the promisor's primary legal duty. In general, it is not available as a remedy for breach of contract. It is only available in certain circumstances, for example, when damages are inadequate,[64] and there is no need for constant supervision by the courts.[65] However, even in cases where these circumstances exist, the courts will not, in general, order as a default remedy the specific performance of an employment contract.[66]

The courts say that one of the reasons for this is that such contracts depend on mutual confidence and respect and specific performance becomes unworkable when these conditions have been undermined.[67] Another reason given is that, in some

[63] Many textbooks are unclear about whether the courts have the power to enforce such clauses. See, for example, Andrew Burrows, *Remedies for Torts and Breach of Contract* (3rd edn, Oxford University Press 2004) 505; Donald Harris, David Campbell, and Roger Halson, *Remedies in Contract and Tort* (2nd edn, Cambridge University Press 2005) 194–95. Andrew Burrows has, however, confirmed that he agrees that such clauses cannot be enforced: 'A court has no power whatever to grant specific performance contrary to the mandatory provisions of s 236.' E-mail from Andrew Burrows to author (30 November 2006).

[64] *Ryan v Mutual Tontine Westminster Chambers Association* [1893] 1 Ch 116, 128.

[65] ibid 123, 128.

[66] *De Francesco v Barnum* (1890) 45 Ch D 430, (specific performance denied against an employee); *Johnson v Shrewsbury and Birmingham Rly Co* (1853) 3 De GM & G 914, 43 ER 358, (against an employer); *Scott v Rayment* (1868) LR 7 Eq 112 (partnership).

[67] *Robb v Hammersmith and Fulham London Borough Council* [1991] ICR 514, 512.

cases, the courts cannot judge whether an order for specific performance is being complied with, for example, where services are artistic in nature.[68]

However, as Andrew Burrows points out, these considerations are incidental to a 'more fundamental' objection: specific performance of contracts of personal service amounts to 'involuntary servitude' or slavery.[69] The leading case is *De Francesco v Barnum*:[70] an infant agreed to became the apprentice of the claimant, a teacher of stage dancing, for seven years. The claimant agreed to teach the infant stage dancing and in return the infant promised that she would not accept any professional engagement during the term of the contract without the claimant's consent. However, in violation of the agreement she accepted another engagement. The claimant tried to enforce the agreement directly. The Court said that it would deny such a remedy. Fry LJ explained why:

> I have a strong impression and a strong feeling that it is not in the interest of mankind that the rule of specific performance should be extended to such cases. I think the Courts are bound to be jealous, lest they should turn contracts of service into contracts of slavery; and therefore, speaking for myself, I should lean against the extension of the doctrine of specific performance and injunction in such a manner.[71]

To grant specific performance would have had the effect of locking the infant into a contractual relationship; this would have eliminated her freedom to trade, and in so doing exposed her to the exercise of the arbitrary will and judgment of the claimant over central areas of her life; damaging not only her self-respect but also risking her material welfare.

Therefore, whereas a restraint of trade might lock someone into an employment contract *indirectly*, that is, because it has a chilling effect, specific performance for breach might lock someone in *directly*. Both restraint of trade and specific performance have the same effect: they subject the employee to the arbitrary will and judgment of the employer, with potentially far-reaching and seriously damaging consequences for her wellbeing: if the employee has no choice but to work for the employer then the employer has no incentive to treat the employee fairly by, for example, improving her pay and conditions.

I argued, when discussing restraint of trade, that the extent to which freedom in the republican sense is limited by such clauses was a matter of degree: it depended for example on their scope, the area they covered, the length of time over which they operated, and so on. What mattered was the extent to which the clauses had the effect of locking the employee into a contract with the employer. Where due to the scope of the restraint, the area it covered, and so forth, the risk that it would lock the employee into the contract was low and the employer was protecting a legitimate interest, I argued that the courts would be more inclined to uphold such clauses as reasonable.[72]

[68] *Southern Foundries (1926) Ltd v Shirlaw* [1940] AC 701, 722; *Giles & Co Ltd v Morris* [1972] 1 WLR 307, 318; Burrows, *Remedies for Torts and Breach of Contract* (n 63) 482.

[69] Burrows, *Remedies for Torts and Breach of Contract* (n 63) 482. See also Robert J Sharpe, *Injunctions and Specific Performance* (3rd edn, Canada Law Book Inc 2000) paras 7.780–7.790.

[70] *De Francesco v Barnum* (n 66).

[71] ibid 438.

[72] See text to nn 41–51.

However, as I have said, in the specific performance context, there is, post the Trade Union and Labour Relations (Consolidation) Act 1992, s 236, no room for judicial discretion: the courts cannot, under any circumstances, 'compel an employee to do any work or attend at any place for the doing of any work'.

Arguably, by way of analogy with the restraint of trade context, the approach adopted by statute here toward specific performance is too blunt. Though it was true in *De Francesco*, that specific performance would have meant that the infant would have had to work with the dance teacher for seven years and not pursue any professional engagement without his consent, one can easily imagine cases where specific performance would not have such serious or drastic consequences, and where the capacity of the employer to exercise his arbitrary will over the employee would be more constrained. What if, for instance, the contract lasted for only seven weeks, and the dancer could accept some (or most) engagements without the teacher's consent?

Potentially, the blanket rule against specific performance against employees is open to criticism. However, it is arguably justified by the fact that specific performance in these cases would lock employees into employment contracts *directly*. In contrast, an unreasonable restraint of trade has an *indirect* effect, that is, it has the practical effect of making an employee continue to work for her current employer (because she cannot work for someone else or set up business on her own), but she does have the choice of not working for her employer (even though this may mean that she does not work for anyone at all). Specific performance for breach of an employment contract would deny employees any viable choice: they have to work for their current employer or risk being in contempt of court. In that sense specific performance is more draconian, and, therefore, there is more reason to have a blanket rule against it in these contexts.

Against an employer

I have argued that specific performance should not be awarded against employees because this subjects the employee to the arbitrary will of her employer. However, do these concerns also militate against specific performance being awarded against employers? In one sense they should, because specific performance eliminates the employer's freedom to escape a contract with an employee that the employer wants to no longer employ or work with (unless the employee is in breach of contract). This is reflected by the fact that, generally speaking, employees cannot in law obtain specific performance against their employer.

However, there are reasons on the republican view why the courts should perhaps worry less about specific performance being granted against employers. First, although the freedom of the employer to get rid of her employee is limited, it is limited for good reasons, in particular to protect the employment rights of the employee. Secondly, making the employer specifically perform does not have the same element of subjugation that making an employee specifically perform does. This is because, typically, in an employment relationship the employee is subordinate to and takes instruction and direction from the employer. The employer is in control and has power over the employee. It is this inequality that carries with it the risk of dominium. However, this element is lacking in the context of specific performance against the employer.

For these two reasons the courts should consider taking a more lenient attitude to granting specific performance against employers. Indeed, in recent cases the courts have begun to do just this.[73]

4.2 Injunctions

The courts will not grant an injunction for breach of a negative covenant where it would amount to specific performance of an employment contract that could not be specifically enforced directly, even if the contract provides for such a mechanism of enforcement in the event of breach. In *Warner Bros Pictures Inc v Nelson*,[74] the defendant agreed to a clause entitling the claimant to an injunction for breach of a negative covenant in an employment contract that could not be specifically enforced. Branson J said that the 'parties cannot contract themselves out of the law'.[75]

The common law position is now reinforced by statute: the Trade Union and Labour Relations (Consolidation) Act 1992, s 236, provides that no court shall by injunction restraining a breach or threatened breach of an employment contract 'compel an employee to do any work or attend at any place for the doing of any work'.

The rationale for the rule is to prevent, 'by the back door', specific enforcement of employment contracts, and so prevent the law being used to constitute relationships of slavery or servitude.[76] So, for example, in *Lumley v Wagner*,[77] Mlle Wagner agreed to sing for three months at the claimant's theatre and promised that during that period she would not sing anywhere else without the claimant's permission. However, in breach of the contract, she sang at a rival's theatre. An injunction was granted restraining her from singing for anyone other than the claimant. This is compatible with a republican approach, because the practical effect of granting the injunction was not to force her to comply with her positive duty to sing for the claimant; it was not tantamount to indirect specific performance: 'in continuing the injunction, I disclaim doing indirectly what I cannot do directly'.[78]

[73] *Irani v Southampton and South West Hampshire Health Authority* [1985] ICR 590; *Robb v Hammersmith and Fulham London Borough Council* (n 67).

[74] *Warner Bros Pictures Inc v Nelson* [1937] 1 KB 209.

[75] However, the existence of the clause assisted 'on the question of evidence as to the applicability of an injunction'. ibid 221. See also the US case of *Stokes v Moore* 262 Ala 59, 64; 77 So 2d 331, 335 (Ala S Ct 1955).

[76] Harris, Campbell, and Halson, *Remedies in Contract and Tort* (n 63) 205. The same rationale explains the Canadian case law. Clifford Ian Kyer, 'A Case Study in Party Stipulation of Remedy: The NHL Standard Player's Contract' (1981) 39 University of Toronto Faculty Law Review 1, 27: 'At bottom it seems that what the courts are really concerned about is forcing someone against his will to resume a personal relationship. The American cases talk in terms of "involuntary servitude". We might be more inclined to speak of slavery.'

[77] *Lumley v Wagner* (1852) 21 LJ Ch 898.

[78] ibid 902. See also: *Whitwood Chemical Co v Hardman* [1891] 2 Ch 416, 427; *Ehrman v Bartholemew* [1898] 1 Ch 671, 674; *Mortimer v Beckett* [1920] 1 Ch 571, 581; *Page One Records Ltd v Britton* [1968] 1 WLR 157, 166–67.

In *Warner Bros Inc v Nelson*, the actress Bette Davis agreed that she would work for the claimant film studio, Warner Bros, and promised that she would not during the time she was under contract with Warner Bros agree to work for any other studio. However, in breach she entered into a contract with another studio. The court granted Warner Bros an injunction preventing Davis from performing for anyone else for three years. Again, as in *Lumley*, the test was whether granting the injunction would amount to indirect specific performance. The court would not:

> true to the principle that specific performance of a contract of personal service will never be ordered, grant an injunction in the case of such a contract to enforce negative covenants if the effect of so doing would be to drive the defendant either to starvation or to specific performance of the positive covenants.[79]

Branson J reasoned that an injunction was not tantamount to indirect specific performance because although it restrained Davis from working for another as an actress it did not prevent her from pursuing other kinds of work:

> no evidence was addressed to show that, if enjoined from doing the specified acts otherwise than for the plaintiffs, she will not be able to employ herself both usefully and remuneratively in other spheres of activity, though not as remuneratively as in her special line. She will not be driven, although she may be tempted, to perform the contract, and the fact that she may be so tempted is no objection to the grant of an injunction.[80]

The decision to grant an injunction in *Warner Bros* has been criticized. In *Warren v Mendy*,[81] an injunction was sought against a boxing manager for inducing the boxer Nigel Benn to break his management contract with the claimant boxing promoter, Frank Warren. As Warren would have sought an injunction against any third party who undertook to manage Benn, the court decided that the same principles should apply as would have applied if the injunction was sought against Benn himself. The court felt that allowing the injunction would amount to indirect specific performance and on that ground refused to allow it. This was despite the fact that an injunction would only have prevented Benn from working as a boxer and that other employment was open to him, such as, for example, working as a security guard.[82] The reason was that boxing required special skill 'whose continued display is essential to the psychological and material, and sometimes to the physical, well-being of the servant', and that 'the human necessity of maintaining the skill or talent

[79] *Warner Bros Pictures Inc v Nelson* (n 74) 216. [80] ibid 219–20.

[81] *Warren v Mendy* [1989] 1 WLR 853.

[82] *Warren v Mendy* should not be considered a special case just because the injunction was sought against a third party and not the servant himself. In *Mortimer v Beckett* (n 78), although a boxer promised not to box for anyone else, he did not promise not to work for anyone else, and yet, the injunction was refused. In *Page One Records Ltd v Britton* (n 78), a pop group breached their management contract by entering into a new contract with another manager. The court refused an injunction against them even though their original promise only related to not making records for anyone else. In *Nichols Advanced Vehicle Systems Inc v De Angelis* (unreported, 21 December 1979), an injunction was refused against a motor racing driver who, in breach of promise, drove for a third party. This was despite the fact that the original promise was only not to compete in a racing car other than the claimant's; it was not, therefore, a promise not to undertake any work whatsoever.

may practically bind the servant to the contract, compelling him to perform it'.[83] Nourse LJ criticized Branson J's finding in *Warner Bros*, that Davis would not have been compelled to perform her contract:

> that judge's view that Miss Bette Davis might employ herself both usefully and remuneratively in other spheres of activity for a period of up to three years appears to have been extraordinarily unrealistic. It could hardly have been thought to be a real possibility that an actress of her then youth and soaring talent would be able to forego screen and stage for such a period.[84]

Nourse LJ distinguished *Lumley*, on the basis that in *Lumley* the contractual period was short: it was for three months, and less than two months were remaining when the injunction was granted. Not performing for two months would not have harmed her skill or ability to perform in the future. Therefore, it is less likely that she would have been compelled to perform for the claimant. The likelihood of indirect specific performance was far higher in Benn's case, because the injunction would have been for two years or longer.[85]

Nourse LJ's approach is more realistic and therefore preferable.[86] Nonetheless, all of the cases are agreed as to the underlying principle: injunctions should not be granted where they cause indirect specific performance of employment contracts.[87] The reason for that is the same as the reason why courts will not grant specific performance of such contracts, that is, to prevent the employee from being subjugated to the arbitrary will and judgement of the employer.

An analogy can be made with restraint of trade. In this chapter I have argued that the reasonableness of a restraint of trade in the employer-employee context depended on the extent to which it had a chilling effect: did the restraint have the effect of (indirectly) 'forcing' the employee to continue to work for the employer? In general, the wider the scope of the restraint (the more or kinds of things it prevented the employee from doing), the larger the geographical area it covered, and the longer it lasted, the more likely it was to deter the employee from seeking work elsewhere, and, therefore, lock the employee into an unequal and potentially harmful relationship with her current employer. The courts are keen to declare such restraints unreasonable.[88]

[83] *Warren v Mendy* (n 81) 857.

[84] ibid 865. See also *Page One Records Ltd v Britton* (n 78) 166–67.

[85] *Warren v Mendy* (n 81) 865–66. See also Burrows, *Remedies for Torts and Breach of Contract* (n 63) 532; Oliver J in *Nichols Advanced Vehicle Systems Inc v De Angelis* (n 82): 'It simply does not, with respect, seem to me to be realistic to say that nothing short of idleness and starvation is compulsive, and therefore no injunction which involves anything less than that can be said to infringe the principle that the court will not specifically enforce a contract of personal services. The injunction in *Warner Bros* did not in practice leave the defendant in that case much freedom of choice if she wanted to pursue her chosen profession. No doubt it might have been quite otherwise if, as in the other previous cases in which similar injunctions had been granted, the contract had been a very short-term one', cited by Nourse LJ in *Warren v Mendy* (n 81) 864–65.

[86] Harris, Campbell, and Halson, *Remedies in Contract and Tort* (n 63) 206; Burrows, *Remedies for Torts and Breach of Contract* (n 63) 532.

[87] Disagreement relates only to the question of which circumstances will practically compel the promisor to perform the original agreement.

[88] See text to nn 41–51.

These same considerations are relevant to the question whether a court grants an injunction to prevent breach of a negative obligation in an employment contract. Fundamentally, the question is: will the injunction have the practical effect of forcing the employee into the hands of the employer; will it amount to indirect specific performance?

As with restraint of trade, the following factors are relevant in answering the question: the scope of the negative obligation, that is, what it prevented the employee from doing; the geographical area covered; and, the length of the contract period. If these factors are applied to the facts of *Warren*, it is clear why no injunction was granted: the negative obligation prevented Benn from boxing, an activity which was fundamental to his wellbeing; it prevented him boxing anywhere in the world; and, if any injunction were granted, it would have lasted for at least two years (in which time, if Benn were out of boxing, his ability and prospects as a boxer would undoubtedly have suffered).

In these circumstances, an injunction would have practically compelled Benn to work for Warren; this would amount to indirect specific performance. Having to work for Warren would have meant that Benn was subject to Warren's arbitrary will and judgment, which would have struck at Benn's confidence, his sense of self-respect, and his ability to plan his life.

Given these clear parallels in the employer-employee context between restraint of trade and injunctions to restrain the breach of negative obligations, the courts should more explicitly draw these parallels to ensure consistency and rationality in decision-making; recognize the underlying concern to prevent domination; and rely on those considerations which most affect whether an employee will feel compelled to continue to work for her current employer (for example, scope, geographical area, length, and so forth).

In contrast, in the US, the orthodox view is that injunctions are not granted in these contexts for economic reasons. The North American approach is that an injunction should be granted only where the promisor seeks to work for a competitor of the claimant. The rationale is that, in these cases, the claimant has a 'separate legitimate interest' to that of inducing the defendant to specifically perform.[89] So, for example, in *Lumley*, it was right to grant an injunction because Wagner sought work with a rival theatre. The claimant had an interest in restraining the defendant

[89] The approach was first advocated in Samuel Williston and George J Thompson, *A Treatise on the Law of Contracts* (rev edn, Baker, Voorhis & Company 1936–1938) 4051: 'In most of the decisions, however, the negative undertaking of the defendant had importance to the plaintiff apart from the pressure which its enforcement would put upon the defendant to perform his affirmative undertaking, and if the defendant's performance of his negative obligation has no value to the plaintiff in itself an injunction will not generally be granted.... In general, it is not the mere taking of new employment but unfair competition which equity enjoins.' See also American Law Institute, *Restatement of the Law of Contracts* (American Law Institute Publishers 1932) s 380(1)(a); David Tannenbaum, 'Enforcement of Personal Service Contracts in the Entertainment Industry' (1954) 42 California Law Review 18, 20–21; Harris, Campbell, and Halson, *Remedies in Contract and Tort* (n 63) 206. In Canada, Williston's approach was defended obiter by McRuer CJ in *Detroit Football Co v Dublinski* [1956] OR 744. Kyer, 'A Case Study in Party Stipulation of Remedy: The NHL Standard Player's Contract' (n 76) 24–25.

which went beyond wanting the defendant to perform for him, this interest resided in making sure his audience would not be diverted to a rival theatre.[90]

As a matter of English law, this approach was explicitly rejected in *Marco Productions v Pagola*.[91] The defendants were theatrical performers who promised the claimants that they would not perform for anyone else. But they subsequently threatened to perform for one of the claimant's rivals. The defendants claimed that an injunction should not be granted against them because the claimants could not show that any damage would flow from breach of the negative stipulation. Hallet J rejected that argument: 'I am not satisfied that the plaintiffs must prove that by performing for the rival producer the defendants may cause more damage to them than by remaining idle.'[92] Therefore, the claimants were not required to show that they had a 'separate legitimate interest' to that of getting specific performance to get an injunction.

Nor can the US approach explain the facts and outcomes of the English cases: injunctions have been refused even though the defendant has undertaken work with a competitor of the claimant: so, for example, in *Warren*, Benn signed for a rival boxing manager; in *Page One Records Ltd v Britton*,[93] 'The Troggs' pop group entered into a management contract with a rival music producer; and in *Nichols Advanced Vehicle Systems Inc v De Angelis*, a motor racing driver, in breach, drove a rival motor car.[94]

The US approach should, as a matter of principle, be rejected. Economic considerations cannot justify putting employees in these contexts into circumstances of servitude or domination. Moreover, even if we accept that economic reasoning should play a role in determining whether injunctions should be awarded, it is largely unclear why on economic grounds employers should be protected from competition. The dominant view in modern economics is that wealth is maximized when there *is* competition. It is very unclear what the economic rationale of the US approach actually is.

5. Achieving Integrity

The cases considered in this chapter typically appear in contract law textbooks under the separate headings of 'illegality' and 'specific remedies'. The advantage of the approach defended here is that it shows that these cases are founded upon a common rationale, that is, to prevent dominium.

[90] Burrows, *Remedies for Torts and Breach of Contract* (n 63) 534. Harris, Campbell, and Halson also explain *Whitwood Chemical Co v Hardman* (n 78), (the claimant did not have any interest in restricting competition) and the *Warner Bros* case (Davis went to work for a competitor) according to this approach. Harris, Campbell, and Halson, *Remedies in Contract and Tort* (n 63) 206.

[91] *Marco Productions v Pagola* [1945] KB 111.

[92] ibid 114.

[93] *Page One Records Ltd v Britton* (n 78).

[94] *Nichols Advanced Vehicle Systems Inc v De Angelis* (n 82). See also *Grimston v Cuningham* [1894] 1 QB 125.

Emphasizing the common rationale of these cases could lead to greater consistency in their treatment. So, as I have argued in this chapter, the reasonableness requirement for restraint of trade could be applied to the equitable relief cases too. Recall, that the validity of a restraint of trade depends on its reasonableness which is determined by factors such as the scope, geographical area covered, and length of the restraint. This reasonableness requirement is explained by the prevention of domination principle—not all restraints will effectively force the employee into the clutches of the other party; whether they do will depend on the scope of the restraint, the area it covers, and so forth.

There is a blanket statutory prohibition of specific performance for breach against employees (Trade Union and Labour Relations (Consolidation) Act 1992, s 236). Unlike restraint of trade, there is no requirement on courts to consider the reasonableness of awarding specific performance. Arguably though considerations such as the scope of a specific performance order, the geographical area it covers, and its duration, should be relevant to determining whether courts make such orders in the employment context.

Similarly, these considerations should be relevant in the context of whether courts award injunctions to prevent the breach of negative obligations in employment contexts. Awarding an injunction in these cases may have the same effect as upholding and enforcing a restraint of trade: potentially, awarding an injunction may have the indirect effect of forcing the employee to carry on working for her employer by denying her the chance to employ her skill and talent elsewhere. Thereby they indirectly bring about the subjugation of the employee to the arbitrary will and judgment of the employer.

By and large, as argued in this chapter, the courts do, at the level of the facts and outcomes of the cases, take these considerations into account in the injunctions context (compare the *Lumley* case,[95] with *Warren*).[96] However, unlike in restraint of trade, they do this far less explicitly. To ensure integrity in this area of law (or as we saw in Chapter 4 what Dworkin calls 'local priority'),[97] the courts should endeavour to treat restraint of trade and injunctions in the same way. They should explicitly recognize the underlying concern to prevent non-domination; and explicitly rely, in determining whether to award injunctions in these contexts, on those considerations which most affect whether an employee will feel compelled to continue to work for her current employer (for example, scope, geographical area, and length).

6. Conclusion

In conclusion, at the heart of the republican theory of contract law is a conception of freedom which requires citizen participation in social and political life. Unlike the liberal, for the republican freedom in any meaningful sense does not reside in the absence of interference by others, but rather involves the constraints imposed by the

[95] *Lumley v Wagner* (n 77). [96] *Warren v Mendy* (n 81). [97] See ch 4, s 4.

presence of others and our civil and political duties to ensure that they are treated with equal concern and respect.

The threat to this type of freedom is not interference by others per se; but, rather, the risk that the state or other individuals or groups in society will interfere with our lives on an arbitrary or unprincipled basis, which takes no account of our shared interests and what we perceive those to be. In this chapter, I have focused on one way that contract law might be abused by others to constitute relationships of dominium between contractual parties. Typically, this occurs when one contractual party cedes or transfers too much control to the other party over central aspects of her life. The use and abuse of contract law in this way subverts its focal purpose which is to structure in a distinctive and unique way intrinsically valuable forms of cooperative activity based on the values of trust, equality, and respect; and instead creating relations based on control, inequality, and subjugation.

The state through its courts has a duty not to assist or be complicit in the abuse of contractual principles like promise and freedom of contract to engineer these forms of servitude. This is either done directly through the use of specific performance to enforce employment contracts or indirectly through reliance on restraints of trade which prevent employees from employing their skill and talent elsewhere or through the use of injunctions to restrain the breach of negative obligations in employment contracts. In these indirect cases, such clauses and the use of injunctions to enforce them have a chilling effect: the undesirable consequences of breach, that is, the inability to find alternative work, have the effect of forcing the promisor to continue to work with her original employer.

The cases and doctrines considered in this chapter on restraint of trade and the limits on the availability of equitable relief show how the courts reach beyond contractual principles such as promise and freedom of contract to the focal aim or purpose of contract law to justify the invalidity and non-enforcement of contracts or contractual clauses that constitute these forms of domination. This is perhaps the best example of how the constitutive purpose of contract law may at the limit function as a side-constraint when it is directly contradicted, even though, as I have argued, this purpose is largely underdetermined and capable of being pursued through a multiplicity of (potentially conflicting) rules and doctrines.

It is important for reasons of achieving local priority or integrity in this area of law that the courts explicitly recognize that underpinning the cases and doctrines is the republican concern to prevent dominium. It is this underlying rationale which explains the inability (and indeed inappropriateness) of using economic analysis to explain these cases. As I have argued, the existence of dominium is a matter of degree depending on factors such as the scope of the activities under the employer's control, the duration over which the power lasts, the geographical area it covers, and so forth. Such factors, as we have seen, are explicitly taken into account in determining the reasonableness of restraints of trade, and to ensure equal treatment the courts should endeavour to explicitly recognize much more than they currently do the important role they play in the equitable relief context too.

8

The Penalties Rule and Compensation*

1. The Challenge

It is a well-established rule in contract law that clauses which stipulate the monetary remedy for breach of contract ('agreed damages clauses') are invalid as 'penalty clauses' if they require the payment of sums which are 'extravagant and unconscionable' when compared to the largest loss that the parties could conceivably have envisaged as flowing from breach at the time that the contract was entered. Loss is defined broadly here to include direct and indirect losses, and pecuniary and non-pecuniary losses. In such cases, the courts award the 'default' measure of damages (that is, the damages that would have been awarded had there been no agreed damages clause). If, on the other hand, the agreed damages clause represents a genuine pre-estimate of the loss (broadly defined) it is enforceable as 'liquidated damages'.[1]

The rule against penalties ('the penalties rule') poses a challenge to the 'promise theory' of contract. If contracts are promises, a penalty clause represents a promise by the promisor to pay the penalty if she breaches. Promissory logic would require that promise to be kept and for the courts to enforce it if it is not. Moreover, the enforcement of penalty clauses is likely to deter the promisor from breaching her primary duties, which are also based on promises. This is an additional reason for why the promise principle would support the enforcement of these clauses. According to the promise principle, what matters most is that promises are kept. The enforcement of penalty clauses ensures not only that promises relating to one's *remedial* or *secondary* duties are kept, but also provides an incentive to perform one's promise-based *performance* or *primary* obligations.

* This chapter is based on and largely reproduces, but with some significant revisions and adaptations, the text of a previously published article of mine entitled 'The Penalties Rule and the Promise Theory of Contract', which appeared in The Canadian Journal of Law and Jurisprudence 26 (2013), 443, copyright © 2013 Canadian Journal of Law and Jurisprudence. The text is used with kind permission of Cambridge University Press.

[1] *Clydebank Engineering & Shipbuilding Co Ltd v Don Jose Ramos Yzquierdo y Castaneda* [1905] AC 6, 10, 19–20; *Dunlop Pneumatic Tyre Co Ltd v New Garage and Motor Co Ltd* [1915] AC 79, 86–88, 91–92; *Cavendish Square Holding BV v Talal El Makdessi and ParkingEye Limited v Beavis* [2015] UKSC 67, [23]–[24], [28]–[29], [31]–[32], [97]–[101]. See also *Uniform Commercial Code* § 2-718 (1); American Law Institute, *Restatement (Second) of Contracts* (American Law Institute Publishers 1981) § 356 (1).

At least prima facie, this looks like a case of divergence between contract and promise.[2] Making matters worse, law and economics has seized on this apparent divergence with promissory morality. What promise struggles to explain, economic analysis has a ready account of. The reason, on such views, why penalty clauses are not enforced is that they hamper efficiency, that is, the movement of commodities from those who value them less to those who value them more, by preventing so called 'efficient breaches'.[3] So, for example, if D promises to sell a book to C for £30, but before performance Y says to D that she will buy the book from D for £45, efficiency may require D to break her contract with C and sell to Y. Efficiency requires this where Y places a higher value on the book than C. So, if the value that C attaches to the book is £39, efficiency requires D to breach the contract she has with C, sell the book for £45 to Y and give C £9 damages. Penalty clauses may preclude these sorts of efficient breaches. If there were a penalty clause of say £18 in C's and D's contract, an efficient breach is prevented because D is going to be worse off if she breaches.[4]

Promise theory cannot accept an efficiency-based account of the penalties rule. It would entail that even small gains in efficiency may require the breach of promissory obligations. This would negate the very idea that promises create rights and obligations, that is, reasons that cannot be defeated by the routine pursuit of collective goals such as the promotion of social utility or economic efficiency.[5] As Seana Shiffrin says: 'It is an important moral aspect of a promise that you commit to doing what you have promised, even when a better opportunity comes along, unless your promisee releases you from your commitment.'[6] The prospect that efficiency

[2] Seana Valentine Shiffrin, 'The Divergence of Contract and Promise' (2007) 120 Harvard Law Review 708, 726. Shiffrin cites as other examples of divergence the fact that expectation damages rather than specific performance is the primary remedy for breach of contract and the remoteness and mitigation doctrines (ibid 722–27). All of these doctrines seem out of keeping with promissory morality because they shift the burden of breach away from the defendant and on to the innocent promisee.

[3] Robert L Birmingham, 'Breach of Contract, Damage Measures, and Economic Efficiency' (1969–1970) 24 Rutgers Law Review 273, 284; James P Fenton, 'Liquidated Damages as Prima Facie Evidence' (1975) 51 Indiana Law Journal 189, 191–92.

[4] The example, which I have varied slightly, is borrowed from Andrew Burrows, *Remedies for Torts and Breach of Contract* (3rd edn, Oxford University Press 2004) 450. Not every efficiency theorist agrees that penalty clauses are inefficient. See Charles J Goetz and Robert E Scott, 'Liquidated Damages, Penalties and the Just Compensation Principle: Some Notes on an Enforcement Model and a Theory of Efficient Breach' (1977) 77 Columbia Law Review 554; and for the application of this analysis by Judge Richard Posner see *Lake River Corp v Carborundum Co* 769 F 2d 1284 (7th Cir 1985) 1288–89. However, for the purposes of this chapter I put these disagreements aside.

[5] Ronald Dworkin, *Taking Rights Seriously* (Duckworth 1977) 92.

[6] Seana Valentine Shiffrin, 'Is a Contract a Promise?' in Andrei Marmor (ed), *The Routledge Companion to Philosophy of Law* (Routledge 2012) 243. Promissory obligations would, however, still make sense if the claim were that promises may be defeated by large gains in social utility or economic efficiency. This is because they would continue to carry special weight against considerations relating to the pursuit of collective goals. The weight of these collective considerations would have to cross a high threshold before they could outweigh the rights and duties generated by promising. See Dworkin, *Taking Rights Seriously* (n 5) 92; Jules L Coleman, 'Tort Law and the Demands of Corrective Justice' (1992) 67 Indiana Law Journal 349, 361–62; Thomas Nagel, 'Personal Rights and Public Space' (1995) 24 Philosophy & Public Affairs 83, 88–89. However, this is not the kind of argument that the efficiency theorist makes to justify the penalties rule. The claim is that even small gains in efficiency require 'breach' of promissory obligations.

is the justification for the penalties rule has led Shiffrin to doubt whether the rule is compatible with the promise theory.[7]

2. Responses

The prima facie incompatibility of the penalties rule with the promise theory, coupled with the fact that law and economics seems to explain it fairly easily, means that the rule poses a challenge to the promise theory.

There are two main ways the promise theorist might respond. They track the two prominent ways discussed earlier in Chapters 2 and 3 for how promise theorists make out the claim that promise is the foundation of contract law or plays a normatively special role in justifying rules and doctrines in the domain. First, they might defend what I called the 'justificatory primacy' of the promise principle in this context, by claiming that the penalties rule does indeed diverge from promissory morality and should for that reason be 'repudiated', because the demands of the promise principle override those of any competing principle in the contractual domain.[8] Alternatively, they might argue that the justificatory primacy of promise is achieved in this context, by 'inflating' the promise principle in such a way that it is able to 'accommodate' the rule by, for example, 'swallowing up' the competing considerations that justify its presence in contract law. Primacy is achieved for promise because by enlarging its scope, it becomes the only principle in play.[9]

The second plausible way in which the promise theorist might respond is by embracing what I called 'justificatory presumptiveness'. Recall, on this view promise plays a special role in contract because any divergence between contract and promise justifies an epistemic presumption that the divergent rule or doctrine is unjustified. The presumption explains why promise is special, without precluding the possibility that instances of divergence might on closer inspection be justified by appeal to the legal context in which these doctrines operate.[10]

These are some of the familiar stock responses of the promise theorist to the problem of divergence.[11] In Chapter 3, I gave general reasons why these approaches are unconvincing. In this chapter, I argue that they also fail in the particular context of explaining how promise plays a special or foundational role in justifying the penalties rule; and also that by recognizing that the promise principle—though relevant—does not play a special role in contract suggests a way forward for justifying the penalties rule.

[7] Shiffrin, 'The Divergence of Contract and Promise' (n 2) 726–27, 731–32.

[8] See ch 2, s 3.2. [9] See text to ch 3, nn 12–14. [10] See ch 2, s 3.3.

[11] cf Shiffrin arguing that the problem of divergence for promise theory should not be exaggerated, because the promise theorist can '1) dispute the critic's underlying view of promise ... ; or 2) regard these doctrines as targets of criticism; or 3) take these divergent doctrines to be explained by reasons distinctive to features of legal enforcement or regulation that render it sensible for the legal treatment of such promises to differ from their moral treatment'. Shiffrin, 'Is a Contract a Promise?' (n 6) 249.

3. Justificatory Primacy

3.1 Justificatory primacy by repudiation

As I have said, one way the promise theorist might respond to the penalties rule is to assert the primacy of the promise principle over other considerations in this context, and simply 'bite the bullet' by admitting that there is real (not just apparent) divergence between promise and the penalties rule, and that therefore the legal doctrine—however longstanding—should be repudiated from the law of contract. This is the strategy adopted by the promise theorist Jody Kraus. According to the promise principle, promises ought to be kept, and if the defendant promised that she would pay the penalty should she breach, she has a moral obligation to pay if she does indeed go on to breach. To the extent that contract law refuses to enforce the penalty clause, it is defective because, Kraus argues, it 'clearly fails to enforce the parties' moral obligations'.[12]

This response though to the challenge posed by the penalties rule is hardly convincing. Say, for example, that I hire for £50 a builder to put up some curtain poles in my house and that I extract a promise from her that if she fails to perform she has to pay me a penalty of £1 million.[13] Even though the builder made a valid promise, it would, nevertheless, be clearly unjust should she breach to require her to pay £1 million in stipulated damages for breaching what was, after all, only a £50 contract to put up curtain poles. However, according to the response advocated by Kraus the promise should be enforced. Although this response is consistent with promissory logic, it reaches a result that is deeply at odds with common sense notions of what justice would require in this situation. This suggests that the rule against penalties has, despite Kraus' protestations, a moral justification.

3.2 Justificatory primacy by inflation

According to justificatory primacy by repudiation the promise principle *conflicts* with the penalties rule, and this is why the rule must be ejected from contract law. However, it is possible to rely on justificatory primacy as a way of justifying or saving the penalties rule. The promise theorist might argue that, despite appearances, there is in fact *no conflict* between the promise principle and the rule, because the scope of the promise principle can be widened or inflated to accommodate the rule. In this

[12] Jody S Kraus, 'The Correspondence of Contract and Promise' (2009) 109 Columbia Law Review 1603, 1635 n 63, 1643. Charles Fried seems to take a similar line. Charles Fried, 'The Ambitions of Contract as Promise' in Gregory Klass, George Letsas, and Prince Saprai (eds), *Philosophical Foundations of Contract Law* (Oxford University Press 2014) 27–28, 33. See similarly Sarah Worthington, 'Common Law Values: The Role of Party Autonomy in Private Law' in Andrew Robertson and Michael Tilbury (eds), *The Common Law of Obligations: Divergence and Unity* (Hart Publishing 2015).

[13] The example (which I have varied slightly) is one made famous by Lord Halsbury in *Clydebank Engineering & Shipbuilding Co Ltd v Don Jose Ramos Yzquierdo y Castaneda* (n 1) 10.

way, the promise principle retains its foundational status because it becomes the only principle we need to rely on to justify the rule.

This inflationist argument might plausibly take one of two forms. First, that a promise to pay a penalty clause is usually involuntary and therefore not a real promise. I will call this the 'no promise' argument. Second, that even if a promise to pay a penalty clause is a real promise, the promise principle prohibits its legal enforcement. I will call this the 'no legally enforceable promise' argument.

According to the first no promise view, the courts refuse to enforce promises to pay penalty clauses because they are very often made involuntarily. Although not a promise theorist, Melvin Eisenberg made this kind of argument to explain why the courts regulate these clauses. Promisors do not adequately exercise their will in these cases because they are significantly more likely to make cognitive mistakes. For most contracting parties the application of a penalty clause is a remote possibility. This makes it potentially very difficult and costly for them to anticipate when and how these clauses might apply. Moreover, promisors tend to be overly optimistic that they will comply with their primary obligations, and they unduly discount the future costs of breach. The result is that they tend systematically to overlook the existence and full implications of these clauses.[14]

The promise theorist could adopt this line of reasoning to argue that when making a promise to pay a penalty clause, the promisor lacks sufficient capacity to make a fully informed decision. This invalidates the promise that they make.

Even if it is true that in many cases parties do not deliberate sufficiently on the existence and implications of penalty clauses, this argument cannot explain the rule against penalties. That rule applies even in cases where the promisor did have sufficient notice of the clause and understood its implications fully. Take again the builder example I gave above. Even if I made it painstakingly clear to the builder before she entered into the agreement that the £1 million penalty clause would apply to the £50 building contract should she breach, the courts would nevertheless refuse to enforce the clause. Moreover, I think that most would agree that the clause should not be enforced even though the builder was fully aware of it.

The counterargument could be made that the rule applies in this case because there is a need to have a clear rule. However, why would not a rule which said that the penalties rule applies *unless* the penalty clause is specifically brought to the attention of the promisor be sufficiently clear? It is no different from other rules that are commonplace in the law of contract, for example, a contract is binding *unless* the promisor can show duress, misrepresentation, mistake, and so forth. We do not

[14] Melvin Aron Eisenberg, 'The Limits of Cognition and the Limits of Contract' (1995) 47 Stanford Law Review 211, 227–28. cf Mindy Chen-Wishart, 'Controlling the Power to Agree Damages' in Peter Birks (ed), *Wrongs and Remedies in the Twenty-First Century* (Clarendon Press 1996) 290: 'Agreed damages clauses may be thought to contain high risks of cognitive error since they involve contingent future obligations which are often difficult to assess and, where accurately assessed are frequently not given their proper weight. There is a psychological tendency to discount far off possibilities, coupled with an over-optimism that the contingency will not eventuate.' Hugh Beale, *Remedies for Breach of Contract* (Sweet & Maxwell 1980) 59; Stephen A Smith, *Contract Theory* (Oxford University Press 2004) 308.

say that contracts should not be set-aside for duress, misrepresentation, and so on, because that would make the rule that contracts are binding less clear.

The promise theorist might claim that a qualified rule of this nature might be justified. They could argue that in the usual case, for example, a transaction involving a penalty clause between a business and a consumer, it is highly likely that the consumer was not adequately aware of the existence and implications of the clause. The penalties rule should apply. However, an exception is justified, in, for example, commercial transactions, where the parties are likely to have been fully aware of any penalty clause. In these cases, such clauses should be enforced.[15] Such a qualified rule would be perfectly clear and coherent.

My claim is not to deny this, but rather just to point out that such a qualified rule would be incompatible with the legal position. According to the law as it stands, penalty clauses are not enforced even when there is perfect awareness of them by the contracting parties. Of course, the promise theorist could argue that the law should be reformed, and a more qualified rule adopted. However, if that were the case the promise theorist would no longer be using the promise principle to accommodate or explain the rule. Instead, promise theory would be repudiating the existing rule, and I have already explained the problem with that strategy—it contradicts our moral convictions.

I now move onto the second way that the promise theory might accommodate the penalties rule, the no legally enforceable promise view. Unlike the previous argument, this position does not dispute that penalty clauses are valid promises. Rather, the claim is that despite their validity they should not be enforced by law because their enforcement corrupts the moral practice of promising. Recall from Chapter 5 that Dori Kimel used a similar argument to justify the intention to create legal relations doctrine.[16] The argument may take either an 'expressive' or 'empirical cast'.[17] Behind the expressivist interpretation would be the worry that the legal enforcement of penalty clauses expresses the view that people should perform their promises for the reason that if they do not they will face onerous external sanctions, such as the enforcement of penalty clauses by the courts. This 'clouds out' the real reason for why promisors should perform their promises, which is to demonstrate special concern for the interests of promisees.[18]

The empirical version of the argument claims that whether or not a message is conveyed by the law the practical effect of enforcing penalty clauses is that people's motivations for performing their promissory duties are, or are at least perceived by promisees to be, 'crowded out' by their self-interested concern to avoid the external

[15] Some support for this analysis may be found in obiter dicta of Lord Woolf in *Philips Hong Kong Ltd v Attorney General of Hong Kong* (1993) 61 BLR 41, 58, suggesting that the penalties rule might not apply in the commercial context.

[16] See text to ch 5 nn 49–53.

[17] I borrow this distinction from Shiffrin, who makes it in relation to the claim that the legal enforcement of promises generally (not just penalty clauses) corrupts promising. Shiffrin, 'Is a Contract a Promise?' (n 6) 252.

[18] ibid; Stephen A Smith, 'Performance, Punishment and the Nature of Contractual Obligation' (1997) 60 Modern Law Review 360, 367–69.

sanction of having a penalty clause enforced by the courts.[19] This corrupts the practice of promising, because one of the basic functions of promising is to enable trusting relationships to develop, which is only possible if the promisor performs her promises, and is perceived by the promisee to perform her promises, not out of concern for herself but rather out of the special concern she attaches to the interests of the promisee.[20]

Both versions of this argument claim that the reason why the courts do not enforce penalty clauses is that if they did it would corrupt the moral practice of promising, either because of the message that the law would send out, or because of the practical effect legal enforcement would have, or be perceived by promisees to have, on the motivations of promisors.

Taking the expressive view first. The claim that the legal enforcement of penalty clauses would send out the message that people should perform their promises to avoid harsh external sanctions seems implausible. There may be other reasons for enforcing these clauses, for example, assuring promisees that the promisor will at least be made to conform to her promissory obligations even if she fails to comply with them for the right (moral) reasons. This does not imply that promisors should perform their promises out of concern to avoid these external sanctions, rather than out of respect for the rights of the promisee. In the same way that the fact that murder carries a life sentence is not meant to convey the thought that the reason why you should not murder is because you will go to jail for a long time if you do. The purpose of the life sentence may just acknowledge the reality that some people are insufficiently motivated by moral considerations not to murder, and therefore external sanctions are needed to give them additional reasons not to kill. This does not suggest that people should cast aside their moral reasons for not murdering and replace them with their self-interested concern to avoid external sanctions.[21]

The empirical version of the corruption argument is also problematic. According to it, even if the law does not aim to displace the moral reasons that promisors have for performing their promises, the enforcement of penalty clauses may nevertheless

[19] I borrow the distinction between 'clouding out' and 'crowding out' from Shiffrin. It tracks her distinction between expressive and empirical versions of the argument (which I've already relied on) that promises should not be legally enforced. Shiffrin, 'Is a Contract a Promise?' (n 6) 252–53.

[20] Stephen Smith seems to make this empirical argument in the context of a discussion about whether punitive damages should be awarded by contract law. Smith, 'Performance, Punishment and the Nature of Contractual Obligation' (n 18) 372. cf Daniel Markovits, 'Contract and Collaboration' (2004) 113 Yale Law Journal 1417, 1509. Markovits argues that punitive damages may also encourage the promisee to welcome breach and take steps to bring it about. This too would undermine the development of certain forms of respectful recognition between the promisor and the promisee, because the promisee would have an incentive to reject the promisor's efforts to establish a bond with the promisee by performing her promissory obligations.

[21] I follow Shiffrin here who makes these arguments against the expressivist who claims that promises in general (not just those relating to penalty clauses) should not be enforced by law. Shiffrin, 'Is a Contract a Promise?' (n 6) 253. cf Anthony Duff arguing in the context of criminal punishment that the threat of hard treatment is a concession to human frailty and weakness of will. Antony R Duff, 'Penal Communications: Recent Work in the Philosophy of Punishment' (1996) 20 Crime and Justice 1, 41–42. See also Uma Narayan, 'Appropriate Responses and Preventive Benefits: Justifying Censure and Hard Treatment in Legal Punishment' (1993) 13 Oxford Journal of Legal Studies 166, 181.

empirically-speaking lead to promisors acting on their legal reason to avoid a harsh sanction rather than the moral concern that should motivate them which is the respect that they owe to the rights of the promisee. Also, there is the danger that the enforcement of penalty clauses will encourage promisees to think that promisors are motivated primarily by legal reasons, which will hinder the development of trusting relationships, regardless of whether promisors are actually motivated by these concerns or not. This explains why, according to this argument, penalty clauses are not enforced.

I follow Shiffrin in doubting how serious these empirical concerns about the legal enforcement of promises are. First, although there is a need for empirical research to be presented on this, it seems highly improbable that the reason that people do not murder is the fact that this crime carries a life sentence. Far more likely is that people are motivated not to murder because it is morally wrong. Therefore, the claim that legal sanctions displace people's motivations for complying with their moral obligations is highly questionable. Nor, Shiffrin argues, is there any reason to suppose that the link between sanctions and motivations would be stronger in contract law, than it is in criminal, or tort law.[22]

Second, Shiffrin rightly makes the point that even if such an empirical link could be established, that does not necessarily mean that promises should not be enforced by the law. The law could instead just make clear that it does not aim to displace one's moral reasons for performing one's promises, but rather that it is motivated by other considerations, such as providing assurance to promisees. The effectiveness of these less drastic responses to the crowding out concern would need to be explored, and they may well mean that there is no need for promises such as those relating to penalty clauses not to be enforced by the courts.[23]

Even if the objections raised above to both versions of the no legally enforceable promise view could be overcome, there would be a further serious problem. The claim that penalty clauses are not enforced because enforcement corrupts the moral practice of promising is over-inclusive. As we saw in Chapter 5, it is an argument not only against the enforcement of penalty clauses but arguably the legal enforcement of promises per se. Even the standard contractual remedy of expectation damages could corrupt the morality of promising either by clouding out the motives that should govern the relations between promisor and promisee, or by having the practical effect of crowding out the moral reasons that promisors would otherwise have for performing their promises, or at least leading to the perception among promisees that these reasons have been crowded out. This is problematic because the no legally enforceable promise view explains the compatibility of the penalties rule with the promise theory, but only at the expense of explaining other rules and doctrines, such as the rule that expectation damages is the standard remedy for breach of contract.[24]

[22] Shiffrin, 'Is a Contract a Promise?' (n 6) 253. [23] ibid 253–54.

[24] Smith who seems to defend the empirical version of the no legally enforceable promise view to explain why punitive damages are not awarded for breach of contract acknowledges this defect in the theory. Smith, 'Performance, Punishment and the Nature of Contractual Obligation' (n 18) 371. See also Dori Kimel, *From Promise to Contract: Towards a Liberal Theory of Contract* (Hart Publishing 2003) 98. Smith does try to avoid this unattractive conclusion by saying that alongside the 'intangible' bond-creating (promissory) function that contract serves, contract also has a 'tangible' function

To sum up, the penalties rule cannot be accommodated by inflating the promise principle. The no promise view which claims that promises to pay penalty clauses are invalid because they are involuntary, cannot explain why the penalties rule applies even in cases where it is clear that the promisor made a fully informed decision. The promise theorist might claim that the rule should only apply in the consumer context, but that there is an exception for cases, such as commercial transactions, where the parties are more likely to be fully aware of the penalty clause. However, this does not account for the current legal position, which is that penalty clauses are not enforced even when the parties are fully aware of them. This argument amounts not to accommodating the current penalties rule, but rather repudiating it and as I explained in the last subsection such a stance conflicts with our moral intuitions.

The no legally enforceable promise view, which claims that such promises though valid should not be enforced by the courts because they corrupt the morality of promising is also open to serious doubt. The expressive version of the view is unpersuasive because the enforcement of penalty clauses by the courts does not imply that people should not perform their promises out of other-regarding concern for the interests of promisees. There is a paucity of empirical evidence to make out the empirical version of this view, and indeed it seems implausible from the point of view of common-sense intuitions about the relationship between sanctions and motivating reasons in other fields such as criminal law. Even if an empirical link between sanctions and motives could be established, it is unclear why the crowding out concern would require the non-enforcement of promises to pay penalty clauses, rather than the less drastic measure of requiring the law to clarify that its aims are not to displace people's moral motives for performing their promises. Furthermore, the no legally enforceable promise view, whether in its expressive or empirical cast, is over-inclusive. It explains why penalty clauses should not be enforced, but at the expense of making the highly implausible claim that expectation damages—the standard remedy for breach of contract—is unjustified.

4. Justificatory Presumptiveness

The second way that promise might play a special role in justifying the penalties rule is what I have called justificatory presumptiveness. This 'foundationalist' view accepts that there is a genuine conflict between the promise principle and the penalties rule, which justifies an epistemic presumption that the legal rule is unjustified. However,

which is to ensure that the promisee receives what she contracted for. Smith argues that although the intangible harm caused by breach cannot be remedied, the tangible harm can through the award of expectation damages, and that therefore this remedy should be awarded (ibid). However, this argument for expectation damages is deeply problematic because it involves putting the pursuit of the tangible function of contract ahead of the intangible function. On this view, the award of expectation damages undermines the bond-creating function of contract. Smith makes a case for expectation damages by claiming that contract serves another function alongside its promissory function, but then this brings into question his own assertion that: 'Contracts are, *first of all*, promises' (ibid 369, emphasis added). If that is truly the case it is unclear why Smith is happy to undermine the promissory function of contract for its more concrete function of securing exchange.

it allows for the possibility that on closer inspection the legal context in which the rule operates might justify the divergence.

Like justificatory primacy by repudiation, justificatory presumptiveness does not deny that there is a real conflict between promise and the penalties rule. It does not attempt, like justificatory primacy by inflation, to dissolve the conflict by claiming that promises to pay penalties for breach of contract are not genuine promises (what I called earlier the no promise view), or that though valid they are promises that should not be legally enforced because they corrupt the moral practice of promising (the no legally enforceable promise view).

Rather, justificatory presumptiveness accepts that a genuine promise was made which the courts have a pro tanto duty to enforce (that is, it is a genuine duty, but it may be defeated by competing considerations).[25] The conflict between promise and the penalties rule generates an epistemic presumption that the rule is unjustified. However, justificatory presumptiveness is open to the possibility that there may be facts about the specifically legal context within which this promissory duty applies that might justify the courts departing from their pro tanto moral obligation to enforce penalty clauses.

On this view, divergence is accounted for 'by a distinctively *legal* normative argument', which is 'a moral argument whose range is specifically tailored to the special, normatively salient properties of law and its appropriate content and shape'.[26] Justificatory presumptiveness admits that there is divergence between law and promissory morality, but claims that it is potentially not problematic because the departure from what morality (generally conceived) requires could be justified by the specifically legal context within which the duty to enforce promissory obligations arises.

In the context of the enforcement of penalty clauses, what might these specifically legal arguments be? Shiffrin has attempted to justify the rule on rule of law grounds. She argues that the public has an interest that the adjudication of disputes and the remedial consequences of legal wrongs be determined by independent and impartial tribunals capable of tailoring fair remedies according to the nature and importance of the breach in question and the specific circumstances in which it took place. The trouble with penalty clauses is that they are an attempt to displace or substitute the impartial judgment of a court on 'the public significance of legal wrongs' with the partial view of private parties.[27] As such, they deprive the promisee of an opportunity to have a 'public recognition and an impartial resolution' of the legal wrong done to her and the circumstances in which it was done:

[25] Shelly Kagan, *The Limits of Morality* (Clarendon Press 1989) 17. On the pro tanto nature of promissory obligations see Richard Bronaugh, 'A Secret Paradox of the Common Law' (1983) 2 Law and Philosophy 193, 224–26; Richard Bronaugh, 'Promises' in Lawrence C Becker and Charlotte B Becker (eds), *Encyclopedia of Ethics* (2nd edn, Routledge 2001) 1389.

[26] Shiffrin, 'The Divergence of Contract and Promise' (n 2) 733. See also Charles Fried, 'The Convergence of Contract and Promise' (2007) 120 Harvard Law Review Forum 1, 4.

[27] Seana Valentine Shiffrin, 'Remedial Clauses: The Overprivatization of Private Law' (2016) 67 Hastings Law Journal 407, 411.

They require promisees to absorb the significance of an abrogation of duty before it has happened, before the specific circumstances and motivations of the breach are known, and during the period in which the parties are correctly more focused on arranging mutually satisfactory circumstances for performance. Having to absorb the significance of breach, as a general, hypothetical matter seems potentially insensitive to the reasonable promisee's reaction to the actual occasion of breach.[28]

Given that these clauses have a punitive dimension, this raises further worries about their enforcement relating to issues of horizontal equity or the danger that like cases won't be treated alike; the proportionality of these responses to the legal wrongs in question; and, the fact that legal punishment which is meant to express *public* censure for wrongs done against the community is being commandeered for distinctly *private* ends or purposes, such as retaliation or deterrence.[29]

The trouble though with Shiffrin's argument is that the reason why penalty clauses are objectionable seems to go beyond such rule of law or public concerns. Take again the builder example used earlier in this chapter. Imagine that I say to the builder that although I want her to promise me that she will pay me the £1 million as a penalty if she fails to do the work, I do not want the agreement to be legally binding. In these circumstances should the builder fail to do the work, the promise to pay the penalty cannot be legally enforced because there is no contract (as there is no intention to create a legal relationship).[30] Therefore, no specifically legal or public reasons come into the picture to explain why the promise should not be enforced. They do not have to, because due to the lack of a contract the courts have no pro tanto duty to enforce the agreement.

And yet, the promise to pay the penalty still seems troubling at a general moral level. Even though the builder has no *legal* obligation to pay the penalty, the idea that she nevertheless has a *moral* obligation to pay seems wrong. True enough she made a valid promise that she would pay the penalty if she breached, and so from the point of view of the promise principle taken alone she clearly has a moral obligation to pay. But it still seems overly severe to say that morality requires her to pay. Our instincts seem to suggest that she does not have even a moral obligation to pay this huge penalty for breaching what was after all only an agreement to put up some curtain poles. The conclusion that we should reach is that it is not, or at least not only, specifically legal concerns which explain what we find so troubling about penalty clauses, but rather some more general moral concern or concerns.

5. Composite Doctrines

The promise theory's stock responses to divergent contract law rules and doctrines cannot deal successfully with the challenge posed by the penalties rule. Their failure

[28] ibid 432.

[29] Shiffrin, 'The Divergence of Contract and Promise' (n 2) 734; Shiffrin, 'Remedial Clauses: The Overprivatization of Private Law' (n 27) 422–25.

[30] *Balfour v Balfour* [1919] 2 KB 571, discussed in Chapter 5.

teaches us something about the rule. The fact that justificatory primacy cannot be achieved in this context by inflating the promise principle, suggests that the rule does conflict with that principle taken alone. That conflict with promise though does not as we have seen mean that justificatory primacy should be achieved by repudiating the penalties doctrine, which tells us that the rule is justified by some other (non-promissory) concern. That this concern cannot be explained by a strategy of justificatory presumptiveness indicates that the moral principle justifying the rule is *general* rather than one *specific* to the context of legal enforcement.

These considerations seem to lend support to the efficiency theory, which can lay claim to be the missing part of the puzzle. The reason that penalty clauses are not enforced is that they are inefficient. This explains why the promise principle is incompatible with the rule, why nevertheless the rule is justified, and why there is reason to worry about these clauses even outside legal contexts: we have reasons to promote efficiency in all aspects of our lives not just when it comes to law.

The failure of the promise theory to explain the penalties rule though does not lead ineluctably to the conclusion that the only explanation for the existence of the doctrine is efficiency. The promise theory rests on a fundamental mistake, which is that the promise principle plays a special role in justifying contract law rules and doctrines. This restricts the responses the promise theorist might give to explain the presence of the doctrine in contract. The promise theorist has to justify the doctrine, whilst at the same time showing that the promise principle plays a special role in providing that justification, because for example of its justificatory primacy or presumptiveness over other moral principles and standards in the contractual context. But as we have seen such strategies fail.

The difficulty of providing a non-economic account of the penalties rule disappear once we accept that promise plays no special role in contract. Contract law is constituted by an irreducible plurality of moral principles, including not only the promise principle, but other principles relating for example to freedom, exploitation, coercion, deceit, fairness, and many others. The promise principle competes and interacts with these other moral principles in a multiplicity of ways. Principles may defeat, qualify, reinforce, and supplement each other. The weight and significance of these principles varies depending on the particular context, and it is not possible to say in the abstract that one or any set of these principles is more important than others in contract. By mistakenly attaching special importance to promise, the promise theory suffers a built-in tendency to overvalue the significance of promise and miss out or undervalue the role played by other moral concerns in shaping contract law rules and doctrines.

The result is that promise theorists routinely mishandle contract law rules and doctrines. As I have argued in previous chapters, many contract law doctrines are 'composite' in nature. They are the product of the interaction between at least two moral principles. Ronald Dworkin uses the example of adverse possession to make a similar point about legal rules in general. According to the rule, a trespasser can acquire a right to own land by occupying it for a long period of time. This seems to conflict with the principle against profiting from one's own wrong. However, this overlooks the fact that the no profiting from wrongs principle plays a role in shaping the rule. It explains why a trespasser has to occupy land for a long period of time before she acquires title. Had that principle not applied, the time period may have been significantly shorter. The doctrine is therefore the product of the interaction between a property principle which confers ownership rights on the trespasser and the principle against profiting from one's own wrong. Legal rules, Dworkin argues, 'often represent a kind of compromise amongst competing principles in this way'.[31]

Perceiving this blocks the claim that efficiency is the only way to justify contract doctrines that diverge from the promise principle and that cannot be explained by specifically legal concerns. As I have argued in previous chapters, the republican view of contract defended in this book is much more sensitive to the irreducible multiplicity of moral concerns and principles that forge contract doctrine because unlike 'top-down' accounts of contract law like economic efficiency and the promise theory, it works from the 'bottom-up' by attempting to uncover the particular scheme of principle that underpins the contract law of particular jurisdictions at particular times. Although on the republican view contract law serves constitutive ends, such as trust-based cooperation in the English context, these ends are themselves rooted in local circumstances and cultures, and they are indeterminate in nature, thus requiring the courts to play a crucial role in settling how they might be achieved.

Recall from Chapter 6 how the republican view explains the undue influence doctrine. According to the doctrine of undue influence, the promisor has a right to rescind (set-aside) a contract that was procured by the promisee taking advantage of the relationship of influence that she had with the promisor.[32] The doctrine conflicts with the promise principle taken alone because it applies even in cases where there is no doubt that the promisor made a valid promise.[33] Does this divergence with promise mean that the undue influence doctrine cannot be justified? Only if, like the promise theorist, you are myopic about the values that play a role in contract. To be sure, the promise principle plays a role in shaping many contract doctrines, but so do other normative concerns and moral principles, such as the principle against exploitation. As I argued in Chapter 6, in cases of undue influence, the promise principle, which requires promises to be performed, is defeated by the principle against exploitation, which justifies the promisor's breach of his contractual obligations. The duty generated by the promise was only pro tanto, that is, real but not conclusive, and was outweighed by the reasons against exploitation.[34]

This does not mean that the promisor's defeated duty to keep his promise has no normative bite. It was a genuine duty, and even though all things considered he is justified in breaching it, nevertheless his failure to comply has normative

[31] Dworkin, *Taking Rights Seriously* (n 5) 77.

[32] See *Royal Bank of Scotland Plc v Etridge (No 2)* [2002] 2 AC 773, 794–97; Edwin Peel, *The Law of Contract* (13th edn, Sweet & Maxwell 2011) 459; *Restatement (Second) of Contracts* (n 1) § 177.

[33] See, for example, *Allcard v Skinner* [1887] 36 Ch 145; *Credit Lyonnais Bank Nederland NV v Burch* [1997] 1 All ER 144.

[34] Principles, Dworkin says, state reasons that argue 'in one direction', but that does not mean that they 'necessitate a particular decision'. Dworkin, *Taking Rights Seriously* (n 5) 26. They may be outweighed by conflicting principles.

consequences. It may, for example, be a reason for regret on his part or a ground for resentment on the promisee's.[35]

Undue influence is a composite doctrine. It can only be explained by the interaction between the promise principle and the principle against exploitation. No single principle accounts for the doctrine. The promise principle alone cannot explain why the promisor has a justification for not performing a promise extracted through exploitation. From its lights, the promisor made a valid promise and therefore performance is required. On the other hand, the principle against exploitation alone cannot explain why if the promisor fails to raise a defence of undue influence to a breach of contract claim the promisee can go ahead and enforce the contract. The contract is enforceable because the promisor made a genuine promise, albeit one that may be set-aside at the option of the promisor because of the promisee's exploitative conduct. Only by considering how the promise principle interacts with the principle against exploitation can we explain the doctrine.

6. Justifying the Penalties Rule

Like the undue influence doctrine, the rule against penalties conflicts with the promise principle taken alone. As with undue influence, this does not, however, mean that the penalties rule necessarily diverges from morality, and can only be explained by efficiency considerations. In this section, I argue that the penalties rule is a composite doctrine.

6.1 Shiffrin's constraint

As I argued earlier, it is Shiffrin's view that the penalties rule despite its conflict with promise is justified by distinctively legal arguments, and in particular the public interest in making sure that legal wrongs which are wrongs against the community are dealt with by impartial and independent courts. Shiffrin claims that penalty clauses are objectionable because they amount to attempts by private parties to interfere with the community's right to recognize the significance of and respond appropriately to legal wrongs.

Shiffrin says that this social interest in recognizing and responding to legal wrongs in a public way has a parallel in morality. She argues that typically morality prevents agents from controlling the seriousness of their moral wrongs and how others react to them: 'the moral status of conduct that is truly misconduct is usually independent of agents' attitudes or will'.[36] This moral constraint applies generally and is not specific to any particular branch of morality. So, for example, because of this constraint we may not be entitled to stipulate in advance how others should react if we murder,

[35] Joseph Raz, *Practical Reason and Norms* (Oxford University Press 1999) 202–03; Dworkin, *Taking Rights Seriously* (n 5) 35, 77; John Gardner, *Offences and Defences: Selected Essays in the Philosophy of Criminal Law* (Oxford University Press 2007) 81.

[36] Shiffrin, 'The Divergence of Contract and Promise' (n 2) 726–27, 729.

torture, or defame someone, and we may not be entitled to control how our friends will feel if we betray them.

Similarly, in the promissory context, Shiffrin doubts that we can 'alter by declaration or by agreement the moral significance of a broken promise ... the power to alter the significance and appropriateness of *others*' reactions to a broken obligation is not within the power of the promisor'.[37] Shiffrin does not rely on this general moral constraint to justify the penalties rule, preferring, as previously noted, to focus on rule of law considerations to justify the doctrine. I have argued that her explanation of the doctrine is inadequate because the prohibition on penalty clauses seems to respond to a more general (and not specifically legal) moral concern. In light of that critique, it may be that the more general moral constraint that Shiffrin says parallels the rule of law concerns she relies on to justify the penalties rule is worth exploring as a justification for the rule in its own right. Shiffrin herself does moot this as a possibility. Perhaps the law simply tracks or reflects private morality in this context?[38]

The argument would be that penalty clauses are invalid and not enforced by courts because they are an effort by a promisor to control in advance the way others will react to her breach of promise and this is something there is a general moral prohibition against. On this view, the penalties rule is a composite doctrine, that is, the product of at least two interacting moral principles. The rule can be explained by the interaction between the promise principle and the constraint (which is an independent moral principle). The constraint qualifies the promise principle to produce a rule that says that promises are binding unless they seek to specify the moral significance of a broken promise and control how others react to it. If a promise does violate the constraint, it will be invalid and unenforceable.

This is a distinct line of argument to justificatory primacy by inflation considered above. The inflationist would seek to explain the penalties rule on the ground that there is no conflict between it and the promise principle or promissory morality taken alone. By contrast, an argument for the rule based on this more general moral constraint acknowledges that the penalties rule does conflict with promise taken alone, but nevertheless claims that the rule is justified by the interaction between the promise principle and another independent moral principle. In other words, the rule is a composite doctrine.

Although I agree that the justification for the penalties rule may depend on the interaction between the promise principle and another distinct moral principle, I disagree that the other moral principle is the constraint against controlling the moral significance of one's conduct and how others react to it.

This is because, in the context of penalty clauses, it is rarely the case that the promisor will be seeking to control the moral significance of her failure to perform and how the promisee reacts to it by inserting a penalty clause into the contract. Usually it is the promisee who insists on the clause, and typically the promisor would

[37] ibid 729. [38] ibid 726.

have preferred for it to be absent from the contract. In that context, it stretches reality to suggest that the *promisor* may be acting impermissibly.

One might reply that what matters is not what the promisor's intentions are but the effect that the clause has. If the clause, whichever party insisted on it, has the effect of controlling the reaction of others to the breach then it may be impermissible. However, even if that is correct, it is unclear that penalty clauses do have this effect. Rather, penalty clauses are designed to control the content of the secondary or remedial duty that arises on breach. The fact that a penalty clause determines the content of that duty need not mean that it also has the effect of controlling how the promisee reacts to the breach. Even if penalty clauses were enforced, the promisee would still be free to feel outraged or let down by the promisor's breach of duty, and would remain free to express forgiveness for that wrong.

It is unclear whether the general moral constraint that Shiffrin identifies is concerned more with preventing wrongdoers controlling the reactions of others to their breaches of duty, or whether it is more concerned with the impermissibility of efforts to control the content of remedial duties.[39] Even if the concern is with the latter, there are still problems with using this constraint to explain the penalties rule.

Shiffrin expresses the following important doubt about relying on this general moral constraint to justify the penalties doctrine. Even if it is the case that we cannot control the content of our remedial duties when we steal from someone or knock them over, that does not necessarily mean that we cannot control the content of our remedial duties in a promissory context. The promissory domain is unlike most other moral domains, in that the duties it imposes on agents are self-imposed: agents choose to make promises, and thereby choose to restrict the range of options that they have in the future. If agents are permitted to create duties for themselves in this way, then it seems reasonable to assume that they also have the right to determine the content of these obligations, and the consequences of breach. So much is entailed by the fact that the primary duty to perform arose in the first place because of a voluntary undertaking.[40]

Related to this is the point that relying on the general moral constraint to justify the penalties rule does not explain why the courts are willing to enforce liquidated damages clauses, that is, agreed remedy clauses that represent genuine pre-estimates of the loss caused by breach. Unlike penalty clauses, there is nothing intuitively objectionable about liquidated damages. If we go back to the example of the £50 contract for putting up curtain poles, imagine that instead of stipulating £1 million as agreed damages, the builder agreed to pay £70 for breach. If a court enforced that remedy clause, few would object. And yet, if the penalties rule does rely for its justification on the general moral constraint Shiffrin identifies, enforcement could be incompatible with what morality requires. That argument for why penalty clauses may be objectionable is, therefore, over-inclusive: it seems to catch cases where parties seek to control remedial duties that are intuitively unobjectionable.

[39] Kraus argues that Shiffrin conflates these two concerns. Kraus, 'The Correspondence of Contract and Promise' (n 12) 1630 n 53.

[40] Shiffrin, 'The Divergence of Contract and Promise' (n 2) 726.

The claim therefore that the penalties rule might be explained by the interaction between the promise principle and the general moral constraint against agents controlling the significance of their moral wrongs is in the end unsatisfactory because that explanation does not capture what is distinctively wrong about the enforcement of penalty clauses, and because of this misidentification the logic of that argument may well entail criticism of the settled legal practice of enforcing liquidated damages clauses, which few would claim is morally problematic.

6.2 The compensation principle

The principle against controlling the significance of and how others react to one's moral wrongs may be used as Shiffrin herself moots to explain the penalties rule as a composite doctrine, that is, as the product of the interaction between the promise principle and another moral principle. In the end though, Shiffrin dismisses this account and for the reasons considered in the previous section she is, I believe, right to do so. Despite this, I think the penalties rule is a composite doctrine. The moral principle that helps to forge the rule though is not the one that Shiffrin moots only to dismiss, but rather another much more familiar moral principle. It is the compensation principle.

As I have argued, the promise principle taken alone would require one to perform one's promise to pay a penalty clause. However, when a penalty clause is inserted into a contract, the promise principle comes into direct conflict with the compensation principle. According to the compensation principle, one has a duty to compensate those whom one has wronged. So, for example, if I negligently run over your foot I now have a duty to compensate you for my breach of duty, that is, having failed to comply with a duty that I owed to you, I now have a duty to do 'the next best thing'.[41]

I cannot of course unrun over your foot, and it may in the circumstances be very unclear what the next best thing actually is. This is because of a form of 'normative pluralism' that I called in Chapter 5 'interpretive pluralism'.[42] Recall, due to interpretive pluralism there may be an irreducible plurality of ways in which to interpret the requirements of a particular value. Although we know the compensation principle requires us to compensate or do the next best thing, bar ruling out obviously inappropriate courses of action (for example, I buy you a private jet), there may be a range of rationally defensible courses of action available to me as forms of compensation, such as, for example, offering proportionate monetary compensation for the loss suffered, or taking it upon myself to carry out tasks that you will now find it impossible or very difficult to perform, or offering to pay for a restful holiday to help you recuperate from the injury, and so forth. These are all

[41] Joseph Raz, 'Personal Practical Conflicts' in Peter Baumann and Monika Betzler (eds), *Practical Conflicts: New Philosophical Essays* (Cambridge University Press 2004) 189, 191. John Gardner, 'What is Tort Law For? Part 1. The Place of Corrective Justice' (2011) 30 Law and Philosophy 1. James E Penner, 'Voluntary Obligations and the Scope of the Law of Contract' (1996) 2 Legal Theory 325, 351–52.

[42] See text to ch 5, nn 109–13.

perfectly legitimate forms of imperfect compliance with the reasons I had for my original duty not to negligently run over your foot.

Similarly, in the promissory context if I fail to perform my promise, I will have a duty to do the next best thing—but what that actually involves is often far from obvious. I promise to take my daughter to the cinema but let her down. What should I now do? Take her to the next showing? Take her out for dinner? Get a DVD to watch together at home? Buy her flowers? These all seem like perfectly legitimate ways of interpreting what the compensation principle might require in the circumstances. There is no uniquely appropriate form of compliance with my duty to compensate.

Matters get even more complex due to the other form of normative pluralism that I identified in Chapter 5 which I called 'value pluralism'.[43] In deciding how to compensate you after my breach of duty, I have to take account of countervailing considerations that compete and conflict with my reasons for doing the next best thing (whatever that might be). So, for example, assuming that the next best thing, having breached my promise to take my daughter to the cinema, is to take her to the next screening of the movie, my reasons for complying with what compensation requires, might conflict with other reasons I have, such as, for example, if the next screening is at a time when I am meant to be carrying out charity work. There exists an irreducible plurality of values, and when conflicts between them arise, there may be no single appropriate way to resolve them, but rather a range of rationally defensible rankings that might be made.

As I argued in Chapter 5, in the context of our personal or private lives the way we interpret the values that bear on us and how we rank values when they conflict is constitutive of the types of people we become and the relationships we form with others. Things though are different in the public or legal sphere. In that context, how values are interpreted and how they rank when they conflict with other values are matters that are authoritatively settled by legislatures and courts. Unlike in our personal lives where how we manage normative pluralism is largely left as an 'open' matter, for us to determine ourselves, the law provides a largely 'closed' system where such matters are authoritatively determined by legal institutions.[44]

So, the lack of clarity about what compensation requires when a promise is broken in the context of our private lives, can be contrasted with a good deal of certainty when promises that are also contracts are broken in our public or legal lives. When a contract is broken we are mostly aware that our duty to compensate or do the next best thing usually involves paying expectation damages, that is, putting the innocent party into the financial position she would have been in had the promise been fulfilled.[45]

[43] See text to ch 5, nn 113–16.
[44] ibid nn 115–24.
[45] Although clearly underlain by the compensatory principle, the expectation damages doctrine is itself an example of a composite doctrine; its contours no doubt being shaped by a ranking of competing values. So, for example, the House of Lords has cited a variety of reasons for preferring expectation damages over specific performance as the standard remedy for breach of contract including the fact that in certain contexts specific performance is difficult and costly to supervise, can lead to slavery, and may be oppressive. See *Co-operative Insurance Society Ltd v Argyll Stores (Holdings) Ltd* [1998] AC 1.

The law then has, broadly speaking, authoritatively resolved or settled the issue of what compensation requires when a contract is broken. The default is that the next best thing to performing a contract is usually paying expectation damages. With that in place, the difficulty the law has with penalty clauses begins to come into view. If the contracting parties have themselves stipulated in the contract that a penal sum is payable for breach, then on breach there is a clear conflict between the promise principle and the compensation principle that underpins the expectation damages doctrine. According to promissory logic, the defendant has a duty to perform her promise, that is, pay the penalty. According to the way the duty to compensate has been interpreted and ranked as a matter of law, the defendant who has breached her contract standardly has a duty to pay expectation damages.[46]

What the rule against penalty clauses shows is that when these principles conflict, the compensation principle which underpins the expectation damages remedy is weightier and prevails over the promise principle. This is why penalty clauses are invalid. However, this does not mean that the promise principle is completely wiped out. Principles, Dworkin said, 'survive intact when they do not prevail', and these defeated principles may play a role in shaping legal rules and doctrines.[47] Like adverse possession and undue influence, the penalties rule is also a compromise between competing moral principles. In the case of the penalties rule, the primary interaction is between promise and compensation.

6.3 Liquidated damages

In what way is the rule against penalties a compromise? Prima facie, it's unclear whether the promise principle plays any role in shaping the rule; it seems to just get completely trumped by the compensation principle. Where the agreed damages clause extravagantly overcompensates the promisee it is invalid and not enforced by the courts, and the remedy clause plays no role in determining what the defendant's liabilities will be. In that context, how can it be said that the promise principle has anything to add in explaining the rule?

[46] One could argue that there is no conflict here because you cannot promise to do that which you already have a moral obligation to do, for example, pay compensation. Richard Bronaugh discusses this problem in the context of whether there is consideration for a promise to a third party to perform an existing contractual obligation owed to the second party. Bronaugh, 'A Secret Paradox of the Common Law' (n 25). Bronaugh claims that consideration does exist, because the promise to the third party entails a change in normative position. It is beyond the scope of this chapter to discuss this debate in any depth. Instead, I will assume for the sake of argument that there is no power to make such a promise. If that is the case, one could argue that you cannot promise to pay a sum for breach when there exists already a pre-existing obligation to pay compensation. However, this conclusion is fallacious for three reasons. First, the promise to pay the sum is made *before* there is any duty to pay compensation. There is no pre-existing duty to pay compensation. Second, the content of the promise to pay the sum and the content of the obligation to pay compensation are very likely to differ; the promise does not replicate the compensatory duty. Finally, the argument appears to be over-inclusive, there does not seem to be anything intuitively problematic about a liquidated damages clause, and yet according to this argument such clauses do not create a duty.

[47] Dworkin, *Taking Rights Seriously* (n 5) 35, 77.

The key lies in the word 'extravagantly'. If it were true that all that mattered from the point of view of explaining the rule were the compensation principle, we would expect the rule to invalidate not only clauses that are grossly or extravagantly over-compensatory but also clauses that are over-compensatory simpliciter. But, the law does not do this, and this reflects the influence of the promise principle.

As I said above, although the courts do not enforce penalty clauses, they do enforce liquidated damages clauses, that is, clauses that represent genuine pre-estimates of the loss caused by breach.[48] This is the flipside of the penalties rule. Provided an agreed damages clause is not *extravagantly* over-compensatory, the courts will uphold and enforce it, even though as a matter of fact it may overcompensate the promisee.

Neither Kraus nor Shiffrin can explain why liquidated damages are treated differently from penalty clauses. For Kraus, who adopts the strategy of achieving the justificatory primacy of promise by repudiating the penalties doctrine, both penalty clauses and liquidated damages should be enforced because that is what is required by the promise principle. Shiffrin, on the other hand, relying on justificatory presumptiveness to vindicate the promise theory, argues that the penalties rule is justified to uphold the public or social interest in ensuring that the response to legal wrongs is made by its own impartial and independent courts. But if that is the explanation for the rule, it would also require the non-enforcement of liquidated damages clauses.

The asymmetry between penalty clauses and liquidated damages clauses exists because the promise principle interacts with the compensation principle. The product of that interaction is a compromise. The compensation principle overrides the promise principle where the agreed damages clause manifestly or extravagantly overcompensates the promisee against the legally determined standard of compensation. However, where overcompensation is not extravagant, the promise principle is given a degree of slack by the compensation principle. The slack exists, because these cases do not constitute serious violations of the weightier compensation principle, in the way that the enforcement of penalty clauses would. This explains why the courts uphold and enforce liquidated damages clauses.

However, a potential problem for my theory is that it does not appear to sit well with the insistence in English law that the permissibility of agreed damages clauses must be assessed at the time that the contract was entered.[49] The courts judge whether the sums stipulated were genuine pre-estimates of what the parties at the time that the contract was entered could reasonably foresee to be the greatest loss that could flow from breach.[50] From the perspective of my explanation this looks odd. If the penalties rule is a compromise between the promise and the compensation principles,

[48] See text to n 1.

[49] The position in US law is not as strict. According to the *Uniform Commercial Code* § 2-718 (1), the reasonableness of agreed damages clauses should be assessed 'in light of the anticipated *or* actual harm caused by the breach' (emphasis added).

[50] *Dunlop Pneumatic Tyre Co Ltd v New Garage and Motor Co Ltd* (n 1) 86–87, 101. There is some uncertainty over whether the loss that must be envisaged by the parties is the actual or the legally recoverable loss. See Burrows, *Remedies for Torts and Breach of Contract* (n 4) 446–47.

then from the point of view of the compensation principle what should matter is the proportionality between the promised amount and the *actual* loss, rather than what the parties at the time that they formed the contract reasonably envisaged that the greatest loss from breach would be. This is because the compensation principle is concerned with repairing the actual losses caused by breaches of duty (subject to other considerations justifying doctrines such as mitigation and remoteness which restrict the recovery of actual losses) and not *potential* losses. There is also no reason why promissory logic should stand in the way of a focus on actual losses, and so this aspect of the rule cannot be explained away by appealing to the interaction between the two principles.

One response would be to say that the current judicial focus on the losses that the parties foresaw at the time that they entered into the contract is misguided, and the law should be reformed. However, such a response may be too quick. I should clarify that my claim is not that the penalties rule is *exclusively* the product of the interaction between the promise and compensation principles. Rather it is the more modest claim that it is *primarily* the product of the interaction between these two principles. I did not mean to deny that other principles and normative concerns may play a role in shaping the contours of the rule. Furthermore, how these principles interact and the weight they carry has to be evaluated against the background of the constitutive purpose of English contract law, which as I have argued in earlier chapters, is the promotion of trust-based cooperation.

One of the great virtues of liquidated damages clauses is that they promote commercial certainty. The parties at the time of entering into the contract will know exactly what will happen if one or both of them breach. Provided that the parties stipulate a sum that is not grossly in excess of the greatest conceivable loss that may flow from breach, they are saved from the possible vagaries of judicial assessment and can rest assured that they know in advance the risks that they are running. This plays a crucial role in giving parties the confidence they need to enter into legally binding trust-based cooperative relations with one another.

If contract is to achieve its constitutive function of promoting trust-based cooperation which, as argued in Chapter 4, is a critical component for achieving the goods of social solidarity, community cohesion, and social stability, it must give contracting parties the power to reduce or manage their litigation risks and costs and, more generally, plan their commercial affairs. This will also promote the rule of law by saving the courts the time and expense of assessing liability.[51]

These commercial certainty and rule of law gains would however be lost if the courts shifted their focus away from the proportionality between the agreed sum and the losses that the parties foresaw at the time of entry into the contract, and focused instead on the actual losses caused by breach. Due to the fact that it is impossible to know in advance what the actual losses caused by a particular breach will be, this will reintroduce the uncertainty that liquidated damages do so well to dispel.

[51] Burrows, *Remedies for Torts and Breach of Contract* (n 4) 449; *Kemble v Farren* (1829) 6 Bing 141, 148: 'In many cases, such an agreement fixes that which is almost impossible to be accurately ascertained; and in all cases, it saves the expense and difficulty of bringing witnesses to that point.'

Therefore, the explanation for this aspect of the penalties rule may lie in a concern for promoting commercial certainty and the rule of law. Relying on these principles to explain this aspect of the penalties rule is not at odds with my claim that the rule is *primarily* explained by the interaction between the promise and compensation principles. Promise and compensation explain the main features of the rule. However, its various contours may have been shaped by other principles, such as commercial certainty and the rule of law, and the constitutive end of contract law which is to promote trust-based cooperation.

6.4 The requirement of breach

My explanation also explains the rigid requirement of breach. This is the most controversial aspect of the penalties rule. The courts have insisted that the rule only applies where payment is required because of a breach of contract.[52] This is considered problematic, because a promisee can easily evade the rule by making payment conditional on an act or an omission that does not amount to breach. In this way, payment of what is in effect a penalty becomes a *primary* term of the contract. For convenience, I will call these 'breach-avoiding clauses'.

So, for example, in *Euro London Appointments Ltd v Claessens International Ltd*, the contract stipulated that the defendant company, which hired employees from the claimant, would receive a discount if it paid its invoices within seven days of receipt. When it failed to pay within seven days, the defendant claimed that the loss of the discount amounted to an invalid penalty clause. However, the Court of Appeal upheld the clause, because it was not activated by an event that amounted to a breach of contract. The defendant company had no duty to pay within seven days, and it was not in breach of contract when it failed to do so. Absent breach, the penalties rule did not apply.[53]

As Mindy Chen-Wishart has pointed out, aside from discounts there are a variety of other types of breach-avoiding clause embodied in traditional contract law doctrines such as compromise, accord and satisfaction, and an action for the agreed sum. This has led her to worry that the requirement of breach is unjust.[54]

[52] *Export Credits Guarantee Department v Universal Oil Products Co* [1983] 1 WLR 399.

[53] *Euro London Appointments Ltd v Claessens International Ltd* [2006] EWCA Civ 385 (CA). See also *Alder v Moore* [1961] 2 QB 57. In a recent case, *Andrews v Australia and New Zealand Banking Group Ltd* [2012] HCA 30, the Australian High Court decided that the penalties rule *might* apply in cases where there is no breach of contract. This was justified on the basis of the rule's equitable origins in regulating the enforcement of bonds where breach of duty was not required to activate the application of a penalty. The court, however, stated that the rule would not apply to cases where the parties had agreed to an option to pay more for receiving further benefits under the contract. It called these 'alternative stipulations' following John Pomeroy. John Norton Pomeroy, *A Treatise on Equity Jurisprudence*, vol 2 (5th edn, Bancroft-Whitney and Lawyers Cooperative 1941) § 437. This seems to preserve the distinction between what I call breach-avoiding clauses and penalty clauses. The decision may not therefore be as dramatic a change in the law as it at first might appear. Thank you to Katy Barnett for alerting me to the case and for her analysis of the decision. Email correspondence on the Obligations Discussion Group available at <http://www.ucc.ie/law/odg/home.htm> accessed 10 September 2012.

[54] Chen-Wishart, 'Controlling the Power to Agree Damages' (n 14) 285.

My explanation of the penalties rule shows why that requirement is defensible. The courts refuse to enforce penalty clauses because they contravene the compensation principle, which requires compensation, usually in the form of expectation damages, to be paid for breach of contract. If, however, a breach-avoiding clause is used, there will be no breach, and, therefore, the compensation principle will not apply. Instead, the promise principle is free to exert itself and that explains why the courts tend to enforce these clauses.[55]

My analysis here is supported by a recent discussion of the status of the breach requirement by the Supreme Court in the case *Cavendish Square Holding BV v Talal El Makdessi*, which was part of a conjoined appeal.[56] The case concerned the sale by the defendant of a controlling stake in a communications group, the defendant agreeing to restrictive covenants guaranteeing the goodwill of the business, which if breached would deprive the defendant of the final two instalments of the price and require him to sell the remaining shares to the claimant at a price excluding the value of the goodwill. The question was whether this aspect of the agreement amounted to a penalty clause.

The court said that the penalties doctrine did not apply because even though the reductions in the price of the business arose on breach of the restrictive covenants they were nevertheless part of the primary obligations of the contract adjusting the consideration or price payable for the business in light of the breaches by the defendant. This would suggest that the requirement of breach is only a necessary and not a sufficient condition for the application of the penalties rule, and that in addition it must be shown that the purpose of any payment or price reduction triggered by breach is compensatory in nature.[57]

This is perfectly in line with my claim that the motivating concern behind the penalties rule is the violation of the compensation principle. It is only when a payment clause triggered by breach aims specifically at compensating the innocent party that the compensation principle is under threat and the penalties doctrine triggered.

6.5 Forfeitures

My theory of the penalties rule explains two of its most salient features: first, its flipside, that although penalty clauses are not enforced, liquidated damages are; and, second, the requirement of breach. Both of these aspects of the rule reflect the fact that the rule is the product of the interaction between the compensation and promise principles. The compensation principle outweighs the promise principle and explains why penalty clauses are invalid, but it does not extinguish the promise

[55] This is not to say that the concerns about this aspect of the penalties rule are entirely misplaced. They may reflect the existence of other reasons for why the courts should be wary of these clauses, such as the protection of reasonable expectations, inequality of bargaining power, and the prevention of exploitation.

[56] *Cavendish Square Holding BV v Talal El Makdessi and ParkingEye Limited v Beavis* (n 1).

[57] ibid [73]–[74], [82]–[83].

principle. Although defeated, the promise principle continues to exert its normative pull. This explains why liquidated damages and breach-avoiding clauses, despite their apparent incompatibility with the compensation principle, continue to be enforced by the courts.

However, a serious objection to my theory is the asymmetry between how the courts regulate penalty clauses on the one hand, and forfeiture clauses on the other. Penalty clauses involve promises to pay sums of money upon breach of contract. In contrast, forfeiture clauses involve the payment of sums to the promisee *in advance* of performance ('advance payments'), either as a 'deposit' or an 'instalment', which the parties have agreed will be 'forfeit' to the promisee on breach.

The courts are, however, less ready to strike down a forfeiture clause than they are a penalty.[58] Even if a forfeiture clause grossly overcompensates the promisee for breach of contract, the courts will enforce it unless *in addition* the clause is either unreasonable (the test used for deposits),[59] or unconscionable (the test applied to instalments).[60]

From the point of view of the compensation principle, this difference of treatment is inexplicable. Both penalty clauses and grossly over-compensatory forfeiture clauses have the same effect. The only difference is in the time of payment. If it is the case, therefore, that the compensation principle prevails over the promise principle in the context of penalty clauses, it should do the same in the case of grossly over-compensatory forfeiture clauses. My theory does seem, therefore, to require the rule against penalties to apply to forfeiture clauses.

I think that is correct, and that there is a strong case for law reform here.[61] However, I want tentatively to suggest the possibility that there may be a distinction between penalty and forfeiture clauses, which justifies the asymmetry of treatment.

Advance payments serve two very important functions, which penalty clauses do not. First, they may be a source of working capital for the payee, which the payee may need to perform her obligations under the contract. And, second, they protect the payee against the insolvency of the promisor.[62] Both of these benefits flow from the fact that these payments are made in advance of performance, and their effect is that they make it more likely that the promisee will enter into contractual exchanges with the promisor.

This is important from the point of view of what I have argued is the constitutive purpose of contract which is to promote trust-based cooperation. As argued in Chapter 4, the intrinsic value of contract resides in the fact that it enables parties to achieve their ends in a spirit of cooperation based on trust and mutual respect. If the penalties rule applied to forfeiture clauses, this might discourage these forms of

[58] *Howe v Smith* (1884) 27 Ch D 89; *Linggi Plantations Ltd v Jagatheesan* [1972] 1 MLJ 89.

[59] *Workers Trust and Merchant Bank Ltd v Dojap Investments Ltd* [1993] AC 573, 578.

[60] *Stockloser v Johnson* [1954] 1 QB 476, 490.

[61] The Law Commission came to the same view after concluding that there was no rational way to distinguish between these two types of clause. Law Commission, *Penalty Clauses and Forfeitures* (Law Com No 61, 1975) para 59.

[62] Donald Harris, David Campbell, and Roger Halson, *Remedies in Contract and Tort* (2nd edn, Cambridge University Press 2005) 147.

cooperation, so important for achieving social solidarity, community cohesion, and so on, because promisees may be less likely to cooperate with promisors because they lack working capital and fear the promisor's insolvency.

Although, therefore, it is difficult to see why from the point of view of the compensation principle the penalties rule should not apply to forfeiture clauses, it may be that the less restrictive approach of the courts toward forfeiture clauses is justified given the constitutive function of contract law which is to promote trust-based cooperation.

7. Conclusion

In conclusion, I argue that the penalties rule poses a challenge to the promise theory of contract, because promissory logic seems to require the enforcement of these clauses. The stock responses of the promise theory to what seem like divergent contract doctrines all fall short in the penalties context. The primacy of promise cannot be achieved in this context, because promise cannot either repudiate what looks like a justified rule or, because of the rule's contours, accommodate it by artificially stretching the promise principle. Nor can the promise theorist rely on a strategy of justificatory presumptiveness, because features specific to the legal context within which the penalties rule operates fall short of explaining the scope of the moral problem that the rule addresses.

The promise theory struggles to explain the rule because of its commitment to the idea that promise plays a special normative role in contract law. However, as I have argued, many contract doctrines are composite in nature, that is, the product of the interaction between the promise principle and other general moral principles.

The rule against penalties is also a composite doctrine. It is primarily the product of the interaction between the promise principle and the compensation principle. The compensation principle outweighs the promise principle and explains why the courts should not enforce penalty clauses, and why breach of contract is a condition for the application of the rule. The fact that the compensation principle prevails, however, does not mean that the promise principle is extinguished. Its presence is felt in particular in the enforcement of liquidated damages and breach-avoiding clauses.

Other principles may intrude on the primary interaction between the compensation and promise principle, and explain some of the contours of the penalties rule. So, for example, I have argued that the principles relating to the promotion of commercial certainty and the rule of law set against the background of promoting trust-based cooperation—contract's constitutive end—explain why the courts assess the validity of agreed damages clauses by reference to the reasonably foreseeable losses that the parties envisaged at the time that they entered into the contract, rather than the actual losses caused by breach. I have also (tentatively) suggested that promoting trust-based cooperation may explain why the rule against penalties does not apply to forfeiture clauses.

Therefore, a richer conception of the general moral principles that bear on contract law and how they interact with one another explains the penalties rule.

The alternative to foundationalism need not be economic efficiency. To see this though involves perceiving that the law cannot and should not be sealed off from the complexity that we find in morality. The next chapter deals with another remedial doctrine that the promise theory has struggled with—mitigation—and provides a further example of how the true morality of contract doctrine depends on the rejection of foundationalism.

9

Mitigation and Fairness*

1. Mitigation and Loss Sharing

1.1 Failure to act

Consider the following case:

I. A promises B to drive her to the airport but she fails to turn up.

Few would deny that A has breached a moral duty owed to B, and that A has secondary obligations toward B as a result of that breach. At the very least, A has a duty to apologize and to express regret. This is so whether or not B suffers loss as a result of the breach. But now let's assume that the promisee has suffered loss:

II. A promises B to drive her to the airport but she fails to turn up. B misses her flight, which costs her £1,000.

Do A's secondary obligations include the duty to cover the promisee's loss? That seems like a plausible or legitimate interpretation of what the compensation principle discussed in Chapter 8 might require in this context. At the very least, we can say, *other things being equal*, A is responsible and to blame for B's loss (putting aside what A should now do in light of her responsibility). But what if things are not equal? Consider this case:

III. A promises B to drive her to the airport but she fails to turn up. B can take a £50 cab to the airport and make the flight. However, she chooses to do nothing and she misses the flight, which costs her £1,000.

Is A responsible and to blame for the whole of B's loss in this case? It seems far less clear that she is, because B could have easily made her flight by taking the cab. Let's stipulate that it makes no difference to B whether A drives her or whether she takes a cab. What seems to be important here is that the promisee can *easily* bring about the same state of affairs that A was under a promissory obligation to bring about. Had

* This chapter is based on and largely reproduces, but with some important revisions and adaptations, the text of a previously published chapter co-authored with George Letsas entitled 'Mitigation, Fairness, and Contract Law', which appeared in Gregory Klass, George Letsas, and Prince Saprai (eds), *Philosophical Foundations of Contract Law* (Oxford University Press 2014) 319, copyright © The several contributors 2014. The text is used with kind permission of my co-author, Oxford University Press, and the editors of that volume.

she done so, she would also have avoided the loss that would have occurred if she did nothing. This can be shown by contrasting III with cases where it is *difficult* for the promisee to bring about the promised state of affairs. Consider the following case:

IV. A promises B to drive her to the airport but she fails to turn up. B can only get a cab by doing a two-hour-long walk (she lives in a remote location). She chooses to do nothing and she misses the flight, which costs her £1,000.

Here it is clear that A is responsible for the whole loss caused when B misses the flight. Although B could have brought about the same state of affairs that A promised, doing so would have been burdensome for B. It would have required her to undertake a two-hour-long walk. Moreover, we would not take a different view if the cost of the flight were to be substantially higher (say, £10,000). The two-hour walk would not become less burdensome, the higher the cost of the flight. A two-hour walk is an unreasonable means of bringing about the promised state of affairs regardless of the size of the loss that would be avoided. By unreasonable I simply mean that this is not an alternative that most people would expect to take, given the nature of the promised performance and the effect that taking the alternative would normally have on people's plans. Even if the promisee were a marathon runner, for whom a two-hour walk is a piece of cake, it would still count as a burden since it is not a substitute that most people would expect to use for getting to the airport. My notion of burdensomeness is, therefore, agent-neutral.[1]

Going back to the republican theme of non-domination discussed in Chapter 7, if the responsibility for the loss caused in case IV above were to be shared, it would unduly subject B and her life plans to the arbitrary will and judgment of the promise-breaker. By breaking her promise, A subjects B to a risk of incurring a very significant responsibility for a loss, which usually people in B's position can only avoid by altering their life plans in a significant way. This seems like an unfair restraint on B's freedom.

The operative principle here is not efficiency, since efficiency would require comparing the cost of walking, which we should quantify, with the cost of alternatives, including the alternative in which the promisee does nothing and suffers loss. Efficiency would *require* the promisee to walk, if walking was the most cost-effective option, or would impose the cost of any losses on her if she chose not to walk.

Still, there will be cases where the alternative way of securing performance is not at all burdensome, but its cost exceeds the cost of the losses that would otherwise flow from the breach. Consider this case:

V. A promises B to drive her to the airport but she fails to turn up. The only way B could have made the flight was by hiring a £10,000 helicopter to take her to the airport. B chooses to do nothing and misses the flight, which costs her £1,000.

[1] My approach may be conceived of as majoritarian in nature: appealing to whether the majority of people similarly situated would regard the alternative to be burdensome. Majoritarianism is often used to justify default rules in contract law. I am, however, not committed to standard normative justifications offered in favour of majoritarianism, such as that majoritarianism is a rule of thumb for maximizing efficiency.

Here, the existence of an alternative way to secure performance the cost of which exceeds the cost of the losses that flow from the breach, does not affect the responsibility of the promisor. So, the size of the loss appears to have some relevance for determining the responsibility of the promisor.

Cases I–V support the following mitigation principle:

MP1: When a promise is broken, *and* (1) there is an alternative way to secure the state affairs promised by the promisor, *and* (2) it does not matter to the promisee whether the promisor or someone else performs, *and* (3) the promisee can easily take that alternative, *and* (4) the cost of that alternative does not exceed the loss that would occur if the promisee did nothing, *and* (5) the promisee fails to take it, *then* the promisor is not responsible for the whole of the losses that flow from her breach.

There will also be cases, however, where there is no easily available alternative open to the promisee to secure the promised state of affairs, but there is an easily available means for avoiding the loss that would otherwise flow from the promisor's breach.[2] So, for example, imagine that after A's breach there was no available means for B to get to the airport, but she could easily phone the airline to cancel the flight and obtain a significant refund. This is a type of what I shall call a 'pure loss-avoidance' case. At the cost of completeness, but to avoid undue complexity, I will not discuss those cases here. Suffice it to say that I believe a similar mitigation principle applies in these cases, the main difference being that it refers to the promisee avoiding the loss that would be caused by the breach of promise, rather than to securing the state of affairs promised.

According to MP1, the existence of alternatives, which the promisee can easily take but fails to do so, mitigates the responsibility that the promisor has for the promisee's losses. In cases like III, the promisor is not responsible for the *entire* loss caused by her breach of duty. Surely, however, the promisor is not completely off the moral hook for these losses? She committed a wrong and must bear at least *some* of the responsibility for the loss. This leads to a loss-sharing principle:

LS1: When MP1 applies, the promisor shares some responsibility for the loss caused by the broken promise with the promisee.

MP1 mitigates the responsibility of the promisor for the loss, and LS1 requires the promisee, when MP1 applies, to share some of the responsibility for the loss caused with the promisor.

1.2 Action taken

So far, I have been considering cases where the promisee does *not* take an easily available alternative that would have secured the promised state of affairs. What if, however, the promisee *had* successfully taken such action?

[2] Thank you to Ben McFarlane and Seana Shiffrin for drawing my attention to these cases.

VI. A promises B to drive her to the airport but she fails to turn up. B takes a £50 cab to the airport and makes the £1,000 flight.

Here it is clear that A is responsible for B's loss. After all, it is because A breached her promise that B had to take a cab. Though B would have lost £1,000 if she hadn't, her loss now is only £50. A is responsible for B's actual loss, not the loss she would have incurred had she acted otherwise. Normally one is not responsible for a loss that hasn't obtained.

Consider now the following case:

VII. A promises B to drive her to the airport but she fails to turn up. B could have taken a £50 cab to the airport, but instead hires a £500 chauffeur-driven limousine to take her to the airport. B makes the £1,000 flight.

It seems clear that A is not responsible for the full cost of the limousine, because there was a cheaper alternative, easily available to B, to obtain the state of affairs that would have obtained had A performed her promise.

Now, consider the following case:

VIII. A promises B to drive her to the airport but she fails to turn up. B could undertake a two-hour-long walk and then get a cab (she lives in remote location), but instead hires a £500 chauffeur-driven limousine to take her to the airport. There were no other ways of getting to the airport on time. B makes the £1,000 flight.

Here it seems A is responsible for the full cost of the limousine, because it would have been burdensome for B to undertake the walk. The walk was not an easily available alternative means of securing the state of affairs that A had promised.

Cases VI–VIII suggest the following mitigation principle:

MP2: When a promise is broken, *and* (1) the promisee successfully takes action to bring about the state of affairs that would have obtained had the promise been performed, *and* there was (2) an easily available, *and* (3) cheaper alternative way of securing the promised performance, *then* the promisor is not responsible for the whole of the losses that flow from her breach.

A similar mitigation principle applies where it is no longer possible for the promisee to secure performance, and she takes action instead which avoids the loss that would otherwise be caused by breach. In such circumstances, the promisor's responsibility for the loss is mitigated, if there was, open to the promisee, an easily available and cheaper alternative way of avoiding that loss. So, for example, assume that after A's breach, there is no available means for B to catch the flight, but that she could easily obtain a significant refund on the price of the ticket by calling the airline to cancel the flight. Instead of calling, however, which is cheap, B hires an expensive cab to take her to the airport to cancel the ticket in person. In such circumstances, A's responsibility for the cost of the cab is mitigated. This is another type of pure loss avoidance case. To avoid making things too complex, I will not go into the detail of the mitigation principle that applies to this case.

Let's go back to the cases where the promisee takes action to secure the promised state of affairs. Consider the following case:

IX. A promises B to drive her to the airport but she fails to turn up. The only way B could make the flight is by hiring a £10,000 helicopter to take her to the airport. B chooses to hire the helicopter and catches the flight on time. Had she missed the flight she would have suffered a loss of £1,000.

It is clear here that A's responsibility for the loss caused is mitigated. The promisor is not responsible for the entire cost of the course of action that the promisee took in order to secure the promised performance when the cost of that action exceeds the loss that would otherwise have been caused by breach.

This case suggests the following mitigation principle:

MP3: When a promise is broken, *and* (1) the promisee successfully takes action to bring about the state of affairs that would have obtained had the promise been performed, *and* (2) the cost of the course of action taken by the promisee exceeds the loss that would have occurred had the promisee done nothing, *then* the promisor is not responsible for the whole of the losses that flow from her breach.

A similar principle exists in cases where the promisee can no longer secure the promised state of affairs, but instead takes action to avoid the loss that would otherwise be caused by breach, but the cost of that action exceeds the loss that would have occurred had the promisee done nothing. This is another type of pure loss avoidance case. Again, to avoid undue complexity, I will not go into the detail of these cases here.

Let's go back to cases where B does successfully take action to secure the promised state of affairs. We have seen that in these cases, A's responsibility for the loss caused by her breach of promise is mitigated if principle MP2 or MP3 applies.

However, in cases like VIII and IX should A be responsible for at least *some* of the loss caused to B? It seems fair that she should be. This leads to a second loss-sharing principle:

LS2: When MP2 or MP3 apply, the promisor shares some responsibility for the loss caused by the broken promise with the promisee.

1.3 Summary

The MP and LS principles above tell us that when a promise is broken and loss caused to the promisee, responsibility for that loss is shared by the promisor and the promisee in three types of case. First, cases where the promisee fails to take some easily available course of action that would have secured the promised state of affairs. Second, where the promisee does successfully take action to bring about the promised state of affairs, but there was a cheaper and easily available alternative course of action that could have been taken to secure that state of affairs. Third, when the promisee does successfully take action to bring about the promised state of affairs, but the costs of that action exceed the loss that would have occurred had the promisee not acted.

So far this is all at the level of systematizing our intuitions about who should bear responsibility for loss caused in particular cases of breach of promise. What justifies having those intuitions and the principles to which they lead? Let's turn now to this question.

2. Justification: Altruism vs Fairness

In MP1, the promisee takes no action to bring about the promised state of affairs, even though she could have done so easily. According to MP1, the existence of easily available alternatives is relevant for determining the responsibility of the promisor for losses caused by her breach. MP1, however, is silent on whether the promisee has a *duty* to take the easily available alternative. All that MP1 says is that *if* the promisee fails to take the easily available alternative, then the promisor's responsibility for the promisee's losses is mitigated.

Now, one way to try and justify MP1 is to argue that the promisee has a moral *duty* to take the easily available alternative, and that breach of that duty mitigates the responsibility of the promisor. This is the view taken by Charles Fried. For Fried, the moral foundation of that duty lies in the idea of altruism: the promisee's position is analogous to that of a Good Samaritan; there is a relation of trust between the promisor and the promisee which makes 'the two parties neighbors rather than strangers'.[3] Fried argues that when such relations of trust hold, they give rise to duties to save the other party 'from serious loss when the actor can do so with little trouble, risk of loss, or harm to himself'.[4]

The logic of Fried's argument seeks to justify MP1 in two steps. First, it postulates a duty on the part of the promisee to act in order to reduce a loss for which, it is assumed, the promisor is pro tanto responsible. Second, it argues that the breach of that duty has the normative effect of mitigating the responsibility of the promisor for the loss she has caused. Though the promisor remains responsible for the losses caused by not performing her promissory obligation, her responsibility is now outweighed, qualified, or cancelled, by the fact that the promisee failed to act as a Good Samaritan would.

Let's start by granting, arguendo, that the promisee has a duty of altruism to help the promisor by reducing the losses caused by the breach of her promissory obligation. So, let's assume that at *t1*, when A fails to turn up to drive B to the airport, B *ought* (in the sense of has a mandatory reason to) take a cab with a view to reduce the losses for which A is pro tanto responsible. At *t2*, the promisee has sat back and done nothing, breaching her duty to help the promisor and allowing losses to accumulate. How would the promisee's breach of her duty to help the promisor have the normative effect of altering the promisor's responsibility for the losses caused by non-performance?

The normative explanation would, I think, run as follows. Upon breaching her duty to help the promisor, the promisee would be under an obligation to compensate

[3] Charles Fried, 'The Convergence of Contract and Promise' (2007) 120 Harvard Law Review Forum 1, 8.

[4] ibid 7–8.

the promisor or do 'the next best thing'.[5] This is normally thought to involve putting the person to whom one owes the compensatory obligation into the position she would have been in had one not breached. In this case, had B not breached her duty to help A, that is, had B taken a cab to make her flight, A would be responsible for the much smaller loss (£50), than the one she is now responsible for (£1,000). In order to put A in the position she would have been in had B complied with her duty of altruism, B would need to make it the case that A is responsible for £50 rather than £1,000. B can achieve this by exercising a normative power: she can waive any claim she might have against A for missing the flight (a loss for which B assumes responsibility). So, B's secondary obligation would require her to waive any claim she has against A for the amount of £950.

According to the argument from the duty of altruism, the promisor is pro tanto responsible for the loss caused by her breach of promise but, at the same time, she has a valid moral claim that the promisee waive her right to hold the promisor responsible for the difference between the actual loss and the one that would have occurred had the promisee complied with her duty of altruism. Both the promisor and the promisee are wrongdoers. By combining the secondary obligations that they owe to each other, in virtue of their wrongdoing, we can conclude that the promisor's responsibility for the actual loss suffered is diminished and shared with the promisee, which is what MP1 and LS1 require. Moreover, and this goes beyond justifying MP1 and LS1, the argument from the duty of altruism tells us exactly how the promisor and the promisee are to share the losses: the promisor's share of responsibility consists in the loss that would have arisen had the promisee complied with her duty of altruism. The responsibility for the rest of the losses is assumed by the promisee.

The duty of altruism, if true, provides normative support for MP1 and LS1. It also provides normative support for MP2 and LS2, that is, for cases where the promisee took action to bring about the promised state of affairs. Where there was an alternative course of action that the promisee could have taken to bring about the same state of affairs which was cheaper than the course taken, easily available, and not more costly than doing nothing, then the promisee is under an altruistic duty to take it. The promisee should avoid taking courses of action that needlessly impose costs on the promisor. If, in these circumstances, the promisee fails to take the cheaper alternative she is then under a duty to waive any claim she has to hold the promisor responsible for losses that accrue as a result of the promisee not taking the cheaper route. The promisor's responsibility for loss is limited to the loss that would have arisen had the promisee taken the cheaper course of action.

Finally, MP3 and LS2 would be explained as follows. When the cost of the only available action to secure the promised state of affairs exceeds the cost of inaction, the promisee has a duty of altruism not to do anything and to suffer the smaller

[5] For the explanation why see Joseph Raz, 'Personal Practical Conflicts' in Peter Baumann and Monika Betzler (eds), *Practical Conflicts: New Philosophical Essays* (Cambridge University Press 2004); John Gardner, 'What is Tort Law For? Part 1. The Place of Corrective Justice' (2011) 30 Law and Philosophy 1.

loss. When the promisee fails to do so, taking the action that results in a loss whose cost is greater than inaction (in example IX by taking a helicopter), then she has a duty to waive her claim against the promisor by that amount which represents the loss that she could have avoided by not taking any action. The promisor's overall responsibility is then limited to the loss that would have arisen had the promisee taken no action at all. This is because the promisee having failed to comply with her altruistic duty is now required to do the next best thing, which arguably in the circumstances is to waive any claim she has to hold the promisor responsible for the losses that arose as a result of her failure to comply with that duty.

Many philosophers have challenged the claim that a duty of altruism exists in this context. Why should the promisee be under a duty to *help* the promisor by waiving the claim she has against her as a victim of her wrongdoing? Normally, altruistic duties to assist others hold between people who are in a special or intimate relationship like friendship, love, or family. The idea that promises, as a matter of fact, trigger such relationships is questionable. The making of a promise may, but need not, bring the promisor closer to the promisee in terms of ethical values such as intimacy or friendship. Whether it does so is a *contingent* matter. Promising a stranger that I will watch her bag while she makes a phone call will, of course, not necessarily bring us closer together in such ways.

Those, like Fried, who defend altruism may, however, have in mind a stronger, *non-contingent*, connection between promise and the value of trust, according to which the very making of a promise invokes trust between the promisor and the promisee, thereby triggering altruistic duties of assistance, over and above the duty to perform what was promised. On this view, there is a *necessary* connection between the existence of a promissory obligation and the existence of trust between the promisor and the promisee.[6] The promissory obligation in part *consists* in there being a relationship of trust between two parties. For example, on Thomas Scanlon's view, there is no promissory obligation in cases where the promisee does not believe that the promisor will perform.[7]

Nevertheless, even on the non-contingent account, it is not clear why the existence of trust between the promisor and the promisee should ground duties *in addition* to the duty to perform what was promised. This takes us back to a point I made at the start of Chapter 6.[8] Fried, along with other 'promise theorists' of contract law, have largely overlooked or attached insufficient weight to a central insight of Lon Fuller's that there may be different degrees of trust between those who enter into promissory relations with each other—the amount of trust between the parties varying depending on the nature of the background relationship between the parties and the context in which the promise is made.

[6] I take this to be Fried's position. Charles Fried, *Contract as Promise: A Theory of Contractual Obligation* (Harvard University Press 1981) 8.

[7] TM Scanlon, *What We Owe to Each Other* (Belknap Press of Harvard University Press 1998) 312, 314, (using his famous example of the profligate pal to illustrate the point).

[8] See ch 6, s 1.

As I argued in Chapter 6, when promises are made in the context of special or intimate relationships of friendship, family, and so forth, there exists what I called 'thick', or a high degree of, trust between the parties, which triggers altruistic duties on the part of the promisee—the presence of such duties explains, again argued in that chapter, the undue influence doctrine in contract law which regulates contracts made in the context of special relationships. Many promises though, and this is typically the case with contractual promises, are not made against the background of pre-existing relationships between the parties of this intimate or close kind.[9] That does not mean that in these contexts there is normally *no* trust between the parties—contra those like Dori Kimel who offer a 'divisionist' or 'separatist' picture of the relationship between contract and promise.[10] I agree with both Fried and Scanlon that the connection between promise and trust is non-contingent or necessary. Rather, it means that the trust that obtains in these contexts is trust in a 'thin' or restricted sense. In other words, the promisor invites the promisee to trust that she will perform her contractual obligations, but she has no duty to go beyond this.[11]

Fried's mistake and the mistake of many promise theorists who have followed him was to pay insufficient attention to the different context in which promises are made between contractual parties. In the contractual context, there is usually no intimate or special pre-existing relationship between the parties, and hence there is only thin trust between the parties which does not trigger altruistic duties. The failure to properly perceive this difference has led promise theorists like Fried to mishandle contract doctrine. I shall return to these points about contract law later in this chapter.

For now, it is enough to say that the mere fact that promises have been made and trust invoked between parties to these promises does not necessarily mean that the promisee incurs altruistic duties toward the promisor. Whether that conclusion follows depends on the precise nature of the trusting relationship that obtains between the parties.

Moreover, there are further worries about the duty of altruism as the explanation for the mitigation and loss sharing principles I identified in the first section of this chapter. Why should the promisor's responsibility for the losses she caused be limited to the amount of the least costly alternative available to the promisee? It seems harsh that the promisee, by failing to help the promisor, might end up shouldering responsibility for the biggest part of the actual losses suffered.

Leaving aside for the moment whether the duty of altruism holds between the promisor and promisee, I want to explore whether there can be an alternative justification for MP1–MP3 and LS1–LS2, which does not turn on there being a moral duty on the part of the promisee to act in a particular way, following the

[9] cf James E Penner, 'Voluntary Obligations and the Scope of the Law of Contract' (1996) 2 Legal Theory 325, 335–39 (making a similar point but about the different contexts within which agreements, which he distinguishes from promises, are made).

[10] See ch 5, s 4.

[11] cf Daniel Markovits, 'Good Faith as Contract's Core Value' in Gregory Klass, George Letsas, and Prince Saprai (eds), *Philosophical Foundations of Contract Law* (Oxford University Press 2014) 292. And see similarly Penner, 'Voluntary Obligations and the Scope of the Law of Contract' (n 9) 337–38, 354.

promisor's breach. Private lawyers sometimes say that the innocent party has no 'duty' to mitigate but that, if she doesn't mitigate, then she loses the right to claim full damages.[12] I want to explore this intuition at the moral level.

Consider again *t1*, when the promisor has either breached or has informed the promisee that she will breach. Why would it follow, upon the fact of breach of promise, that the promisee has a duty to take a particular course of action? Surely, the promisee is free to decide that she no longer wishes to bring about the state of affairs promised. In my example, B may decide that she no longer wishes to travel but that she will not hold A responsible for her decision. Or she may decide that she now feels like taking a more expensive means of transport to the airport (a limousine), without expecting the promisor to cover it. Such decisions would not violate any duty on her part. If they did, that would violate the republican principle of non-domination (defended in Chapter 7), which seeks to protect citizens from having their lives or interests set back by the arbitrary will and judgment of others. In this context, the promisor's own wrong would incongruously impose constraints on the freedom of the innocent promisee.

In fact, it seems that the promisee has a right to make these decisions. It would be odd to say that the promisee has a duty to travel, or a duty to take the cheapest means of getting to the airport. She has a right 'to treat herself', so to speak, as well as a right to change her preferences. What appears morally problematic is the case where the promisee decides to do those things *and* seeks to blame or hold the promisor responsible for the whole cost of them. This suggests that there is a moral duty not to claim the cost of losses from the promisor that the promisee could have easily avoided, rather than a duty not to incur these losses. But what could the foundation of that moral duty be? Altruism is ruled out since altruism postulates a duty to avoid losses rather than a duty not to claim for losses that one could have easily avoided.

I believe that the foundation lies in the principle of fairness. It would be unfair if the promisee were entitled to hold the promisor responsible for losses that she could easily have avoided, while obtaining what was promised. A cannot complain when B fails to take a cab to the airport and misses the flight, if B makes no claim against A. She cannot tell B: 'why didn't you follow through on what my promise was meant to help you achieve, when you could have done just that?'

But it is unfair for B to choose to sit back and miss her flight, which she can easily make by getting a cab, and then blame or hold A responsible for it, seeking compensation. Upon passing up on less costly alternatives ways of securing the promised performance that are easily available, the moral profile of the promisor and the promisee changes. The principle of fairness bars the promisee from blaming the promisor for those easily avoidable losses or claiming compensation for them,

[12] See, for example, Robert Stevens, *Torts and Rights* (Oxford University Press 2007) 170. There are also plenty of judicial statements that support this view in the case law. See, for example, *Darbishire v Warran* [1963] 1 WLR 1067, 1075: 'The plaintiff is not under any actual obligation to adopt the cheaper method: if he wishes to adopt the more expensive method, he is at liberty to do so and by doing so he commits no wrong against the defendant or anyone else.' See also, *Sotiros Shipping Inc v Sameiet Solholt (The Solholt)* [1983] 1 Lloyd's Rep 605, 608. Thank you to Andy Summers for highlighting these case law references.

at the same time as extinguishing the promisor's responsibility for them. The promisee has no right to claim these losses and, correlatively, the promisor is not responsible for them. This is so even though the promisee was under no duty to minimize or not to exacerbate losses.

By appealing to the principle of fairness, I am availing myself of the well-known method of asking which normative principles people would choose if they did not know their position in the relevant normative relationship.[13] In the present case, I am asking what principles promissory parties would choose if they did not know whether they are the guilty promisor or the innocent promisee. And, I assume, that this method may lead parties to select principles simply on the basis that they are fair and not on the basis of some other value, such as equality or efficiency.[14] In other words, the fairness-based approach is not just a heuristic device for discovering what other values require.

According to the fairness-based explanation, when passing up on less costly alternatives (as in MP1), the promisee is exercising a choice rather than suffering a loss.[15] The principle of fairness is indifferent about how the promisee exercises that choice. It simply bars a claim on the promisee's part and extinguishes part of the promisor's responsibility for losses caused following her breach. It's not the case that the promisee *assists* the promisor in any way, as the altruism-based approach suggests. This is because the cost of the choice not taken is not, from a normative standpoint, a loss for which the promisor is even pro tanto responsible. The promisor's position is, therefore, no better off if the promisee chooses action over inaction in a case like III. It is not that the promisor would be worse off if the promisee failed to take action, since if she were to do so, then the promisor would not be responsible for the loss resulting from inaction. Hence, the promisee's inaction is not a failure to assist the promisor, nor is her taking the easily available alternative a helping hand toward the promisor. In a way, the promisee could not help the promisor even if she wanted to. If fairness is the correct normative explanation of MP1–MP3 and LS1–LS2, then mitigation has nothing to do with assistance.

It should also be noted here that if fairness is the correct explanation of mitigation, then the subject matter of the mitigation is the promisor's responsibility, rather than the losses caused by her breach. According to the fairness-based account, what gets mitigated when the promisee takes the easily available alternative is the promisor's

[13] A method familiar of course in political philosophy, thanks to the work of John Rawls. John Rawls, *A Theory of Justice* (rev edn, Oxford University Press 1999) 15–19.

[14] Goetz and Scott, for example, use joint cost minimization as a basis for determining which mitigation principle parties would select. Charles J Goetz and Robert E Scott, 'The Mitigation Principle: Toward a General Theory of Contractual Obligation' (1983) 69 Virginia Law Review 967, 973.

[15] It can be claimed that by exercising this choice, the promisee 'breaks the chain of causation' or constitutes an intervening cause. This claim relies on a common-sense notion of causation, according to which the test for whether the promisee's conduct is an intervening cause is whether her conduct is fully voluntary. But it would be a mistake to argue that the promisor is not responsible because the promisee has caused the relevant loss. In my view, this gets matters backwards. Whether the promisee's failure to act constitutes an intervening cause in this sense, depends on the prior question of whether it is fair for the promisee to share losses with the promisor. Causation here tracks responsibility, not the other way around.

responsibility for breaching her promise, rather than the losses caused as a result of the breach.

The normative explanation based on fairness has the same structure as arguments justifying estoppel. So, to use a common example, I see you building a house on my land, mistakenly thinking that the land is your own, and instead of informing you of your mistake I allow you to continue building. Although I had no duty to inform you of your mistake, it would be unfair for me to rely on my right over the land in order to benefit from what you built, say by acquiring property rights over it. Property lawyers would say that I'm *estopped* from relying on my property rights against you or that by not informing you I waived those rights. These are alternative ways of making the same point, namely that my failure to inform you changes our moral profiles and extinguishes rights that I would otherwise have had against you and creates new ones.[16]

3. Advantages of the Fairness-based Approach

There are three distinct advantages to the fairness-based explanation of mitigation. First, it explains the intuition that when a promise is broken in a case like III above, the promisee is under no obligation to take the cab and make the flight. The promisee chose not to travel, even though she could easily have done so, and, therefore, is barred from claiming the cost of her choice from the promise-breaker. So, by failing to take easily available alternative courses of action, the promisee does not breach a duty and hence has nothing to regret or apologize for. By contrast, on Fried's view, the promisee would have reasons to feel regret and to make an apology even when she complies with her secondary obligation to waive her claim against the promisor. This is because she ought not to have allowed the losses to accumulate in the first place.

A second advantage of the fairness-based account is that it doesn't presuppose any specifically altruistic duties between the promisor and the promisee. It therefore avoids all of the objections against Fried's account that promises do not necessarily create such duties. All that the principle of fairness requires is that promisees not claim compensation from the promisor for losses that they could have easily avoided. It's therefore compatible with cases where the two parties are in no special or intimate relationship with one another wherein what I have called thick trust obtains and altruistic duties are triggered. The absence of these sorts of pre-existing relationships is typical of promises made in contractual contexts, where usually only thin trust obtains between the parties.

[16] The argument does not rely on the property owner deriving any kind of benefit from her silence. The relevant normative concern here is not unjust enrichment. For an example in law of a successful estoppel claim even in the absence of such benefit, see *Jackson v Cator* (1800) 5 Ves Jr 688, which involved an owner remaining silent out of spite. Loughborough LC asked rhetorically 'Is it not just as competent to the Court to prevent an injury arising from mere spite as to prevent him from doing it in order to put money in his pocket?' (ibid 691). Thank you to Ben McFarlane for the reference.

A third advantage of this normative explanation is that it can justify mitigation in non-promissory contexts. Mitigation and loss sharing principles seem to apply beyond the realm of promising. Consider, for example, moral wrongs other than breach of promise. If you negligently injure me, and I choose not to treat my injuries even though it was fairly easy for me to do so, then it is unfair for me to blame you for the resulting harm and seek to recover the cost from you. Here it would make no sense to argue that I have a duty of altruism toward you to reduce the extent of the harm you caused me. Though I do have a strong reason to reduce the harm you caused me, this is not because by doing so I comply with a duty I have to assist you. Duties of assistance arise only when there is a special or close relationship between the parties, and one could not even begin to argue that there is a special relationship of this kind between the negligent injurer and her victim. It is interesting, though of course not in itself an argument in favour of fairness, that mitigation in tort law works no differently than in contract law.[17]

Finally, I should make clear that the argument advanced here relies on fairness as a general moral principle to explain mitigation. This is another example of promise interacting with general moral principles—I have already considered in previous chapters how it interacts with other general moral principles like exploitation, compensation, freedom, and so forth. In other words, the mitigation doctrine is another example of what I have called earlier in the book a 'composite doctrine'. Fairness is a foundational value that is pro tanto relevant each and every time a promise is made (unlike altruism which only applies when promises are made in the context of certain pre-existing relationships), and, in the context of mitigation, it changes the moral position of the parties. The application of the principle of fairness doesn't presuppose any institutional background (for example, the existence of the state or courts). Nor is it limited to a practical or economic concern about how to shift losses caused by a breach of promise. Recall that the principle of fairness also requires the promisee not to blame the promisor for losses that she could easily have avoided.

In sum, unlike the duty of altruism, the structure of the explanation from fairness is one that applies to all cases where there are secondary obligations arising out of the breach of a primary obligation. It qualifies or cancels part of the wrongdoer's responsibility for the loss caused by her breach. Unlike the duty of altruism, it construes cases of failure to avoid losses as a choice on the part of the innocent party rather than as a breach of a duty. In that respect, it offers a more direct normative justification for principles MP1–MP3 and LS1–LS2, than the duty of altruism. I now argue that, by and large, these mitigation and loss sharing principles explain existing contract law doctrine.

[17] *McAuley v London Transport Executive* [1957] 2 Lloyd's Rep 500, (worker's injury to hand resulting from employer's negligence, but worker's unreasonable failure to get medical treatment meant that employer was not responsible for loss that worker could have easily avoided. Worker could have avoided loss of earnings from point when injured hand would have recovered from medical intervention).

4. Contract Law

The mitigation and loss sharing principles that we find in morality are also present in the common law mitigation doctrine. When a contract is broken, the legal responsibility of the promisor for any loss caused by her breach is mitigated in two types of case. First, there are those cases that Andrew Burrows describes as cases of 'unreasonable inaction'. These are cases where the promisee is precluded from recovering any losses from the promisor that the promisee 'could reasonably have avoided but has failed to avoid'.[18] Secondly, there are cases where the claimant takes 'unreasonable action' in avoiding losses caused by a breach of promise. The claimant cannot recover for expenses unreasonably incurred.

According to the common law doctrine, the promisor's responsibility for loss is limited to the losses that the promisee would have suffered had the promisee taken reasonable action to bring about the state of affairs that would have obtained had the contract been performed.

Burrows, as well as the other leading contract lawyers,[19] says that whether reasonable steps should have been taken 'depends on the particular facts in question'.[20] When lawyers say that this determination is a matter of fact, I am unclear about what exactly this means. If it means that it is an extra-legal or purely factual question, and that no underlying legal principle determines whether or not the promisor's responsibility for loss in cases of this type is mitigated, then I disagree with their interpretation of the law. If, on the other hand, the claim is that there is an underlying legal principle, but that we have to look at the facts of a particular case to determine whether the conditions for the application of that principle are satisfied, then I agree.[21] I think that the cases clearly demonstrate that the courts interpret and apply the mitigation and loss sharing principles that we find in morality to determine at least in part the responsibility of the promisor for the loss caused by her breach of contract.

[18] Andrew Burrows, *Remedies for Torts and Breach of Contract* (3rd edn, Oxford University Press 2004) 122. Burrows cites for this proposition Viscount Haldane LC's classic statement of the principle in *British Westinghouse Electric v Underground Electric Railways Co of London Ltd* [1912] AC 673. The law said Haldane 'imposes on a plaintiff the duty of taking all reasonable steps to mitigate the loss consequent on the breach and debars him from claiming any part of the damage which is due to his neglect to take such steps' (ibid 689).

[19] See, for example, Mindy Chen-Wishart, *Contract Law* (4th edn, Oxford University Press 2012) 510; Ewan McKendrick, *Contract Law: Text, Cases, and Materials* (5th edn, Oxford University Press 2012) 895.

[20] Burrows, *Remedies for Torts and Breach of Contract* (n 18) 123.

[21] There is reason to think that Burrows does mean the latter. He says that examination of the cases demonstrates the presence of certain 'factors' which are relevant to the question of whether the promisor's responsibility for the loss should be mitigated. ibid.

4.1 Unreasonable inaction

Recall, I've argued that in cases where the promisee has failed to act, the promisor's responsibility for the loss caused by breach is shared if the promisee could have taken an easily available alternative course of action to secure the promised state of affairs (assuming that the cost of taking that alternative does not exceed the loss that results from the promisee's inaction). It is unfair for the promisee to place the entire burden of this loss on the promisor's doorstep. I will now attempt to show that this principle, or, to be more accurate, combination of principles MP1 and LS1, underpins the legal cases where responsibility was shared from those where it wasn't.

Take, for example, the case of *Payzu Ltd v Saunders*.[22] The defendant, in breach of contract, refused to deliver silk in instalments to the claimants unless they agreed to pay cash on delivery of each instalment. The claimants declined these terms, and instead brought an action for breach of contract claiming the difference between the contract and market price of the silk. The market price of the silk had risen. The Court of Appeal, however, held that the defendant did not have to pay the difference, because the claimants should have accepted the defendant's offer to pay cash. Instead, the claimants were awarded damages to reflect the residual loss that they would have suffered had they accepted the offer. The defendant's responsibility was mitigated, because the claimants:

> were in fact in a position to pay cash for the goods, but instead of accepting the defendant's offer, which was made perfectly bona fide, the plaintiffs permitted themselves to sustain a large measure of loss which as prudent and reasonable people they ought to have avoided.[23]

In other words, the claimants had an easily available alternative course of action open to them for securing the state of affairs that would have obtained had the promise been performed. They had no difficulty paying cash, and that would have led to them receiving the performance due under the contract, that is, receiving the silk.[24]

The critical issue is whether the alternative or substitute, if available, is *easy* for the promisee to take. This explains why the law tends to take what Tomlinson J described as a 'tender approach to those who have been placed in a predicament by a breach of contract'.[25] The approach is 'tender', because if the alternative imposes any serious difficulty on the claimant, then the courts will not mitigate the defendant's responsibility. In such circumstances, it is not unfair for the promisee to place the burden for the loss onto the promisor. This is brought out in Scrutton LJ's judgment in *Payzu*, when he distinguishes commercial contracts from contracts of personal service:

> In certain cases of personal service it may be unreasonable to expect a plaintiff to consider an offer from the other party who has grossly injured him; but in commercial contracts it

[22] *Payzu Ltd v Saunders* [1919] 2 KB 581. [23] ibid 586.

[24] See also *The Solholt* (n 12), (buyer should have accepted late delivery of a ship, which was still perfectly suitable for buyer's purposes).

[25] *Britvic Soft Drinks Ltd v Messer UK Ltd* [2002] 1 Lloyd's Rep 20, 46.

is generally reasonable to accept an offer from the party in default. However, it is always a question of fact. About the law there is no difficulty.[26]

The reason why the defendant's responsibility is harder to mitigate in contracts of personal service is that usually it will be much more burdensome for the claimant to accept the defendant's offer to renegotiate in that context. The main reason being that the relationship between the parties may already have broken down, because, for example, the dismissal occurred in circumstances that were humiliating or an attack on the employee's integrity, and, in that context, re-employment may impose a significant burden on the claimant, who may have to continue to work with the defendant.[27]

It is important, however, to stress Scrutton LJ's remark that the issue of burdensomeness is a question of fact to be determined on a case-by-case basis. There will be cases of commercial contracts where renegotiation would be burdensome,[28] and cases of personal service contracts where it would not be.[29] Scrutton LJ is just making the point that, as a general rule, renegotiation is likely to be easier in a commercial, rather than personal service, context. The underlying principle is that mitigation of the defendant's responsibility for the loss depends on whether the claimant had an easily available alternative way of securing the promised performance.

A personal service case where the defendant's responsibility was not mitigated by an offer to renegotiate and which illustrates the application of this principle is the decision of Blain J in *Yetton v Eastwoods Froy Ltd*.[30] The managing director of a company was wrongfully dismissed by his employer, and then offered reemployment as an assistant managing director by the same company. The claimant's refusal to accept the offer did not reduce the defendant's liability. Blain J stated the principle on which the case rested as follows:

> the opportunity to reduce damages by finding reasonable (I repeat reasonable) alternative employment should be taken and, indeed, sought, whether such employment is by the same defaulting employer or by someone else; in either case the test being whether it is reasonable to refuse it or not in the circumstances of each case.[31]

This is the same principle that underpinned the decision in *Payzu*. The key issue was whether it was reasonable to expect the claimant to accept the revised terms offered. Blain J repeated the point made by Scrutton LJ in *Payzu*, that renegotiation with the defendant may be much more of a burden in the context of an employment contract:

[26] *Payzu Ltd v Saunders* (n 22) 589.

[27] Similar considerations explain why restraints of trade are less likely to be enforced in employment contexts than in the case of business sales. See ch 7, s 3.1-2.

[28] So, for example, the claimant does not in a sale of goods context have to accept goods of a lower quality. *Heaven & Kesterton Ltd v Et Francois Albiac & Cie* [1956] 2 Lloyd's Rep 316.

[29] *Bruce v Calder* [1895] 2 KB 581, 589.

[30] *Yetton v Eastwoods Froy Ltd* [1967] 1 WLR 104.

[31] ibid 115.

personal factors clearly are more likely to be of weight or are likely to be of greater weight in cases of personal services than in (for want of a better word) what I call soulless cases of sale of goods contracts where money may often be the only important factor.[32]

On the facts, Blain J decided that it was not unreasonable for the claimant to refuse the offer. Essential to this finding was that the new job offered by the defendant to the claimant was a significant step-down from the position the employee had occupied, and that relations between the parties had broken down to such an extent that it was unclear how they could now work together. It is clear from the decision, that requiring the claimant to accept the offer would have imposed a significant burden on him.

4.2 Unreasonable action

Remember that when considering the moral position I claimed that the promisor's responsibility for the loss caused by her breach of promise is shared in cases where the promisee successfully takes action after breach to bring about the promised state of affairs, but the promisee could have taken an alternative course of action to obtain that same state affairs which was easily available and cheaper than the course of action actually taken.

This principle, or to be more accurate combination of principles MP2 and LS2, explains, I believe, the decisions reached in the contract cases where the promisee takes action to secure the promised state of affairs. The common law rule is that the promisee cannot recover expenses that were unreasonably incurred, and the promisor's liability is capped at the loss that would have arisen had the promisee acted reasonably in bringing about the promised state of affairs.

The MP2 principle identified earlier underpins when the courts find the promisee's action in these legal cases unreasonable. Take, for example, the case of *Compania Financiera Soleada SA v Hamoor Tanker Corp Inc (The Borag)*,[33] where the claimant ship owners took out a very high interest rate loan in order to secure the release of a ship wrongfully detained because of a breach of contract by the ship managers. Lord Templeman LJ in his judgment, said on the issue of mitigation that the ship managers were not liable to cover the expenses associated with the high interest loan, because the ship owners had easily available to them cheaper alternative ways of securing the release of the ship:

the owners could and should have adopted a form of mitigation which was reasonable either by refusing to pay the interest charges to their bankers or by seeking a guarantee elsewhere or by some other available form of securing the release of the vessel more cheaply.[34]

This is a clear application of the MP2 principle that we find in morality. Given the existence of easily available and cheaper alternative methods for securing the performance, the promise-breaker is not responsible for covering the entire loss

[32] ibid 118.
[33] *Compania Financiera Soleada SA v Hamoor Tanker Corp Inc (The Borag)* [1981] 1 WLR 274.
[34] ibid 285.

caused by the breach, and it is unfair for the promisee to claim damages for that loss from the promise-breaker.

The same or very similar principles are applied in cases where the promisee's actions either to secure the promised performance or, where that is no longer possible, to avoid the losses caused by the promisor's breach are held to be reasonable. So, for example, in *Britvic Soft Drinks Ltd v Messer UK Ltd*,[35] ingredients contaminated with benzene, which is carcinogenic, were supplied to a soft drinks manufacturer. It was no longer possible to secure the promised performance, and instead the manufacturer took action to reduce the consequential loss caused by the breach. In other words, this was what I called earlier a pure loss avoidance case.[36] Even though the levels of benzene in the ingredients did not pose a risk to health, the Court of Appeal decided that the manufacturer acted reasonably in destroying and withdrawing products that contained those ingredients, because that was the only way to preserve its commercial reputation. The supplier was responsible for covering the costs incurred by the manufacturer.[37] There was no easily available and cheaper alternative course of action that the manufacturer could have taken to preserve its commercial reputation, and, therefore, the courts refused to mitigate the responsibility of the supplier for the loss caused, and it was fair for the manufacturer to claim damages for that loss from the supplier.

Recall, I said earlier that in cases where a promise is broken and the promisee successfully takes action to secure the state of affairs that would have obtained had the promise been performed, there is a separate moral principle that I called MP3 which mitigates the responsibility of the promisor for the loss caused where the costs of the action taken exceed the loss that would have occurred had the promisee not taken any action to bring about the state of affairs. LS2 also applies in this type of case and requires loss sharing. According to *Treitel's The Law of Contract*, the common law mitigation doctrine contains a similar principle. *Treitel* formulates the principle in the following terms: '[the promisee] should not ... spend more on curing a defect in performance than the subject matter without the defect would be worth'.[38]

The principle was applied in *Grant v Dawkins and Others*.[39] The case concerned a contract for the sale of a house free from incumbrances. However, the house was subject to two mortgages. The purchaser wanted specific performance, and an order to allow him to pay off the mortgages and claim as damages any loss that exceeded the purchase price. Goff J granted the order but said that the damages recoverable

[35] *Britvic Soft Drinks Ltd v Messer UK Ltd* (n 25).

[36] Strictly speaking, therefore, this is not a case where MP2 would apply, because MP2 involves cases where the promisee takes action to bring about the promised state of affairs. However, as I said in s 1.2, a similar principle to MP2 applies to cover cases of action taken to reduce or avoid consequential loss. As with MP2, central to whether the promisor's responsibility is mitigated in these pure loss avoidance cases is whether there was an easily available and cheaper alternative course of action that the promisee could have taken. The main difference is that the promisee's action in these pure loss avoidance cases relates to avoiding or reducing loss, rather than securing substitute performance.

[37] *Britvic Soft Drinks Ltd v Messer UK Ltd* (n 25) [114].

[38] Edwin Peel, *Treitel on The Law of Contract* (13th edn, Sweet & Maxwell 2011) 1064–65.

[39] *Grant v Dawkins and Others* [1973] 1 WLR 1406.

to the extent that they could not be compensated by the purchase price of the house were capped by the value of the house.[40] This is a clear application of the MP3 and LS2 principles. Responsibility for loss caused by the broken promise is shared when the promisee takes action to secure the promised state of affairs, in this case paying off the two mortgages, the costs of which exceed the loss that would have been suffered by the promisee had the promisee done nothing, in this case that loss is represented by the value of the house. It was unfair, in these circumstances, for the purchaser to claim the entire cost of discharging the mortgages from the vendor.

Another example of the application of these principles is the tort case *Darbishire v Warran*.[41] The defendant negligently damaged the claimant's car. The claimant had the car repaired and claimed, as damages from the defendant, the costs of repair which were £192 (minus an £80 insurance payout that he had received) and the costs of a hire car which he used while his car was being repaired. However, the costs of repairing the car exceeded the market value of the car, which was £85. The Court of Appeal declined to award the claimant the costs of the repairs carried out on the basis that 'the cost of repairs greatly exceeds the value in the market of the damaged article'.[42] Instead, the market value of the car and the costs of the hire car capped the sum that could be recovered. Responsibility for the loss caused by the defendant's negligence was shared between the parties.

There may be cases where due to the unique nature of the good it may be reasonable to incur the cost of securing the promised performance, even though it exceeds the market value of the good. So, for example, the costs of repairing a car were awarded in *O'Grady v Westminster Scaffolding Ltd*, even though they massively exceeded the market value of the car.[43] The reason was that the car in that case was unique. Before the crash that led to the car being damaged the claimant spent between £300 and £400 per annum maintaining the car, and he had replaced the engine three times, put in new coachwork, and, among other things, carried out work on the wheels, the hood, and the steering column.

The decision in this case is compatible with the moral principle MP3. According to that principle, the costs incurred by the promisee in securing the promised performance, should not exceed the loss that would be suffered if the promisee took no action. Loss has to be understood broadly here to include both pecuniary and non-pecuniary loss.[44] In a case like *O'Grady*, the loss that the claimant would have suffered had he not repaired the car would have been huge given the unique nature of the car. Therefore, even though the cost of repairs exceeded the market value of the car, they did not exceed the loss that the claimant would have suffered had he not undertaken them. What this case shows is that the market value of the subject matter in question does not exhaust its value to the claimant, or the loss that the

40 ibid 1411. 41 *Darbishire v Warran* (n 12). 42 ibid 1071.

43 *O'Grady v Westminster Scaffolding Ltd* [1962] 2 Lloyd's Rep 238.

44 Lawyers distinguish between pecuniary and non-pecuniary losses. I am making the same distinction here, and clearly it is very important in morality and law to see that pecuniary loss does not exhaust the category of loss.

claimant would suffer if the state of affairs to which the claimant is entitled does not materialize.[45] In such cases, the defendant is responsible for all of the losses that flow from her breach of contract. MP3 is not satisfied in cases of this kind, which is why the decision in *O'Grady* does not contradict that principle.[46]

5. The Convergence of Contract and Morality

In the previous section, I argued that the doctrine of mitigation as it is found in English law satisfies principles MP1–MP3 and LS1–LS2. The fact that it does is, of course, no argument for the merits of those principles. In section 2 of this chapter, I argued that these principles are morally defensible either on the grounds of altruism or on the basis of fairness. I opted for the fairness-based explanation on the grounds that: first, it explains the intuition that the promisee has no duty to reduce losses; second, that it does not presuppose any special or close relationship between the promisor and the promisee; and, third, that it explains why mitigation principles apply to other moral wrongs and not just promise-breaking. If fairness provides support for MP1–MP3 and LS1–LS2, and the doctrine of mitigation as it exists in contract law satisfies these principles, then there is *convergence* between morality and contract law.

However, in recent times a number of contract theorists have argued that the doctrine of mitigation *diverges* from what *promissory* morality would require. This is only, of course, a problem for promise theorists who claim that promise plays a special justificatory role in contract. This alleged divergence is welcomed by those I called 'divisionists' in Chapter 5, who claim that promise and contract exist in entirely separate or distinct spheres.[47] The promise theorist who embraces 'justificatory primacy', will argue that if there is divergence between promise and contract in this context, the promise principle should prevail, and the mitigation doctrine should be repudiated or reformed.[48]

As I've argued, in my view there is convergence between contract law and morality. My view though differs from Fried's justification in that I propose the principle of fairness as the best normative justification of the doctrine, rather than altruism. Fried is, of course, a promise theorist, but unusually he believes there is a necessary connection between the promise principle and altruism. On his view, every time a promise is made—in whatever context—the mere fact that a promise is made and accepted creates a relationship of trust between the parties that necessarily triggers altruistic duties. I have argued that Fried paid insufficient attention to the different contexts in which promises are made and that altruistic duties only arise

[45] See similarly *Ruxley Electronics and Construction Ltd v Forsyth* [1996] AC 344; *Farley v Skinner* [2002] AC 732.

[46] Therefore, the comparison between the cost of repairs and the market value of the good in question in *Darbishire* was too narrow. *Treitel's* formulation which focuses on what the subject matter would be worth, not just what it is worth on the market, is broader, and captures O'Grady, where the focus was on what the subject matter was worth to the promisee rather than what it was worth on the market.

[47] See ch 5, text to nn 3–7.

[48] See ch 2, s 3.2.

when promises are made in the context of close or special pre-existing relationships between the parties involving what I have called thick trust. Such relationships are not typical in the contractual context, and when contracts do take place against the backdrop of a special or close relationship, then, as we saw in Chapter 6 on the doctrine of undue influence, the law is shaped by the presence of the altruistic obligations that exist in these contexts.

It may be that Fried's view here about the relationship between promise and altruism is an example of what I have called in previous chapters 'justificatory primacy by inflation', that is, establishing the primacy of promise in contract by expanding the scope of the promise principle to accommodate other principles like altruism to explain existing doctrine.[49] In my view, this not only distorts promise (by relying on a necessary connection between promise and altruism, when the actual connection is only contingent), but also leads to an inaccurate portrayal of the nature of the mitigation doctrine. Nevertheless, Fried's account of mitigation has proven to be enormously influential. Indeed, I will argue that those promise theorists and divisionists who have claimed that the mitigation doctrine diverges from promissory morality have been led to this view by the problems with Fried's account. If we reject Fried's account of mitigation and replace it with the fairness-based account I have advocated in this chapter, we see that contract law actually converges with morality (broadly conceived).

Let's begin with the promise theorist Seana Shiffrin's critique of the mitigation doctrine. Shiffrin's argument relies on a number of premises. First, she argues that morality does not normally impose a duty on the promisee to accept alternatives. Second, when morality exceptionally requires the promisee to accept an alternative, then it is usually the promisor's duty to provide it. Third, the exceptional cases, where it might be argued that the promisee has a moral duty to avoid losses by taking alternatives, turn on a limited range of factors such as: 'the closeness of the relationship, the history of the relationship, the reason for breach, the reason the promisor wants to shift the burden, and how cumbersome mitigation activities would be'.[50] Shiffrin finds that the doctrine of mitigation in contract law diverges from all three of these features of promissory morality. On her view, contract law imposes a *general* duty on the promisee not only to accept alternatives but also to seek them out, and to do so whether or not there are exceptional circumstances that—morally speaking—would justify a duty of assistance. She concludes that the effect of this divergence is to make the doctrine of mitigation morally objectionable. This is because it enables the promisor who commits a wrong by breaching her promise to impose a duty on the innocent promisee, the aim of which is to benefit the promise-breaker, that is, the guilty party. Why would one have a duty to help the person who wronged one? This looks morally perverse. As Shiffrin puts it: 'It is morally distasteful to expect the promisee to do work that could be done by the promisor when the occasion for the work is the promisor's own wrongdoing.'[51]

[49] See ch 3, text to nn 12–14.
[50] Seana Valentine Shiffrin, 'The Divergence of Contract and Promise' (2007) 120 Harvard Law Review 708, 725.
[51] ibid 724–25.

Critiques like Shiffrin's above are motivated by hostility toward altruism-based accounts of mitigation, such as Fried's. Shiffrin finds it 'distasteful' that the innocent party should be expected to be altruistic toward the person who wronged her, particularly in cases where the wrongdoer did so without any excuse or justification. If there is a reason to help promise-breakers, this is usually because of a moral value (for example, friendship, charity, and so forth) other than promise. Fried's response is to 'bite the bullet' and say that the promissory bond is special enough to trigger general duties of altruism, and that the more in the wrong the promisor is, the more altruistic the promisee's act of loss-avoidance would be.[52]

In my view, the Shiffrin-Fried debate presupposes that the candidate normative explanation for the doctrine of mitigation is an altruistic duty imposed on the innocent promisee to help or render assistance to the guilty promisor. Shiffrin disputes the existence of such a duty and criticizes contract law, whereas Fried argues in favour of the duty and defends existing doctrine. But what if the candidate normative explanation is not based on altruism, but is based instead on the principle of fairness? Recall that, according to the fairness-based explanation, the promisee has no *duty* to avoid losses but rather is *barred* from claiming damages that could have been easily avoided. Would Shiffrin's critique of the mitigation doctrine apply, were the fairness-based account correct? It is clear that it would not.

First, contra Shiffrin, it does not follow from the existing case law that the promisee has a moral duty to avoid losses. As I have shown above, principles MP1–MP3 and LS1–LS2, which underpin existing case law, are compatible with the view that the promisee has no duty to avoid losses. In fact, the dominant reading of cases amongst private lawyers is that the so-called 'duty to mitigate' is a misleading label, because no legal liability attaches when this 'duty' is breached.[53] It follows that it cannot be assumed that the question of whether the doctrine of mitigation diverges from promissory morality turns exclusively on whether the duty to avoid losses is morally defensible. Another possibility is that the law's position is morally defensible, without assuming the existence of a duty on the part of the promisee to avoid losses, let alone a duty based on altruism.

Second, the fairness-based account renders redundant Shiffrin's complaint that the mitigation doctrine is morally perverse. The basis of this complaint is that the promisee is under a legal duty to assist the person who has wronged her, which in moral terms is indefensible. As I argued earlier, under the fairness-based account, there is no moral duty of assistance on the part of the promisee. The promisee is morally free to sit back and not to seek alternatives. All that she is prevented from doing is claiming damages for losses she could have easily avoided.[54] In fact, according to the fairness-based account, the promisee is unable to help the promisor even if she wanted to. If it is true that the promisor is not morally responsible for losses that

[52] Fried, *Contract as Promise: A Theory of Contractual Obligation* (n 6) 131.

[53] See, for example, J Beatson, A Burrows, and J Cartwright, *Anson's Law of Contract* (29th edn, Oxford University Press 2010) 555; Chen-Wishart, *Contract Law* (n 19) 509; Peel, *Treitel on The Law of Contract* (n 38) 1062; Stevens, *Torts and Rights* (n 12) 170.

[54] See text to nn 9–14.

the promisee could have easily avoided, then by avoiding them the promisee helps no one but herself.

Third, Shiffrin takes Fried to task for proliferating the circumstances in which altruistic duties to assist arise. On her view, such duties are exceptional and depend on a number of factors that go beyond the mere existence of a promise. But this complaint has no bite against the fairness-based account, which does not presuppose the existence of a special relationship between the promisor and the promisee, let alone one in which duties to assist necessarily obtain.

In sum, none of Shiffrin's objections cut against the fairness-based justification of the doctrine of mitigation. Even if she is right—as I think she is—to dismiss altruism as a morally defensible account of the mitigation doctrine, we should not assume that altruism is the only candidate justification. Moreover, I have shown that the principle of fairness not only supports principles of mitigation of the promisor's responsibility and loss sharing at the moral level, but also explains existing doctrines and cases that would otherwise appear morally problematic.

The claim that the mitigation doctrine diverges from what interpersonal morality would require is also made by divisionists who claim that contract law is not based on the morality of promising. So, for example, Kimel has claimed, making arguments that are similar to Shiffrin's, that Fried's altruism-focused account of the mitigation doctrine is defective. First, Kimel argues that the promissory relation alone cannot explain the existence of these kinds of altruistic duties, because in the promissory context they only arise when other relational facts obtain, for example, when the parties are friends.[55] The mitigation doctrine is, however, as we saw earlier, insensitive to the presence of these facts, that is, responsibility for loss caused by the promise-breaker may be mitigated even if the only way that the parties are connected is by the promise.

Second, Kimel argues, following Patrick Atiyah, that given that altruism has a limited role in contract law, it looks incongruous that when it does make an appearance it requires the promisee to render assistance to the promisor who has wronged her.[56]

Kimel's critique of Fried's account of mitigation suggests that there is divergence between promissory morality (broadly conceived to include other interpersonal moral principles that interact with the promise principle) and the mitigation doctrine. However, Kimel thinks that the mitigation doctrine may nevertheless be justified. The doctrine is justified in law by the harm principle which requires the courts to refrain 'from the imposition of a certain remedial duty where this could not be justified as the least demanding or restrictive way of preventing or redressing a given harm'.[57] Kimel's argument is that imposing responsibility for the entire loss on the breaching party, is an 'unnecessary and excessive interference with this

[55] Kimel argues that these facts do typically obtain in the promissory context, because promises are usually made in the context of on-going relationships. Dori Kimel, *From Promise to Contract: Towards a Liberal Theory of Contract* (Hart Publishing 2003) 110.

[56] ibid 110–11, citing PS Atiyah, *Essays on Contract* (Clarendon Press 1986) 124.

[57] ibid 111.

party's freedom' in circumstances where the harm caused by the breach can be easily avoided by the innocent party.[58]

I am not going to evaluate Kimel's own account of the mitigation doctrine here. Instead, I just want to point out that the suggestion that there is divergence between law and promissory morality here, presupposes Fried's claim that the candidate moral justification for the mitigation doctrine is the duty of altruism. Kimel's objections, like Shiffrin's, that the duty of altruism cannot explain mitigation in law, have no force against the fairness-based account of the mitigation doctrine that I have offered. First, my account does not require there to be a special relationship, like that of friendship, between the promisor and the promisee. It is sufficient for the promisee's claim to damages to be barred that she had an opportunity to easily avoid the loss. Secondly, the fairness-based account involves no incongruity. The promisee, as I have argued, is under no duty to assist the promise-breaker, but, rather, is blocked on the basis of fairness from claiming losses that she could easily have avoided.[59]

Therefore, although the objections made by Shiffrin and Kimel to the altruism-focused justification of the mitigation doctrine may well be sound, they are insufficient to establish that there is any divergence between the law and promissory morality (broadly conceived). In particular, those objections have no bite against the fairness-based account of the mitigation doctrine. This account establishes that contract doctrine is morally defensible at the level of first-order moral principles. One can justify the doctrine of mitigation without appealing to considerations that apply uniquely in the context of institutional action or the taking of coercive measures.[60]

In other words, there is no divergence between what promissory morality (broadly conceived) requires and what contract law enforces. The appearance of divergence is a symptom of the 'promise theory', which, in an effort to explain the

[58] ibid.

[59] It may be that Kimel's account is compatible with mine. However, his account is distinct. Kimel relies on an aspect of *political* morality, to do with liberal constraints on state coercion, to justify the doctrine. I claim that an appeal to political morality is unnecessary to justify the doctrine, and that it can be justified on the grounds of what *interpersonal* morality requires alone. Kimel seems, at least in the promissory context, to deny this. See Kimel, *From Promise to Contract: Towards a Liberal Theory of Contract* (n 55) 110.

[60] In his most recent work Fried has been tempted by an institutional justification for the mitigation doctrine based on considerations relating to justice and the rule of law. He claims that mitigation can be explained by reasons to minimize judicial intervention (such as cost and availability of resources). Fried says: 'The objective theory advocated by Barnett, like the regime of default rules, the requirement of mitigation, and much else, are practical necessities if the government is to become involved in enforcing agreements at all.' Charles Fried, 'The Ambitions of *Contract as Promise*' in Gregory Klass, George Letsas, and Prince Saprai (eds), *Philosophical Foundations of Contract Law* (Oxford University Press 2014) 34. This may reflect a shift on Fried's part from relying on earlier unsatisfactory attempts to explain mitigation based on the justificatory primacy of promise, and a move toward a new strategy of relying on what I have called in previous chapters 'justificatory presumptiveness', that is, the acceptance that contract and promise diverge in this context raising an epistemic presumption that contract doctrine is unsound, but that it may be saved or justified on closer inspection by, for example, factors special to contract law and its enforcement. See ch 2, s 3.3. In my view, relying on institutional considerations of this kind is not only unnecessary but distorts the true nature of the doctrine.

mitigation doctrine on the basis of the special role played by promise in contract law, not only distorts the true nature of that doctrine, but also the requirements of morality itself.

6. Conclusion

In conclusion, I argue that the principles MP1–MP3 and LS1–LS2 identified in the first section of this chapter are morally defensible on the grounds of fairness. Fairness requires that the promisor is not responsible for losses that the promisee could have easily avoided. I have also argued that these principles justify contract doctrine and case law, and that there is, therefore, no divergence between promissory morality (broadly conceived) and contract law.

The argument that the mitigation doctrine diverges from promissory morality has focused on the claim, famously made by Fried, that the point of mitigation is to get the promisee to assist the promise-breaker on the grounds of altruism. This may have been an attempt by Fried to establish the justificatory primacy of promise in contract law by inflating the promise principle's scope to accommodate other principles necessary for explaining doctrine.

Fried's explanation though has rightly faced criticism from those on both sides of the 'contract and promise debate'. I have offered an alternative rationale based on the principle of fairness. This alternative account does not depend on the claim that the promisee has a duty of altruism to assist the promisor, and avoids the objections made to the altruism-based explanation of the mitigation doctrine. If successful, my account dissolves the apparent divergence between the mitigation doctrine and morality (broadly conceived), at the level of first-order moral reasoning.

The debate about mitigation we have been considering reflects a broader debate about whether contract doctrine diverges or converges with promissory morality, which has taken centre stage in contract theory in the past decade or so. The doctrine of mitigation, like doctrines such as intent to contract, undue influence, the penalties rule, consideration, expectation damages, and so forth, appears to contradict the claim that the promise principle is the foundation of contract. In response to the perceived contradiction, contract theorists have reacted either by rejecting these doctrines as morally unjustifiable (like Shiffrin in relation to remedies,[61] and Fried in his early work with respect to the consideration doctrine),[62] or by rejecting the view that contracts are promises (like James Penner,[63] Randy Barnett,[64] and Dori Kimel).[65] I find both of these reactions too quick. What the fairness-based account of mitigation can teach us, alongside the other accounts of contract doctrines I have offered in previous chapters, is that seemingly divergent doctrines of contract law

61 Shiffrin, 'The Divergence of Contract and Promise' (n 50) 722–27.
62 Fried, *Contract as Promise: A Theory of Contractual Obligation* (n 6) ch 3.
63 James E Penner, 'Voluntary Obligations and the Scope of the Law of Contract' (n 9).
64 Randy E Barnett, 'A Consent Theory of Contract' (1986) 86 Columbia Law Review 269.
65 Kimel, *From Promise to Contract: Towards a Liberal Theory of Contract* (n 55).

can be justified if one considers the interaction between the promise principle and other moral principles, at the level of first-order moral reasoning. In other words, they are examples of what I have called composite doctrines. When attempting to justify contract doctrine, we ought to consider the interaction between the promise principle and other first-order moral principles without assuming that the promise principle has any special role to play in that interaction.

10

Contract Law Beyond the State*

1. Introduction

It has been a central claim in this book that law is by its very nature a local phenomenon; it is rooted in social facts and political practices that emerge from the existence of distinct political communities at particular times and places. In the context of contract law, comparative lawyers have for years unearthed the divergences in legal rules and doctrines that result from the fact that law is anchored and emerges from the local customs and practices of particular political communities (most often those that we call 'nation states'). By divergence, I mean that even though the relevant facts of cases to be decided may be roughly the same between jurisdictions, the rules, principles, and doctrines that are relied on by the courts to decide cases differ in important respects. I don't mean that the outcome—who wins and who loses—necessarily differs between jurisdictions. It may be that the outcomes are the same. Yet, there may still be divergence. The outcomes may be the same, but the applicable rules and doctrines may nevertheless differ. Those differences may manifest themselves by affecting outcomes in future cases.[1]

Comparisons between English and French law provide a treasure trove of examples. In English law a contract is only enforceable if there is an exchange, or something of value, or 'consideration' is given by the promisee in return for the promise. In contrast, French law recognizes the gratuitous promise as a category of contract (*contrats à titre gratuit*). In France, the absence of a bargain does not prevent a contract from coming into existence.[2]

* This chapter is based on and largely reproduces, but with significant additions, revisions, and adaptations, the text of a previously published article: Prince Saprai, 'The Convergence of Contract Law in Europe and the Problem of Legitimacy: A Common Lawyer's Perspective'; in *European Review of Contract Law*, 12(2), Berlin/Boston: De Gruyter, 2016, 96–135, copyright © 2016 Walter de Gruyter GmbH, Berlin/Boston. The text is used with kind permission of de Gruyter.

1 Hence, I don't adopt the prevailing 'functional' approach to comparative law. See K Zweigert and H Kötz, *An Introduction to Comparative Law* (Tony Weir tr, 3rd edn, Oxford University Press 1998) 34. According to which, the test for divergence is whether when the facts of cases are the same between jurisdictions, the outcomes differ or are the same. When they are the same, there is convergence, because although the applicable rules or doctrines may differ they achieve the same result or perform the same function. I believe such approaches are liable to mislead. This is because the outcome may be the same in particular cases, but it may be based on divergent rules and doctrines which may lead to different results in future cases. These approaches fail to take these rules and doctrines seriously.

2 Articles 1105–1106 Code Civil; Anne de Moor, 'Contract and Agreement in English and French Law' (1986) 6 Oxford Journal of Legal Studies 275, 281–82.

In England, the availability of damages on a 'cost of cure' basis, that is, the cost of obtaining the bargained for performance from a third party, is in certain contexts severely curtailed by a reasonableness requirement. So, for example, in the famous case of *Ruxley Electronics & Construction Ltd v Forsyth*, the promisee could not claim damages on a cost of cure basis when his swimming pool was built shallower than the contractually specified depth. The House of Lords judged that the depth of the pool did not affect its use, and for that reason it would be unreasonable and disproportionate to award cost of cure damages, which would have amounted to more than £21,000.[3] In contrast, in French law, awards of cost of cure damages are not similarly curtailed. In a recent and important monograph comparing English and French approaches to remedies for breach of contract, Soléne Rowan cites examples of French cases, which suggest strongly that had *Ruxley* been decided in France cost of cure would have been awarded.[4] So, for example, cost of cure was awarded by the Cour de cassation when a house was built a metre or so lower than the height specified in the contract. This breach did not affect the use of the house, but nevertheless cost of cure was deemed the appropriate measure of damages.[5]

There are many other examples of divergence between English and French contract law, relating, for example, to the interpretation of contracts and mistake,[6] the availability of damages for non-pecuniary loss,[7] the enforceability of penalty clauses,[8] the availability of specific performance,[9] and whether the promisee is required to mitigate her loss.[10]

There are of course significant divergences not just between English and French contract law, but also between the contract laws of many states. In an era of free

[3] *Ruxley Electronics and Construction Ltd v Forsyth* [1996] AC 344.

[4] Solène Rowan, *Remedies for Breach of Contract: A Comparative Analysis of the Protection of Performance* (Oxford University Press 2012) 117–18.

[5] Cass Civ 3e, 5 December 1979, JCP 1981, II, 19605, cited by Rowan, *Remedies for Breach of Contract: A Comparative Analysis of the Protection of Performance* (n 4) 118.

[6] Catherine Valcke, 'On Comparing French and English Contract Law: Insights from Social Contract Theory' (2009) 4 Journal of Comparative Law 69; Anne de Moor, 'Are Contracts Promises?' in John Eekelaar and John Bell (eds), *Oxford Essays in Jurisprudence: Third Series* (Clarendon Press 1987) 117.

[7] Rowan, *Remedies for Breach of Contract: A Comparative Analysis of the Protection of Performance* (n 4) 121–28: 'Whilst compensation for non-pecuniary loss is heavily circumscribed in England, it is widely available in France' (121).

[8] Lucinda Miller, 'Penalty Clauses In England And France: A Comparative Study' (2004) 53 International and Comparative Law Quarterly 79; Rowan, *Remedies for Breach of Contract: A Comparative Analysis of the Protection of Performance* (n 4) 184–88, 197–98.

[9] Lucinda Miller, 'Specific Performance in the Common and Civil Law: Some Lessons for Harmonisation' in Paula Giliker (ed), *Re-examining Contract and Unjust Enrichment: Anglo-Canadian Perspectives* (Martinus Nijhoff Publishers 2007) 287–88: 'in the common law the primary remedy for breach is damages, and specific performance is awarded only very exceptionally. In contrast, in civilian jurisdictions, specific performance receives a far more favourable reception and, where the victim of the breach opts to pursue this remedy, the court will rarely choose to substitute it with damages'. See also Rowan, *Remedies for Breach of Contract: A Comparative Analysis of the Protection of Performance* (n 4) 17–55.

[10] Rowan, *Remedies for Breach of Contract: A Comparative Analysis of the Protection of Performance* (n 4) 142–55: 'English law restricts damages through the [mitigation] principle, requiring the injured promisee to take reasonable steps to avoid loss.... In contrast, there is presently no place for loss mitigation in French law' (154–55).

trade, market liberalization, and globalization, governments around the world have increasingly felt that these differences between contract law regimes are major obstacles to economic efficiency; creating transaction costs which inhibit free trade and diminish the prosperity of nations. This has led to increased efforts between nations at both global and regional levels to bring about the greater convergence, or alignment, of their varied contract law regimes.[11] These transnational developments are potentially hugely important and may lead to significant change in the existing contract law regimes of the nations that participate.

Despite this, philosophers of contract law have had little to say about them. I suspect there are two reasons for the neglect. First, these initiatives have largely been justified by states or international organizations on economic, or efficiency, grounds alone, without engaging in broader normative or philosophical issues. Second, and as I argue in this book, the two dominant theories of contract law—economic analysis and the 'promise theory'—both typically presuppose a 'top-down' view of the law of contract according to which there is a 'blueprint', either economic or moral, to which the 'structure' of *all* contract law in whatever jurisdiction it might be found should seek to conform.[12] From the perspective of the top-down model of contract theory, there seems nothing wrong with these transnational efforts and indeed they seem entirely desirable—assuming of course that those in charge follow the correct (economic or moral) blueprint.

My aim in this book has been to attempt to disrupt this top-down way of theorizing about contract law, by pointing out the fact of 'normative pluralism' and the important role that local beliefs, conventions, and practices play in navigating the domain of value, shaping legal rules and doctrines, and establishing the rule of law. On this 'bottom-up' approach toward law, the divergence of contract law between jurisdictions does not present a moral problem, but is something more like a moral necessity or inevitability—the legitimacy of each state depends on its ability and its effort at seeking to make past political practice into a coherent and integrated whole capable of expressing equal concern and respect toward each and every citizen of that particular political community. From this perspective, these transnational

[11] For example: UN Convention on Contracts for the International Sale of Goods (11 April 1980) 1489 UNTS 3, *entered into force* 1 January 1988 [CISG]; International Institute for the Unification of Private Law, *Principles of International Commercial Contracts* (3rd edn, Transnational 2010) [PICC]. Regional efforts include South America, Asia, and South Africa. For South America, see Rodrigo Momberg and Stefan Vogenauer (eds), *The Future of Contract Law in Latin America: The Principles of Latin American Contract Law* (Bloomsbury Publishing 2017); Rodrigo Momberg and Stefan Vogenauer, *'The Principles of Latin American Contract Law: Text, Translation, and Introduction'* (2018) 23 Uniform Law Review 144. For Asia, see Shiyuan Han, 'Principles of Asian Contract Law: An Endeavor of Regional Harmonization of Contract Law in East Asia' (2013) 58 Villanova Law Review 589. For South Africa, see OHADA, Acte Uniform portant sur le Droit Commercial Général, OHADA Official Gazette, No 21 (15 February 2011), available at<http://www.ohada.org/index.php/en/official-gazette/official-gazette-n-21> accessed 13 November 2018, English translation available at <http://www.ohadalegis.com/anglais/audrtcomgb1.htm> accessed 13 November 2018.

[12] I borrow this metaphor of morality as a 'blueprint' and law as a 'structure' from Tony Honoré, 'The Dependence of Morality on Law' (1993) 13 Oxford Journal of Legal Studies 1, 3. I agree with Honoré that despite the huge influence of this way of thinking, it is seriously misleading about the nature of morality and law.

efforts to harmonize the law of contract seem in tension with the very nature of law and the conditions for its legitimacy.

My aim in this final chapter is not to condemn the emergence of these efforts to bring about the greater alignment of contract law regimes. There may indeed be good economic reasons for pursuing these projects. Rather, my purpose is to show why—if the thesis of my book is correct—these transnational initiatives face a significant moral obstacle which has been largely neglected or only opaquely addressed in the literature on these reforms. It is the problem of legitimacy, and I argue it arises precisely because contract law is forged and shaped by local beliefs, customs, conventions, and so forth about how to handle the fact of normative pluralism, that is, the fact that there is no uniquely correct answer to the problem of how morally underdetermined values should be interpreted (what I have called in previous chapters 'interpretive pluralism') and how irreducibly plural values should be ranked or weighted when they conflict (which I've been calling the problem of 'value pluralism').

This problem of legitimacy in the face of normative pluralism afflicts to some degree any effort to harmonize or bring about the greater convergence of contract law whether on a regional or global basis. To illustrate the problems that arise, I focus in this chapter on attempts by the European Union ('EU') to bring about the greater convergence of the general law of contract between its constituent Member States. I choose the EU as a case study to make these more general points largely because of my greater familiarity with these European efforts, but also because they represent perhaps the most sustained, sophisticated, and ambitious attempt yet to bring about this type of convergence in the contract law regimes of sovereign states.

2. The Emergence of European Contract Law

For over a decade now, there has been a serious debate in both academic and policy circles about whether and how to eliminate divergences in the contract law regimes of Member States of the EU. It was triggered by the European Commission's consultation document *Communication on European Contract Law*,[13] and has now led to the development of a Draft Common Frame of Reference ('DCFR'), which aimed to establish a common set of contract law rules and principles for the Member States.[14]

The DCFR had a threefold purpose. First, improve the coherence of European contract law legislation, known as the *acquis*. Second, guide Member States in the development of their own contract law. And third, serve as the foundation for a non-sector specific 'Optional Instrument'.[15] Until recently, it looked like this Optional

[13] Commission, 'Communication from the Commission to the Council and the European Parliament on European Contract Law' COM (2001) 398 final. See also the Commission's response to the consultation, 'A More Coherent European Contract Law, an Action Plan' COM (2003) 68 final.

[14] Christian von Bar and Eric Clive (eds), *Principles, Definitions and Model Rules of European Private Law: Draft Common Frame of Reference (DCFR)* (Oxford University Press 2010).

[15] Commission, 'A More Coherence European Contract Law, an Action Plan' (n 13), para 62.

Instrument would implement a Common European Sales Law ('CESL'), which contracting parties could opt into using a choice of law clause.[16] However, that proposal has now been withdrawn.[17] Replacing it are proposals for two Directives, one covering the supply of digital content, and the other the online sale of goods. Together, they will, according to the Commission, 'fully harmonise in a targeted way the key mandatory rights and obligations of the parties to a contract for the supply of digital content and the online sales of goods'.[18] These new proposals form part of the Commission's Digital Market Strategy.[19]

The European Commission hoped, by means of the DCFR, to bring about the greater convergence of contract law in Europe. The focus was on the general law of contract, and not as in the past specific areas of contract, such as consumer law.[20] This alone makes these developments hugely significant, regardless of how convergence is ultimately brought about, that is, through the use of an optional or binding instrument.[21] The justification given was economic: divergence was seen as a significant barrier to cross-border trade within the EU, and hence an obstacle to the creation of an internal market.

I am not going to attempt here to offer a detailed commentary on this process of harmonization, or its likely chances of success.[22] Nor am I going to discuss the particular ways in which the DCFR might be used to promote harmonization. There are a number already on the table, from its use as the basis for an Optional Instrument for cross-border transactions, or as a 'toolbox' or set of non-binding guidelines for European legislators, or most radically as the foundation of a European Civil Code.[23]

The issue of *how* convergence is brought about is, of course, extremely important, and bears on whether convergence *should* happen. However, I'm going to try and focus in this chapter just on the latter should question without getting too involved with the *how* question. I do this for purely pragmatic reasons. My primary purpose here is just to clarify the nature of the problems that normative pluralism or a bottom-up republican view of contract law presents to harmonization efforts of this

[16] Commission, 'Proposal for a Regulation on a Common European Sales Law' COM (2011) 635 final.

[17] Commission, 'Work Programme 2015: A New Start' COM (2014) 910 final, Annex 2, 12.

[18] Commission, 'Digital Contracts for Europe : Unleashing the Potential for E-commerce' COM (2015) 633 final, 3.

[19] Commission, 'A Digital Market Strategy for Europe' COM (2015) 192 final, 4–5.

[20] Martijn W Hesselink, 'European Contract Law: A Matter of Consumer Protection, Citizenship, or Justice?' (2007) 15 European Review of Private Law 323, 344.

[21] Ruth Sefton-Green, 'Sense and Sensibilities: The DCFR and the Preservation of Cultural and Linguistic Plurality' (2008) 4 European Review of Contract Law 281, 289.

[22] For an excellent account see Lucinda Miller, *The Emergence of EU Contract Law: Exploring Europeanization* (Oxford University Press 2011). For a longer-term perspective see Martijn W Hesselink, 'Roman Law and the Harmonisation of Private Law in Europe' in Arthur S Hartkamp and others (eds), *Towards a European Civil Code* (4th edn, Kluwer Law International 2011).

[23] According to Stefan Vogenauer the latter option was clearly what the drafters of the DCFR intended. See European Union Committee, *European Contract Law: the Draft Common Frame of Reference 12th Report* (HL 2008–2009, 95) s12, para 21. However, politically speaking, it is the least likely outcome. See s 26, para 83.

kind, and I believe that these problems largely persist no matter how harmonization is actually pursued or implemented (although I acknowledge that certain ways of harmonizing, for example, in the European context through the creation of a European Civil Code, would face them far more acutely than others).[24]

I will make three claims. First, the central problem that a harmonization project of this nature faces is the problem of legitimacy. The problem arises because of the existence of normative pluralism, and the value of state sovereignty.

Second, contrary to widely held and prevailing assumptions the problem of legitimacy goes beyond the issue of state consent, that is, whether treaty provisions provide for the harmonization of contract law. Rather, and as I argue in Chapter 4, the central condition for the legitimacy of any legal regime is whether a political community exists in which members and legal officials strive to treat citizens with equal concern and respect. The law of such a regime will display integrity or principled consistency in how it is interpreted, applied, and enforced. The main objection to attempts to harmonize contract law in Europe is the absence of *any* political community, even a 'bare' or 'de facto' political community bound together by the contingencies of history and geography—never mind a political community in the strong sense of a 'community of principle' that embraces a rights-respecting culture of the kind necessary to justify a right to rule.[25]

Finally, I will argue that legitimacy is not the only obstacle to convergence in this context. Even if the conditions of legitimacy could be met, that would only establish a right to rule, and it is a further question whether that right should be exercised. The main argument put forward by the EU to justify harmonization has been economic, and is based on the removal of barriers to the creation of an internal market. In this chapter I express some doubts about the plausibility of the economic assumptions behind this argument. Furthermore, I argue that even if convergence had a pro tanto justification, efficacy considerations suggest that it would be extremely difficult to implement in practice.

[24] See Hugh Beale, 'The Future of the Common Frame of Reference' (2007) 3 European Review of Contract Law 257, 267–58. The issue I want to bracket here is one of the precise normative implications of these more general concerns. See Duncan Kennedy, 'Thoughts on Coherence, Social Values and National Tradition in Private Law' in Martijn W Hesselink (ed), *The Politics of a European Civil Code* (Kluwer Law International 2006) 24, claiming that the notion of legal culture or tradition 'might be an argument for limiting the area to be harmonised to avoid areas where conflict in national rules is either great or of great symbolic importance. It might be an argument for harmonising slowly rather than rapidly. And it might be an argument for harmonising by "soft law" rather than "hard law". It might also be an argument for harmonising not by regulatory soft law but by "dialogue" between jurists, professors, judges and others, of different systems.'

[25] For the distinction between a 'de facto' political community (where members 'treat their association as only a de facto accident of history and geography') and a 'community of principle' (where each member 'accepts political integrity as a distinct political ideal and treats the general acceptance of that ideal, even among people who otherwise disagree about political morality, as constitutive of political community') see Ronald Dworkin, *Law's Empire* (Hart Publishing 1998) 208–11.

3. Normative Pluralism and State Sovereignty

Anxiety about state sovereignty is often expressed in the convergence literature.[26] However, what motivates this worry is rarely unpacked. The underlying issue is state freedom. The value of state sovereignty in this context resides in the freedom of states to decide how they interpret and balance the values that shape contract law.[27] This matters because the contract law rules and doctrines chosen by Member States play an important role in constituting and expressing national character or identity.[28] As the Study Group on Social Justice in European Private Law has said: 'any system of contract law expresses a set of values, which strives to be coherent, and which is regarded as fundamental to the political morality of each country'.[29] Against this backdrop, the EU's harmonization programme 'may be regarded as a disproportionate and illegitimate interference with the diversity of national and local political and legal traditions'.[30]

The expressive potential of state sovereignty depends on the existence of normative pluralism. In other words, it depends on the fact that there exists an irreducible plurality of ways in which the values that shape contract law might be interpreted, which I've been calling interpretive pluralism, and an irreducible plurality of ways in which these values might be ranked when they conflict, which I've called value pluralism.

3.1 Interpretive pluralism

By interpretive pluralism, I mean that there exists a multiplicity of irreducibly distinct ways to interpret the values that fashion the rules and doctrines of contract law. Take promise as an example. Few would deny that promise or its entailment the protection of the performance interest plays at least some role in contract law. However, even though it plays a role, it does not play a determinate role, that is, it does not specify precisely which rules and doctrines should govern contractual disputes.

To illustrate this, take the example I cited earlier in this chapter of the purported divergence between English and French law when it comes to awards of cost of cure damages for breach of contract.[31] It is harder to get cost of cure for breach of a

[26] See, for example, Hugh Collins, 'European Private Law and the Cultural Identity of States' (1995) 3 European Review of Private Law 353; Pierre Legrand, 'European Legal Systems are not Converging' (1996) 45 International and Comparative Law Quarterly 52; Pierre Legrand, 'Antivonbar' (2006) 1 Journal of Comparative Law 13.

[27] cf John Tasioulas, 'Human Rights, Legitimacy, and International Law' (2013) 58 The American Journal of Jurisprudence 1, 21–22, discussing the value of freedom or sovereignty as a limitation on the legitimacy of international law. My conception of the value of state sovereignty has been to a large extent influenced by John Tasioulas' important work in the philosophy of human rights and international law.

[28] Study Group on Social Justice in European Private Law, 'Social Justice in European Contract Law: a Manifesto' (2004) 10 European Law Journal 653, 654.

[29] ibid 656.

[30] ibid 669. Strictly speaking, I would argue that it is interference with sovereignty which is the relevant concern in this context, not national legal culture or tradition.

[31] See text to nn 2–5.

building contract in England, because English contract law imposes a reasonableness requirement. No similar restriction is placed in French law.

Is the imposition of a reasonableness requirement on the recovery of cost of cure damages out of step with the promise principle? Rowan clearly thinks that it is: 'There can be little doubt that the exercise of assessing damages in France is significantly more oriented toward the protection of the performance interest than in England.'[32] In English law, Rowan argues, the interests of the promisee, 'appear to be subordinated to those of the promisor',[33] and this leads her to conclude that 'there is scope for improvement in the protection of the performance interest in England'.[34]

I am far less certain. In *Ruxley*, discussed above, instead of awarding cost of cure damages (which would have been £21,560) the House of Lords awarded a smaller sum of loss of amenity damages (£2,500) to reflect the promisee's disappointment at not receiving the pool of the specified depth. Given that the pool was still perfectly safe and usable, it's not at all obvious that this decision reflects a lack of concern in English law for the keeping of promises, or the protection of the performance interest. That interest was largely protected in *Ruxley*: the promisee received a perfectly safe and useable pool, *and* loss of amenity damages for his frustrated expectations at not receiving a pool that met his exact specifications.[35]

My point here is not to defend the English approach. Rather, it is to suggest that it is far from clear which remedy best protects the performance interest. Promise or the protection of the performance interest does not provide a uniquely correct answer. Cost of cure is a good candidate, but so too is loss of amenity damages. No particular interpretation of the value of promise is obviously right or wrong in this context.[36]

This is true also of other moral values which play a role in contract law, such as fairness, the prevention of exploitation, trust, freedom, and so forth. There is no uniquely right way to interpret these values, and they could justify mutually incompatible contract law rules and doctrines.

[32] Rowan, *Remedies for Breach of Contract: A Comparative Analysis of the Protection of Performance* (n 4) 118.

[33] ibid 119. [34] ibid 120.

[35] See *Ruxley Electronics and Construction Ltd v Forsyth* (n 3) 357: 'A failure to achieve the precise contractual objective does not necessarily result in the loss which is occasioned by a total failure.' See also Mindy Chen-Wishart, *Contract Law* (2nd edn, Oxford University Press 2005) 521; Prince Saprai, 'Measuring Expectation Damages' (2010) 6 In-Pactum 184, 190–92.

[36] cf Tasioulas, 'Human Rights, Legitimacy, and International Law' (n 27) 20, discussing the multiple ways in which the right to political participation might be cashed out. There are, he argues, a range of eligible interpretations. See also Allen Buchanan, 'The Legitimacy of International Law' in Samantha Besson and John Tasioulas (eds), *The Philosophy of International Law* (Oxford University Press 2010) 95, making the point that people may reasonably disagree about the specific content of even the most fundamental human rights, such as the right not to be tortured. See also Honoré, 'The Dependence of Morality on Law' (n 12) 5, arguing that the moral duty to pay tax is 'incomplete' or 'inchoate': 'It has no real content until the amount or rate of tax is fixed by an institutional decision, by law.' In this way, Honoré argues, 'morality depends on law'.

3.2 Value pluralism

Another source of under-determinacy in contract law is value pluralism. According to value pluralism, there are a multiplicity of irreducibly distinct moral values that play a role in contract law, and no uniquely correct way to rank these values when they conflict. Instead, there exist a variety of eligible combinations.[37]

As I have said in previous chapters, 'foundationalism' and in particular the 'promise theory' of contract in its various formulations has in recent decades come to dominate philosophical accounts of contract law. On this view, promise plays a special role in the fashioning contract law rules and doctrines.

It is these foundationalist assumptions which have led the promise theorist Seana Shiffrin to be hugely critical of the Anglo-American regime for breach of contract. She argues that it diverges too significantly from what promissory morality would require. So, for example, she claims that as a matter of promissory morality, it is standardly the case that when a promise is broken, the defaulting promisor is required to perform at the next available opportunity. Anglo-American contract law, however, awards expectation damages (the financial equivalent of performance), as the standard remedy for breach, rather than ordering specific performance which would require actual performance. This departure from promissory morality is problematic, she argues, because: 'The law thereby fails to use its distinctive powers and modes of expression to mark the judgment that breach is impermissible as opposed to merely subject to a price.'[38]

Shiffrin, as we saw in the previous chapter, is similarly critical of the mitigation doctrine, also found in Anglo-American contract law. According to the doctrine, the extent to which damages are available for losses caused by breach depends on whether the innocent party took reasonable steps to reduce or minimize those losses, by, for example, finding substitute performance. There is divergence here, she claims, with promissory morality where in her view no such requirement exists: 'It is morally distasteful to expect the promisee to do work that could be done by the promisor when the occasion for the work is the promisor's own wrongdoing.'[39]

Given the special role that Shiffrin assigns to the promise principle in contract law, it is morally problematic when contract law adopts rules and justifications for rules that directly contradict what promissory morality would require.[40] This is the basis for her critique of the remedial regime in Anglo-American contract law. Shiffrin does not engage in a comparative exercise, but it is likely, given her theory, that she would prefer the French regime for breach of contract, where specific performance is the primary remedy for breach of contract,[41] and where there is no requirement that

[37] See Tasioulas, 'Human Rights, Legitimacy, and International Law' (n 27) 19, discussing the thesis generally, and not, as I do, in the context of contract law. See also Leslie Green, 'Jurisprudence for Foxes' (2015) 3 Transnational Legal Theory 150, 155–56; Jeremy Waldron, *'Partly Laws Common to All Mankind': Foreign Law in American Courts* (Yale University Press 2012) 140; Honoré, 'The Dependence of Morality on Law' (n 12) 13–15.

[38] Seana Valentine Shiffrin, 'The Divergence of Contract and Promise' (2007) 120 Harvard Law Review 708, 725.

[39] ibid. [40] ibid 717.

[41] Rowan, *Remedies for Breach of Contract: A Comparative Analysis of the Protection of Performance* (n 4) 39–47, 40: 'Unlike in England, specific performance is a central remedy in French contract law.'

the innocent victim of breach of contract mitigate her loss.[42] These differences have led Rowan to conclude that in France 'moral values are integral', whereas English law is more 'commercially orientated'.[43]

As I have argued in this book, this type of foundationalist critique is problematic because it loses sight of other values, aside from promise, which play an important role in justifying contract doctrines. So, as I claimed in the previous chapter, the mitigation requirement in contract law seems to reflect a principle of fairness in morality that precludes a promisee from recovering losses from a defaulting promisor where the promisee could easily have avoided them.

It is of course open to the promise theorist to deny the relevance or weight that I attach to the fairness principle in explaining the mitigation doctrine. Much of my argument in the previous chapter depended on intuitions, and the promise theorist may not share them or might question their reliability. Indeed, I would accept that we have to be acutely alive to the risk that our intuitions are not fixed apertures and may well even be shaped by legal rules and conventions prevailing in a particular society at a particular time.[44] My purpose is not to deny any of this, but rather to call attention to the fact that there may well be other values aside from promise, such as fairness, that quite plausibly play a role in shaping contract law doctrines. These values are irreducibly distinct and there may be no uniquely correct answer over which of these values should prevail when they conflict.[45]

Indeed, natural lawyers say that this kind of under-determinacy, which we find both as a result of interpretive and value pluralism, is precisely why we need positive law: to flesh out or specify the exact requirements of natural reason, and thereby to guide human conduct. That guidance function can't be performed by natural law alone because it is too open to interpretation. As Jeremy Waldron says, 'The concern is to have something tangible, something we can share and look to as a point of common orientation.'[46] They call the process by which the law makes natural law concrete the determinatio.[47] There may be many eligible ways in which the

Standardly specific performance is available as of right in French law (it is a discretionary remedy in English law), even in the context of contracts for the sale of non-unique goods and building contracts.

[42] ibid 147–51; Solène Le Pautremat, 'Mitigation of Damage: A French Perspective' (2006) 55 International and Comparative Law Quarterly 205.

[43] Rowan, *Remedies for Breach of Contract: A Comparative Analysis of the Protection of Performance* (n 4) 54–55. See also Anthony Ogus, 'Remedies, English Report' in Donald Harris and Denis Tallon (eds), *Contract Law Today: Anglo-French Comparisons* (Clarendon Press 1989); Miller, 'Specific Performance in the Common and Civil Law: Some Lessons for Harmonisation' (n 9) 301–07. Rowan is at pains to stress though that this does not mean that moral considerations are not important in England, or that commercial factors don't play a role in shaping French doctrine. There is just a difference in orientation.

[44] Honoré, 'The Dependence of Morality on Law' (n 12) 3.

[45] cf JM Finnis, 'On "The Critical Legal Studies Movement"' (1985) 30 The American Journal of Jurisprudence 21, 39.

[46] Jeremy Waldron, 'Torture, Suicide and Determinatio' (2010) 55 The American Journal of Jurisprudence 1, 10. See also Tasioulas, 'Human Rights, Legitimacy, and International Law' (n 27) 17: 'when reason leaves a number of interpretations open, reason itself can demand an act of individual or collective will to identify the one that is to serve as a basis for co-ordination'.

[47] See ch 4, text to nn 98–101. And see: Waldron, 'Torture, Suicide and Determinatio' (n 46) 2, 9; Finnis, 'On "The Critical Legal Studies Movement"' (n 45) 23; Hugh Collins, 'Cosmopolitanism and Transnational Private Law' (2012) 8 European Review of Contract Law 311, 314; Honoré, 'The Dependence of Morality on Law' (n 12) 4–5.

positive law specifies, or renders determinate, by case law precedents and legislative enactment, the content of natural law. As John Finnis says using contract law as an example:

> one might reasonably defend a set of rules and doctrines authoritatively established in the 'legal materials' (say, the current rules and doctrines of an American law of Contract), and defend them as 'embodying' and 'sustaining' a 'defensible' conception (say, of fair 'market' relationships), without claiming that, in all or even most respects, they are the *uniquely* reasonable rules and doctrines available for such embodiment and sustenance, or that such a conception is the *only* 'defensible' conception of a fair market.[48]

The presence of interpretive and value pluralism justifies the existence of positive law, and they also explain why state sovereignty is a powerful objection to the EU contract law harmonization programme.

3.3 State sovereignty

The value of state sovereignty in this context resides in the freedom of states to decide how they interpret and balance the various competing values that fashion contract law rules and doctrines.[49]

As I have said, there are numerous ways in which these values might be legitimately interpreted or balanced. States should, on the whole, be free to decide how to interpret and balance these values. Of course, this does not mean that they can adopt interpretations and rankings that are manifestly unreasonable or unfair. But it does mean that provided that their interpretation or ordering of values falls within a reasonable range, and even in some cases outside of that range, it should be respected even though there may be alternative or even superior interpretations and orderings. This is because of the instrumental and intrinsic value of states making these choices freely.[50]

The instrumental value rests in the fact that states may be better placed to fashion contract law rules and doctrines that meet local needs and expectations.[51] Furthermore, as Timothy Endicott reminds us, external actors 'are not generally good at interfering with the state'.[52] For these reasons, the rules that a state itself creates may be more likely to promote valuable goals and ends, and achieve widespread acceptance from the local population, which is essential for their efficacy and legitimacy.

This freedom also has an intrinsic value.[53] The choices that states make about how these values are interpreted and ranked may help to forge and express a sense

[48] Finnis, 'On "The Critical Legal Studies Movement"' (n 45) 23, see also 37–38.

[49] cf Tasioulas, 'Human Rights, Legitimacy, and International Law' (n 27) 21–22, discussing the value of freedom or sovereignty as a limitation on the legitimacy of international law.

[50] ibid 20. John Tasioulas, 'The Legitimacy of International Law' in Samantha Besson and John Tasioulas (eds), *The Philosophy of International Law* (Oxford University Press 2010) 113; Timothy Endicott, 'The Logic of Freedom and Power' in Samantha Besson and John Tasioulas (eds), *The Philosophy of International Law* (Oxford University Press 2010) 255.

[51] Tasioulas, 'The Legitimacy of International Law' (n 50) 106.

[52] Endicott, 'The Logic of Freedom and Power' (n 50) 255.

[53] Tasioulas, 'Human Rights, Legitimacy, and International Law' (n 27) 20.

of national identity. As Hugh Collins has argued, different systems of private law reflect distinct mixes of values relating, for example, to autonomy, welfare, and externalities. These mixes amount to national political settlements on matters of social justice, which confer legitimacy on these systems of private law, and reflect a sense of collective identity that promotes community cohesion.[54] Similarly, the Study Group on Social Justice in European Private Law says 'private law still performs its role as a national statement of the basic principles of justice and social ordering in a market society',[55] and 'what is revealed by comparative studies is that national legal systems have made divergent political decisions with respect to the question of how basic values should be reconciled'.[56]

I agree with both Collins and the Study Group here that private law involves the choice between fundamental values, and that this plays a role in constituting national identity. However, the focus on politics and social justice in these passages is too narrow. The widespread presence of interpretive and value pluralism allows for the expression of a broader set of commitments. So, for example, French contract law expresses vividly the importance of keeping one's word. This may be the product of a political compromise, but it may also reflect something deep in the French psyche that goes well beyond the domain of politics or social justice.

Take again the doctrine of mitigation. As I pointed out, unlike in English law, there is no similar mitigation doctrine in French law. It may be that both of these alternatives, that is, having a mitigation requirement or not having one, are equally rational or based on undefeated reasons. It may be that our intuitions about such matters are unreliable and themselves influenced by social conventions and legal practices. However, whether a state chooses to lay down a mitigation doctrine expresses something about the national character of that state, that is, the values, beliefs, and ideals that it attaches particular salience to. By embracing mitigation, it may be that the English courts attach less priority to the promise principle, and more, as I argued in Chapter 9, to the value of fairness. However, in France greater priority may have been attached to the value of fidelity to one's promises. This is not merely a political value, but one that reaches into every corner of life. By not having a mitigation doctrine, the promisor is incentivized to perform. Either way, it seems plausible to conclude that one value is being justifiably sacrificed at the altar of another.

The values at stake here are likely incommensurate, or irreducibly plural, and so it may be that no particular ordering of these values is uniquely correct.[57] Rationality might under-determine whether the promisee should be required to mitigate. In such circumstances, national courts or legislators may be faced with a choice

[54] Collins, 'Cosmopolitanism and Transnational Private Law' (n 47) 320–21.

[55] Study Group on Social Justice in European Private Law, 'Social Justice in European Contract Law: a Manifesto' (n 28) 654.

[56] ibid 663.

[57] As Herbert Hart said, 'because a plurality of such principles is always possible it cannot be *demonstrated* that a [judicial] decision is uniquely correct'. HLA Hart, *The Concept of Law* (3rd edn, Oxford University Press 2012) 205, cited by Green, 'Jurisprudence for Foxes' (n 37) 155. See also Honoré, 'The Dependence of Morality on Law' (n 12) 14.

between undefeated reasons. So, for example, they might have to choose between a value like fairness by requiring the promisee to mitigate, or they might decide to incentivize promise-keeping by not having a mitigation requirement. If these reasons are undefeated, the way the state chooses to act says something about the national character. It is a form of boundary-marking, and, as Joseph Weiler has argued, this is how a sense of nationhood is fostered:

At a societal level, nationhood involves the drawing of boundaries by which the nation will be defined and separated from others. The categories of boundary-drawing are myriad: linguistic, ethnic, geographic, religious, etc. The *drawing* of the boundaries is exactly that: a constitutive act, which decides that certain boundaries are meaningful both for the sense of belonging and for the original contribution of the nation.... Of course, with time, the boundaries, especially the non-geographical ones, write themselves on collective and individual consciousness with such intensity that they appear as natural.[58]

For Weiler nationhood creates a sense of belonging and provides an opportunity for the development of original ways of realizing human potential. Nationhood arises partly out of the kind of boundaries that are drawn when states make choices between values.[59] In the legal context, these choices are made when judges decide cases, when politicians enact legislation, and when scholars write textbooks. As Martijn Hesselink comments, 'scholars and politicians do not *find* national private law but *create* it'.[60] Over time when a sense of nationhood or political community takes root it may actually determine how a state exercises these choices. This is because, as I argued in Chapter 4, the emergence of a political community imposes duties on legal officials and members to treat all citizens with equal concern and respect, which means that political and legal decisions must cohere or demonstrate principled consistency with past political and legal practice. In this way, a growing sense of community requires courts and legislatures to select certain values over others.[61]

This shows how a sense of national identity is forged, reflected, and expressed by the rules, principles, and doctrines that constitute national private law. This can only happen if states are free from external interference when it comes to making decisions about how values should be interpreted and balanced.[62] The nation has a moral right to self-determination in this sphere. That right is a ground, or justification, for the doctrine of state sovereignty.[63]

[58] JHH Weiler, *The Constitution of Europe: 'Do the New Clothes Have an Emperor?' and other Essays on European Integration* (Cambridge University Press 1999) 340.

[59] As Michael Green says '[a] civilization ... attempts to melt down different peoples, ethnic groups, and cultures who do not share the same fundamental beliefs, values and attitudes into a common framework of beliefs and values'. Michael Green, 'Codes of Civilization and Codes of Culture' in Roberta Kevelson (ed), *Codes and Customs: Millennial Perspectives* (Peter Lang 1994) 112, cited by Pierre Legrand, 'Against a European Civil Code' (1997) 60 Modern Law Review 44, 61. See also Karl W Deutsch, *Nationalism and Social Communication: An Inquiry into the Foundations of Nationality* (2nd edn, MIT Press 1966).

[60] Hesselink, 'European Contract Law: A Matter of Consumer Protection, Citizenship, or Justice?' (n 20) 345.

[61] John Tasioulas, 'Mercy' (2004) 103 Proceedings of the Aristotelian Society 101, 128–32.

[62] Tasioulas, 'The Legitimacy of International Law' (n 50) 112.

[63] ibid 113; Endicott, 'The Logic of Freedom and Power' (n 50) 255.

One objection might be that if the concern is with self-determination, it may be a problem for this argument that most decisions about the rules and doctrines of national private law are made by un-elected judges, or, in states with civil codes, by committees of jurists. The thought is that for the argument from self-determination to have any purchase, these decisions should have been taken democratically or by elected officials.[64] The fact that citizens did not have a say in these rules diminishes the argument that external interference with them compromises the right to self-determination.[65]

For two reasons, this line of attack is not convincing. First, self-determination should not be equated with democracy. As Waldron says: 'The right of self-determination is prior to democracy, for it includes the right to decide whether to have a democracy around here, and if so, what sort of democracy to have.'[66] Second, even when officials are unelected, they may nevertheless represent the political community or nation, or at the least reflect in their decision-making a sense of national consciousness or priorities. In this way, they can still express the will of the people that they serve, and indeed play a role in shaping and forging it. For these two reasons, outside interference with this kind of decision-making may be problematic from the perspective of the right to self-determination, whether or not these decisions are the product of democratic processes.

In summary, sovereignty protects the valuable freedom of states to interpret and rank the values that play a role in contract law. This is in part how collective or national identities are forged, and it is important for the efficacy and legitimacy of systems of national private law. It is this background doctrine of state sovereignty, which activates the central problem of the legitimacy of EU efforts to harmonize contract law, to which I now turn.

4. Legitimacy

4.1 The nature of legitimacy

In the previous section, I defended the doctrine of state sovereignty when it comes to decision-making about the rules and doctrines of national contract law. I based the defence on the moral right to national self-determination. It is this defence of state sovereignty which gives rise to the problem of the legitimacy of the EU's project to bring about the convergence of contract law through the DCFR. The pertinent question is: can the EU justify its interference with national sovereignty in this particular domain? Another way of putting this is whether the EU has established

64 Thanks to Dan Priel and Octavio Ferraz for pressing me on this point.

65 In the case of civil codes, Reinhard Zimmermann claims that citizens are largely unaware of their provisions and characteristics. Reinhard Zimmermann, 'Codification: The Civilian Experience Reconsidered on the Eve of a Common European Sales Law' (2012) 8 European Review of Contract Law 367, 380.

66 Jeremy Waldron, 'Two Conceptions of Self-Determination' in Samantha Besson and John Tasioulas (eds), *The Philosophy of International Law* (Oxford University Press 2010) 408.

the right to rule in this area, that is, the right to lay down authoritative directives which when exercised member states have a moral duty to obey?[67]

There is of course an immediate objection to the way I have set up the problem of legitimacy here. It assumes the Westphalian primacy of the sovereign state, when arguably the EU is a transnational enterprise. In a recent article, Neil Walker set out the various competing conceptions of what the EU is:

> They are, in turn, a neo-federalist position, treating Europe's destiny as involving some approximation of a continental state. At the other extreme, is a statist position, which comprehends the European good as ultimately reducible, rather like the typical international regime, to the inter-governmentally negotiated aggregate interests of the Member States. Located between these two, is a supranational, or in some conceptions, transnational position, which envisages the new Europe not as a trade-off between different levels of state or state-like authority but as transcending the logic of statehood in a new model of political design.[68]

It is beyond the scope of this chapter to evaluate these rival interpretations. Instead, I do indeed assume here that the nation state is the basic political unit in the EU context. With that in my mind, my analysis of legitimacy is traditional from the point of view of international law theory, and it is aimed primarily at the two extremes presented by Walker, namely the 'neo-federalist' and 'statist' positions. Inevitably, this leaves my presentation of the issues open to the criticism that the EU is a *tertium quid*.[69] I concede that this is a limitation of my argument.

In defence of my approach, there is value in highlighting what the legitimacy constraints are from the point of view of orthodox international law theory, according to which, the EU is an international organization born of international law (albeit one that is unprecedented in its scale, scope, and powers). I would make three points. First, understanding the legitimacy constraints such a conception faces is important, because the neo-federalist and statist interpretations have been incredibly influential.[70]

[67] Tasioulas, 'The Legitimacy of International Law' (n 50) 97–98, drawing on Joseph Raz, *The Morality of Freedom* (Clarendon Press 1986) ch 2, and Joseph Raz, 'The Problem of Authority: Revisiting the Service Conception' (2006) 90 Minnesota Law Review 1003.

[68] Neil Walker, 'The Philosophy of European Law' in Anthony Arnull and Damain Chalmers (eds), *The Oxford Handbook of European Union Law* (Oxford University Press 2015) 7–8.

[69] For a sophisticated defence of this conception see JHH Weiler and Ulrich R Haltern, 'Constitutional or International? The Foundations of the Community Legal Order and the Question of Judicial Kompetenz-Kompetenz' in Anne-Marie Slaughter, Alec Stone Sweet, and Joseph Weiler (eds), *The European Court and National Courts: Doctrine & Jurisprudence* (Hart Publishing 1998).

[70] Varieties of the neo-federalist position were held by two of the founding fathers of the project, Jean Monnet and Robert Schuman. Walker, 'The Philosophy of European Law' (n 68) 8–9. See also Francis Jacobs and Kenneth Karst, 'The "Federal" Legal Order: The U.S.A. and Europe Compared: A Juridical Perspective' in Mauro Cappelleti, Monica Seccombe, and Joseph Weiler (eds), *Integration Through Law: Europe and the American Federal Experience*, vol 1 (Walter de Gruyter 1986). Statism has a long pedigree in the tradition of German ordoliberalism, according to which 'Europe should be no more than a delegated market-making framework, enhancing the common pool of resources and economic welfare of all Member States'. Walker, 'The Philosophy of European Law' (n 68) 8–9. For a recent defence of the statist picture see Bruno de Witte, 'The European Union as an International Legal Experiment' in Gráinne de Búrca and JHH Weiler (eds), *The Worlds of European Constitutionalism* (Cambridge University Press 2011). See also Trevor C Hartley, 'International Law and the Law of the European Union—A Reassessment' (2002) 72 British Yearbook of International Law 1.

Secondly, as Walker stresses, this trio of approaches are not hermetically sealed off from one another, rather they exist along a spectrum.[71] Although the wind now is behind the transnational understanding,[72] no plausible account of the EU could ignore the political reality of the importance attached to state sovereignty in the EU context. Indeed, as Perry Anderson argues, historically at the heart of the very idea of Europe is a 'unique equilibrium' between its constituent states.[73] Therefore, the legitimacy constraints imposed by state sovereignty, are to some degree going to be relevant whichever approach to the EU is undertaken.

Finally, the transnational approach is far from achieving a settled understanding; it is highly contested what the conception is, and against that background it makes sense to begin legitimacy assessments with the neo-federalist and statist positions which are well established and better understood.

Another objection might be that it makes no sense to subject contract law alone in this context to a legitimacy assessment. Allen Buchanan has argued that when making legitimacy assessments the primary issue is whether a particular legal institution, such as the EU, is legitimate, because that is what the legitimacy of all of its particular laws depends on.[74] On his view, 'international laws are legitimate *only* if the institutions that make them are legitimate'.[75] This view is too strong, and indeed mistaken. There is of course a huge literature on the issue of the legitimacy of the EU, about its 'democratic deficit', and so forth. It seems clear that this question about the legitimacy of the EU as a whole is separate from the question about whether the EU has legitimacy in particular spheres, for example, labour law, environmental protection, consumer law, and so on. The fact that we constantly make legitimacy assessments in these particular contexts, and that they seem perfectly apt, bears this out. Therefore, it seems that whatever the case may be with respect to whether the EU as an institution is legitimate, it is a further question whether the EU's attempts to harmonize say contract law or consumer law are legitimate.[76]

It is important to stress that the issue of the legitimacy of the EU's contract law harmonization programme does not exhaust the normative questions that arise in this context. It is a separate question, for example, whether the content of the rules contained in the DCFR is just, efficient, and so on. Therefore, even if we reach the conclusion that the process is legitimate, that is, that the EU has the right to lay down authoritative directives with a view to bringing about the convergence of

[71] Walker, 'The Philosophy of European Law' (n 68) 8.

[72] ibid; de Witte, 'The European Union as an International Legal Experiment' (n 70) 20; Sionaidh Douglas-Scott, *Constitutional Law of the European Union* (Longman 2002) 260.

[73] Perry Anderson, *The New Old World* (Verso 2009) 477. See also Walker, 'The Philosophy of European Law' (n 68) 6: 'the political recognition of Europe as a discrete object could only be of an entity whose basic structure and distinctive configuration was one of prior and embedded political plurality'.

[74] Buchanan, 'The Legitimacy of International Law' (n 36) 79–80 (emphasis added).

[75] ibid 80.

[76] cf Tasioulas, 'The Legitimacy of International Law' (n 50) 102–03, and 103 n 13 suggesting, furthermore, that the legitimacy of domains may actually be primary. See also the distinction between 'integrated' and 'disaggregated' approaches to legitimacy in Walker, 'The Philosophy of European Law' (n 68) 12–15.

contract law in Europe, this does not mean that the EU *should* legislate in this area. In the last section of this chapter, I illustrate this issue with a focus on efficiency and efficacy considerations.[77]

That said, legitimacy does play a special role in debates about convergence. It functions to borrow Robert Nozick's famous phrase about rights as a 'side-constraint'.[78] By this I mean that we have to settle the issue of the legitimacy of the contract law harmonization programme before we get into the question of whether convergence would be a good idea. Legitimacy is a threshold: no matter what convergence has going for it, it is not something that the EU is permitted to pursue, if it does not have legitimate authority in this sphere. In the next section, I consider what the conditions of legitimacy are in this context, and I raise some preliminary doubts about whether they have been satisfied.

4.2 The conditions of legitimacy

Having established the nature of legitimacy, and the fact that it applies to domains as well as institutions, we can now investigate the conditions of legitimacy, that is, the circumstances under which a right to rule exists.

In Chapter 4 of this book, I followed Ronald Dworkin in defending a republican conception of legitimacy according to which the central condition for the legitimacy of any state is whether legal officials and other members of the political community strive to treat all other members of that community with equal concern and respect. This entails that the law of the community be interpreted, applied, and enforced with principled consistency or what Dworkin called integrity. This is what elevates a 'bare' or 'de facto' political community to the ideal of what Dworkin called a 'community of principle'.[79] It is, as I argued in Chapter 7, the ability of citizens in such a regime to challenge the exercise of arbitrary power by the state and other citizens that constitutes their (republican) freedom.[80] My central worry about EU efforts to harmonize the general law of contract is that this distinctly republican legitimacy condition for law has not been satisfied, and the central reason for this is not that EU law in this sphere lacks integrity, but rather and more fundamentally that there does not exist in Europe even a bare political community of the sort necessary to justify such a wide-scale and ambitious process of harmonization.

However, before I turn to these doubts about the EU effort, it is necessary to deal with the claim that, in the EU context at least, the central condition for legitimacy is not republican or based on the notion of fraternity, but rather consent. This has been the central plank of the European Commission's own justification for its legitimacy in this field, and it reflects the orthodox Hobbesian conception of the legitimacy of the nation state which following Dworkin I rejected in Chapter 4.

[77] The point I am making here is a general one: the existence of a right does not entail that it should be exercised.

[78] Robert Nozick, *Anarchy, State, and Utopia* (Basil Blackwell 1974) 28–30.

[79] Dworkin, *Law's Empire* (n 25) 208–11

[80] See ch 7, s 1.

This argument from consent is based on the notion of 'constitutional legitimacy', or the idea in this context that Member States of the EU consented to give away their sovereign rights over contract law by signing up to and ratifying various EU treaties. This argument though is problematic for two important reasons.

First, the claim that Member States when they signed these treaties consented to the prospect of the convergence of the general law of contract in Europe is completely implausible. The Treaty on the Functioning of the European Union ('TFEU') provides no explicit mandate for a contract law harmonization programme. Instead, the Commission has sought to establish competence on the basis of provisions, in particular Article 114 TFEU, ex Article 95 Treaty Establishing the European Community ('TEC'), relating to the promotion of an internal market. However, it seems unlikely in the extreme that when states agreed to these, they ever envisaged that they could be used by the Commission to embark on a programme for the harmonization of the general law of contract. Given this, it cannot be said that states consented.[81]

There is a second, much more fundamental point. Even if, contrary to the political reality, states *did* consent to the contract law harmonization process, this would not establish the legitimacy of the Commission's programme. Consent is neither a *necessary*, nor a *sufficient* condition for the legitimacy of international law.[82] The existence of customary international law shows that consent is not necessary. There are states that did not even exist when some of these customs emerged, and yet, even though they could not possibly have consented, they are nevertheless subject to them.[83]

Nor is consent sufficient for legitimacy. As Scott Hershovitz has argued, consenting to be subject to the dictates of a wicked authority 'is akin to promising to do something morally atrocious; neither generates the reasons it might under more felicitous conditions'.[84] So, in the international context if states enter into a treaty to wage an unjust war, that treaty would lack legitimacy regardless of consent.

I am not saying that consent plays no important role or is altogether irrelevant to assessments of legitimacy. Such a claim would be too strong. Rather, the point is that it is not a *fundamental* condition of legitimacy. This does not preclude saying that it plays a *derivative* role, in relation to the fulfilment of the true or more basic conditions of legitimacy.[85]

For these reasons, consent does not even get off the ground as a plausible basis for legitimacy in this context. Having put consent aside, let's now consider whether the legitimacy of the EU programme can be established on the republican view of contract law that this book endorses and defends.

[81] This raises the more general problem of what Buchanan calls the 'bureaucratic distance' between states that have by treaty established global governance institutions like the EU and the continuous rule-making activities that these institutions engage in. To say that states have consented to all of these individual acts of rule-making unduly stretches the notion of consent. Buchanan, 'The Legitimacy of International Law' (n 36) 91.

[82] ibid 90–93. [83] ibid 92.

[84] Scott Hershovitz, 'Legitimacy, Democracy, and Razian Authority' (2003) 9 Legal Theory 201, 215.

[85] Tasioulas, 'The Legitimacy of International Law' (n 50) 101–02.

The republican view is, as I have argued, based or grounded on the ideal of fraternity. On this view, the legitimacy of the EU effort to harmonize contract law would depend on the existence of a Pan-European political community requiring or demanding convergence. The basic idea would be that European citizens form a political community, and as such they have the right to equal treatment from European and national institutions when it comes to the creation and enforcement of contract law rights.

On this analysis, divergence of contract law raises an issue of fairness or integrity, because similarly situated people involved in contract disputes are treated differently depending on the jurisdiction in which their dispute arises. So, for example, we saw earlier that in England the innocent victim of a breach of contract has a so-called duty to mitigate her loss caused by the breach, but that no such requirement exists in France. This has the consequence that the victim of a breach of contract in England will be treated differently, that is, is under a duty to mitigate, even though her case is similar in all relevant respects to a case decided in France, where no duty to mitigate is imposed. She might complain that this is unfair. It is unfair that she has to bear the burdens of this rule, when the victims of breach in France don't.[86]

There is an obvious objection. Usually, complaints of unfairness or lack of principled consistency arise when a single agent or institution is responsible for the differential treatment. However, in the mitigation example, it is not the same agent or institution responsible. Waldron makes an analogy (in the human rights context) that makes the point clear:

> It is like a child who complains that her friends are allowed to stay up late on Sundays whereas she has to go to bed at 7:30: 'It's not fair!' she says. And we respond that no one is being unfair; other parents' practices are not binding here; that's not how we do things in this house. We don't determine the bedtime of your friend, so we are not being unfair to you when we send you to bed at a different time.[87]

Similarly, in the mitigation example, the English courts don't decide French contract law, and the French courts don't decide English contract law, therefore litigants in either jurisdiction can't complain that they are being treated unfairly vis-à-vis litigants in the other jurisdiction. No single authority is responsible for the differential treatment.

It could be argued that in the EU context national courts are now European courts, because they enforce European law, thus creating a single agency. However, the legislative competence of the EU is circumscribed by treaty, and as I have said does not extend to the general law of contract.[88] Therefore, litigants cannot complain that a single agent is enforcing, for example, differential mitigation requirements.

[86] Waldron, *'Partly Laws Common to All Mankind': Foreign Law in American Courts* (n 37) 124–25.

[87] ibid 126.

[88] Although a fairness-based claim could be made in spheres where the EU clearly does have competence such as consumer law. This is an example of the derivative role that consent plays in determining questions of legitimacy. See text to nn 84–85.

However, Waldron has argued that the absence of a single agent is not fatal to a claim that differential treatment is unfair. He uses the following example to explain why:

> Imagine a large refugee camp after a famine or humanitarian emergency, where, as often happens, several aid agencies and NGOs are working side by side with the same large population in the same camp. Suppose one of the organizations becomes aware that the provision it is offering the refugees is quite different in quantity and quality from the provision that the other aid agencies are offering to members of the same population in the same camp. Oxfam, for example, is giving two meals a day to the people in the north part of the camp, and other agencies are giving one meal a day to people in the southern sector, even though the people in the north are no more needy and no more deserving than those in the south.... The people in the south are likely to be distressed by the disparate treatment. They are likely to complain that their treatment is unfair.... And that demand does not presuppose a single agency responsible for all the treatment, although—and this is important—the complaint about unfairness may become the basis for a demand that the various agencies should start to behave as a unit. In other words, the demand for fairness could be a reason for the various entities to begin working as a system; their working as a system is not a precondition for the legitimacy of the demand.[89]

The basis for the complaint of unfairness in the example, Waldron argues, is that there exists a community of people who are sufficiently related to one another to make these complaints seem reasonable.[90] Waldron uses this analogy to argue for greater consistency in human rights law between jurisdictions. This is because there is now a transnational community of people, which is committed 'specifically to advancing the idea of human rights for all, to pressuring governments (from whom we all have a lot to fear in this regard as well as a lot to hope for) to take rights seriously, and to watching out for each other when it comes to rights'.[91]
The existence of this interconnectedness of peoples when it comes to human rights issues, and the awareness by members of this community that human rights are not given the same level of protection across jurisdictions, leads to the demand, based on a principle of fairness, that governments converge when it comes to protecting human rights.[92]

It is important to see here that Waldron's argument relies on a key or fundamental *empirical* premise, which is that as a sociological matter a community of people who identify with one another in relevant respects must actually exist in order to get the demand for fairness off the ground. In Dworkinian terminology, the emergence of a community of principle depends, first and foremost, on the existence of a 'bare' or 'de facto' political community.[93]

The question arises: does a transnational community exist in Europe that might justify a claim of equal treatment when it comes to the creation and enforcement of contract law rights? The formation of collective identity depends on whether a group 'accepts a fundamental and consequential sameness that causes them to feel

[89] Waldron, *'Partly Laws Common to All Mankind': Foreign Law in American Courts* (n 37) 131–32.
[90] ibid 132. [91] ibid 133. [92] ibid.
[93] Dworkin, *Law's Empire* (n 25) 208–11.

solidarity amongst themselves'.[94] In the European context, what is required is akin to a sense of national identity.[95] National identifications rely on the acceptance by disparate social groups of a shared narrative, usually combining a variety of elements, including history, religion, myth, ethnicity, and so forth, 'into a potent vision of human identity and community'.[96]

Such a narrative may well be available for Europe. Emerging as it did in 1951 from the ashes of world war, Weiler argues that the heart of the European community is a fundamental commitment to celebrate the virtues of the liberal nation state, while keeping its excesses in check, 'especially, but not only, its propensity to violent conflict'.[97] In an important sense, the European project is a 'post-national' enterprise.[98] Priority is attached to the individual above the nation state, the upholding of human rights, non-discrimination on the basis of nationality, social solidarity, sustainable development, and the virtue of tolerance.[99] According to Weiler, the idea of Europe represents 'the ability of the individual to rise above his or her national closet'.[100]

As I have said, it goes beyond my purpose in this chapter to evaluate this type of post-national conception of what the EU is for. However, whatever its merits might be, it can be said, with some confidence—particularly in the current political climate—that this vision has not been *embraced*. Rather, it has been *imposed* by elites in pursuit of admittedly laudable political and economic ends, including the creation of an internal market, the prevention of war, and the geopolitical strategic

[94] Neil Fligstein, 'Who Are the Europeans and how Does this Matter for Politics?' in Jeffrey T Checkel and Peter J Katzenstein (eds), *European Identity* (Cambridge University Press 2009) 134.

[95] Historically, it is interesting to note that movements toward the convergence of private law have followed hot on the heels of the development of a sense of national identity. See Zimmermann, 'Codification: The Civilian Experience Reconsidered on the Eve of a Common European Sales Law' (n 65) 374, 390.

[96] Anthony D Smith, 'National Identity and the Idea of European Unity' (1992) 68 International Affairs 55, 61. See also Fligstein, 'Who Are the Europeans and how Does this Matter for Politics?' (n 94) 135–36, relying on Deutsch, *Nationalism and Social Communication: An Inquiry into the Foundations of Nationality* (n 59).

[97] Weiler, *The Constitution of Europe: 'Do the New Clothes Have an Emperor?' and other Essays on European Integration* (n 58) 341.

[98] Smith, 'National Identity and the Idea of European Unity' (n 96) 67.

[99] Weiler, *The Constitution of Europe: 'Do the New Clothes Have an Emperor?' and other Essays on European Integration* (n 58) 344–45. Hugh Collins, 'Harmonisation of European Contract Law: Citizenship, Diversity and Effectiveness' (2005) 7 Cambridge Yearbook of European Legal Studies 81, 89–90. Martijn W Hesselink, 'The Case for a Common European Sales Law in an Age of Rising Nationalism' (2012) 8 European Review of Contract Law 342, 359–60, arguing that in the contractual context looking out for the interests of the other party is a key component of European identity. See also Kennedy, 'Thoughts on Coherence, Social Values and National Tradition in Private Law' (n 24) 19–20, arguing that currently solidarity with weaker parties is a key theme of European private law; Ole Lando, 'The Structure and the Legal Values of the Common Frame of Reference (CFR)' (2007) 3 European Review of Contract Law 245, 251.

[100] Weiler, *The Constitution of Europe: 'Do the New Clothes Have an Emperor?' and other Essays on European Integration* (n 58) 343. For a longer-term picture of this sense of European identity, see Anthony Pagden, 'Europe: Conceptualizing a Continent' in Anthony Pagden (ed), *The Idea of Europe: From Antiquity to the European Union* (Cambridge University Press 2002); Anderson, *The New Old World* (n 73) ch 9.

needed to provide a counterweight to the East and the West.[101] It lacks the bottom-up impetus that is vital for the creation of a collective consciousness.[102] As Neil Fligstein has shown, 87.3 per cent of people in Europe conceive of themselves mostly in terms of their national rather than European identity.[103] People are divided on class-based lines: 'People who tend to think of themselves as European represent the more privileged members of society, while people who tend to think of themselves as mainly national in identity tend to be less privileged.'[104] As Anthony Smith says, Europe's failure 'only underlines the distance between the European ideal and its rootedness in the popular consciousness of Europe's national populations'.[105]

Against this background, it is difficult to see how in the European context Waldron's empirical premise, the existence of a bare political community, can be said to exist, with the result that the argument from fairness will struggle to get off the ground. This is not to say that a European identity will not emerge, but the political reality in the foreseeable future at least is, as Fligstein argues, that our national self-understandings will 'continue to trump' our European ones.[106]

4.3 Summary

In summary, I have argued that the attempt by the EU to harmonize the general law of contract in Europe involves an interference with state sovereignty which is the freedom of a state to decide for itself how to interpret and balance the irreducible plurality of values that shape contract law rules and doctrines, and that such interference has not, and arguably cannot—in current circumstances at least—be shown to be legitimate. The EU has focused attention on the issue of consent by Member States to the harmonization programme, but consent, as I have argued, is not a fundamental or basic condition for legitimacy. On the republican view defended in this book, legitimacy depends on the existence of political communities that make demands by members based on values of fairness or equality reasonable. However, it is difficult to see how legitimacy can be established on this basis, given that there is an insufficiently robust sense of European identity embraced by the people of Europe, which is needed to justify such a claim.

5. The Merits of Convergence

In the previous section, I raised some serious doubts about the legitimacy of the EU project to harmonize the general law of contract. Consent is not a fundamental condition for legitimacy, and on the republican view defended in this book

[101] The achievement of these ends through the creation of economic and political institutions was the central plank of the Pan-European project. See Smith, 'National Identity and the Idea of European Unity' (n 96) 67.

[102] ibid 72–73.

[103] Fligstein, 'Who Are the Europeans and how Does this Matter for Politics?' (n 94) 140.

[104] ibid 137.

[105] Smith, 'National Identity and the Idea of European Unity' (n 96) 73.

[106] Fligstein, 'Who Are the Europeans and how Does this Matter for Politics?' (n 94) 158.

convergence cannot be shown to be legitimate, because of the non-existence of a relevant Pan-European political community. This is *the* fundamental problem that the emergence of a contract law for Europe faces.

As I said earlier, analytically it is important to distinguish the issue of legitimacy from the issue of the merits of convergence. Establishing that an authority has the right to rule does not necessarily mean that they should exercise that power. We have to weigh up the costs and benefits that ruling might have.

In this section, I want to put aside the issue of legitimacy, and assume arguendo that the EU effort to harmonize contract law does, or will in the foreseeable future, satisfy the republican conditions for legitimate authority—perhaps a collective consciousness in Europe will emerge.[107] Even if the EU contract law harmonization project were legitimate, it still leaves open the question of whether it is justified or desirable or even possible to achieve. As I have said, the main argument that the EU has given for convergence is economic. I will show that it is based on questionable assumptions, and that the economic benefits of convergence are hardly clear-cut or beyond doubt. Furthermore, I will argue that there are serious efficacy constraints on whether convergence in this sphere is even possible.

5.1 Economic efficiency

The economic case for convergence is the central justification given by the European Commission for convergence. The Commission claims that divergence between the contract law regimes of Member States of the EU is a significant barrier to cross-border trade.[108] Convergence would, the argument goes, remove these barriers and promote free trade and the creation of an internal market between European nations. An implicit premise of the claim here being that it is *only* through the EU that coordinated action is possible to bring about this type of convergence. This is due mainly to the tendency of Member States to obey EU directives.[109]

How convincing is the economic case for convergence? It is beyond the scope of this chapter to provide a full-scale economic analysis of the issues. Indeed, much depends on the method of convergence adopted. There is a nascent literature on this topic, and it is fair to say that the jury is still out.[110] However, I will express some

[107] Fligstein speculates on how a particular event, such as a terrorist atrocity affecting multiple EU states, might in the future bring about a sense of togetherness. ibid 158–59.

[108] Commission, 'A More Coherent European Contract Law, an Action Plan' (n 13) paras 25–51.

[109] Tasioulas calls this an 'executive' advantage that public international law may have. It arises from its ability in certain cases to bring about the achievement of common goals, due to the tendency of states to comply with it: 'All states face problems—epidemics, economic instability, environmental degradation, the proliferation of weapons of mass destruction, refugee movements, etc—that cannot be adequately addressed by individual states acting alone but only through a framework for co-operation and co-ordination. PIL [public international law] can provide such a framework, largely in virtue of the propensity of states to obey it.' Tasioulas, 'The Legitimacy of International Law' (n 50) 102.

[110] See, for example, Gerhard Wagner, 'The Economics of Harmonisation: The Case of Contract Law' (2002) 39 Common Market Law Review 995; Fernando Gómez, 'The Harmonization of Contract Law through European Rules: A Law and Economics Perspective' (2008) 4 European Review of Contract Law 89; Erin O'Hara O'Connor, 'The Limits of Contract Law Harmonization' (2012) 33 European Journal of Law and Economics 505. See also contributions to a special issue of the *Common*

preliminary doubts about the economic arguments the Commission itself has put forward, if only to show that the economic case is far from obvious. As such, it is a risk to base the case for convergence on these economic arguments alone.

The Commission claims that there are two main ways that divergence inhibits cross-border trade. First, divergence discourages consumers from shopping across borders, because they cannot be sure what level of consumer protection they will receive in the state in which they are making a purchase. The EU has relied on this argument in the past to justify directives that seek to harmonize consumer law,[111] and it was used recently to justify the review of the consumer *acquis*.[112] The basic idea, according to Lucinda Miller, is that:

> the EU steps in to reduce such unequal substantive rights by (re)regulating consumer contract law in the form of harmonising Directives thereby restoring the confidence of consumers to shop in other EU states.[113]

Second, divergence by creating legal uncertainty deters businesses, due to higher transaction costs, from engaging in cross-border trade. In a recent article, Hugh Beale, a leading figure in the preparation of the DCFR, fleshes out the worry:

> it seems self-evident that having to deal with a variety of legal systems must add to the cost, or the risk, of anything except the simplest cross-border transaction. The business will want to know, what difference will it make to us if the other party insists on the contract being governed by their law (or indeed the law of some third country)? Will our standard contract 'work' as well under that law as it does under our own law? Perhaps even more important is that for many business people, differences between legal systems create a psychological barrier.[114]

Market Law Review on the theme of economic approaches to European contract law. Common Market Law Review 50 (2013) issue 1/2.

111 See, for example, Recital 5 of the Council Directive 99/44/EC of 25 May 1999 on Certain Aspects of the Sale of Consumer Goods and Associated Guarantees [1999] OJ L171/12: 'Whereas the creation of a common set of minimum rules of consumer law, valid no matter where goods are purchased within the Community, will strengthen consumer confidence and enable consumers to make the most of the internal market', cited by Miller, *The Emergence of EU Contract Law: Exploring Europeanization* (n 22) 49.

112 See the Commission Green Paper on the Review of the Consumer *Acquis* COM (2006) 744 final, 4, cited by Miller, *The Emergence of EU Contract Law: Exploring Europeanization* (n 22) 49. See also Recital 6 of the Council Directive 2011/83/EU of 25 October 2011 on Consumer Rights [2011] OJ L304/64.

113 Miller, *The Emergence of EU Contract Law: Exploring Europeanization* (n 22) 49.

114 Hugh Beale, 'A Common European Sales Law (CESL) for Business-to-Business Contracts' in Luigi Moccia (ed), *The Making of European Private Law: Why, How, What, Who* (Sellier European Law Publishers 2013) 67. Collins, 'Harmonisation of European Contract Law: Citizenship, Diversity and Effectiveness' (n 99) 94, arguing that a significant obstacle to trade in the EU is the fact that different Member States adopt different rules about when standard form contracts are enforceable or valid. This creates uncertainty for businesses engaged in cross-border trade. Ole Lando, 'Is Codification Needed in Europe? Principles of European Contract Law and the Relationship to Dutch law' (1993) 1 European Review of Private Law 157; Commission, 'A More Coherent European Contract Law, an Action Plan' (n 13) paras 27–51.

So, for example, in the context of business-to-consumer transactions, businesses that sell their goods across borders are subject to the consumer protection laws of each member state in which they operate:[115]

> This means that a business advertising its goods across Europe, for instance via a website 'e-shop', must be prepared to deal with the consumer protection rules of at least 28 different jurisdictions.[116]

Beale argues that these problems pose a particularly acute challenge to small and medium-sized enterprises, which do not have access to the same legal expertise about foreign law as bigger firms, and don't have the resources to take the same risks that larger firms can.[117]

These twin concerns about consumer confidence and the effects on business are the foundation of the EU's justification for its programme of contract law harmonization.[118] They were reiterated recently in Recital 7 of the Proposal for a Directive on Consumer Rights:

> These disparities create significant internal market barriers affecting business and consumers. They increase compliance costs to business wishing to engage in cross border sale of goods or provision of services. Fragmentation also undermines consumer confidence in the internal market. The negative effect on consumer confidence is strengthened by an uneven level of consumer protection across the Community.[119]

And yet, as Miller has pointed out, these arguments are almost entirely 'under-analysed' and routinely taken for granted in the academic literature.[120] If we scratch beneath their surface, two problems quickly come into view.

First, as Miller says, there is an 'astonishing' lack of empirical evidence provided by the Commission to support the contention that divergence negatively impacts cross-border trade:[121] 'Instead, the assumption that variations in contract laws do create obstacles to cross-border trade transactions is allowed to remain unproven'.[122]

[115] This is due to art 6, Council Regulation (EC) 593/2008 of 17 June 2008 on the law applicable to contractual obligations (Rome 1) [2008] OJ L177/6.

[116] Beale, 'A Common European Sales Law (CESL) for Business-to-Business Contracts' (n 114) 65. See also Wagner, 'The Economics of Harmonisation: The Case of Contract Law' (n 110) 1013–14: 'It should be obvious that such a state of affairs places additional costs on the dealings of a truly European enterprise marketing its goods and services in every jurisdiction of the Union.... it is no exaggeration to say that legal diversity places a tax on European business, a tax that creates no benefits either for firms or for consumers but only benefits for lawyers'.

[117] Beale, 'A Common European Sales Law (CESL) for Business-to-Business Contracts' (n 114) 67. See also Wagner, 'The Economics of Harmonisation: The Case of Contract Law' (n 110) 1014–15; Beale, 'The Future of the Common Frame of Reference' (n 24) 270–71; Hesselink, 'European Contract Law: A Matter of Consumer Protection, Citizenship, or Justice?' (n 20) 353.

[118] Miller, *The Emergence of EU Contract Law: Exploring Europeanization* (n 22) 59.

[119] Commission, 'Proposal for a Directive of the European Parliament and of the Council on consumer rights' COM (2008) 614 final, cited by Miller, *The Emergence of EU Contract Law: Exploring Europeanization* (n 22) 60.

[120] Miller, *The Emergency of EU Contract Law: Exploring Europeanization* (n 22) 59.

[121] ibid 60.

[122] ibid 60–61. See also: Wagner, 'The Economics of Harmonisation: The Case of Contract Law' (n 110) 1016; Gómez, 'The Harmonization of Contract Law through European Rules: A Law and Economics Perspective' (n 110) 109–11, 115; European Union Committee, *European Contract Law: the*

This is particularly problematic given that we know that trade has flourished between jurisdictions with divergent contract laws. Think, for example, of trade between England and Scotland, or between American states.[123] This experience suggests that, at the very least, it is unclear that differences in legal rules necessarily inhibit cross-border trade. It may well be that other factors such as linguistic and cultural differences, or absence of trust in legal enforcement mechanisms in other jurisdictions, or the practicalities of pursuing redress abroad, play a more significant role.[124]

Even if empirical evidence were available to support the claim that divergences in contract law were a significant deterrent to cross-border trade, there is a second problem with the economic case. The fact that divergence may be a barrier to cross-border trade does not necessarily mean that the *general* law of contract should converge throughout Europe.

As has been pointed out by the Study Group on Social Justice in European Private Law, there are less drastic solutions. First, certain areas of contract law, such as the sale of goods, commercial law, and consumer law, are more likely to be affected by these kinds of economic concerns than others. Therefore, whilst there may be a case for a sector-specific harmonization of contract law, it is difficult to extend that economic argument to justify the convergence of the *whole* of contract law in Europe. Secondly, many of the problems thrown up by divergence can already be solved by market actors through, for example, the use of choice of law clauses. By altering their contracts 'traders can avoid most potential barriers to cross-border commerce'.[125]

Hence, it is unclear why even if divergence is problematic on economic grounds, the solution proposed is the harmonization of the general law of contract. The Commission seems to want to use a sledgehammer to crack a nut.[126]

These two flaws, that it is uncertain that divergence is a barrier to cross-border trade, and that even if it is, it is unclear that the convergence of the general law of contract is the solution, suggest that the economic case presented by the Commission is far from watertight. Even if the EU has the right to rule in this area (and I have explained in the last section why I think this is unlikely), the economic rationale it presents for exercising that right simply does not stand up to critical scrutiny.

Draft Common Frame of Reference 12th Report (n 23) para 83. The criticism has been acknowledged by Hugh Beale. Hugh Beale, 'Finding the Remaining Traps Instead of Unifying Contract Law' in Stefan Grundmann and Jules Stuyck (eds), *An Academic Green Paper on European Contract Law* (Kluwer Law International 2002).

[123] Miller, *The Emergence of EU Contract Law: Exploring Europeanization* (n 22) 61.

[124] ibid 62–63; Wagner, 'The Economics of Harmonisation: The Case of Contract Law' (n 110) 1016–17; Zimmermann, 'Codification: The Civilian Experience Reconsidered on the Eve of a Common European Sales Law' (n 65) 391; European Union Committee, *European Contract Law: the Draft Common Frame of Reference 12th Report* (n 23) para 51.

[125] Study Group on Social Justice in European Private Law, 'Social Justice in European Contract Law: a Manifesto' (n 28) 656.

[126] This has led the Study Group to be suspicious of the motives of the Commission. They worry that the economic case may be a Trojan horse for a broader political agenda. ibid 656–57.

5.2 Efficacy and normative pluralism

As I argued in the previous section, it is far from clear that there is a convincing justification for why the Commission is pursuing such an ambitious and radical programme of harmonization in the field of contract law. Furthermore, there are efficacy considerations or practical barriers that seriously call into question whether any such programme can possibly achieve its objectives.

The worry about efficacy that I want to pursue here relates to the difficulty of ensuring consistent interpretation of the DCFR across twenty-eight separate jurisdictions. There is an extensive literature on this issue, which has highlighted a number of potential obstacles. There is the problem of ensuring accurate translation of the DCFR text that is in English into the twenty-three official languages of the EU.[127] Then there is the fact that the DCFR uses 'an astonishing number of vague and ambiguous terms'.[128] Another source of confusion is that the DCFR contains some badly drafted provisions.[129]

These issues to do with translation, vague terms, and poor drafting make consistent interpretation an uphill task. I want to focus though on another related concern that links with the arguments I have made in this book about the implications of normative pluralism for contract law.

In an important article, Pierre Legrand made the following point:

> a code leads the jurist astray by suggesting that to have knowledge of the law is to have knowledge of the rules (and that to have knowledge of the rules is to have knowledge of the law!). Assuredly, ... *jus* is not reducible to *lex*.[130]

Legrand relies here on Jacques Derrida's broader theory of interpretation, and in particular on a distinction Derrida drew between the 'graphical' surface level of a text and what he called its unseen 'trace' element, which 'indicate the presence of other discourses of which they are vestiges'.[131]

Legrand's thought is that rules even when they are clearly formulated are subject to interpretation, which is an evaluative exercise:[132] 'Since they are invisible, the traces await their unfolding or elucidation or unconcealment—their bringing forth—by the text's interpreter'.[133] Where there are multiple legal systems involved,

[127] Sefton-Green, 'Sense and Sensibilities: The DCFR and the Preservation of Cultural and Linguistic Plurality' (n 21) 294, 290.

[128] Stefan Vogenauer's evidence to the European Union Committee on European Contract Law. European Union Committee, *European Contract Law: the Draft Common Frame of Reference 12th Report* (n 23) Minutes of Evidence 14. Sefton-Green, 'Sense and Sensibilities: The DCFR and the Preservation of Cultural and Linguistic Plurality' (n 21) 298.

[129] See, for example, art II-4:105, which prevents reliance on 'No-Oral-Modification' ('NOM') clauses. For criticism of the provision see Florian Wagner-von Papp, 'European Contract Law: Are No Oral Modification Clauses Not Worth the Paper They Are Written On?' (2010) 63 Current Legal Problems 511, 581.

[130] Legrand, 'Against a European Civil Code' (n 59) 59–60.

[131] Pierre Legrand, 'Siting Foreign Law: How Derrida Can Help' (2011) 21 Duke Journal of Comparative & International Law 595, 607; Pierre Legrand, 'Paradoxically, Derrida: For a Comparative Legal Studies' (2005) 27 Cardozo Law Review 631, 674; Jacques Derrida, 'Living On' in Harold Bloom and others (eds), *De-construction and Criticism* (Routledge & Kegan Paul 1979).

[132] Legrand, 'Siting Foreign Law: How Derrida Can Help' (n 131) 609.

[133] ibid.

interpretations will vary depending on the values that those systems embrace: 'What point, then, a unitary text of reference in the absence of a unitary rationality and morality to underwrite and effectuate it?'. There is no Archimedean, or value neutral, vantage point from which to determine the content of law.[134]

Take as an example the mitigation doctrine which I discussed earlier, and which is embraced by the DCFR (Article III-3:705). In Chapter 9 I defended the doctrine on the grounds of fairness, but it has been defended on other grounds too, such as Charles Fried's defence in terms of altruism,[135] or on the basis of loss avoidance.[136] Different jurisdictions will attach different weight to these values. This will influence how they interpret the requirements of the doctrine, and that will lead to divergences in application.[137]

Which values are embraced by a particular state may depend on local conditions. Gunther Teubner has argued that the reception of the good faith doctrine (introduced by the European Directive on Unfair Terms in Consumer Contracts 1994),[138] has been heavily influenced by the type of capitalism that particular Member States embrace. Countries like Germany have a 'business-coordinated market economy', where business plays a dominant role in shaping the economic framework and which is 'characterised by long-term cooperative relations between companies in the market, between companies and their employees, between companies and their owners and the suppliers of financial capital'. Against that backdrop, good faith has an important role to play in balancing 'the risks and opportunities which the mixture of autonomy and trust' create in this regime.[139]

In contrast, the British have a 'liberal market economy', where economic action is largely left to the market and relations between economic actors are characteristically adversarial. This is not a culture in which good faith can flourish.[140] Instead, Teubner says, the doctrine has become a 'legal irritant'. These irritants may bring about change *within* the legal system, but it is likely that the evolutionary development that they catalyse will lead to divergence *between* legal systems.

My point here is just to illustrate how, due to interpretive and value pluralism, rules may be interpreted differently depending on which values a particular society embraces, and local conditions. This makes the prospects for integration around a

[134] Legrand, 'Against a European Civil Code' (n 59) 60. See also Legrand, 'Siting Foreign Law: How Derrida Can Help' (n 131) 601, 607–08; Legrand, 'Paradoxically, Derrida: For a Comparative Legal Studies' (n 131) 674–76. Legrand presents this theory of interpretation as a critique of legal positivism. See similarly Ronald Dworkin's argument from theoretical disagreement in his *Law's Empire* (n 25) ch 1.

[135] Charles Fried, 'The Convergence of Contract and Promise' (2007) 120 Harvard Law Review Forum 1, 7–8. See my critique of this interpretation of the doctrine in ch 9, ss 2–3.

[136] See Charles J Goetz and Robert E Scott, 'The Mitigation Principle: Toward a General Theory of Contractual Obligation' (1983) 69 Virginia Law Review 967, 973.

[137] cf Tasioulas, 'The Legitimacy of International Law' (n 50) 111, discussing the multiple ways of grounding the human right not to be tortured.

[138] Council Directive 93/13/EEC of 5 April 1993 on Unfair Terms in Consumer Contracts [1993] OJEC L95/29.

[139] Gunther Teuber, 'Legal Irritants: Good Faith in British Law or How Unifying Law Ends Up in New Divergencies' (1998) 61 Modern Law Review 11, 25.

[140] ibid 26–27. cf Gómez, 'The Harmonization of Contract Law through European Rules: A Law and Economics Perspective' (n 110) 103.

common contract law in Europe hazardous. Reinhard Zimmermann reminds us that in past centuries the national codification movements in, for example, France and Germany, were supported by strong supreme courts, which ensured consistent interpretation of civil codes. In contrast, Zimmermann, commenting before the withdrawal of the proposed CESL,[141] argued that were it enacted the European Court of Justice ('ECJ') could not in its present form at least 'cope with the flood of requests for preliminary rulings that would result'.[142]

Efficacy constraints of this nature have to be taken on board in taking any decision about whether a right to rule, even if established in this area, should be exercised.

6. Conclusion

The central claim of this book has been that top-down theories of contract law, such as the promise theory or economic analysis—which seek to impose a blueprint of how contract law should look or the structure it should take wherever and whenever it is found—are doomed to collapse. This is because contract law does not have a fixed foundation in any moral principle, value, or normative concern, or any set of such principles, values, or concerns. Rather, contract law, as I have argued, emerges as a response to disputes that arise when people in particular communities such as nation states invoke the practice of promising to pursue their own ends, and the shape that its particular doctrines and rules take depends on how members of these communities—mostly through their courts—grapple with and make their way through a normative landscape in which normative pluralism is a pervasive feature or fact. Against that background, contract law and the values or normative concerns that underpin it are invariably contingent and dependent on local conventions, customs, beliefs, and political practices.

With this in mind, efforts by business, global elites, international organizations, international lawyers, and so forth, to bring about the convergence of contract law between varying jurisdictions and states inevitably run up against a serious moral obstacle, which is the freedom of states embodied in the legal and political concept of state sovereignty to determine for themselves how they handle the pervasive fact of normative pluralism in fashioning the rules and doctrines of contract law, and

[141] On the withdrawal of CESL see text to nn 15–17.

[142] Zimmermann, 'Codification: The Civilian Experience Reconsidered on the Eve of a Common European Sales Law' (n 65) 395. Making similar points about the weaknesses of the current system of judicial administration for the purposes of harmonizing contract doctrine see Walker, 'The Philosophy of European Law' (n 68) 23–24; Wagner, 'The Economics of Harmonisation: The Case of Contract Law' (n 110) 1022: 'a uniform European law of contract is in urgent need of a European system of judicial administration in civil matters that is capable of resolving the many issues of doubt with which any civil code will invariably be afflicted'; Eric A Posner, 'The Questionable Basis of the Common European Sales Law: The Role of an Optional Instrument in Jurisdictional Competition' (2013) 50 (1/2) Common Market Law Review 261, 271, (relying on experience from the divergent ways in which different states have interpreted the UCC in the US); Gómez, 'The Harmonization of Contract Law through European Rules: A Law and Economics Perspective' (n 110) 102, 105–06.

in doing so how they constitute and express themselves as a culture, and political grouping. They have, in other words, a right to their own self-determination.

My purpose in this chapter was not to show that such transnational efforts can never succeed, but rather to illustrate using the EU's attempts to harmonize in this sphere as an example the serious legitimacy burden they face due to the value of state sovereignty. As we have seen, the European Commission's 2001 consultation paper has set in train a process which has as its end the greater convergence of the general law of contract in Europe. It has led to the creation of the DCFR, which clearly has radical ambitions. As Stefan Vogenauer says:

> The DCFR, as published in 2007, is much more than a 'toolbox' for a revision of the *acquis*, and it even goes beyond a potential European Contract Law Instrument. It is clearly meant to be a blueprint of a European Civil Code in the area of patrimonial law.[143]

Politically there is no appetite for a Civil Code, and it is not altogether clear what form harmonization initiatives will take in the future.[144] However, and as I have argued, whichever form they eventually take, it will be an uphill task to show that the EU has a right to rule in this area because on the republican view I have defended throughout this book legitimacy ultimately rests on the existence of political communities that strive to treat their members with equal concern and respect. The basic problem with the EU's harmonization effort in this sphere is the absence of even a bare or de facto political community among those who would be subject to the new legal regime. Without the existence of a polis, the EU's argument for its legitimacy or competence in this area never gets off the ground.

Even if the EU could establish its legitimacy in this sphere, it would have to show that harmonization is justified, and, as I have argued, the economic case it has presented is based on assumptions that have not been proven. The fact of normative pluralism presents a problem for the EU in defending its legitimacy in this context, but also in showing that its efforts to harmonize would not be in vain. This is because EU contract law has to be interpreted, and interpretation does not take place in a vacuum, but rather against the background of local conditions, customs, and value commitments. These centrifugal forces make it likely that divergence will remain—although arguably it might be possible to counteract these tendencies through serious institutional reform, involving, in particular, the strengthening of the supervisory jurisdiction of the ECJ.[145]

I do not deny that some of these issues are going to be more or less problematic depending on the form that harmonization takes in the future. So, for example, Hesselink rightly points out that the use of an Optional Instrument that gives contracting parties the right to use European sales law is less of a threat to national

143 European Union Committee, *European Contract Law: the Draft Common Frame of Reference 12th Report* (n 23) Minutes of Evidence 3, para 14.

144 Wagner-von Papp, 'European Contract Law: Are No Oral Modification Clauses Not Worth the Paper They Are Written On?' (n 130) 512–13.

145 Posner, 'The Questionable Basis of the Common European Sales Law: The Role of an Optional Instrument in Jurisdictional Competition' (n 142) 271.

identities than a Civil Code that would replace national contract law regimes.[146] Nevertheless, the harmonization enterprise generally and these initiatives specifically, all face, at least to some degree, questions about pluralism, sovereignty, legitimacy, efficacy, and so forth.

What we are left with is a 'protestant' or what I have preferred to call a republican conception of contract law. On this view, contract law is contingent, functional, under-determined, and pluralistic. It plays a constitutive role not only in fashioning the relationships that we have with others when we make certain promises, but it also, as I have argued in this chapter, constitutes a sense of national or political identity. To truly grasp the practice, one cannot start with a foundation or blueprint, but must instead grapple from the ground up with the legal rules and doctrines that actually regulate contractual transactions in particular jurisdictions and uncover the typically implicit interpretations and value judgments that have led to their formation. That effort though is not just one for judges or lawyers or legal philosophers in the sky; it has to be a collective endeavour wrapped up in our basic commitment as members of the same political community to treat each other with equal concern and respect. In that effort lie the seedlings of a binding contract law.

[146] Hesselink, 'The Case for a Common European Sales Law in an Age of Rising Nationalism' (n 99) 365.

Index